SERVING OUR COUNTRY

Joan Beaumont is Professor Emerita, Strategic and Defence Studies Centre, Coral Bell School of Asia Pacific Affairs, at the Australian National University. Her publications include the critically acclaimed and multiple award-winning *Broken Nation: Australians in the Great War* (2013); with Aaron Pegram and Lachlan Grant, *Beyond Surrender: Australian Prisoners of War in the Twentieth Century* (2015); (ed.) *Australia's War, 1939–45* (1996); *Gull Force: Survival and Leadership in Captivity, 1941–1945* (1988); and *Comrades in Arms: British Aid to Russia, 1941–1945* (1980). In 2011–13 she led the research team for the Department of Veterans' Affairs commemorative website, 'The Thai-Burma Railway and Hellfire Pass'.

Allison Cadzow is a Research Associate at the Australian National University. She co-authored *Rivers and Resilience: Aboriginal people on Sydney's Georges River* (2009) with Heather Goodall (shortlisted for the 2010 NSW Premier's History Awards). She has also co-edited *Nelson Aboriginal Studies* (2012) for HSC Aboriginal Studies teachers and students in NSW with John Maynard, and *Brokers and Boundaries: Colonial Exploration in Indigenous Territory* with Tiffany Shellam, Maria Nugent and Shino Konishi (2016). She has developed community history exhibitions and websites and has also worked at the National Museum of Australia. Her other areas of interest and publication include migrancy and environmental history, as well as women's and gender histories.

This book is dedicated to the Aboriginal and Torres Strait Islander men and women who have served in the national defence forces, in the past and present, and the families of those service people who have told and shared their histories.

SERVING OUR COUNTRY

INDIGENOUS AUSTRALIANS, WAR, DEFENCE AND CITIZENSHIP

EDITED BY
JOAN BEAUMONT & ALLISON CADZOW

NEWSOUTH

A NewSouth book

Published by
NewSouth Publishing
University of New South Wales Press Ltd
University of New South Wales
Sydney NSW 2052
AUSTRALIA
newsouthpublishing.com

First published 2018

10 9 8 7 6 5 4 3 2 1

ISBN: 9781742235394 (paperback)
9781742244174 (ebook)
9781742248592 (ePDF)

NATIONAL LIBRARY OF AUSTRALIA
A catalogue record for this book is available from the National Library of Australia

Design Josephine Pajor-Markus
Cover design Peter Long
Cover images Arthur Murdoch, one of the Barambah Boys who fought in the First World War. *Cherbourg Museum.*
Printer Everbest

This book is printed on paper using fibre supplied from plantation or sustainably managed forests.

UNSW
SYDNEY

Contents

Abbreviations

AAA	Australian Aboriginal Association
AACAP	ATSIC/Army Community Assistance Program
AAL	Australian Aborigines' League
AAPA	Australian Aboriginal Progressive Association
ABC	Australian Broadcasting Corporation
ADF	Australian Defence Force
AIATSIS	Australian Institute of Aboriginal and Torres Strait Islander Studies
AIF	Australian Imperial Force
AMF	Australian Military Forces
AMR&O	Australian Military Regulation and Order
ANU	Australian National University
ANZAC	Australian and New Zealand Army Corps
APA	Aborigines Progressive Association
APB	Aborigines Protection Board
APS	Australian Public Service
ATSIC	Aboriginal and Torres Strait Islander Commission
ATSIVSA	Aboriginal and Torres Strait Islander Veterans and Services Association
AWAS	Australian Women's Army Service
AWOL	Absent Without Leave
AWLA	Australian Women's Land Army
AWM	Australian War Memorial
BCOF	British Commonwealth Occupation Force
CMF	Citizen Military Forces

CWA	Country Women's Association
DAA	Department of Aboriginal Affairs
DIA	Directorate of Indigenous Affairs
DIDP	Defence Indigenous Development Program
DVA	Department of Veterans' Affairs
EP	Elkin papers, University of Sydney Archive
FCAATSI	Federal Council for the Advancement of Aborigines and Torres Strait Islanders
FNQR	Far North Queensland Regiment
INTERFET	International Force for East Timor
IPRC	Indigenous Pre-Recruitment Course
IWM	Imperial War Museum
NAA	National Archives of Australia
NACC	National Aboriginal Consultative Committee
NAIDOC	National Aborigines and Islanders Day Observance Committee
NAOU	North Australian Observer Unit
NCIS	National Centre for Indigenous Studies
NCO	Non-commissioned Officer
NGO	Non-government Organisation
NLA	National Library of Australia
NORFORCE	North-West Mobile Force
NTER	Northern Territory National Emergency Response
NTSRU	Northern Territory Special Reconnaissance Unit
OPAL	One People of Australia League
PIB	Papuan Infantry Battalion
PIR	Pacific Islands Regiment
PROV	Public Record Office Victoria
PTSD	Post Traumatic Stress Disorder
QCAATSI	Queensland Council for the Advancement of Aborigines and Torres Strait Islanders
RAAF	Royal Australian Air Force

RAANC	Royal Australian Army Nursing Corps
RAE	Royal Australian Engineers
RAN	Royal Australian Navy
RAP	Reconciliation Action Plan
RAR	Royal Australian Regiment
RFSU	Regional Force Surveillance Unit
RSL	Returned and Services League of Australia
RSSILA	Returned Sailor's and Soldier's Imperial League of Australia
SAS	Special Air Service Regiment
SLSA	State Library of South Australia
SOC	Serving Our Country project
SROWA	State Records Office of Western Australia
TPI	Totally and Permanently Incapacitated
TSLI	Torres Strait Light Infantry Battalion
UK	United Kingdom
UN	United Nations
UNAMIR	United Nations Assistance Mission in Rwanda
UNIA	United Negro Improvement Association
UNITAF	United Task Force in Somalia
WAAAF	Women's Auxiliary Australian Air Force
WO	Warrant Officer
WRAAC	Women's Royal Australian Army Corps
WRAAF	Women's Royal Australian Air Force
WRANS	Women's Royal Australian Naval Service

Acknowledgments

The authors of this book owe a debt to many people and institutions. The project, 'Serving Our Country: A history of Aboriginal and Torres Strait Islander people in the defence of Australia', was made possible by the generous support of an Australian Research Council (ARC) Linkage Grant and four national Partner Institutions: the Department of Veterans' Affairs; the Department of Defence; the National Archives of Australia; and the Australian War Memorial. The Australian Institute of Aboriginal and Torres Strait Islander Studies was a further institution with whom we collaborated. We thank these organisations and their staff, including Rebecca Bateman, Michael Bell, Anne Bennie, Terence Bligh, Donna Boulton, Bonnie Carter, Anne-Marie Conde, Stewart Crawford, Leith Dewis, Jeff Fairweather, Amy Lay, Eric McDonald, Dylan Daniel-Marsh, Bob Noble, Gary Oakley, Garth O'Connell, Hilary Rowell, Catherine Spooner, Luke Taylor, Russell Taylor, Matthew Trynes, Brett West, Kelly Wiltshire, Anne Wright and Gail Yapp. Their ongoing commitment and interest spoke to the wide national recognition being given, after decades of neglect, to the important subject of Indigenous military service.

We also owe much to the academic institutions that provide our intellectual homes. The project was conceived and based at the Australian National University: especially the National Centre for Indigenous Studies; the Strategic and Defence Studies Centre, in the Coral Bell School of Asia and Pacific Affairs, ANU College of Asia and the Pacific; and the School of History, the Australian Centre for

Indigenous History, and the Australian Dictionary of Biography, all in the ANU College of Arts and Social Sciences. Ann McGrath AM and Allison Cadzow of the School of History, and Doug McNicol and Peter Elford of the CASS Research Office, played a central role in the original conception and grant success of the project. Partner universities were the School of Arts, Australian Catholic University, and the Academic Division, the University of Newcastle.

The story of Indigenous military service belongs to Aboriginal and Torres Strait Islander Australians. In the four years of the Serving Our Country project over 200 men and women gave the time and energy to participate in interviews with our researchers in Yarn Ups. We are also grateful to those Indigenous men and women who previously participated in interviews with Noah Riseman for another research project on Indigenous military service, and who agreed to have their material incorporated into this book. These individuals' names, too numerous to list here, can be found in Appendix 1. Their words and memories inform this book, and without the willingness of these men and women to tell us their own and their families' stories, difficult though these memories sometimes were to revisit, this book could not have been written.

The Serving Our Country Yarn Ups did not just happen. At the ANU the meticulous planning and practical arrangements were managed by the project's Community Consultation Coordinator, Craig Greene, who brought both expertise and sensitivity to the role. He was ably supported by the project team, especially Allison Cadzow. At the community level many institutions generously opened their premises and facilities to our researchers. Their names too are listed on pp. 346–48. Other Indigenous individuals and organisations that were generous with their advice and assistance included: Gary Oakley, Garth O'Connell and David Williams of the Aboriginal and Torres Strait Islander Veterans and Services Association; Harry Allie, who served as our ex-service representative on the project's advisory committee; John Schnaars of Honouring Indigenous War Graves; and Ray Minniecon, organiser of the Redfern Coloured Diggers march.

Integral to the project were two conferences: 'Defending Country: Sharing Stories of Aboriginal and Torres Strait Islander Service', held at the Australian National University, Canberra in December 2014 and organised by Craig Greene and Kate Macfarlane; and 'Brothers and Sisters in Arms: Historicising Indigenous Military Service', held at the Australian Catholic University, Melbourne, in June 2015, and organised by Noah Riseman. The attendance of Indigenous participants at the Canberra conference was assisted by support from Qantas, who also assisted by waiving excess baggage charges that the recording equipment used in Yarn Ups would otherwise have incurred.

The advice and interest of colleagues was, as ever, much valued. We thank particularly: Malcolm Allbrook, Melissa Bellanta, Cath Bishop, Colin Campbell, Jessica Duncan, Doseena Fergie, Cressida Fforde, Hannah Forsyth, Niki Francis, Heather Goodall, Kerrie Hogan, David Horner, Damien Minton, Nell Musgrove, Maggie Nolan, Maria Nugent, Tim Rowse, Margaret Simoes, Shurlee Swain, Kirsten Thorpe, Richard Trembath, Janet Turpie-Johnstone, Annette Twyman, Ellen Warne, Christine Winter, Naomi Wolfe and Linc Yow Yeh. Shannyn Palmer provided meticulous, thoughtful editing, of both Yarn Up interviews and this book, while writing her own chapter at the later stages of the book's preparation. Stephanie Woodbridge and Tristan Moss provided earlier valued work in summarising and tagging interviews.

The oral history interviews collected during this project form a lasting and unique national resource. Many of the interviews are available on the website <ourmobserved.anu.edu.au/>, which has been attentively edited by Luke Hambly. The original data has been stored on the Data Commons at the Australian National University with a view to its being transferred to the Australian Institute for Aboriginal and Torres Strait Islander Studies at a later date. Data management and web design was initially managed by Alex Hayes, whose work was very ably built upon by Luke Hambly. With Craig Greene, Luke also provided oversight of the task of seeking permission from all those quoted in the book. The ongoing and budget management of this complex multi-institutional project was capably provided by Kate Macfarlane, Douglas McNicol, Tim Robbins and Putri Handriantri. Maps were designed by CartoGIS at the Australian National University.

Note on terminology

Indigenous Australians are the first peoples of Australia. They are people of Aboriginal and Torres Strait Islander descent, who identify as Aboriginal or Torres Strait Islander and are accepted as an Aboriginal or Torres Strait Islander person in the community in which they live, or have lived. Aboriginal people are those whose traditional lands are on mainland Australia, Tasmania and other adjacent islands. Torres Strait Islanders are those whose traditional lands are in the Torres Strait that separates Australia from Papua New Guinea. All of these terms, Indigenous, Aboriginal and Torres Strait Islander, represent numerous peoples who had their own identifiers before colonisation.

Some Indigenous Australians use group names for people from a broad area, such as Murri (Queensland) or Noongar (south-west Western Australia). Other terms used relate to language groups, such as Bundjalung (north-east NSW) and Yolngu (Arnhem Land, Northern Territory). We use the more specific mob names when possible and relevant to particular individuals or families.

When referring to Indigenous people beyond Australia, the preferred group names of those communities are used where possible, for example, Sioux (USA) or Māori (NZ). The terms 'First Nations' and 'Native American' are used for the Indigenous peoples of Canada and the USA respectively where the preferred group names are not known. Alternatively when referring to people collectively, from many regions of the world, the term 'Indigenous peoples' is used.

The Returned and Services League (RSL) has undergone numerous name changes since its founding as the Returned Sailor's and Soldier's Imperial League of Australia in 1916. In this book we use the term RSL to refer to all of the previous names of this ex-service organisation.

Note of warning

Much historical documentation uses racialised terminology which is considered offensive today (for example, 'half-caste' and 'full blood'). While recognising that such terms are derogatory, we use them when they appear in historical documents being cited and in specific historical contexts. We do this with a conscious awareness of the problematic nature of these words and the hurt that they often cause to Indigenous people.

Aboriginal and Torres Strait Islander readers are also warned that this book contains images and the names of deceased persons. We advise reading and viewing with caution and apologise for any distress unintentionally caused by the inclusion of these images and words.

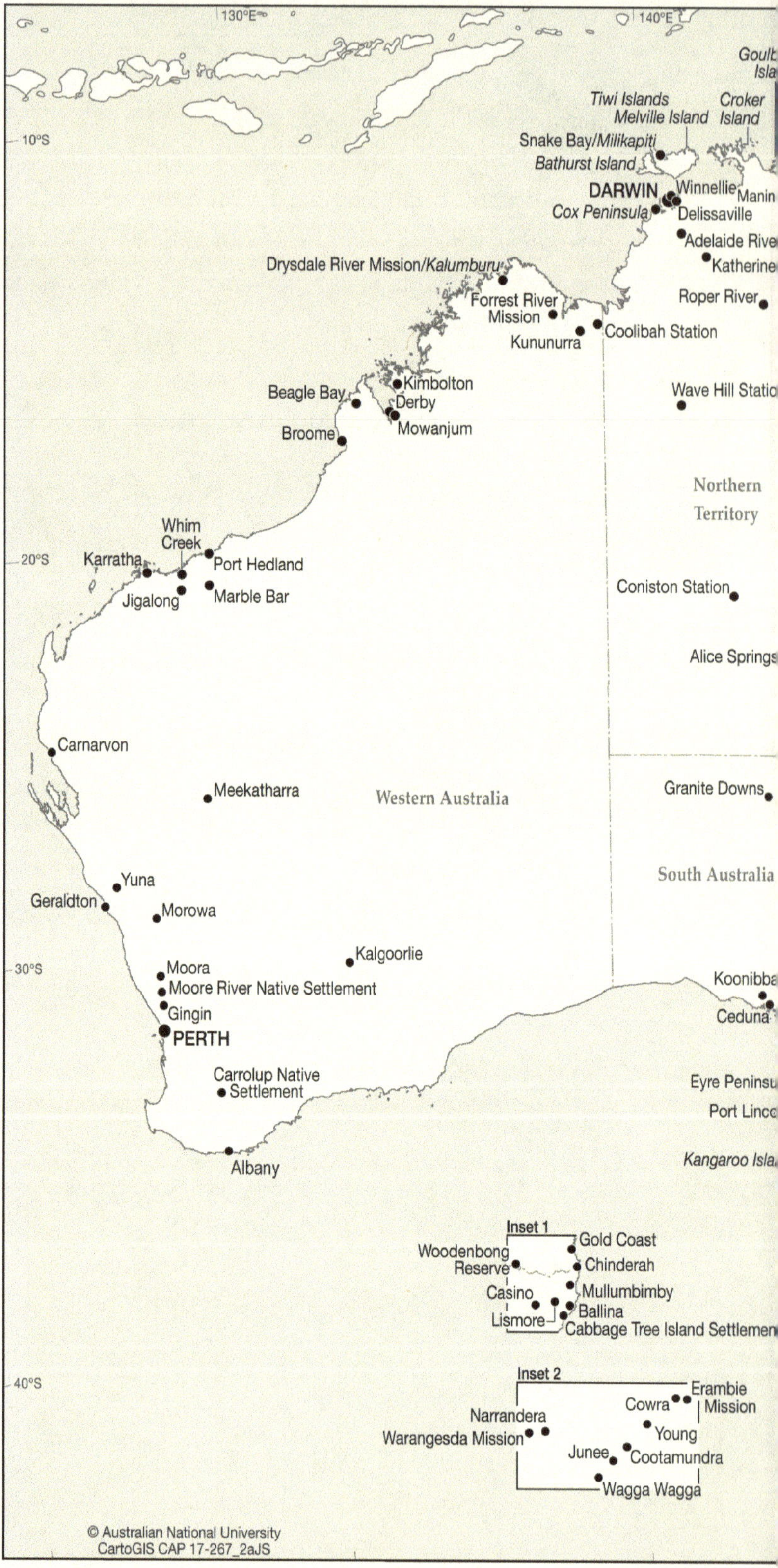

Places of significance, Australia

150°E
160°E
Yam Island
Badu Island
Murray Island/Mer
Thursday Island
Milingimbi
Milingimbi Mission
Elcho Island
Nhulunbuy
Yirrkala
Gove Peninsula
Weipa
Emerald River Mission
Groote Eylandt
Cape Bedford Mission
Mornington Island Mission
Burketown
Mona Mona Mission
Kuranda
Cairns
Yarrabah
Herberton
Ingham
Palm Island/Bwgcolman
Townsville
Charters Towers
Bowen
Queensland
Rockhampton
Woorabinda
Biloela
Taroom Settlement
Wondai
Murgon
Cherbourg/Barambah
Kingaroy
North Stradbroke Island
Deebing Creek
BRISBANE
Warwick
Euraba Mission
Collarenabri
Inset 1
Terry Hie Hie Reserve
Brewarrina Aboriginal Mission
Walgett
Copmanhurst
Grafton
Wilcannia
New South Wales
Caroona Mission
Kinchela
Upper Hunter Valley
Murray Bridge
Tailem Bend
Dubbo
Taree
Ivanhoe
Condobolin
Manning Valley
Forster
Point Pearce
Balaklava
Forbes
Karuah Mission
Merbein
Inset 2
Lithgow
Mount Olive Settlement
Mildura
Moonah Cullah Mission
SYDNEY
ADELAIDE
La Perouse
Lake Boga
Deniliquin
CANBERRA
Salt Pan Creek
Bomaderry
Lake Hindmarsh
Echuca
Cummeragunja Reserve
South Coast
Goolwa
/Raukkan
Victoria
ACT
Braidwood
MELBOURNE
Wallaga Lake
Conmurra
Hamilton
Ballarat
Healesville
Heywood
Corranderrk
Lake Condah Mission
Lake Tyers
Framlingham
Ramahyuck
Colac
Koo Wee Rup
Fort Queenscliff
Flinders Island
Cape Barren Island
Launceston
Tasmania
Claremont
HOBART

Sites of oral history interviews, 2010–17

1

Serving Our Country

Joan Beaumont and Allison Cadzow

'Honour, Recognition and Respect: Lest We Forget'
– *Anzac Day march banner, Redfern, Sydney*

Each Anzac Day the streets of Redfern, Sydney, are filled with Aboriginal and Torres Strait Islander marchers. Their supporters line the footpaths, clapping the service and ex-service men and women, as they move from the war memorial in Redfern Park to the nearby community centre, where a commemorative ceremony is then held.[1] The banner the marchers follow lists the international conflicts in which some have served and the words 'Honour, Recognition and Respect: Lest We Forget'. This vivid event, held since 2007, demands that the service of Aboriginal and Torres Strait Islander Australians in the defence of Australia be recognised after many decades of silence. It is a demand that has echoed across the twentieth century, when Indigenous Australians chose to defy racist restrictions and enlist in the defence forces, only to find that they gained spasmodic recognition and were denied full citizenship rights on their return to civilian life. It is a demand which has inspired this book.

Military service and citizenship

The recognition of Aboriginal and Torres Strait Island military service matters because for many decades their story has been marginalised in the national narratives of war, narratives that have formed a key element in Australia's political culture and its histories. It matters, too, because their service was given voluntarily, and in the face of discrimination which denied many Aboriginal and Torres Strait Islander Australians the right to serve in the defence forces. And it matters because this exclusion of Aboriginal and Torres Strait Islander Australians from military service was a testament to their being denied one of the key elements of citizenship. Across the twentieth century the political and social rights of Australia's Indigenous peoples were limited in multiple ways. Under the abhorrent 'protection' regimes of various state governments, which were initiated in the nineteenth century, but intensified in the twentieth century, many Indigenous Australians were stripped of their land, their mobility, their economic independence – and even their right to care for their own children. For many decades they could not exercise political rights, such as the right to vote in some states. But the denial of the right to join the defence forces was especially significant because historically, military service has been a core element in the contract between the state and its citizens. From the time of the French Revolution on, it was the men that took up arms in defence of the nation, either voluntarily or through being conscripted, who thereby earned their right to be citizens.[2] Women and minorities exempted from this obligation were relegated to an inferior political status for many centuries.

So it was to be with Aboriginal and Torres Strait Islander Australians. From the earliest days of the Australian federation in 1901, they were exempted from compulsory military service for home defence. In a political culture fervently committed to White

Australia, the obligation to serve the nation was placed only on those Australian men who were substantially of European origin or descent. This exclusion continued until 1917 when, under the pressures of the First World War, the military authorities accepted that 'half-castes', to use the racialised language of that time, could be eligible to serve in the Australian Imperial Force (AIF). With the return of peace in late 1918, however, the old policies of exclusion returned, despite vocal demands in the inter-war years by Aboriginal activists, some of whom were returned soldiers, for full citizenship rights. During the Second World War the military authorities reverted to the policy of the earlier war, allowing 'half-castes' but not 'full bloods' to serve. Only when the Australian continent was threatened with invasion in 1941–42 did the authorities finally concede that they needed to mobilise specific Indigenous units and labour forces in the defence of Australia's north. Even then, this was a temporary response to an unprecedented security crisis and the door to military service remained partly closed to Indigenous Australians. In the post-1945 period, some Aboriginal Australians were permitted to join the defence forces, but they were still exempted from the national service schemes of the 1950s and 1960s, thanks partly to continuing confusion about how to define 'Aboriginality'. Only in the late twentieth century were all formal barriers to Indigenous Australians entering the defence forces removed.

Given this history of systemic discrimination, it is remarkable that many thousands of Indigenous Australians were willing to serve in conflicts which Australia fought across the century between the Boer War and Afghanistan. Their exact numbers are not known, but around 1000 served in the First World War and some 3000–4000 (possibly 6000) in the Second World War. At least 300 Indigenous Australians served in the Vietnam War. Even more remarkably, these men and women chose to serve a nation that was the agent of their exclusion and disadvantage and which refused to grant them full citizenship rights even after they had risked their lives in Australia's defence. Moreover, during wartime this same nation controlled and disrupted the lives of the communities from which the Aboriginal servicemen had come, relocating their families to often distant locations, conscripting them for labour units, removing their children and even appropriating their land for soldier settlement schemes.

Why Aboriginal and Torres Strait Islander men and women were willing to volunteer for military service in such a context of disadvantage will always be a matter for conjecture. Many who served in past conflicts left no record of their motivation. However, it seems reasonable to infer that many wished to exercise their own agency: to better their economic situation, to improve their political status, and to demonstrate their equality with other Australians. But, as the oral histories of service personnel and their families testify, many also aspired to serve their 'country', a rich and nuanced term which embraces not only the Australian nation, the traditional focus of patriotism and loyalty, but also the land that has remained so central to the livelihood, culture and spirituality of Indigenous communities.

Between Aboriginal and military history

Although this story of Aboriginal and Torres Strait Islander military service is important, for decades it was neglected by academic historians. It was, as Noah Riseman has said, 'a very niche academic area'.[3] This is perhaps because the subject sits uneasily between two fields of academic history: military history and Aboriginal history. For different reasons neither of these cohorts of historians made the study of Indigenous service in the Australian defence forces a priority. Nor did they often engage with each other in collaborative research or dialogue.

Military historians have tended to focus their research and writing on narratives of war: the command structures, strategic planning, operational manoeuvres and tactical innovations of battle and deployments such as peacekeeping. In these histories what matters is the performance of collective units – such as armies, divisions, battalions and platoons – and the manner in which these have been led, supplied and deployed to achieve the political ends of war. Individuals have always played a part in these narratives: not just the commanders who have tried to determine the outcomes of wars but the soldiers who have lived and died at the so-called 'face of battle'.[4] However, in Australian popular military history at least, the individuals who have featured prominently have been those who have displayed exceptional courage and skill in battle; or those who have been slaughtered in military disasters, commonly attributed to the supposed incompetence of Australia's allies. Of less concern to military historians has been what these and other individuals did before they joined the defence forces. Their ethnicity, class or pre-war cultural identification are all assumed to have been eclipsed by their new collective identity. This, after all, is the purpose of military training: to subsume men and women of diverse cultural and social backgrounds into a unified, even homogenised, whole; and to transform them into a tightly knit collective in which individual differences are erased. In combat particularly, it is argued, the need for small-group cohesion makes any sensitivity to differences of race and class irrelevant and dangerous.

Hence, military historians have been inclined to question whether there is a distinctively 'ethnic' experience within the Australian defence forces. Given the functional demands of battle and the levelling regimes of the armed forces, can we speak of a specifically Aboriginal, Torres Strait Islander – or for that matter Russian-Australian or Chinese-Australian – experience of battle? The occasional monographs that have been written about ethnic minorities in the defence forces suggest not.[5] It is this, in part, which explains the relative indifference among military historians to the question of minorities, including Aboriginal and Torres Strait Islander Australians, within the defence forces.

This indifference also reflects the ethnic composition of Australia's defence institutions. Historically the Australian services have been the preserve of Anglo-Celtic men. Indigenous Australians have always been only a small fraction of the defence forces, as have other ethnic minorities and women.[6] Moreover, the foundational narrative spawned by the Australian experience of the First World War, the Anzac legend, arose at a time when Australia was overwhelmingly Anglo-Celtic. It, too, has been essentially a narrative of white men, despite recent attempts by Australian governments and their commemorative agencies to make this mythic narrative more inclusive on gender and ethnic grounds.[7] The pull towards ethnocentricity in the history of the defence forces has therefore been almost irresistible, especially as the majority of Australian military historians have been white men. Only in the fields of the social history and the memory of war have women been strongly represented.

Yet, if military historians have tended to overlook minorities in the defence forces, so too have scholars of Aboriginal history been slow to give any priority to the question of Indigenous military service. Over the past four decades Aboriginal historiography has become a rich and diverse field.[8] Its focus, naturally, has been on the impact of dispossession, discrimination and racism since the time of white settlement: the destructive legacy of colonialism on Indigenous culture and social organisation; the invidious Protection Acts controlling all dimensions of Indigenous life; the complexity of cross-cultural encounters from the time of white settlement; the forcible removal of children; the exploitation of women doubly marginalised by gender and race; the struggle for self-determination and rights to the land lost to the ever-encroaching European settlement; and, in some anthropologically influenced works, the need to record culture and languages seen to be 'lost'. For historians who are themselves Indigenous, a major concern has been the survival of their peoples, and, to quote John Maynard, the 'restoration and reconnection of Aboriginal people with the largely fragmented, lost and erased sections' of their history.[9] The agency of Aboriginal and Torres Strait Islander people, their resilience and their maintenance of continuities between family, community and country have thus been foregrounded, as have been their hope and distinctive humour developed through adversity.[10] As Maria Nugent has argued, Aboriginal family histories have significantly focused on naming people, providing information about connections between them, and broader understandings of Aboriginal identity and shared history.[11] Broader frameworks incorporating Aboriginal Dreaming stories, which pass important knowledge, cultural values and belief systems between generations, have also been employed in some histories. In these works Aboriginal and Torres Strait Islander voices and interpretations have been given prominence and are valued.[12]

A persistent theme of Aboriginal historiography has been conflict: especially the violence and the power of a racist state. Hence frontier wars; that is, the conflicts between white settlers and the Indigenous communities defending their land, spawned an extensive literature from the 1980s on, including by military historians crossing the genre divide.[13] Frontier wars, after all, even though they involve the difficult histories of the role played by Native Mounted Police in suppressing fellow Aboriginal peoples, lend themselves to the depiction of Indigenous Australians as heroes of resistance and victims of exploitation.[14] These are powerful tropes for historians seeking to support land rights campaigns and to make visible the underlying reasons for continuing Indigenous disadvantage.[15] In contrast, service in the international conflicts on which the Australian state regularly embarked during the twentieth century are less easily accommodated within the oppositional, assimilation-resisting narratives of some Aboriginal historiography. The exception has been the Second World War, which was recognised early on to have had a profound significance, especially for those Indigenous Australians living in Australia's north.[16]

Despite all this, the neglect of Indigenous military service in both Aboriginal and military historiographies should not be overstated. From the mid-1970s works by Chris Coulthard-Clark and David Huggonson signalled an emerging interest in the topic.[17] In the next decade Robert Hall published his pioneering study of 'Black Diggers' in the Second World War in 1989, a definitive work which was followed, in 1995, by his *Fighters from the Fringe*, a study which provided Aboriginal and Torres Strait Islander perspectives by telling stories of six Aboriginal servicemen and women.[18] In 1992, meanwhile, DJ Mulvaney and PJ Grimshaw convened a special issue of the journal, *Aboriginal History*, on 'Aborigines in the Services'. Its content ranged from studies of the now-iconic Aboriginal servicemen of the Second World War, Reginald Saunders and Leonard Waters, to oral histories of the Malayan Emergency and the Vietnam War, and advice on archival material such as anthropologist Donald Thomson's report on the Northern Territory Coastal Patrol and Special Reconnaissance Unit during the Second World War. In the following year Alick Jackomos and Derek Fowell published *Forgotten Heroes: Aborigines at War from the Somme to Vietnam*, a study which drew upon individual and family accounts of cross-generational service.[19] The role of Indigenous Australians in the defence of Australia's north, already examined by Hall, was further explored in Desmond Ball's *Aborigines in the Defence of Australia* (1991); in this the contributing authors examined the legal, demographic and cultural perspectives of both historical and contemporary deployments.[20] The impact of the First World War on Aboriginal soldiers also started to attract some attention, especially as the 75th anniversary of the Gallipoli landing in 1990 triggered an official and popular growth in the memory of Australia's experience of war.[21]

This remarkable memory 'boom', which continues to this day, was fuelled by a dynamic interaction between government, community and individual initiatives of commemoration (see pages 327–38 and Appendix 2). Coinciding with a powerful movement of Aboriginal political activism from the 1970s to 1980s on, the memory boom inspired both the production of films, documentaries and drama showcasing Indigenous military service, and also the publication of the life stories of Indigenous ex-servicemen and women.[22] Complementing these were several state-, or area-based, community studies: Aboriginal journalist Rory O'Connor's *Yugambeh: In Defence of Our Country*, about Aboriginal Gold Coast people who served in Australia; George Bray, Kenny Laughton (an Arrernte ex-serviceman) and Pat Foster's *Aboriginal Ex-servicemen of Central Australia*; and Doreen Kartinyeri's *Ngarrindjeri Anzacs*, which told the stories of soldiers and families, including her relatives from Point McLeay in South Australia.[23]

Academic historians too began to address the question of how Aboriginal service was recognised or neglected. Ken Inglis's seminal study of war memorials noted the exclusion of Aboriginal service from past memorials while deeming more recent and diverse efforts as 'few, modest and late'.[24] Meanwhile Ann Curthoys explored in 2000 the historical exclusion of Aboriginal service from the national mythology of war and remembrance more recently.[25]

The growing momentum of wider Australian war commemoration also empowered Aboriginal and Torres Strait Islander Australians to press for more public recognition of their military service. While local Indigenous communities initiated their own remembrance practices, official agencies such as the Department of Veterans' Affairs, the National Archives of Australia, the Australian War Memorial and the Australian Institute for Aboriginal and Torres Strait Islander Studies (AIATSIS) raised the profile of Indigenous service in their national and state-based commemorative rituals and exhibitions. With the digitisation of the records of First and some Second World War military service by the National Archives of Australia, it also became easier for professional and family historians to conduct detailed research on men who served in Australia's wars: the date and place of their enlistment, their age and previous work experience; their deployments overseas; and, especially, their deaths and injuries. Like many Australians, then, Aboriginal and Torres Strait Islander service personnel were able to become more 'visible'. Their families and communities had long cherished stories of their forebears' service, but now these could be enriched with empirical details. Moreover, family memories could be positioned within the wider, national narrative of war.

In the last two decades, therefore, significant new research has been published on Aboriginal and Torres Strait Islander servicemen and women, including many publications on the First World War by public historian Philippa Scarlett, Jan James's *Forever Warriors*, and a host of state government–supported projects and websites.[26] In 2015 *Aboriginal History* again dedicated a special section to Aboriginal war service, in which the growing breadth of the field was reflected in articles covering the Boer War (John Maynard), the problems of identity and mateship in the First World War (Philippa Scarlett), the aftermath of the war for Aboriginal soldiers in the Western District of Victoria (Jessica Horton), Tasmanian Aboriginal men's service (Andrea Gerrard and Kristyn Harman), and the provision of comforts by white women to Aboriginal soldiers during the Second World War (Kristyn Harman).[27] Other recent academic works have included Noah Riseman's studies of the Indigenous people in the Second World War and (with Richard Trembath) post-1945 conflicts.[28] Riseman has also analysed the links between military service and post-war activism and, like the Canadian/US scholar, Timothy Winegard, has positioned the Aboriginal and Torres Strait Islander military experience within a wider transnational, comparative context, especially that of settler colonialism.[29] As Riseman notes, the growing interest in Indigenous military history has been 'a global postcolonial phenomenon'.[30]

This book builds on these foundations, documenting in a single volume many aspects of the Aboriginal and Torres Strait Islander experiences of military service in war and peace across the twentieth century. Our focus is on the national defence forces, dating from the time of Australian federation, and is not limited to a single state or region. Against this broad canvas we examine the obstructive policies that Aboriginal and Torres Strait Islander peoples had to surmount in order to join the defence forces; their motivations for enlisting despite these obstacles; their experiences of active service and professional employment once they had managed to enter the defence forces; and the legacies of service, for both individuals and Indigenous communities across Australia.

However, our scope is wider than formal service within the Australian defence forces. In the two world wars particularly, the battle and home fronts were in dialogue with each other, events in the one shaping perceptions and actions in the other. In the Second World War the Australian home front in the north literally became a battle front. Hence, we consider those Aboriginal and Torres Strait Islander Australians who stayed at home, and the way their lives were shaped by the social dislocation and economic mobilisation that came with war. Acknowledging, too, that the impact of war continued beyond the end of formal fighting, we trace its physical and emotional legacy. Having served the Australian nation and enjoyed an environment relatively free of racism, Indigenous Australians returned (at least after both world wars) to institutionalised discrimination. Moreover, their adjustment on their return seems to have been exacerbated by the difficulties many encountered in accessing the benefits of military service, such as pensions and soldier settlement, which were available to their non-Aboriginal counterparts.

In telling this complex story, this book draws on both the archival records, on which the history of defence has traditionally relied, and the memoirs and oral history of Aboriginal and Torres Strait Islander peoples. Wherever possible, the story of the experience of war is presented in the voices of the men and women who lived it, and the families who remembered it across the generations.

Telling Aboriginal and Torres Strait Islander stories of service

Giving voice to these Aboriginal and Torres Strait Islander narratives poses some methodological challenges. In the first place, it is simply difficult to identify how many Indigenous men served in past conflicts, and who they were. At no time in the past century have men and women enlisting in Australia's defence forces been required to list their ethnicity. Indigenous volunteers in the First World War were routinely described by the medical officers as 'dark', but this was not a precise or reliable descriptor of ethnicity. In addition, there were multiple, and confusing, definitions of 'Aboriginality' in force at different times within the different states and Commonwealth. Only in recent years has meticulous research by families, historians, the National Archives of Australia and the Australian War Memorial produced something approaching a comprehensive list of over 1000 Indigenous soldiers who served in the First World War. Yet even this list may yet be expanded as more Indigenous families identify ancestors who served without their ethnicity being known or disclosed. Meanwhile, we are far from having any definitive list of Aboriginal and Torres Strait Islander Australians who served in the Second World War.

To this problem of the bureaucratic invisibility of Aboriginal and Torres Strait Islander peoples within the defence forces must be added their relatively limited presence in many written sources, such as memoirs, diaries and autobiographies. Certainly Indigenous servicemen sent letters and postcards home from the front, some of which are quoted in this volume, but like most Australian service personnel, they left few written memoirs of their service.[31] As Peter Dennis and Jean Bou say in their 2015 study of the 1st AIF: 'the individual stories of most Indigenous members of the AIF, like the AIF as a whole, are known only to their immediate families, or, in some cases, to their communities, or to a small but growing band of researchers who have sought to make their service more widely known'.[32]

Ultimately, however, it is not written text but oral communication which is at the heart of Indigenous historiography. This has been the mode of transmission of knowledge within Indigenous communities over the centuries, and it continues to be important today. Oral history, too, has long been recognised by historians as a means of capturing the perspectives of those often excluded from written sources: the poor, the illiterate, women and other marginalised groups. Oral history is not a simple recovery exercise, however. It involves a complex dialogue between interviewee and interviewer, and between the past as it is remembered and present concerns. A 'facts and figures' approach fails to appreciate the unique dimensions of oral history – such as working with interviewees' interpretation of their experience and often emotional content too, as Lynn Abrams has argued.[33] As Alessandro Portelli's frequently quoted work has noted: 'Memory is not a passive depository of facts, but an active process of the creation of meanings.'[34] This 'active process' of making memory is influenced by the responses of particular audiences, narrative frameworks available to the narrator at different points in time and cultural memory – in forms such as film and other cultural media. Alistair Thomson's work on First World War veterans has shown, for example, the tendency of veterans to reshape their individual life stories in accordance with dominant collective narratives, as well as how their stories altered over time.[35] Oral history, then, has the undeniable value of revealing how the events of the past are shaped, framed, interpreted and invested with significance by those individuals and communities recalling them.

Hence, it was to oral history that the authors of this book, like many recent scholars of Aboriginal history, turned in their search to capture Aboriginal and Torres Strait Islander voices and memories of war. In some cases oral history interviews had been conducted by the authors or other scholars on earlier occasions. But the majority of interviews informing this book were conducted by a team of multi-disciplinary scholars who participated in an Australian Research Council Linkage project, Serving Our Country. With the support of five partner institutions – the Australian Institute for Aboriginal and Torres Strait Islander Studies, the Australian War Memorial, the Department of Defence, the Department of Veterans' Affairs, and the National Archives of Australia – we undertook in 2014 to 2017 a series of interviews with current and ex-service personnel, and their families and their descendants. These Yarn Ups – a conversational and welcoming term devised by the project's Community Consultation Coordinator, to avoid any connotations of the perfunctory 'consultation' by government practice – were held at 41 locations across Australia (see map p. xviii). In all, some 184 interviews were conducted. Participants were self-selected, responding to a variety of invitations: personal requests by the project's Community Consultation Coordinator, flyers circulated through community contacts, notices posted on the website and Facebook page of the project, Our Mob Served, and publicity provided through Aboriginal radio stations, the Special Broadcasting Service, the Australian Broadcasting Corporation, the *Koori Mail* and other local publications.[36] The snowball effect, whereby one interviewee recommended another, widened our reach. Interviews also provided the names of people who were otherwise not identified as

Aboriginal or Torres Strait Islander people in the official records of military service.

Of those interviewed in these Yarn Ups, 85 had records of defence service, including national service and in the reserves; 34 had undergone active service overseas: in the Second World War, Korea, Confrontation with Indonesia, Vietnam, Somalia, Timor-Leste, Iraq and Afghanistan. Six of these 34 men had served in more than one conflict. Women were a minority of those with military service: this is unsurprising given that they carried the double marginalisation of race and gender. However, women made up the majority (73 of 118) of those who, while not serving themselves, chose to take on the responsibility for passing on family history and sharing collective memories. In informal environments – venues such as community cultural centres, local organisations and Aboriginal-run radio stations – these people told their stories of war and military service, sometimes for the first time in public, and shared photos or other memorabilia that illuminated their oral histories. In cases where mobility was an issue, people were interviewed in their homes.

The readiness with which these community members shared their often deeply personal testimonies spoke to the value of some members of the initial contact and interview team being Indigenous: Yawuru Aboriginal public figure, Mick Dodson, Worimi historian John Maynard and Gurindji/Warlpiri Community Consultation Coordinator, Craig Greene. These men brought to the interview process a cultural 'short hand', and in Maynard's case considerable experience with Aboriginal oral history, which put those being interviewed at ease. The commitment of time and energy to the project by Dodson, a former counsel assisting the Royal Commission into Aboriginal Deaths in Custody, Aboriginal and Torres Strait Islander Social Justice Commissioner for the Bringing them Home hearings and a member of the United Nations Working

Group on Indigenous Populations, affirmed the seriousness and gravitas of the project. Where non-Indigenous oral historians like Allison Cadzow, and the highly experienced Noah Riseman and Mary Anne Jebb, conducted the interviews, they deliberately framed the experience as a semi-structured dialogue, working off Lorina Barker's yarnin' research methodology.[37] They took their cues from the interviewees, allowing them to tell their story as they saw fit, with an occasional prompt. Questions were open-ended, covering a range of topics including motivation for joining the defence forces, experiences before and after service, and later memory-making and remembrance.

Many of the stories told in these interviews inform the chapters that follow.[38] Naturally, given the coverage of the project across many decades and multiple armed conflicts, the interviews are diverse. The voices of the Yarn Ups become more prominent in the more recent conflicts being considered. No one who fought in the First World War remains alive and the numbers of Second World War and Korea veterans is rapidly declining: we interviewed only one from each conflict. For these earlier wars families are now the custodians of memory.

Whether it was servicemen and women, or families recalling what they had been told across the generations, the message was common: these Aboriginal men and women take fierce pride in their own and their forebears' military service. Always there was a desire to make the story of Indigenous military service better known to the wider Australian public and to gain appropriate recognition. Furthermore, many of those who served spoke positively of the opportunities the defence forces had offered them: the chance to acquire professional skills denied them in civilian life, and to make cross-cultural friendships in an environment surprisingly free from racial prejudice. Yet some spoke also, more negatively, of painful recollections of combat; the scars left by the war (including Post

Traumatic Stress Disorder), and the strategies they had developed to cope with the aftermath of war. Others manifested a reticence, even a silence, about episodes of the past, which was itself telling about how these men and women have reconstructed their personal histories.

Families and descendants, likewise, recalled narratives of combat, in this case distilled through the stories passed down across the generations. They spoke too of the impact of war trauma on the families of which they were part. This trauma was often compounded by events not directly related to military service: government policies that cut through family and community structures, children being abducted while family members were serving outside their community, service personnel being refused alcohol service in hotels on their return, and doors to some of the clubs of the Returned and Services League (RSL) being closed. Such memories were, of course, not always the family members' 'own', but they were burned into their minds as children and grandchildren. They represent what a scholar of the Holocaust, Marianne Hirsch, has called post-memory, or 'the relationship that the "generation after" bears to the personal, collective, and cultural trauma of those who came before'. Children and grandchildren, though not actual participants, 'remembered' experiences by means of the stories, images and behaviours among which they grew up; these experiences have been transmitted to them 'so deeply and affectively as to seem to constitute memories in their own right'.[39]

Recognition and respect

From this rich archive of interviews (now available for public access) and the archival research conducted during this project, there emerges a narrative which is both familiar and new, complex and ambiguous.[40] Across the twentieth century Australian governments and military authorities consistently adopted policies towards military service which ensured that this important path to full citizenship rights was officially denied to Australia's Indigenous peoples. Yet, in practice, thousands of Aboriginal and Torres Strait Islander Australians remained willing, even eager, to serve. They managed to evade policy restrictions and join the defence forces. Many more were caught up in the mobilisation of Australian society during the two world wars. For some Aboriginal and Torres Strait Islander people this military service and wartime labour, in the Second World War particularly, provided an opportunity to acquire valuable skills and training. Moreover, it provided a deep sense of empowerment, especially as Indigenous Australians were integrated into defence services which, for all their inherent hierarchy, were relatively free at the operational levels of the racism so deeply entrenched in wider Australian society.

However, this 'equality' was qualified. The historical record shows that few Aboriginal and Torres Strait Islander Australians were able to surmount their structural disadvantage and gain commissioned rank during the two world wars, as well as Korea and Vietnam. And when military units were stationed in Australia during the Second World War, as opposed to being on overseas service, Indigenous soldiers seem to have found it difficult to escape the constraints imposed by the local Protection legislation, such as bans on drinking alcohol and curfews restricting Aboriginal peoples' movements.[41]

Furthermore, when Aboriginal and Torres Strait Islander servicemen and women returned home from service in the two world wars, they found that their political and social status had not been transformed. Individuals may have been empowered by their personal experiences of war, but their service in itself did not prove sufficient to drive structural change in Australia's military institutions and wider political culture. Aboriginal servicemen in the First

World War were not granted full citizenship rights on their return and few gained access to the land made available to ex-servicemen under the soldier settlement schemes. Indeed, land was taken from Aboriginal communities to be given to white ex-servicemen, while the many harsh controls of the state Protection regimes remained in place. It was this that led some Aboriginal ex-servicemen and their families to join the burgeoning protest movements of the 1920s and 1930s.

Service in the Second World War, meanwhile, did bring a significant political gain that was directly attributable to military service, in that Aboriginal and Torres Strait Islander servicemen and women were granted in the mid and late 1940s a qualified right to vote in Western Australian and Commonwealth elections. But while the door to Indigenous recruitment to the defence forces opened a little in the 1950s and 1960s, there was still no clear-cut obligation on these peoples to undertake national service. The activism of Indigenous ex-servicemen and women in the 1960s also did not succeed in changing the policy framework of the Australian defence forces. This transformation only came in the late twentieth century when new societal norms, and the wider civil rights movement, both within Australia and internationally, made the overtly racist policies of the past obnoxious and anachronistic.

Hence, in recent years the Australian Defence Force (ADF) has been proactive in seeking to attract Indigenous men and women to the three services, the Army, the Royal Australian Navy and the Royal Australian Air Force. Their efforts have included encouraging Indigenous participation in Regional Force Surveillance Units (RFSUs) in remote northern Australia, such as NORFORCE (North-West Mobile Force), and offering dedicated pre-recruitment training programs for young Indigenous Australians. However, for all its commendable efforts to reverse its long history of discrimination, the ADF is failing to meet the participation targets set in its Reconciliation Action Plans. Perhaps, so long as wider societal structural disadvantage continues, for example, in lower levels of Indigenous educational achievement, it will be difficult to achieve the representation of Aboriginal and Torres Strait Islander Australians in the nation's defence forces that is commensurate with their numbers in the wider population.

Yet, if these structural issues (which also inhibit the ADF achieving gender balance and multicultural diversity) remain intractable, there have been major advances in recent decades in the national recognition of Indigenous military service. As mentioned, those interviewed for the Serving Our Country project spoke often of the pride that they take in their personal and family histories of service. They also demanded the recognition and respect to which they believe this service entitles them and their communities. In many ways this recognition is now being accorded, not just in the new rituals of remembrance which have sprung up in Indigenous communities across Australia, but also in state and national commemoration. Working with Indigenous communities, the Australian War Memorial, the Department of Veterans' Affairs, the National Archives of Australia and many other public agencies have granted Aboriginal and Torres Strait Islander military service a prominent place in their commemorative rituals and historical exhibitions. Most notably, since 2015 the dawn service on Anzac Day in Canberra, has opened with the evocative playing of the didgeridoo from the parapets of the Australian War Memorial, the key institution in the national memory of war. Such recognition, it should be said, has not come at the expense of honouring non-Indigenous service personnel. Rather it has illuminated the diversity of those Australians who have contributed to the national war effort over the past century, countering the perceptions that the Anzacs of the past were exclusively white. It has also given a new visibility to the role that Aboriginal and Torres Strait Islander Australians have played in the defence of the nation, a subject about which many Australians may have previously known little.

However, this is only part of the story that needs to be told. The same recognition needs to be accorded to the violent encounters between white settlers and Indigenous communities, as both peoples fought to control land and resources from 1788 onwards. The institutions of the Australian state currently refuse to accord these battles the same recognition as service in the nation's defence forces, but in the memories of some of those interviewed for this project, and some Aboriginal historians, the two narratives of conflict are interconnected.[42] The violence of wars, at home and internationally, together with another act of profound violence, the Stolen Generations, have a seamless continuity in individual and community memories. Those interviewed for this book are not alone in making such connections. In 2011 a contingent from the Aboriginal Tent Embassy outside Old Parliament House Canberra joined the rear of the Anzac Day march proceeding along Anzac Parade towards the Australian War Memorial. They carried a banner declaring 'Lest We Forget the Frontier Wars'. Their leader meanwhile not only wore the medals that his grandfather had won before being killed in the First World War; he carried a boomerang and nulla nulla, weapons that could have been used in frontier conflict. This powerful demonstration of 'dual commemoration', as Fiona Nicoll has called it, continues to this day.[43] On the 2017 Anzac Day march in Canberra, a contingent of Aboriginal and Torres Strait Islander servicemen and women, past and current, led the official march for the first time. But again at the rear a group of Aboriginal and Torres Strait Islander people and supporters stood silent with their flags and a banner proclaiming, 'Lest We Forget the Frontier Wars'. On this traditional day of state remembrance and on the official mall of war memory, Anzac Parade, both conflicts were present and powerfully represented.

Perhaps, then, it is too narrow to frame the Indigenous experience of war, as this project itself does, as a series of episodes and policies relating to military conflicts fought by the Australian state. Important and overdue though recognition of this defence service is, it should not serve to inhibit the national remembering of a more difficult past in which violence, physical and institutional, profoundly and persistently distorted and damaged the lives of Australia's Indigenous communities, who, despite it all, have survived and are willing to share their histories of defending their country.

2

Race, citizenship and military service

Siobhan McDonnell and Mick Dodson

The play *Black Diggers* opens in a recruiting office during the First World War. Ern, an Aboriginal man, approaches the recruiting officer and the scene unfolds:

> Recruiting CPL: Age and place of birth?
> Ern: Nineteen, Barambah.
> Recruiting CPL: Barambah? [Looks up for the first time] Jesus Christ! Pardon the profanity. You can't come in here.
> Ern: Why not?
> Recruiting CPL: Well, you're … you're not a citizen.
> Ern: Subject of His Majesty.
> Recruiting CPL: Smart alec eh? Here. Here's your form. It'll go down a treat at the protector's office.
> Ern: 'Deficient Physique'. What does that mean?
> Recruiting CPL: It's all there. Next!
> Ern: 'Reason: Of Strongly Aboriginal Appearance'.[1]

Here, Ern's attempt to enlist for military service is denied on two grounds: first, his political status; he is 'not a citizen' and second, his race; he is 'of strongly Aboriginal Appearance'. In response Ern argues that he is a British subject and is told by the recruiting officer that he is being 'a smart alec' and that he needs to report to the protector's office. Although a work of fiction, this compact, eloquently written scene introduces the complex intersections of race, citizenship and military service in Australia – themes that are explored in this chapter.

Table 2.1
Indigenous and defence policy, citizenship and rights

1816	Governor Macquarie (NSW) issues a proclamation that Aboriginal people are protected by British law.
1837	A British Parliamentary Select Committee recommends that 'Protectors of Aborigines' be appointed.
1869	*Aborigines Protection Board Act 1869* (Vic): establishes a Board for the Protection of Aborigines.
1886	*Aborigines Protection Act 1886* (WA): establishes an Aborigines Protection Board.
1897	*Protection of Aboriginals and the Restriction of the Sale of Opium Act 1897* (QLD): establishes powers over Aboriginal and 'half-caste' inhabitants of the colony.
1899–1902	The Boer War.
1901	1 January: Federation of Australia.
1903	*Defence Act 1903* (Cth): establishes small permanent army and volunteer citizens' militia.
1905	*Aborigines Act 1905* (WA): establishes a 'Chief Protector' as legal guardian of every Aboriginal and 'half-caste' child under 16 years of age.
1909	*Aborigines Protection Act 1909* (NSW): establishes a Board for the Protection of Aborigines. *Defence Act 1909* (Cth): introduces compulsory military training but exempts men 'not substantially of European origin or descent'.
1910	*Northern Territory Aboriginals Act 1910* (SA): establishes the NT Aboriginals Department. The Chief Protector may undertake the care, custody or control of any 'Aboriginal' or 'half-caste'.
1910	*Naval Defence Act 1910* (Cth).
1911	*Aborigines Act 1911* (SA): establishes the Chief Protector of Aboriginals and a system of regional protectors.

1912	*Cape Barren Island Reserve Act 1912* (Tas.): creates Cape Barren Island as a subdivided reserve for Aboriginal people.
1914	August: The First World War begins.
1915	*Aborigines Amending Act 1915* (NSW): removes the requirement that an Aboriginal child had to be neglected in order to be removed.
1917	Military regulations altered to allow enlistment of 'half-castes' in the Australian Imperial Force.
1918	*Aboriginals Ordinance 1918* (NT): gives the Chief Protector wide powers over Aboriginal people by broadening the definition of who was deemed to be 'Aboriginal'.
1923	Royal Australian Air Force created. *Aborigines (Training of Children) Act 1923* (SA): expands the definition of 'Aboriginal' and 'half-caste'; provides for the removal of an 'Aboriginal child' upon decision by the Chief Protector that the child was neglected.
1934	*Protection of Aboriginals and the Restriction of the Sale of Opium Act Amendment 1934* (QLD): extends the powers of the Chief Protector 'to any person who is the grandchild of an Aboriginal or half caste', and 'any person of Aboriginal or Pacific Islander extraction who lives or associates with aboriginals'. A 'half-caste' could also be exempted from the provisions of the Act.
1936	*Aborigines Protection Amendment Act 1936* (NSW): broadens the definition of 'Aborigine'. *Native Administration Act 1936* (WA): broadens the definition of 'native' to include 'any person of less than full blood excluding a quadroon' under 21 who did not associate with 'full bloods'.
1937	21–23 April: emergence of explicit assimilation agenda at Conference of Commonwealth and State Aboriginal Authorities which states 'This conference believes that the destiny of the natives of aboriginal origin, but not of the full blood, lies in their ultimate absorption by the people of the Commonwealth.'
1938	26 January: The Australian Aborigines Conference, Sydney, marks a Day of Mourning on the 150th anniversary of the settlement of NSW.

1939	September: Second World War begins. 'New Deal' policy released, based upon the economic and social absorption of Aboriginal people. The Native Affairs Branch established and Chief Protector of Aboriginals abolished and replaced by the Director of Native Affairs. (NT)
1940	*Aborigines Protection Amendment Act 1940* (NSW): The Protection Board is replaced by the Aborigines Welfare Board. Any Aboriginal child found to be neglected to become a 'ward of the Board'. (NSW) May: Recruitment to 2nd Australian Imperial Force restricted to those 'substantially of European origin and descent'.
1941	*Native Administration Amendment Act 1941* (WA): restricts the right of Aboriginal people to move from north to south of the state.
1944	*Native (Citizenship Rights) Act 1944* (WA): allows applications by a 'native' for a 'certificate of citizenship' of the state. Application includes a statutory declaration stating that for at least two years the applicant has dissolved 'tribal and native association' and 'that he has served in the Naval, Military or Air Force and has received or is entitled to receive an honourable discharge'. The holder of a certificate shall be deemed to be 'no longer a native or aborigine'.
1947	Regular Australian Army established.
1949	Extension of Commonwealth franchise to Indigenous veterans and serving members.
1950	Australia commits forces to the Korean War.
1951	*National Service Act 1951* (Cth): Indigenous Australians not required to register.
1953	Aboriginal populations affected by atomic bomb testing carried out at Emu and Maralinga, SA.
1954	*Native Welfare Act 1954* (WA): The Commissioner of the Department of Native Affairs becomes the Commissioner of the Native Welfare, retains powers as the legal guardian of native children.

1957	*Aborigines Act 1957* (Vic): establishes the Aboriginal Welfare Board 'to promote the moral, intellectual and physical welfare of aborigines (full blood and half-caste) with a view to their assimilation in the general community'. Changes to the *Licensing Act 1957* (Vic), Aboriginal people have the right to drink and sell alcohol.
1960	*Native Welfare Act 1963* (WA): 'quadroons' exempted from the definition of 'native'.
1961	Native Welfare Conference defines its assimilation policy as: 'all aborigines and part-aborigines are expected eventually to attain the same manner of living as other Australians and to live as members of a single Australian community enjoying the same rights and privileges, accepting the same responsibilities, observing the same customs and influenced by the same beliefs, hopes and loyalties as other Australians'.
1962	The Aborigines Protection Board (SA) replaced by the Aboriginal Affairs Board. The new Board ceases to be the legal guardian of Aboriginal children. *Electoral Act Amendments 1962* (Cth): allows Aboriginal and Torres Strait Islanders to vote in federal elections.
1963	*Aborigines Protection Amendment Act 1963* (NSW): repeal of provisions allowing magistrates to place 'mixed blood' Aborigines under control of the Board; allows Aboriginal and non-Aboriginal people to live together. *Native Welfare Act 1963* (WA): The Commissioner ceases to be the guardian of 'native minors'. Only 'natives' and specified persons may remain on reserves. Regulations may be made for the care or control of the 'children of natives'.
1964	Restrictions on the sale of alcohol to Aboriginal people are lifted. (NT) *National Service Act 1964* (Cth): Indigenous Australians not required to register.
1965	*Aboriginal and Torres Strait Islander Affairs Act 1965* (QLD): establishes a Director of Aboriginal and Islander Affairs in place of the Director of Native Welfare. The Director no longer the legal guardian of Aboriginal and Torres Strait Islander children. Extension of the franchise in WA and QLD. Australia commits infantry to Vietnam War.

1966	NT: The Australian Workers' Union brings a case to the Commonwealth Arbitration Commission, seeking equal wages for Aboriginal pastoral workers in the Northern Territory. Equal wages implemented in 1968.
1967	Referendum to amend the race power in the Constitution to allow the Commonwealth to pass special laws with respect to Aboriginal people. As initially drafted, section 51(xxvi) empowered the parliament to make laws with respect to 'The people of any race, *other than the aboriginal race in any State*, for whom it is deemed necessary to make special laws.' The referendum vote deleted the words in italics.
1969	NSW: repeal of the remaining various *Protection Act* provisions still in place.
1971	*Aborigines Act 1971* (QLD): abolishes the status of an 'assisted Aborigine'. An offence to be on a reserve unless entitled to be under the Act. Regulations are made under the Act to promote the policy of assimilation. WA: repeal of remaining restrictions on Aboriginal people drinking alcohol.
1975	*Racial Discrimination Act* (Cth)
1976	*Aboriginal Land Rights Act* (NT)
1989	*Aboriginal and Torres Strait Islander Commission Act* (Cth)
1992	*Defence Legislation Amendment Act 1992* (Cth): removes clause exempting Indigenous men from national service in time of war.
1992–4	1992 Mabo decision overturns the doctrine of 'terra nullius' and recognises Native Title.
1997	*Bringing Them Home* report presented to Parliament, detailing the impact of policies of child removal upon Aboriginal and Torres Strait Islander families.
2007	Northern Territory Emergency Response (Intervention).
2008	Prime Minister Kevin Rudd apologises to the Stolen Generations.

Military service by 'black diggers' must be located in the broader history of the treatment of Aboriginal and Torres Strait Islander people in Australian society. This chapter provides an overview of the laws that governed the lives of Indigenous people across a 150-year period (see Table 2.1). It charts the discrimination faced by Indigenous Australians under the oppressive regulatory and bureaucratic regimes established during the late nineteenth and early twentieth centuries, primarily via the various Protection Acts. Though these were implemented at the state level, they provided the context within which Aboriginal enlistment and service in the Commonwealth defence forces took place.

Despite the restrictions which the authorities placed on the enlistment of Indigenous men for military service, many did manage to serve in the First and Second World Wars and during the Korean and Vietnam Wars. Their service suggests that while few Aboriginal and Torres Strait Islanders were immune from the discriminatory regimes, they were able to express varying degrees of agency in circumventing the controls exercised over their lives.

In Australia citizenship does not automatically confer civil rights. In 1901 the Australian Constitution declared all Australians, including Indigenous people, to be British subjects. In spite of this overarching status, in practice the rights afforded to Indigenous people were negotiated through legislative arrangements between various states and the Commonwealth. This meant that Aboriginal and Torres Strait Islander people often held the status of lesser subjects whose civil rights were more restricted than other Australians, evident particularly in the restrictions in the franchise. However, from the 1940s onwards military service became a basis for the recognition of civil rights for Aboriginal and Torres Strait Islander Australians both in citizenship legislation adopted in Western Australian law and, subsequently, by the Commonwealth.

Early Protection Acts

For much of the twentieth century, many Aboriginal people lived under restrictive legislation commonly called Protection Acts. The idea of protection evolved in the early nineteenth century, influenced by British anti-slavery movements that campaigned for an inquiry by a British Parliamentary Select Committee.[2] The Committee Report in 1837 drew attention to the violence of Australian colonial settlement, recommending the appointment of 'protectors' to provide for the benevolent care of 'uncivilised' natives.[3] Protectors were subsequently appointed in the Port Phillip district of New South Wales (later Victoria), and in South Australia and Western Australia. However, they were often resented by the settler population, especially in Port Phillip where the protectorate was disbanded in 1849.[4]

During the mid-nineteenth century these early administrative arrangements around 'protectors' evolved as colonies were granted responsible government by the British parliament. Colonial jurisdictions devised legislation that, while framed in terms of 'protecting aborigines', was actually designed to promote the interests of settler populations by continuing the widespread dispossession of Aboriginal people of their land. Together these Acts, often referred to as 'Aborigines Protection Acts', established the legislative basis for the draconian regulatory and bureaucratic regimes which governed the lives of Aboriginal and Torres Strait Islander people well into the twentieth century with enduring and traumatic historical legacies.

Formal protection regimes were established in three jurisdictions in the mid- to late nineteenth century: Victoria in 1869; Western Australia in 1886; and Queensland in 1897. Where legislative schemes were not in place, or not enforced, such as in the Northern Territory, Aboriginal people continued to live a reasonably independent existence depending on their proximity to the colonial frontier or mission stations. Differing settler land uses impacted on the likelihood of co-existence in New South Wales, influencing the degree of independence and access to land that Aboriginal people were able to negotiate.[5]

The first Protection Board was established in Victoria in 1869.[6] For the next 90 years the board oversaw the operation of Aboriginal reserves and mission stations across Victoria, which in 1874 covered a combined population of around 500 Aboriginal people located in communities at Coranderrk, Framlingham, Lake Condah, Lake Hindmarsh, Ramahyuck and Lake Tyers. The principal roles for the Victorian Protection Board were to determine the location where any Aboriginal group could reside; provide custody and education for Aboriginal children; distribute bedding, clothing and other articles; and maintain bans on the sale of alcohol to the Aboriginal population. Although precise provisions varied between jurisdictions, the core arrangements of various Protection Acts largely replicated this early Victorian model.

The colonial (later state) governments adopted numerous and conflicting definitions of 'Aboriginality', sometimes excluding 'half-caste' people from specific provisions and at other times including them. In 1884 the Victorian Protection Board argued that 'half-caste' people should be excluded from Aboriginal reserves with the intention that they would then assimilate with the wider population.[7] Subsequent amendments to the Victorian *Aborigines Protection Act 1886* differentiated between the treatment of 'full-blood' and 'half-caste' Aboriginal people, resulting in the expulsion of 'some forty families' from reserve areas.[8] Such definitions of Aboriginality later informed policy and law around Aboriginal peoples' eligibility to serve in the defence forces, where distinctions between people were also based on blood quantum.

Another focus of early protection regimes was ensuring that Aboriginal people were not forced into slavery.[9] In Queensland the

Aboriginal Protection and Prevention of the Sale of Opium Act 1897 (hereafter the Queensland Act) regulated the use of Aboriginal labour, developed work permits for Aboriginal people and required that employment of any Aboriginal woman be approved by a protector.[10] Over the next century many jurisdictions remained preoccupied with regulating Aboriginal employment.

The Queensland Act of 1897 also mandated the relocation of Aboriginal people to reserves and missions for their 'protection' and prohibited the sale of opium and alcohol to the Aboriginal population.[11] The effect of the Queensland Act, like the earlier Victorian Act, was to strip Aboriginal Australians of their rights as British subjects and to make them effectively wards of the state.[12] The Act operated as government policy for the next 40 years, and was largely replicated across three separate jurisdictions: Western Australia, South Australia and the Northern Territory.

Race, citizenship and the Australian Constitution

The correct terminology for the citizenship status ascribed to Indigenous people in the late nineteenth and early twentieth centuries has been a matter of academic debate. In their study of the ways in which Aboriginal and Torres Strait Islander people were excluded from the rights of Australian citizenship between the 1880s and 1990s, John Chesterman and Brian Galligan refer to Indigenous Australians as 'citizens without rights'.[13] Federation debates held in the lead-up to 1901 contained minimal reference to Aboriginal people largely because, following the received wisdom of the day, it was believed that Aboriginal people were a 'dying race'. Despite this general lack of attention, the resulting text of the Constitution refers to Aboriginal people in two places. Article 51(xxvi) of the Constitution stated that the parliament should have the power to make laws for the peace, order and good government of the Commonwealth with respect to '[t]he people of any race, other than the aboriginal race in any State, for whom it is deemed necessary to make special laws'. Section 127 of the Constitution stated that '[i]n reckoning the numbers of people of the Commonwealth, or of a State or other part of the Commonwealth, aboriginal natives shall not be counted'. The records of the debates fail to indicate the basis for the inclusion of these clauses although Robert Garran, who officiated at federation conferences, suggested the reference to 'the aboriginal race' in Article 51(xxvi) was an afterthought.[14] Another reason for the exclusion of Aboriginal people was the entrenched idea of ethnic nationalism. Russell McGregor argues that '[w]hiteness was also a badge of Britishness, and it was Britishness that underpinned Australia's nationhood'.[15] Concepts of race and of ethnic nationalism appear regularly in early federation debates, with Henry Parkes evocatively presaging the importance of the 'crimson thread of kinship' imagined as the ethnic solidarity of white Australians, both with each other and with their British ancestry.[16]

Debates prior to federation also record the rejection of the idea of defining citizenship within the Constitution. This meant that at federation Aboriginal people, like other Australians, were understood to be 'British subjects' by virtue of having been born in Australia. Rather than this status automatically conferring a set of civil rights, the rights accorded to Aboriginal subjects were defined largely by state legislation. The effect of Article 51(xxvi) was that the right to legislate with respect to Aboriginal people was retained by the states, thereby allowing the ongoing operation of various protection regimes.[17]

State legislation routinely denied the Aboriginal people the civil rights commonly associated with citizenship, including the franchise and the right to enlist for military service. At federation, Article 41 of the Constitution held that no person eligible to vote in a state election should be prevented from voting in a Commonwealth election. However, in the early twentieth century, Queensland and Western Australia formally prevented Aboriginal people from voting in elections, while other states established legislation that, in effect, created the same result. In New South Wales in 1912 anyone in receipt of charity was prohibited from voting, meaning that in 1922 it was estimated that only 175 Aboriginal people were entitled to vote in Commonwealth elections.[18] In the Northern Territory, electoral regulations passed in 1922 denied the vote to every 'aboriginal native of Australia' with the exception of those permitted to vote under Article 41 of the Constitution.[19]

Federation was quickly followed by the passing of the *Federal Franchise Act* of 1902 which, while granting the franchise to women, also stated that 'no aboriginal native of Australia' shall have their name placed on the electoral roll unless entitled to under Article 41. The then secretary for the attorney-general, Robert Garran, offered a restrictive interpretation of Article 41; that the franchise only applied to a very small number of Aboriginal people placed on the electoral roll before 1902.[20] This decision combined with state legislation effectively denied almost all Aboriginal people the right to vote, suggesting that Aboriginal and Torres Strait Islanders were routinely stripped of civil rights through decision making by bureaucrats and procedures established by governments.

Defining the term 'aboriginal native' also became of instrumental importance, given the exclusionary effect of Article 127 of the Constitution on the rights of Aboriginal people. In interpreting the meaning of 'aboriginal native' within Article 127, the then attorney-general Alfred Deakin held that 'half-castes' were not 'aboriginal natives'.[21] This definition of 'aboriginal natives' was subsequently applied in interpreting the *Electoral Act 1905* (Cth) such that 'half-castes are not disqualified' from voting. However, Garran advised that 'all persons in whom aboriginal blood preponderates are disqualified'.[22] This blood-quantum distinction was widely accepted and was still being used by the Commonwealth Electoral Office until 1961.[23] The wording of the Franchise Act excluding 'aboriginal natives' was replicated in legislation relating to both citizenship and entitlements to pensions included in the *Invalid and Old-Age Pension Act 1908* (Cth) and the *Maternity Allowance Act 1912* (Cth). The significance of the establishment of these racial categories was that, once established, 'the exclusionary regime of "aboriginal native" was developed by generations of ministers, and bureaucrats' informing the development of both Protection Acts and the *Defence Act*, as discussed below.[24]

Protection and increasing control

Rather than being defined in the Constitution, the citizenship status of Aboriginal people was determined by a piecemeal tapestry of various Protection Acts and Commonwealth laws. Various Protection Acts repeated provisions from one jurisdiction to another, creating a relatively consistent approach to Aboriginal affairs in which administrators had wide-ranging control over the Aboriginal population. However, state legislation in the early twentieth century sometimes adopted different approaches, which wavered between protection, segregation and the absorption of the Aboriginal race into the broader population.[25] In broad terms, Queensland adopted a policy largely based on racial segregation, while New South Wales and Victoria vacillated between partial absorption, as well as elements of segregation and protection.[26] Across all jurisdictions, protection legislation was used to control the movement and location of Aboriginal people; remove Aboriginal children; and to dictate the terms of employment of Aboriginal people as well as who they could marry.[27] While these restrictions were not uniformly enforced, and Aboriginal people exercised agency in creatively circumventing the controls in place over their lives, such as sheltering extended family and refusing to work for rations, it is evident nonetheless that the restrictions were considerable. As later chapters illustrate, it is difficult to know precisely what motivated Aboriginal and Torres Strait Islander people to choose to volunteer for military service in the national defence forces. However, it seems that some desired to escape the oppressive control exercised over their lives by Protection Boards. In Victoria, for example, enlisting for military service was one of the few acts an Aboriginal man could take on his own accord without needing the permission of the Protection Board.[28]

From 1901 to the 1930s state and territory protection regimes became increasingly regressive, coinciding with the First World War and the subsequent return of Indigenous servicemen to Australia. Queensland's Protection Act was amended in 1904 to specifically include reference to Torres Strait Islanders. Queensland's protection regime influenced legislators in Western Australia such that the *Aborigines Act 1905* (WA), and later amendments in 1911 and 1936, allowed for the Aboriginal population to be moved to reserve areas.

Protection Acts were introduced in New South Wales in 1909; the Northern Territory in 1910 and South Australia in 1911. The only jurisdiction without such legislation was Tasmania, where the official position was that the state had no Aboriginal people. Legislators did, however, pass two Acts which demonstrated a tacit recognition of the existence of Tasmanian Aboriginal people: the *Licensing Act* of 1908 which restricted the sale of alcohol to 'half-castes'; and the *Cape Barren Island Reserve Act 1912* (section 23) which allowed 'half-castes and their descendants' to reside on Cape Barren Island. Under the Act any woman living on Cape Barren Island who married a 'white man' would forgo her rights to lease a block of land on the island.

Following from earlier interpretations of the term 'aboriginal native', Protection Acts in South Australia and the Northern Territory drew a stark legal distinction between 'half-castes' and 'Aborigines' and allowed protectors to segregate Aborigines to reserve areas, representing an intensification in the control exercised over the lives of Aboriginal people. The Northern Territory *Aboriginals Ordinance* of 1918, passed after the territory came under Commonwealth jurisdiction in 1911, saw Aboriginal people prevented from entering areas declared to be 'prohibited', which included hotels. Aboriginal people could not be 'at large' in any town after sunset without written permission on risk of imprisonment. Under the *Northern Territory Aboriginals Act 1910* the Chief Protector could undertake any activities in the care, custody or control of any 'Aboriginal' or 'half-caste' including transferring children to an 'aboriginal institution'. This quickly developed into efforts to promote the conversion of 'half-caste' children to Christianity by removing them from their families and placing them in dormitories where contact with their families was strictly limited.[29]

Amendments to the Victorian Act in 1916 suggest an obsession with blood quantum as the basis of definitions of 'aboriginality'. These amendments suggest a policy of segregation by extending the Protection Board's powers such that 'all quadroon, octoroon and half-caste lads over 18 shall leave and not be allowed to return to any station or reserve'. This amendment allowed for the removal of large numbers of Aboriginal people from reserve areas and resulted in the separation of families, including those of Aboriginal servicemen.

Early twentieth–century Protection Acts established strict controls over the employment and wages of Aboriginal people. Beginning in Victoria from 1916 the Protection Board could oversee employment contracts for all Aboriginal people; determine the wages they were paid; and even hold half of all wages paid to Indigenous apprentices until the end of the term of their apprenticeship. These employment arrangements, and similar ones in other states, suggest that Indigenous men may have been attracted to military service because it offered a regular wage and access to other benefits such as a pension, conditions which compared favourably with other intermittent sources of income and wages that were often controlled by Protection Boards.

The scale of the discrimination against Aboriginal peoples was apparent in the powers of Protection Boards to forcibly remove Aboriginal children. By 1899 Victoria's Protection Board had the power to remove any Aboriginal child without needing to prove that the child was 'neglected' or 'unprotected'.[30] In 1911 the Western Australian Chief Protector became the guardian of Aboriginal and 'half-caste' children, a power extended to 'exclude the rights of the mother of any illegitimate half-caste child'.[31] In New South Wales in 1911 the Protection Board regularly placed Aboriginal children in apprentice schemes where children were treated as indentured slaves.[32] Under the schemes young children were taken from their families and 'apprenticed' as domestic servants or agricultural labourers.[33]

In 1915, at the same time Aboriginal men were serving overseas in the 1st Australian Imperial Force, sweeping changes were proposed to the New South Wales Protection Act, consistent with Victorian policy, such that children could be removed without any court determination of neglect. Contemporary parliamentary debates suggest that some members of parliament viewed these changes as the 'reintroduction of slavery'.[34] In spite of these arguments, amendments were passed in 1915 empowering the board to 'assume full control and custody of the child of any aborigine, if after due inquiry it is satisfied that such a course is in the interest of the moral and physical welfare of such child'.[35]

In New South Wales young Aboriginal girls were targeted for removal for the purposes of becoming domestic servants.[36] These young women were particularly vulnerable to sexual exploitation and the rate of births among young apprenticed domestics was extremely high.[37] The power of the Protection Board to remove Aboriginal children without evidence of 'neglect' remained in force until 1940. The enduring effects of the forced removal of Aboriginal children from their families are discussed in harrowing detail in the 1997 *Bringing Them Home* report.

Enlisting: A matter of race

Eligibility for military service was based on the existing racial categories entrenched in Protection Acts and Commonwealth legislation. While the earliest Commonwealth *Defence Act*, passed in 1903, establishing a small permanent army and a volunteer citizens' militia force said nothing about the ethnicity of the members of these forces, this changed in 1909. The 1909 amendments to the *Defence Act* which introduced compulsory military training of all men aged between 12 and 25 specifically exempted men 'who are not substantially of European origin or descent, of which the medical authorities appointed in that behalf under the regulations shall be the judges'.[38] In 1910, this exemption was further extended to cover any future wartime conscription, effectively restricting those who were not 'substantially of European origin or descent' from compulsory military service.[39] While not specifically directed at the Indigenous population, these amendments were followed by policy detailed in the military recruiters' handbook which stated that 'Aborigines and half-castes are not to be enlisted'.[40]

Meanwhile, the *Naval Defence Act* of 1910, while requiring permanent naval personnel to serve overseas, incorporated those parts of the *Defence Act* which exempted from compulsory military training for those of non-European origin or descent.[41] Likewise the Australian Flying Corps, which served as part of the Australian Imperial Force during the First World War and would become the

Royal Australian Air Force in 1923, was governed by the provisions of the *Defence Act*.[42]

Hence, when the First World War broke out in 1914, Aboriginal and Torres Strait Islander men who attempted to volunteer to serve in the Australian Imperial Force were often identified by medical officers as unfit to serve because of their skin colour or race. Medical forms include the words 'unsuitable physique aboriginal' or 'unsuitable physical colour', pointing to the preoccupation of military authorities with racial categories.[43] However, a number of recruiters and medical officers allowed Aboriginal men to enlist in spite of the regulations.

In a continuation of earlier ideas of the 'Aboriginal native', an individual's racial category was viewed as being based on their genealogy, so a 'half-caste' Aboriginal person was viewed as European. Accordingly, by May 1917 under the pressures of the war, the military regulations were altered to allow the enlistment of 'half-castes' provided that 'one of the parents is white and of European origin'.[44] Each of these men made an attestation, such as this:

> I Willie Cummings do solemnly and sincerely declare that I am anxious to enlist in the Australian Imperial Force. My age is 19 years. My father was a white man born in Queensland and my mother was a half-caste … I have lived all my life with white people. I am not of German, Austrian, Turkish or Bulgarian descent.[45]

Cummings' statement illustrates that just as Aboriginal and Torres Strait Islander people were barred from service based on racial characteristics, the justification for their eligibility to serve was also based on blood quantum and the assimilationist ideas of established associations with white people.[46]

Protection guided by forced assimilation

From the 1930s onwards the various state and territory protection regimes were increasingly guided by the idea of assimilation, meaning the collection of government policies and regulations which were designed to ensure the cultural, and in some discussions biological, absorption of the Aboriginal population within the broader Australian population.[47] While assimilation ideas were discussed in Australia over a long period of time, and are still debated today, they became the established policy framework for protection at a conference held between the Commonwealth and state Aboriginal protection authorities in 1937. Conference delegates unilaterally supported the following resolution:

> This conference believes that the destiny of *the* natives of aboriginal origin, but not of the full blood, lies in their ultimate absorption by the people of the Commonwealth, and it therefore recommends that all efforts be directed to that end.[48]

This commitment to assimilation is evident in the obsessive preoccupation in various Protection Acts with defining racial categories to either include or exclude people from the category of 'Aboriginal'.

In Queensland in 1939 the adoption of the ideas of assimilation meant that legislators broadening in the category of 'Aboriginal' to include 'half-castes' or people who lived or associated with Aboriginal people – this resulted in a larger group of people being brought under the control of the Chief Protector.[49] Torres Strait Islanders were governed from 1939 by the *Torres Strait Islanders Act* which, while echoing many of the provisions of the *Aboriginals Preservation and Protection Act*, also enabled the establishment of island courts and an elected island council. Both of these Acts remained in force until 1965, with the effect that some Aboriginal men and women needed to seek permission from the Protector or state guardians to enlist.[50]

Throughout the 1930s and 1940s the Aboriginal and Torres Strait Islander populations of Queensland had their lives 'regulated even more comprehensively than they had ever been in the previous century'.[51] No Aboriginal person could be employed or married without the approval of the Protector, an Aboriginal person could be moved to a reserve at any time, and the Director of Native Affairs retained the powers for the care and custody of Aboriginal children. In a continuance of colonial laws, the employment of Aboriginal people was heavily regulated, Aboriginal people had no right to vote and the Aboriginal population remained prohibited from drinking alcohol.

During this period Protection Acts across Australia increasingly established strict controls over the employment and wages of Aboriginal people. Protection Boards restricted some spouses' and relatives' access to Aboriginal soldiers' pay. Once again, Aboriginal peoples' access to their own income and allowances became entangled in intersecting state and Commonwealth bureaucratic rulings. John Lovett from Heywood in Victoria described his father Herbert's motivation for enlisting in the Second World War, after having already served in the First World War, as being compelled by the need to provide for his family.[52] Such motivations are understandable, given that in 1939 the unemployment rate across Australia was 11 per cent and many Aboriginal men faced acute difficulty in finding work and supporting their families.

Military service and citizenship

Deprived of equal status to other Australians, Aboriginal people who served in the First World War began to assert their rights to citizenship on the basis of their military service. From the 1920s

Aboriginal activists made overt the links between citizenship and military service, calling for an end to the discriminatory treatment under the Protection Acts and arguing for the franchise (see chapter 6). In 1939, on the eve of the Second World War, William Cooper of the Australian Aborigines League argued that given the poor treatment of Aboriginal servicemen after the First World War there should be 'no enlistment without citizenship'.[53]

Aboriginal men were still excluded from the defence forces at the commencement of the Second World War in September 1939. In 1932 an Australian Military Regulation and Order had confirmed that no person could voluntarily enlist who was not substantially of European origin or descent. This meant that Aboriginal and Torres Strait Islander men continued to be exempt from compulsory military service when it was reintroduced (after a hiatus during the Depression years) in September 1939. Indigenous men were also deemed to be ineligible to volunteer for the 2nd Australian Imperial Force, which was deployed overseas in 1940. On 6 May 1940, a Military Board memorandum was issued to Army Commands stating that recruiters should exclude 'British subjects of non-European origin or descent'.[54] Subsequent instructions suggested that the enlistment of 'half-caste' Aboriginal people was 'not advisable'. At the same time, however, Indigenous Australians were eligible to enlist in the Royal Australian Air Force. Furthermore, when the Japanese forces seemed poised to invade Australia in 1941–42, the restrictions on the employment of Aboriginal and Torres Strait Islander people in the Army and various auxiliary forces were relaxed.

Military service by Aboriginal and Torres Strait Islander men and women brought some change in government attitudes, at least with respect to the franchise. During the Second World War Aboriginal people who were employed by the defence forces were enfranchised. Unfortunately these rights were conditional on active service and so lasted only six months after the war ended.[55]

Western Australia also recognised the franchise as an entitlement associated with military service. While legislators in the state remained staunchly opposed to allowing the broader Aboriginal population to vote, they were prepared to extend the franchise to people awarded a 'Certificate of Citizenship'. In 1944 the Western Australian *Natives (Citizenship Rights) Act* allowed Aboriginal people to apply for a 'Certificate of Citizenship' which, if granted, would allow a person to 'be deemed no longer a native or aborigine' conferring instead the rights and privileges of a British subject. This Act made overt the link between military service and the legal recognition of citizenship. Applications for certificates needed to include character references as well as making explicit the applicant's military service in either the Navy, Army or Air Force. People who were granted citizenship were deemed to cease to be 'a native or an aborigine' and were therefore entitled to vote in Western Australian elections, but not Commonwealth elections until after 1948. Citizenship status could, however, be lost if people did not adopt the manners and habits of a 'civilised life', which included rejection of their 'tribal associations', meaning that they should cease to have any relationships with Aboriginal people. The fact that citizenship status could be lost through any assertion of Aboriginal identity suggests both the precarious nature of these supposed 'rights' and the way in which this broader policy was informed by ideas of assimilation.

A definition of citizenship was formally introduced into Commonwealth law with the passing of the *Nationality and Citizenship Act* in 1948. In practice the Act maintained the distinction between Australians who were conferred full citizenship rights, and those whose citizenship was effectively limited by Commonwealth and state legislation, including Aboriginal and Torres Strait Islander people. For example, in 1948 while Aboriginal people in Queensland were now termed 'citizens', in practice they continued to be denied the right to vote.[56] Clearly, citizenship did not automatically confer rights on Aboriginal people. Legislation at a state and territory level actively discriminated against Aboriginal people by continuing to restrict their access to a broad range of civil rights.

The links between military service and citizenship became further entrenched in 1949 when the Commonwealth franchise was extended to Aboriginal people who were currently, or who had previously served, in the defence force. In addition, the changes to the *Commonwealth Electoral Act 1949* made clear, for the first time, that the Commonwealth vote was extended to those Aboriginal people who were entitled to vote at a state level. The ability for Aboriginal people to vote was therefore dependent on if they had either a record of service in the defence force, or the franchise in the state where they resided.

The actual capacity of Indigenous Australians to acquire a record of military service continued to be restricted in the decades after the Second World War. In 1947 the Army became, for the first time in Australian history, a permanent regular force, as opposed to a volunteer force raised to serve in particular conflicts. In 1948 the earlier colour bar restricting Indigenous Australians from volunteering to serve was removed. Although Aboriginal and Torres Strait Islander soldiers were now theoretically eligible to serve on a regular basis, the Army decided to accept them on a case-by-case basis. The Navy and Air Force continued to exclude Indigenous enlistments until 1951, when amendments to the *Defence Act* repealed section 138, which had exempted those 'not substantially of European origin or descent' from compulsory service. Even then Indigenous Australians remained exempt from any obligation to register when compulsory military service schemes were reintroduced in 1951–59 and 1964–72. However, the accompanying regulations and debates over the meanings of 'Aboriginality' left many men still liable, including during the Vietnam War. It was only in 1992 that the clause in the

Defence Act exempting Aboriginal men from compulsory call-up in a time of war was finally removed.

Extending the franchise to Aboriginal people after the Second World War formed part of a growing movement of political support for civil rights that emerged in the 1950s and gathered momentum in the 1960s as Aboriginal people were participating in the Vietnam War. Representatives from the Commonwealth and all states met in 1951 to discuss 'native welfare', agreeing that assimilation was 'the objective of native welfare measures, [central to the] desire to see all persons born in Australia enjoying full citizenship'.[57] This resolution suggested acceptance by delegates of the status of Aboriginal people as less than equal citizens.

Aboriginal and Torres Strait Islanders continued to hold the status of lesser citizens through the operation of discriminatory legislation. Regulation often created a circular logic whereby Protection Acts restricting the rights of Aboriginal people became the basis for discrimination in other subsequent legislation. For example, until 1959 many social security payments, such as the old age pension (1908) and the maternity allowance (1912) were not made available to Aboriginal people unless they were exempt from the provisions of Aboriginal Protection legislation.[58] By 1942 invalid and old age pensions were made available to Aboriginal people, but only to those not living under the Act.[59] In 1959 these social security provisions were reviewed and linked more closely to aspects of Aboriginal identity, thus the Act stated that:

> An aboriginal native of Australia who follows a mode of life that is, in the opinion of the Director-General, nomadic and primitive is not entitled to a pension, allowance, endowment or benefit under this Act.[60]

These assimilationist provisions restricting access to social security for 'primitive' Aboriginal people remained in place until 1966, impacting upon some of the Aboriginal men who served in the defence forces and their families.

The status of a person and their associated rights was similarly linked in Northern Territory legislation to the operation of various state Protection Acts. Enacted in 1951, the Northern Territory *Welfare Ordinance Act 1953* deemed people to be 'wards' on the basis of: their manner of living, their supposed ability to manage their own affairs, their standard of behaviour and their 'personal associations', which meant ongoing relationships with Aboriginal kin. Any person previously governed by protection legislation in Queensland, South Australia or Western Australia automatically became a ward upon entering the Northern Territory, a restriction that was obviously only applicable to Aboriginal people. Under the Act (section 8) the Director of Welfare had considerable powers over wards' custody, relationships, employment and wages. In 1957 Aboriginal people could only vote if they were not declared a ward.[61] Many of these provisions show a continuity with the regulations established in various Protection Acts almost 100 years earlier, and they remained in place until at least 1978.

In summary, the history of the entwined restrictions placed in the *Defence Act* as well as other Commonwealth, state and territory legislation meant that Indigenous Australians who chose to enlist in the Boer War, First World War and Second World War were British subjects whose lives were governed by various 'protection' regimes. Indigenous Australians who enlisted to fight in the Korean and Vietnam wars were British subjects and also Australian citizens, after the passing of the *Nationality and Citizenship Act* in 1948, however, this status did not automatically confer the civil rights associated with citizenship.

The path to more equal citizenship rights

In practice, discriminatory legislation continued to operate in many Australian states until well into the 1960s, with some legislation not being repealed until the late 1980s. In the early 1960s legislative restrictions continued to prevent Aboriginal people in Western Australia, Queensland and the Northern Territory from voting in federal elections unless they had served in the military, meaning that in 1961 in the Northern Territory only 72 Aboriginal people were entitled to vote. A House of Representatives Select Committee established in 1961 found, for example, that only 57 of the 659 members of the Torres Strait Islander Light Infantry Battalion were aware of their right to vote in a federal election and had enrolled.[62] While these Torres Strait Islanders who had undertaken military service could vote in federal elections they, and all other Aboriginal and Torres Strait Islanders who had served in the military, were still banned from voting in Queensland elections.

In Australia in the 1960s increasing attention was being paid to the state and territory legislatures' restrictions on the civil rights of Aboriginal people. In 1962 the Commonwealth finally passed amendments to the *Electoral Act* to allow Aboriginal and Torres Strait Islanders the vote in federal elections in spite of discriminatory state laws. Western Australia finally amended its *Electoral Act* in 1962 to allow Aboriginal people the vote. Three years after the Commonwealth Act was passed, Queensland legislators finally removed the restrictions on Aboriginal people voting in state elections.

In the context of ongoing discrimination, amendments were proposed to the Constitution in 1967 to allow the Commonwealth the power to legislate for Aboriginal people and to include Aboriginal people in the census. Returning to the original discussion of the text of the Constitution in this chapter, the referendum proposed: (1) removing the words 'other than the aboriginal race in any State' from section 51(xxvi) such that the Commonwealth had powers to legislate with respect to Aboriginal people, and (2) removing the entire text of section 127 which stated that 'aboriginal natives shall not be counted'. The referendum produced a groundswell of support and resulted in a 90.77 per cent 'yes' vote. For many Aboriginal people the amendment was deeply politically significant and symbolic. The 1967 referendum did not, however, substantially alter the legal status of Aboriginal people, nor did it herald a new era of formal equality as citizenship status continued to be largely regulated by the states.[63]

The political momentum associated with the referendum may, however, have prompted many of the recalcitrant state legislators, particularly in Western Australia and Queensland, to begin to remove many of the more overt pieces of discriminatory legislation including limitations on the franchise. In 1971 the Western Australian *Native (Citizenship Rights) Act* was finally repealed and in 1972 it became legal for Aboriginal people to consume alcohol. Being denied service in hotels was a particularly searing experience recalled by many Aboriginal ex-servicemen, the 'right to drink' seen as symbolic of equality, mateship and belonging to the (male) nation.[64]

In Queensland the case was less clear cut. Queensland did extend the vote to Aboriginal people in 1965. However, in 1971 it introduced two new Acts: the *Aborigines Act* and the *Torres Strait Islander Act* which retained significant controls over the lives of Aboriginal and Torres Strait Islander people. For instance, the Acts gave broad powers to the Director to inspect reserve areas, the minister had the power to authorise mining in any reserve areas and various by-laws which promulgated regulations over the minutiae of people's daily lives.[65] This legislation remained in force until 1984.

While the 1960s heralded a new era in the recognition of civil rights, restrictions on Aboriginal and Torres Strait Islander people engaging in national service remained in place. When national service was introduced in 1951, and reintroduced in 1964, the Commonwealth government formally exempted Aboriginal people from the requirement of compulsory service, insisting instead that they apply for military service on a case-by-case basis (see chapter 10). This meant that the National Service Acts of 1951 and 1964 did not require Aboriginal and Torres Strait Islanders to register. However, debates over the definition of Aboriginality meant many men and women did serve, including during the Korean and Vietnam wars.

The 1970s ushered in an era of new legislation that recognised specific rights accorded to Indigenous people, as well as offering broader protection for political rights. The international decolonisation movement and civil rights movements influenced the Commonwealth to pass the *Racial Discrimination Act* in 1975. The Act prevents discrimination against minority groups, and specifically against Aboriginal people, representing the 'first serious attempt by the Commonwealth government to do more for Aborigines than simply remove the restrictions that had prevented their attainment of ordinary citizenship rights'.[66] Pressure from Aboriginal activists and their supporters, in a climate of social and political change around race, gender and representation, was key to these developments. This was followed in 1976 by the recognition by the Commonwealth of Aboriginal land rights over large areas of land in the Northern Territory, with New South Wales and other states developing their own land rights legislation in the 1980s.[67] In the 1970s the Commonwealth government also began to create bodies, such as the National Aboriginal Consultative Committee, designed to allow for greater Aboriginal self-determination. This was followed some 17 years later with the establishment of the Aboriginal and Torres Strait Islander Commission (ATSIC), which was a peak elected representative body that also had the power to administer significant government funds.

In the 1990s, with the Mabo and Wik decisions, a growing emphasis on Indigenous rights and culture was apparent, as well as activism around compensation, seen in the Stolen Wages cases and payment of auxiliaries, delivering some justice to those who had served but had not been served fairly by legislation or government in return.[68] Finally, in 1992 with the removal of the clause in the *Defence Act* exempting Aboriginal and Torres Strait Islander men from compulsory service in time of war was finally removed, suggesting that the long history of racially discriminatory treatment in relation to enlisting for military service was finally at an end.

The echoes of protection

The history of Aboriginal and Torres Strait Islander military service has been explored in this chapter with reference to legislation operating at the intersections between ideas of citizenship and race. This discussion shows that Aboriginal and Torres Strait Islander military service can only be understood in the context of the wider entrenched discrimination suffered by Indigenous people through the operation of state and territory Protection Acts.

For most of the twentieth century the civil rights of Aboriginal and Torres Strait Islanders, and the practical citizenship status afforded to people, were defined by state and territory Protection Acts, in consort with discriminatory Commonwealth legislation. The enactment of Protection Acts in the early twentieth century in New South Wales, South Australia and the Northern Territory, and the tightening of existing protection regimes operating in other jurisdictions, meant that a series of punitive regulations were put in place over the lives of Aboriginal and Torres Strait Islander people, at the same time as they were fighting for their country. Restrictive protection regimes were matched at the federal level by a formal exclusion of Aboriginal people from military service through legislation which remained in place until as recently as 1992. The entwined nature of citizenship and military service also meant that from the 1940s onwards military service became a pathway through which Aboriginal people were able to articulate claims for equal citizenship. This link was made explicit in the legislation enacted in Western Australia and by the Commonwealth linking military service to franchise, the foundational right of citizenship.

While this chapter has focused on a historical account of 150 years of legal arrangements, these are not just matters of the past. Understanding the historical context of institutional racial discrimination in Australia remains important for understanding the contemporary experience of Aboriginal and Torres Strait Islander people. The legacy of the institutional discrimination established by protection regimes continues to be experienced by Aboriginal and Torres Strait Islander people across Australia, as acknowledged in the long-term effects of the removal of children documented in the *Bringing Them Home* report, and the apology by Prime Minister Kevin Rudd in 2008 to the Stolen Generations.

Legislation that echoes 'protection'-style regimes remains in place. The passing of the Northern Territory National Emergency Response (NTER) legislation in 2007 was justified on the grounds of needing to protect Aboriginal children. In practice, the package of legislation required the suspension of the operation of the *Racial Discrimination Act*, suggesting that Aboriginal people in the Northern Territory have once again been subjected to discriminatory legislation. We wonder if, in part, it is this historic legacy of legislative discrimination based on race that paves the way for this more recent Commonwealth legislation. We question if a 'protection' regime like the NTER would ever have been applied to any other group of Australians. Which prompts us to ask: is the citizenship status of Aboriginal and Torres Strait Islander people still not equal to that of other Australians?

1.1 Coloured Diggers march, Redfern, Anzac Day 2014.
Source: Craig Greene courtesy of Serving Our Country

1.2 Vietnam veteran Mick Markham being interviewed by Michael Dodson and Allison Cadzow for the Serving Our Country project at his home at Pine Creek, Northern Territory, 14 September 2015.
Source: Craig Greene courtesy of Serving Our Country

LEST WE F
THE FRON
1867
Goulbolba Hill
Massacre
Central Qld
1874

1.3 Protectors gathered in front of the Australian War Memorial behind a banner listing the places and dates of known violent encounters between white settlers and Indigenous communities from 1788 onwards. A prominent large sign reads 'Lest We Forget the Frontier Wars', and other signs held refer to specific battles, wars and massacres. Canberra, ACT, Australia, Anzac Day 2016.

Source: John Janson-Moore

2.1 *Top left* Moore River Native Settlement c. 1924. Established by the Western Australian government in 1918. Many of the children sent to the settlement had been forcibly removed from their families as part of the Stolen Generations. In 1951 the government transferred management of the settlement to the Methodist Overseas Mission, who opened Mogumber Mission on the same site.

Source: AIATSIS COLBUNG.K09.BW-N02692_30

2.2 *Below left* Chief Protector of Aborigines in Queensland, JW Bleakley (left) and Chief Protector of Aborigines Northern Australia, Dr Cecil Cook (right) in the Barkly Tablelands, 1928. In 1927 Prime Minister Stanley Bruce announced a government inquiry into the conditions of 'half-castes' and Aboriginal people in northern and Central Australia, which was undertaken by Bleakley. Bleakley's report included recommendations for improved living conditions and minimum wages for pastoral workers, increased 'protection', closer administration of residents at government institutions and different policies based on degree of Aboriginality and 'civilisation'.

Source: NAA – A263, 7873288

2.3 *Above* Reverend George Garnsey, Lilon Bandler and referendum advocate Faith Bandler at a Census Day demonstration in Martin Place, Sydney, 30 June 1966. Leaflets distributed by protesters included the following: 'Today, 30th June, is Census Day. Today the white population of Australia will be counted. But Aborigines are excluded from the Commonwealth Census by Section 127 of the Constitution. Why should the descendants of the original inhabitants suffer this insult? Because the referendum which was to remove this grave discrimination has not been held'.

Source: AIATSIS HORNER2.J01.BW-N04612_12

3.1 The men of the 4th Contingent, Queensland Imperial Bushmen on their return from the Boer War in August 1901. The very rare, original photo was discovered in 2013 and shows an Aboriginal serviceman in the right side of the photo.

Source: AIATSIS

3.2 Native Mounted Police in Rockhampton, Queensland, December 1864.
Source: Queensland Police Museum

3.3 A studio portrait of Aboriginal trackers and a policeman in Central Australia circa 1900. Printed for circulation as a postcard during the Boer War, this image illustrates that Aboriginal people were represented as trackers at the time.
Source: NLA PIC Album 1197/3 #PIC/15797/5

4.1 *Left* Aboriginal serviceman Trooper William (Willie) Allen, 11th Light Horse Regiment. Originally from Darwin, Allen enlisted on 10 December 1917, and returned to Australia on 20 July 1919. This studio portrait was likely to have been made in Cairo, as the photographer has inserted, in the top left-hand corner of the portrait, a copy of a photograph sent to Allen of the children of the family he worked for in Queensland. The original of the photograph sent to Allen is in a frame standing on the desk. It is very likely Allen had this portrait made to send back to the same family in Queensland.

Source: AWM P00889.021

4.2 *Above* Anzac Day 1944 at Herberton War Memorial in Queensland. Erected in 1922, the memorial is one of the few known monuments from the time to recognise a soldier's Aboriginality. The Honour Roll (inset) notes that William Perrott was an Aboriginal soldier. Perrott worked as a stockman at Evelyn Station prior to enlisting in Cairns in 1917. He later died in hospital in France from bronchitis, which was attributed to his service on the Western Front.

Source: AWM 065880 and Queensland War Memorial Register, Department of Environment and Heritage Protection, contributed by Dennis Stocks and Doug Tanner (inset).

4.3 Colourful local Aboriginal personality 'Black Fanny' with members of the armed services and other local residents of Port Lincoln, South Australia, during the 1914–18 War.

Source: SLSA B27552

4.4 Corporal Harry Thorpe, 1916. Thorpe was born at the Lake Tyers Mission Station, near Lakes Entrance, Victoria. He enlisted at Sale on 12 February 1916, and embarked on 4 April 1916. He joined the 7th Battalion in France in July 1916.

Source: AWM P01695.002

5.1 Private William Reginald Rawlings was born at the Aboriginal station of Framlingham, in the Western District of Victoria. Rawlings enlisted at Warrnambool on 14 March 1916 and embarked on 1 August 1916. He joined the 29th Battalion in France and was killed in action on 9 August 1918, during the capture of Vauvillers, France. He was awarded the Military Medal for bravery.

Source: AWM P01695.001

5.2 Aboriginal soldier settler Percy Pepper (right), in his army uniform, with a fellow returned soldier (wearing a souvenired German uniform), early 1920s. This photograph was taken at the Pepper home at Koo Wee Rup, Victoria. Family members can be seen in the background.

Source: PROV and Glenys Watts

3

The South African 'Boer War'

John Maynard

'The old men felt that they would be equal to the occasion and in their native language they would say, "Let us go".'

– *Matthew Kropinyeri*

Much mystery and myth surrounds the history of Aboriginal involvement in the Second South African Anglo-Boer War (hereafter the Boer War) of 1899–1902. Unquestionably some Aboriginal men went to South Africa and played a part in this conflict, but their numbers, identity and background remain sketchy. This chapter considers some of the known and unknown stories and experiences of Aboriginal people during the Boer War. What do we know of the Aboriginal men who went to South Africa? How did they get there and did they get home? In addressing these issues, I acknowledge the groundbreaking work and perseverance of several scholars including Dale Kerwin, Philippa Scarlett, Colin Renshaw, Bill Woolmore and Peter Bakker, all of whom have conducted work over many years trying to piece together the fragmented record and previously missing place of Aboriginal people associated with the largely forgotten war in South Africa.

Why did they go?

The Boer War arose from a long history of conflict in South Africa between the Boer Afrikaans-speaking white South Africans and the British who had controlled the Cape Colony since 1814. The discovery of gold in the independent Boer South African Republic in 1886 exacerbated tensions as English-speaking immigrants flooded the region. In 1899, the conflict erupted into actual war, which consisted initially of a Boer offensive against British command posts and railway lines. The British then launched a counteroffensive and brought the two Boer republics under their control. But then a Boer guerrilla resistance movement prompted a widespread scorched-earth campaign by the British and the internment and deaths of thousands of Boer civilians in British concentration camps.

In a show of support for the empire, the Australian colonial governments (the conflict began just before federation) offered to raise contingents. Many individual Australians, too, were gripped by imperial loyalty and excitement. The *Brisbane Courier* reported that in February 1902 (at the height of the controversial scorched-earth policy), 'One of the largest public meetings ever held took place in the [Sydney] Town Hall' at which the Premier, John See, and the Leader of the Opposition Charles Lee, gave stirring addresses to a highly supportive crowd'.[1] A resolution was endorsed that stated:

> That this meeting of citizens, assembled under the auspices of the Australian Natives Association [a nationalistic group that campaigned for political reform and patriotic causes], takes this opportunity of expressing its entire confidence in the British Government in the course they are pursuing in connection with the war in South Africa, and also in the Commander-in-Chief of the Imperial federated army engaged therein.[2]

Possibly some 16 000 Australians volunteered to fight in this imperial conflict.[3] From the outset 'men left Australia through rapturous crowds' and as one observer remarked, 'An epidemic of war fever set in.'[4] The crowds witnessing the embarkation were so dense in the streets of Melbourne that one officer noted, 'in places the troops could only pass in single file. Handkerchiefs, sweets, and all kinds of good things were pressed upon us as we passed through the crowd.'[5]

Amid this euphoria, which was manufactured to some degree by colonial authorities, there was little consideration as to whether the Boer War was just, or in the interest of the Australian colonies.[6] Thomas Pakenham's 1979 study of the Boer War concluded that for the Canadians, Australians and New Zealanders, 'blood was thicker than water' and they all 'felt a natural solidarity with the mother country'.[7] Yet there were some Australian politicians and academics prepared to question 'why the colony's soldiers should be expected to "butcher those with whom they have no quarrel and who they knew nothing about"'.[8] Charlie McDonald, a Labor politician in Queensland, was adamant that the war in South Africa was 'the most unjust war England has ever taken part in'.[9] WH Browne, the member for Croydon in Queensland, also declared it unjust 'to send a lot of our young men out to train them up as into a quarrel we had no hand or part in, and which they know nothing about'.[10] But in all of this controversy, voices of dissent were in the minority.

When trying to understand why Aboriginal Australians became involved in this imperial conflict, it is important to recognise that at this time the freedom, movement and enterprise of some Aboriginal people was greater than in subsequent decades. Between 1870 and 1910 the general living conditions of Aboriginal people were complex and not uniform. Despite the restrictive protection regimes in some states, in many areas of the continent Indigenous people had re-established themselves on country. Through a combination of traditional methods of subsistence and European farming they had become effective producers on their land. This was certainly the case across areas of New South Wales, South Australia and Queensland. As prominent historian Heather Goodall has explained, in New South Wales 'Aborigines had resettled small patches of their traditional lands and demanded inalienable, freehold title'.[11] Meanwhile Susan Johnston in her influential 1970 Master's thesis estimated that in the later stages of the nineteenth century around 81 per cent of Aboriginal people in New South Wales were self-sufficient.[12] In contrast to the heavily congested and tightly controlled reserves of the 1930s, these patches of land in most instances consisted of independent farms, run by one or two Aboriginal families. They prospered on areas encompassing 40 to 50 acres (16 to 20 hectares) which they had cleared, fenced and cropped, and on which they had built homesteads and grazed livestock. Examples of this widespread Aboriginal farming success are readily attested to in the archives. At Cabbage Tree Island on the Richmond River a small group of Aboriginal cane farmers had made a profit of some £700 to £800 on their crop.[13] On the Fattorini Island on the north coast of New South Wales, Aboriginal farmer Jimmy Linwood had a return of over £156 on his maize crop and was winning the blue ribbons in the local agricultural shows of the region.[14] At Ulgundahi Island on the Clarence River two Aboriginal families shipped over 30 bags of beans and received a cheque for £103 for their labour.[15] These Aboriginal people, then, were effectively running their own lives and these 'reserves were not an instrument of segregation, as is often assumed, but instead reflected an Aboriginal land rights movement'.[16]

It was during this period that Aboriginal men stepped forward to enlist to fight in the Boer War. When the war broke out in 1899, Australia still constituted six colonies, each with their own militias. Gary Oakley, former Indigenous Liaison Officer at the Australian War Memorial, has argued that there were Aboriginal men serving

Table 3.1
Aboriginal servicemen who served in the Boer War (1899–1902)

Name	Lifespan	Service details
John Alick aka John/Jack Bond	1873–1941	1st Tour: Trooper 1063, 1st Australian Horse; 2nd Tour: Trooper 356, 1st Australian Commonwealth Horse
John Alexander Barnes	1864–1945	Private 493, 'C' Company, 3 NSW Mounted Rifles
John Robert Searle aka Robert John Searle, Robert Charles Searle	1869–1942	Private No. 9, 4th Western Australian Mounted Infantry
Frank Leighton Sinclair	1873–1934	Private 397, 'B' Squadron, First NSW Mounted Rifles; Farrier 55 'A' Squadron, Fifth Australian Commonwealth Horse
William James Stubbings	1879–1957	Trooper 1533, 'D' Squadron, 3rd New South Wales Mounted Rifles
Arthur Wellington	Not known	Private 925, 5th Victorian Mounted Rifles
William Charles Westbury	c.1880–1936	Trooper Corporal 632, 'F' Squadron, No. 4 Troop, 6th S.A. Imperial Bushmen
Alfred Ernest Whye	c.1879–1969	Trooper 3067, No. 4 Squadron, 3rd NSW Mounted Rifles (NSW Drafts)
Stephen Yuille	Not known	Private 712, 3rd Victorian Imperial Bushmen

Note: According to verification research by Peter Bakker (Melbourne) as of June 2017; confirmed by Michael Bell, Australian War Memorial.

in the military from as far back as the 1860s and that some of these men went to South Africa:

> These men would have come out of a community, they would have basically joined the military, served overseas as part of that unit as an equal, then they would have come back to Australia and probably disappeared back into their community.[17]

The number of Aboriginal men who served in South Africa, either as soldiers or trackers, remains debatable. But at least nine Aboriginal men are now confirmed as having served in South Africa (see Table 3.1).[18] A recent addition is William Charles Westbury, a Boandik man from South Australia who served in both the Boer War and the First World War with distinction. Westbury's attestation papers list '1 year's experience with the Lameroo Rifle Club and 18 months in the 5th and 6th South Australian Imperial Bushmen' contingent during the Boer war.[19]

As chapter 5 shows, a sense of imperial loyalty marked Aboriginal involvement in the First World War, with many communities supporting the war effort through contributions to patriotic fund appeals.[20] A similar patriotism was displayed by Aboriginal communities during the Boer War. However, the war also provided a space for Aboriginal men to reclaim some respect and demonstrate their skills. A South Australian journalist reporting an interview with Ngarrindjeri man Matthew Kropinyeri in 1914 stated that when:

> [W]ar was in progress in South Africa a few years ago there was great excitement among the blacks on the mission … I remember when the news came through of some of the mistakes made by the British troops in South Africa because they were not accustomed to the style of warfare adopted, the old men felt that they would be equal to the occasion and in their native language they would say, 'Let us go.'[21]

The Boer War also provided opportunities for Aboriginal men with initiative. For example, the legendary Aboriginal athlete and boxer Jerry Jerome made '£2 a day by breaking horses for the military authorities'.[22] Alfred Polson, from Taree on the mid-north coast of New South Wales, was the horse handler and carriage driver for the local Taree district doctor, Neville Howse. When Howse enlisted in the New South Wales Medical Corps to go to the Boer War, Polson accompanied him as his batman.[23] Howse and Polson were both present at a clash between British and Boer forces near Vredefort in 1900:

> [A]t the height of the fighting as a line of horsemen charged toward the Boer position, Neville Howse noticed a young trumpeter fall from his horse, wounded in the foremost line … Despite the enemy fire being extremely heavy, Howse did not hesitate to mount his white stallion held in readiness by Alfred Polson of Taree. Howse galloped out furiously onto the battlefield to rescue the wounded trumpeter.[24]

Neville Howse received the Victoria Cross for his bravery. As with so many stories of Aboriginal men in the Boer War, given the lack of historical sources available it is hard to unravel myth from fact. But according to John Ramsland, who has conducted historical research within the Manning Valley over many years, Polson was most likely Aboriginal. Aboriginal descendants too remain convinced of his ties to them. Polson's Boer War Dossier Record in the National Archives of Australia reveals that he joined up on 10 February 1902 and served with the Australian medical team. Since Taree was no easy space for an Aboriginal identity, it is possible that the endorsement of Howse had provided Polson with a window of acceptance. Yet, on Polson's death in 1942, although there were a few obituaries in the local newspapers for an obviously well-respected individual, there was no mention of his having Aboriginal background. Maybe the final word rests with Polson's enlistment medical certificate notes which stated: complexion 'Dark' and hair 'Black'.[25]

Why did Aboriginal men want to go? Were they simply caught up in the excitement of the moment or was there something else underlying their desire to fight? The Boer War was both fought as a 'man's war' and covered in the press as a man's war. But where did this situate the Aboriginal man? David Huggonson writes that the challenge facing Aboriginal men at the time was that 'the majority of the general public saw them as a dying race and as a subject of ridicule'.[26] As Patricia O'Brien too has illustrated, the historical record has reinforced and perpetuated some of these long-ingrained misconceptions:

> These writers were influenced by a derogatory stereotype of the Aboriginal male which had been common in early colonial literature in Australia and was (and remains) a prominent colonial stereotype of the 'black man' applied in many other theatres across the globe.[27]

Victoria Haskins has also argued that the 'role of Aboriginal men within their families and the broader Aboriginal communities was denied, displaced, and destroyed by the state'.[28] This may have played a part in encouraging Aboriginal men to step forward and break the shackles that had for so long portrayed them as useless, worthless and less than men. Some Aboriginal men might have wanted the chance to prove that they could ride and shoot as well as any white man and track better than anyone on the planet. This was an opportunity to reclaim a space for respect, both within their own families and communities as well as the wider Australian population.

Aboriginal service in the Boer War

There is some evidence suggesting that several requests and offers were made for Aboriginal trackers and volunteers to go to South Africa but there were significant obstacles in the way of their doing so. For example, Don and Bev Elphick's history of Warangesda mission at Darlington Point records that five Aboriginal men volunteered for the Boer War: they wanted to 'go with the "Bushmans [sic] Contingent" to South Africa as scouts'.[29] But their offer was rejected by the New South Wales Board for the Protection of Aborigines: 'these five Australians were ignored, whilst the white colonials were queuing up to become involved in this "volunteers only" war'.[30] A Noongar man, Fred Mead, complained to the press of unfair treatment:

> Sir. – I wish you to make known that there are a number of half-castes in this colony who would gladly serve under the King's colours in South Africa if they were given the chance … I volunteered once, but was not accepted.[31]

The Chief Protector in Queensland, Archibald Meston, took a different approach to that of the New South Wales Board. In December 1899, it was reported in the *Brisbane Courier* that Meston had written to the Queensland premier offering to organise and lead:

> a small body of fifty bushmen, expert horsemen and dead shots to accompany any further troops sent from Queensland to South Africa. The body … could act as guerrilla fighters and scouts … The Premier has, it is understood, replied to Mr. Meston to the effect that the offer has been referred to the defence force authorities.[32]

In the event, Meston's offer was turned down.

This evidence suggests that Aboriginal attempts to volunteer in the Boer War were rejected, even though experienced Aboriginal men who had already fought in uniform were available. The much-feared Native Police had been created in several Australian colonies during the nineteenth century and had been heavily involved in the 'dispersal' of Aboriginal people during the Australian frontier war period. The often-described 'state of war' between settlers and Aboriginal people had intensified and fluctuated in differing locations and time periods across the continent.[33] In a letter to *The Queenslander* in 1891 a Professor Rentoul stated that the 'quite ruthless and matter-of-fact way in which the "dispersing of the blacks" is described to you is a distinct and ugly fact'.[34] An earlier letter to the editor in *The Queenslander* in 1866 could not have been more explicit: 'a war of extermination is the only policy to pursue'.[35] Their notoriety notwithstanding, the Native Police of Queensland were known to be great shots and excellent horsemen who had served under white commanders, responded well to orders, and were proven killers in the field. Historian Jonathan Richards indeed argues that the clinical and trained Native Police of the late nineteenth century would be likened to a 'Special Forces' unit today: 'the Native Police should be regarded as a military force, albeit an odd or irregular one. Just as it was an exceptional police force, it was an exceptional military force'.[36]

It is possible that some of these men may well have stepped forward to serve in South Africa, as either soldiers or trackers. There is a developing body of scholarship on Aboriginal trackers and explorer guides across Australian history. The recent edited collection *Brokers and Boundaries – Colonial Exploration in Indigenous Territory* by Maria Nugent, Tiffany Shellam, Shino Konishi and Allison Cadzow reveals the complexities of these relationships and experiences. Aboriginal guides and trackers were highly regarded, with an 'unmatched knowledge of their environment, [and] related expertise' including the 'ability to locate water and well grassed country'.[37]

Certainly Aboriginal men fitted the criteria articulated in the British Commander-in-Chief Lord Kitchener's request for men in 1902: besides an ability to 'ride and shoot', 'tracking ability by applicants will be a recommendation'.[38] A telegram from the acting

Police Magistrate of Burketown in Queensland sought to clarify whether 'half-castes' were acceptable as recruits within the Imperial Bushmen's Contingent: 'Will you accept half-castes', 'one is offering and is a good man, he is by a white man and [A]boriginal mother and has received schooling'.[39] There is no further evidence to reveal whether this Aboriginal man was accepted or not.

There has been much speculation as to whether a group of Aboriginal trackers were sent to South Africa and left behind after the conflict ended.[40] It appears that this story stemmed initially from press reports in 1902 that Kitchener had cabled the governor-general of Canada requesting that Indian scouts be provided to assist the British. This drew the ire of some in the Australian press, who complained that Kitchener had clearly overlooked a far superior tracker commodity down under. As the Adelaide *Register* put it:

> [W]e may make bold to say that King Jacky of Turramurra and King Tommy of Binalong, aforetime warriors bold and lusty, could be advantageously employed in South Africa in guiding the rooineks by spruit and kloof to the secret haunt of Stein and his peripatetic 'Government'. The spectacle of one of our [A]borigines in full attire of white clay stripes, fluff, spears, and waddy, suddenly appearing at dawn, would severely bother Botha and perhaps demoralize the most adamantine dopper.[41]

There were other calls in the press for Aboriginal trackers to be unleashed upon the Veldt:

> It might not be amiss to send with the Contingent a squad of black trackers. They must be black, because no white men can track worth mentioning in comparison with the native. And unfortunately, they must be non-combatants. But that will not, after all, matter so much, as it will be found that 'Billy', and

> 'Combo', and 'Jacky' will be able to trek as well as to track when the Mausers begin to sing.[42]

The Australian government, for its part, had earlier communicated with the British parliament to learn what was required by Kitchener for the further prosecution of the South African campaign. There was nothing in this correspondence specific to the provision of Aboriginal trackers, and Kitchener simply replied that he was 'fully satisfied with mounted troops now at his disposal'.[43] However, eight months later, with British losses and reversals in South Africa mounting, dispatches and cables were sent to Prime Minister Edmund Barton requesting Australian 'bushmen and trackers'.[44] In response, Barton offered to 'dispatch 50 Bush Trackers by the S.S. "Euryalus" carrying a consignment of horses'.[45] Again, it was not specified that these men were to be Aboriginal. The Australian term 'bushmen' was in wide circulation at the time, and when the famed Sir Arthur Conan Doyle reported that 'a small force of Australian bushmen' arrived at Rustenburg, he added when 'the balladmakers of Australia seek for a subject, let them turn to Elands River, for there was no finer fighting in the war'.[46] These men established a reputation for the Australian fighting man: 'They did sterling service as scouts: the third, fourth and fifth contingents sent from Australia were labelled as "Bushmen" and were used in pursuit of Boer guerrillas'.[47]

However, if it is improbable that the men proposed by Barton were Aboriginal, it is possible that a couple of Aboriginal trackers were included in this Bushmen's contingent. The Boer War was one of the first wars to receive widespread newspaper coverage. Some of the world's literary giants rushed to South Africa to cover the conflict, including Rudyard Kipling, Arthur Conan Doyle and Australia's Banjo Paterson. Paterson recorded one tongue-in-cheek incident of an Aboriginal tracker in the Boer War:

> One of the Australian regiments brought over a black tracker, and was going to do great things with him. One day news came in that the supply wagons had gone astray. 'Very well,' said the captain, 'send in the black tracker!' 'Please sir, he's lost too!' was the discouraging answer.[48]

With such a high level of media interest, it seems inconceivable that the presence of large numbers of Aboriginal trackers in South Africa would not have been picked up. It suggests that, while Aboriginal men were present, their numbers were not high.

For example, a New Zealand press report of October 1899 noted the presence of an Aboriginal man from the Coromandel Peninsula enlisting with a New Zealand contingent:

> Teddy Collins is a very intelligent Australian black, who has been living here several years. He is reported to be a good black tracker. He is also one of our local crack sprinters. All of the men who have volunteered are general favourites here.[49]

We do not know how Teddy Collins came to be in New Zealand, but Lynette Russell's historical research has identified Aboriginal men working on ships throughout the nineteenth and early twentieth centuries, which resulted in these men travelling widely. She has revealed the 'enterprise and entrepreneurship' of Aboriginal people and in her work 'we see Aboriginal people exerting their individual autonomy and agency as they seek the opportunity to profit from a life at sea'.[50] It is likely that Collins had simply disembarked in New Zealand, liked the place and stayed on.

Two further Aboriginal men, William Stubbings and Jack Alick, have been confirmed as serving in the Boer War. Stubbings served in South Africa with D Squadron of the 3rd Regiment, New South Wales Mounted Rifles between 1899 and 1902. Public historian and website discussant Philippa Scarlett, having spent decades researching Aboriginal military service, indicated that Stubbings' identity was revealed as far back as 1993, when details of his Darug heritage and service in the Boer War was covered in James Kohen's *The Darug and their Neighbours: The Traditional Aboriginal Owners of the Sydney Region.*[51] Peter Bakker is responsible for unearthing Jack Alick as serving 'in the pre-Federation New South Wales First Australian Horse'.[52] Alick had links to 'a well-known Aboriginal family originating in the Braidwood area of New South Wales'. While serving in South Africa, Alick posted a letter home but it is assumed someone else wrote it for him, since on the 1902 form completed when he enlisted he could only make 'his mark'. In this letter he confessed that he had 'seen quite enough fighting and have had some very narrow squeaks'. He was hopeful that he would be returning home 'which I hope won't be long, as I reckon it has lasted long enough'. On his return to Australia, Jack Alick and some of his fellow comrades were given a civic reception by the mayor of Braidwood. It seems that he quickly recovered from his ordeal and homesickness since he volunteered again and went back to South Africa with the 1st Battalion of the Australian Commonwealth Horse.[53] This second foray in February 1902 was short-lived, as peace was declared on 31 May. There was, it seems, no welcome home celebration for Alick then; nor for the Australian Commonwealth Horse. Perhaps, as Scarlett has suggested, there may have been a 'change in the mood in relation to the war in some quarters following the discovery of the mistreatment of Boer civilians'.[54]

Yet another Aboriginal man, John Searle, served in the Boer War as a private with the Western Australian Mounted Infantry. He fought at Stinkhoutboom, the battle of Rhenoster Kop, the great De Wet hunt and the attack on Pietersburg. He survived the war and it is assumed that he returned to Australia on the *Britannia* in

1901. Peter Bakker has concluded that he was 'obviously affected by his time in the Boer War and a bit disillusioned when he came back and he apparently tried to commit suicide'.[55]

Edward Kennedy's *The Black Police of Queensland*, published in 1902, told the story of an Aboriginal tracker named Billy who served in South Africa.[56] Australian claims that Billy could track anything over any terrain were derided by British officers: 'We have heard all these wonderful accounts of reading the ground, and though there may be some shadow of truth in the matter, yet we don't believe more than half your fairy stories.'[57] The Australians countered this scoffing by telling the British officers to 'put their money where their mouth was'. The bet was taken and Billy was given the task of tracking five men, two on foot and three on horseback:

> The tracker, first stating that the men had chosen their various routes over all the hard and rocky ground of the neighbouring veldt, then proceeded to draw five lines in the sand, and descanted on each track: these of the mounted men he had followed at a run – described how one had got off his horse and had then proceeded to light his pipe, producing the half burnt match to prove it.[58]

Billy's account was breathtakingly detailed. It stated that one of the men had been thrown by his horse and another had tied his horse to a tree and 'climbed one of these, presumably to get a view as there was neither "possum" nor "sugar bag" in it said Billy'. He also revealed that one of the men on foot had cut his foot badly. Overall 'Billy proved beyond doubt that he had run and read every track faithfully; and afforded other proofs, by recording many minute finds and incidents that he had done so.' The British officers were convinced, and willingly handed over their bets to the Australians.[59]

A photograph of the 4th Contingent of the Queensland Imperial Bushmen, taken on their return from the Boer War in August 1901, clearly identifies an Aboriginal soldier as part of this contingent:

> The vintage silver gelatin photograph on the original flush-cut mount was in excellent condition. But even more astounding was the Aboriginal serviceman clearly visible in the right side of the photo … initial research suggests the serviceman's name may be Martin Grogan.[60]

The Grogan name belongs to a very well known Queensland Aboriginal family and it appears that this Aboriginal man did go to South Africa. Press coverage in the *Sydney Morning Herald* reported that two Aboriginal trackers 'Davis and F. King have been taken on the strength' to serve in South Africa.[61] Interestingly, neither King nor Davis appear in any official military documentation for South Africa.

Aboriginal trackers fighting in South Africa were more at risk than white soldiers. Kitchener reported in 1901 that a small British patrol had been cut off and forced to surrender to over 200 of the Boer forces; after 'the surrender the Boers shot all the native scouts who accompanied the patrol'.[62] In contrast, after their weapons were removed, the British soldiers were released. Boer general and guerrilla commander Pieter Hendrik Kritzinger went so far as to release a letter stating that he 'will shoot all natives in the employ of the British, whether armed or unarmed'.[63]

In 1901 a number of newspaper articles covered the story about a trooper named Quinlan who disappeared during the march from Johoonda through Pouri Pouri with a destination of Rietfontein. It transpired that he had apparently taken leave of the column to hunt and became lost in the bush. It was certainly no place to be lost or alone and it was reported that some of the troopers had to escape from a lioness who 'prowled around the camp, roaring and growling' through the night.[64] Quinlan, by all accounts, was one of the 'best troopers', and was 'popular with his comrades'.[65] After two unsuccessful search parties were sent out without finding him, it was decided by:

> [T]he officers to not waste further time by keeping the whole column waiting but to push on to Reitfontein [sic]. However, a small group were detached from the main column to stay behind and look for Quinlan. This group comprised Lieutenant French, 'Diamond' (one of our negro-drivers), a black tracker Trooper Phillips (formerly a police tracker in Queensland), and Sergeant-Major Esler.

Quinlan's trail was eventually tracked down in a sandy creek some 17 miles (27 kilometres) from the road. French later stated:

> [H]e would never have found the trail without the assistance he got from Phillips. Examining the trail Phillips said. 'He is getting weak on it, for he is using his rifle as a walking stick.' After a bit they found Quinlan's rifle in the creek, with a message written in ink.

Some four miles (6 kilometres) further on the searchers made the call 'coo-ee' and heard a faint reply. Riding in that direction they spotted Quinlan. He called out to them 'For God's sake give me a drink,' in a hoarse, husky voice and with his tongue protruding dry and swollen from his mouth. Quinlan had been found some three days and some sixty hours since his disappearance from the wagon and column. The searchers, particularly Trooper Phillips, were the heroes of the day.[66]

However, Phillips' Aboriginality has been contested in contemporary discussions of the event. Rob Droogleever on the Desert Column website states:

> Arthur James Phillips was 33 years old when he signed up with the 4th Bushmen. He had worked in New South Wales & Queensland and had gained his knowledge of tracking from the blackfellas there. He had assisted the Queensland police on occasions. Did he have Aboriginal blood in him? I don't know for I do not have his mother's name. I think it unlikely.[67]

Another commentator on the website, Bill Woerlee, revealed that there were two other candidates with the surname Phillips in South Africa: William Henry Phillips, who was apparently invalided back to Australia in 1900, was effectively ruled out, and Arthur James Phillips. If Trooper Phillips was a black tracker and taken to South Africa, he may not have even been officially enlisted.[68] The recent study of Queensland's Native Police, *The Secret War* by Jonathan Richards, has an extensive appendix with a nominal roll of the European members of the Native Police in Queensland and there is no mention of an Arthur Phillips or anyone even with the surname Phillips serving with that notorious contingent.[69] This certainly adds weight to the belief that Phillips was a black tracker; so the jury remains out on this intriguing story.

The aftermath

The numbers of Aboriginal men serving in the Boer War may have been small, and those that did serve may not have returned home to a life as recognised heroes. Indeed, it has been suggested that some may not even have come home at all, rather being refused admission to Australia under the White Australia policy and thus marooned in South Africa. What substance is there in this story of the 'lost trackers'?

A 1907 report by the Commonwealth agent in South Africa, George Valder, compiled information on at least a thousand Australian men, women and children seeking repatriation at home due to the 'dire depression prevailing in South Africa'.[70] It was made plain to the applicants that they 'must undertake to repay the amount expended on their behalf' by the Commonwealth.[71] Since this report revealed that some of the men requesting assistance to return home were Aboriginal, it has fuelled speculation that this was evidence of 'lost trackers'. Indeed, Valder stated that he received several applications 'from coloured people who were natives of Australia, in some instances these were the descendants of American Negroes resident in Australia, others were evidently half caste, and two or three were either Aboriginals, or Aboriginal half castes'.[72] Valder implied that changes to the Australian *Immigration Restriction Act 1901* had locked these people out of their own country. The law was quite clear: 'coloured persons from Australia cannot be allowed to return unless they have, prior to leaving the Commonwealth, obtained a permit'.[73] Despite correspondence from these individuals stating that they had left Australia prior to the Act's introduction, Valder revealed that he had contacted the prime minister for clarification. The reply was blunt: 'that all coloured persons born in Australia must obtain a special permit from the Commonwealth, before they could be permitted to land'.[74] Dale Kerwin has put forward a case that some of the men looking to get home may have been Aboriginal trackers:

> By the decree of the then prime minister of Australia Edmund Barton, and the newly adopted *Immigration Restriction Act 1901*, their repatriation would have required a special permit and there is no evidence that this was issued. The fact that the Aboriginal

> trackers could have paid their own fare back to Australia is unimaginable, as they would have been poorly paid.[75]

The question remains, were the Aboriginal men mentioned in Valder's report veterans from the Boer War in South Africa? Evidence strongly suggests they were, as '80 per cent of the men produced discharges, which showed that they had fought in the South African War and had borne good characters whilst serving with their regiments'.[76] Valder advised the Aboriginal men to make 'applications for permits. As these men have all since obtained employment. They will I believe manage to pay their own fares'.[77] However, it is also possible that some Aboriginal men may have been in South Africa before the war. A good number of Australians had gone there chasing riches and work with the gold and mining boom.[78] Some of these men may have been Aboriginal, given Russell's argument about the mobility of Aboriginal men in search of work and opportunities.

Given that archival sources for an Aboriginal presence in South Africa are limited, the stories of the Boer War experience of Aboriginal soldiers and trackers, and those back at home, have many gaps. Clearly, some Aboriginal men put their hands up to go and some were accepted, while others were turned away. Some people had opportunities because of the war and some Aboriginal communities took an avid interest in the conflict. It has been important to note that Aboriginal people's access to military service, and their freedom to make their own choices in life, were far greater during the Boer War years than was the case later in the twentieth century. The desire to enlist in the Boer War and following First World War may, in fact, have been an Indigenous challenge to the historical emasculation of Aboriginal male identity from the earliest point of

European occupation of the continent. Finally, although the numbers of Aboriginal men serving in South Africa may have been small, they took the opportunity to prove themselves as equal or superior to white men on the biggest level playing arena, the battlefield. It is also significant that some Aboriginal community members carried memories of Aboriginal service in the Boer War long after the event. In a 2GB radio broadcast in 1941, famed Aboriginal activist Pearl Gibbs reminded listeners 'that men of my race served in the Boer War, more so in the 1914–18 War'.[79]

Note: This chapter is an expanded and modified version of an earlier publication, '"Let us go" … it's a "Black-fellows' War": Aborigines and the Boer War', *Aboriginal History*, vol. 39, 2015, pp. 143–62.

4

The First World War

John Maynard

'It was hell on earth.' – *Private Edgar Hite*

The First World War gave rise to an enduring narrative about the soldiers of the Australian Imperial Force (AIF). In the Anzac legend the Australian 'digger' was celebrated as the quintessential citizen-in-arms – affable, courageous, poorly disciplined, a larrikin and a great mate. But where did the Aboriginal soldier sit within this foundational national narrative? We now know that around 1000 Aboriginal men enlisted between 1914 and 1918, many times more than served in the Boer War only a decade or so earlier.[1] With the aid of First World War military records, we can ascertain where these Aboriginal men came from, when they enlisted, and how they were employed at the time they volunteered to serve.[2] Since military regulations excluded Aboriginal men from service until May 1917, it might be assumed that the greatest number of Aboriginal men enlisted after that date, but was this the case? And what happened to Aboriginal men after they joined the AIF, and on their return? This chapter seeks to unravel some of these complexities of Aboriginal experiences during the First World War.

Enlistment: Where, when and why

The First World War was essentially a European conflict into which Australia was drawn after the British government, acting on behalf of the whole Empire, declared war on Germany on 4 August 1914. With the exception of the Australian occupation of German New Guinea in September–October 1914, almost all of the 416 809 Australians who chose to enlist – they were all volunteers – served far from home: at Gallipoli; on the Western Front in France and Belgium; in Sinai and Palestine; and on the high seas with the Royal Australian Navy. What must it have been like for the young Aboriginal men who headed overseas to take part in this conflict? They sailed away from family, community and country, presumably with a mixture of apprehension, excitement and fear. Interviews with descendants a century later spoke of the difficulty that Aboriginal men faced 'leaving community, family and home behind'.[3]

The records of the Aboriginal men who enlisted for the First World War reveal that, as in the Boer War years, some had considerable freedom of movement and a capacity to make their own life decisions. Many Aboriginal people at the turn of the century were not welfare-dependent. Although government controls over Aboriginal life would intensify during the First World War (see chapter 5), all those Aboriginal men who volunteered for the AIF stated on their enlistment forms that they were employed. They listed their occupations, as might be expected: stockmen, labourers, shearers and farm hands. But these records also reveal Aboriginal men working as truck drivers, fettlers, dairymen, clothing cutters, masons, miners, clerks, jockeys, contractors, glass workers, machinists, lime burners, butchers, musicians, fishermen, blacksmiths, bakers, plumbers, railway clerks, nurserymen, train engine drivers, oyster merchants, pattern makers, railway porters, motor mechanics, merchant sailors, mechanical draftsmen, students, orchardists, warehousemen, process engravers, musicians, dental mechanics and a journalist. Gordon Syron, reflecting a century later on his uncles who fought in the First World War, stated that 'his family grew up on farms, they were rugged and good soldiers'.[4]

The precise details of Aboriginal enlistment in the First World War continue to be debated. In the early years of the war there were barriers to Aboriginal enlistment in the AIF, since the *Defence Act* of 1909, which had limited compulsory military service to Australians of substantially European origin or descent, continued to shape official policy (see p. 39). In 1915, the Minister of Defence, Senator George Pearce, stated 'he was not prepared at present to recruit Aborigines'.[5] This was despite accounts advising that 'the smartest horse and cattle men and the best shots in the Territory are the half-castes'.[6] But how effective were these restrictions on Aboriginal enlistment? Previously it has been assumed that it was not until the military authorities relaxed the barriers to Aboriginal enlistment in May 1917, allowing 'half-castes' to enlist, that significant numbers of Aboriginal men joined the AIF.[7] In fact, the records drawn upon in this study reveal that the greatest numbers of Aboriginal men signed up in the years 1914 to 1916. Of the 989 records of Aboriginal men examined, 641 of them had enlisted before 1917. However, it is important to note that in contrast to other states, there was a spike in Queensland enlistment in 1917.[8]

Hence, the relaxation of official barriers to Aboriginal enlistment was likely to have been motivated not by the AIF's need to recruit more men after huge losses in the Battle of the Somme and the failure of the conscription referendum of October 1916, but rather that the military authorities acknowledged that large numbers of Aboriginal men were already fighting overseas – and had proven themselves effective soldiers into the bargain. Unfortunately, we cannot know why the military authorities finally decided to admit Aboriginal men to the AIF. The AIF Correspondence Index Cards in the National Archives of Australia reveal that there was extensive correspondence during the First World War on the question of Aboriginal 'half-castes' and 'coloured' men enlisting. However, none of this correspondence survived the record culls of subsequent decades.[9]

Given the barriers to their enlisting, Aboriginal men who wished to volunteer had to be inventive and proactive in seeking ways to sign up with the AIF. This included moving to regions or localities where there was greater support for and appreciation of Aboriginal people. We know from the records that 677 enlisted from country areas and 312 from the cities. Some simply took on another racial identity: James Lingwoodock identified himself as a Kanaka and gained entry in this way; while Richard Martin from Stradbroke Island identified as Māori and was wounded in action three times before he was killed in action in France on 23 March 1918.[10] Opportunities to enlist also depended on the discretion of the recruiting officer and medical officers at particular locations. As Philippa Scarlett has argued, 'the large number who managed to join up demonstrates the pragmatism of recruiters'.[11]

Were these Indigenous soldiers fighting for 'their country', for Australia or for the British Empire? We cannot know the answer to this question with any certainty, since few of those who served left any record of their motivation for so doing. As previously discussed, the records of Aboriginal men who joined up suggest that they were previously employed in other occupations. This challenges the idea that the prospect of a wage was the major motivation behind their volunteering. Aboriginal men did not go to war simply because they lacked options or choice. Some probably signed up for the same reasons as non-Indigenous men: for travel and adventure; because their mates or brothers had signed up; because they believed in the war effort; or because they were subjected to aggressive recruitment campaigns.[12] However, Aboriginal people during the early twentieth century were also developing a sense of a pan-national Aboriginal identity loosely tied to the rise of a wider Australian national identity. This would come very much to the fore during the 1920s when organised Aboriginal political protest began to emerge. However, like many white Australians, Aboriginal men may have positioned their sense of identity within a wider 'British' loyalty. James Arden and Richard King, on their arrival at the Ballarat military training camp, stated that they were:

> [A]nxious to get to the front as soon as possible in order to fight for the Empire … the natives at the Condah station felt that they were real Britishers, having been born under the Australian flag, and were willing to fight to a man if they were accepted by the military authorities.[13]

Despite their willingness to serve, many of those Aboriginal men who volunteered encountered official obstruction, including after they enlisted. Twenty-two-year-old Tom Cooper, a young Aboriginal man from Kalgoorlie, enlisted in the Light Horse but was discharged after 61 days because he was not 'of substantially European descent': this, despite a supporter declaring that he was 'a splendid rider and rifle shot'.[14] In 1917, 16 very disgruntled Aboriginal would-be diggers from Barambah (later Cherbourg) in Queensland wanted to know why they had been discharged from the AIF on 13 June. As they wrote to the *Cairns Post*, they resented being made to appear as 'slackers' through no fault of their own:

> [T]hey allege that when they were discharged from the military training camp they were told that they would be met at the Central Railway station by the Chief Protector of Aborigines, who would hand over to them their pay and discharge papers. Instead, they were at the station handed over to a police

> escort, and were brought back to their settlement 'like a lot of prisoners.' … It was pointed out that white men have an objection to a 'blackfella' being associated with them at the camp.

In response, the military headquarters in Melbourne explained that it was a condition of approval for 'coloured men' to be enlisted 'that one of the parents was [of] European origin'.[15] This was later qualified to the effect that Aboriginal men also had to demonstrate that they had been associated with white people for 'some time prior to enlistment'. In the case of the manifestly racial exclusion of the Barambah men it was inferred that they 'were not half-castes'– the military authorities stated that 'full-blooded [A]boriginals' were not wanted, as they believed that they would 'not make soldiers'. The military issued a final clause to headquarters in Brisbane that 'half-castes' could be enlisted 'at the discretion of the commandant'.[16]

The experience of war

Once they were admitted to the AIF, the Aboriginal soldiers' experiences of military service and combat were as diverse as those of their non-Indigenous comrades. Many Aboriginal men served with the Light Horse, which gained fame (as dismounted troops) in the Gallipoli campaign of 1915, and then in the subsequent Palestine campaign of 1916–18. Possibly Aboriginal volunteers were deployed to the Light Horse because they had been horsemen in their prewar life: horse breakers, boundary riders, jockeys and stockmen. For many such men their first experience of overseas service was Egypt, the land of pyramids and the Sphinx. This was a completely different cultural landscape from Australia, and a difficult environment and climate; the nights could be bitterly cold, even in summer, and it was a land of sand, dust, heat and flies. One Australian soldier described a 'beast of a day with a hot wind blowing … "Arab's Heaven" and soldier's hell'.[17] For Aboriginal servicemen there could be both humorous and potentially dangerous incidents in the Egyptian towns. Frank Balser, from Lakefield Station, Queensland, was captured at one point by an Indian Cavalry Unit, who were convinced they had captured an Arab spy.[18] Thomas Locke, of Rooty Hill, NSW, was attacked and set upon when returning from leave in Ismailia in 1918: 'Whilst passing the Arab portion of the town, I was assaulted by the natives and received blows on the back of the neck and the left arm, dealt to me by a heavy stick.' Locke called for the assistance of the military police, who transported him to hospital. It is worth noting Locke's reference to his attackers as 'natives' and even more revealing that he had been attacked in the 'public women's quarters' of Ismailia.[19] Yet despite the dangers and hardship of Egypt, Walter Ernest Smith sent a message home to his family from Cairo simply stating that he 'was having the time of his life'.[20]

The legend of the Australian fighting soldier began to be burnt into the national memory with the landing at Gallipoli, on 25 April 1915. Anzac Cove is the site, we are constantly reminded, where Australia 'became a nation' thanks to the incredible sacrifice of its young diggers trying to secure a hold on contested and rugged terrain.[21] Another memory of Gallipoli that has largely lain hidden and been overlooked is the number of young Aboriginal soldiers who served there. Several were killed or wounded alongside their non-Indigenous comrades during the eight-month campaign before the Australian evacuation in December 1915.

One of these men was John Miller from Claremont in Tasmania, who was killed on the first day of the campaign. Miller had had previous military experience before enlisting, having served with the Derwent Regiment. He was initially reported as missing in action, and his wife, Ida, wrote to Victoria Barracks, Melbourne on 7 October 1915, 'I am living in a lonely place with my 4 little children. I am very anxious to hear of my husband.' Miller's body was not found and officially buried until after the war, in 1922, in the Baby 700 Cemetery north-east of Anzac Cove. His identity disc, recovered by the war graves unit, was returned to his wife by the military authorities.[22] James Dickerson from Gingin in Western Australia meanwhile was wounded in action at Lone Pine on 29 August 1915, with a gunshot wound to the buttock and a fractured leg.[23] A day later he died of his wounds and was one of many men to be buried at sea, 50 miles west of Cape Matapan. Arthur Charles Homer, an Aboriginal man from Lismore in New South Wales, was killed at Gallipoli on 28 June 1915.[24] Edgar George Bindoff died of a bomb wound (to the left arm, buttock and fingers) suffered at Lone Pine on 4 September 1915.[25] Arthur Benjamin Brown, a labourer from Surry Hills in Sydney (noted on his attestation papers as being of a 'swarthy' appearance), was also killed at Gallipoli on 8 August 1915, at the age of just 21. He was his mother's only son.[26] Ngarrindjeri man George Karpany fought with distinction at Gallipoli and was later promoted to lance corporal. He would serve on the Western Front, where he was wounded in the leg and forehead from an exploding bomb. He was undoubtedly resilient as he would later receive several other gunshot wounds in action, to the right thigh, left knee, shoulder and right forearm.[27] Sergeant James Ernest Burke too, from Casino in NSW, was wounded, twice at Gallipoli, including once from an exploding bomb that left wounds to his face, neck and hands.[28] Edward Lewis Maynard from Flinders Island in Tasmania was another casualty of the fierce fighting at Lone Pine on 8 August 1915, when the British forces made their last abortive attempt to break the stalemate at Gallipoli.[29] A number of other Aboriginal men, including Alfred Robbins of Junee; Walter Smale from Queensland; Charles Waller, a merchant sailor from Kangaroo Island; and Peter Zeisser from Sydney, were also killed in action at Gallipoli.[30]

The pride of these men and their families in such service was self-evident. Arthur Walker, a Ngarrindjeri man, who fought at Gallipoli until the evacuation in December 1915, was later killed at the 1916 battle of Mouquet Farm, near Pozières, on the Western Front. Arthur's son was named Anzac to commemorate his father's role in the 'famous Australian battle'.[31] Another Ngarrindjeri man, Eustace Garnet Wilson, better known as 'Garney', named his house at Point McLeay (Raukkan), 'Passchendaele, after the famous battle of October-November 1917. A street sign bearing that name, which he must have souvenired from the Western Front, was nailed to the front of his house'.[32] Wilson was among a number of Aboriginal servicemen from the First World War who chose to re-enlist in the Second World War.[33]

Aboriginal men from this author's own local area also fought with great courage during the war. Three Aboriginal brothers, Fred, Alister and Augustus Lester from St Clair Aboriginal mission in the upper Hunter Valley, enlisted with the AIF. Fred was sent to the army camp at Rutherford and, probably fortunately for the family, was discharged after only 69 days: he was declared as medically unfit (he had flat feet).[34] Alister and Augustus both fought in France and were killed in action: Alister on 16 April 1918 and Augustus, on 23 August 1918 after more than two years' service. According to his military record Augustus is buried on the left of a quarry on Bray-Corloe Road in front of Tallie Wood in France.[35]

Worimi Aboriginal man Albert Lilley Knight was another who lost his life in France. His Commanding Officer, Lieutenant AJ Gardiner, wrote in 1918:

> It is with great regret and extreme sorrow I write these few lines … He was killed during an enemy bombardment of our trenches.

> He was highly esteemed by officers and men of his company, a good lad, a fine character, and an excellent soldier … He has a very nice grave in a village called Aubigny.[36]

A few months later another Aboriginal man of the same name, Albert Knight, was awarded the Distinguished Conduct Medal for his role on 30 September 1918 during the attack on the formidable German defences known as the Hindenburg Line when several bombing parties were held up by heavy machine gun fire. As the official citation said:

> Cpl. KNIGHT … proceeded with another N.C.O. to push forward and reconnoitre the enemy position. This necessitated moving over country which afforded no cover, other than shell holes, for a distance of 200 yards. This was carried out in broad daylight and in full view of the enemy lines, and under Heavy Machine Gun fire, Trench Mortar and Artillery fire. In spite of difficulties he succeeded in reaching a position from which he located several Machine Guns and Trench Mortars, which were at the time playing on our position. He then returned to our lines with the valuable information which he had obtained and artillery assistance was brought [t]o bear with success on the positions indicated.[37]

Yet as Aboriginal men displayed such bravery, their letters home also revealed their fears, trauma and homesickness. While convalescing in England, Charles Blackman wrote:

> I don't wish to go back [to France] yet while this big stunt is on. I have seen quite enough of it before … I am putting in the time with new mates because the last time in we had some stiff fighting, my cobbers are away wounded. I were nearly going away

> wounded but I am very lucky. I wish others were as lucky as I am. I am wonderfully lucky.[38]

Similarly, a letter from Private Charles Morgan, originally from Deebing Creek in Queensland, to a friend Bill, was published in the *Queensland Times* in May 1918. In this he stated, 'I wish the war was over, so I can get back to the old home again.' The article itself described Morgan as 'a fine stamp of a man – not quite full blooded, with a beautiful set of natural teeth, and that he would be admired everywhere in his khaki uniform'.[39]

Another young Aboriginal soldier Edward Heath, writing home to his sweetheart, confided that he expected God 'to guard me safely through this strange country … and if he spares me to come back to the homeland, I will come back the same as I left it'. There was a sense of foreboding in the correspondence: he told her this would be his last letter for some time 'but do not get anxious or worry. If the worst should come you know you have one who has proved a soldier to the end, and I will die proud of the one I left behind. Play your part at home and don't worry too much.'[40] Heath was killed on the Western Front on 9 June 1917. His record reveals he had fought for three days in the battle of Messines, his officer noting that he 'showed great courage and did excellent work'.[41]

In a letter to his sister on 23 September 1917, Edgar Hite from Tasmania expressed his deep concern for his family back at home and wanted to ease their worry about himself and his brother Charles:

> It was on easter Sunday poor Charlie got wounded. I have not heard from him since but he was not missing he went to hospital with a bad wound he left me about six o'clock in the morning at the dressing station it was a hard Easter. I will never forget that Sunday morning it was hell on earth. Well Alice I can't tell you any more I know it is hard for you all at home. You need

> not worry about me ... I have not much to tell you this time its I must say good bye with love to all from your ever loving brother.[42]

Charles Hite had been wounded in action with a gunshot wound to the shoulder in France in 1916. He suffered trench fever in January 1917; the symptoms of this disease, transmitted by body lice, include headaches, skin rashes, inflamed eyes and leg pains. Hite was then wounded a second time in France before dying in action on 10 April 1917. A statement by Private Barkworth said:

> On Easter Tuesday ... I was searching the dead and looking for wounded when I came across a man lying face downwards shot through the heart. I turned him over but owing to the condition he was in could not recognise him. I found his disc and recognised the name to be that of an old comrade of mine. I then made a closer inspection of the body and recognised the man to be that of 2843 Pte C.E. Hite of the 12th Battalion.[43]

As these casualties indicate, Aboriginal men took part in some of the fiercest fighting on the Western Front, a theatre where the individual soldier was almost eclipsed by artillery and other weapons of industrialised war. On the night of 24–25 February 1917 Private Fred Briggs took part in a raid on the enemy's trench. To quote his Active Service form:

> while acting as a covering Bomber for the Wire Cutters [Briggs] was severely wounded in the right arm but with great grit and determination he continued bombing with his left arm. He thus prevented the enemy who were in readiness at the point of entry from inflicting further casualties on our Wire Cutters, who were enabled to complete their work.[44]

Briggs was awarded the Military Medal for this action but was ultimately killed in action on 24 September 1917 in Belgium. His name appears on the Menin Gate Memorial in Ypres, which honours over 55 000 dead who had no known graves, including 6100 missing Australians.

Frederick Brook, an Aboriginal horse trainer from the south coast of New South Wales, who was married with two children, died of wounds near Ypres. Eyewitness accounts state that Brook, one of 'the most popular lads in the battalion', was almost buried by an exploding shell fragment. One leg was virtually severed at the knee. He was taken away by two stretcher bearers to the dressing station. One observer recalled that 'He was then still in a conscious condition. He said 'goodbye' to us all and wished us luck and remarked that he felt right for "Blighty". I knew him very well, he came from NSW.' Another eyewitness recalled that Brook's battalion:

> [W]as in trenches about a mile behind the front line east of Ypres. They were to go up to the front line the following evening to attack. During the 3rd October a shell burst overhead and some pieces dropped in the trench killing one man and wounded three others including Brooks who was very badly wounded. Informant saw him hit, being only about 10 yards away. Brooks was carried out by Private Campbell and Charlton, both of whom have since been killed.[45]

Sydney Burgess from Cape Barren Island in Tasmania initially arrived in England from Australia, where he had to be hospitalised for sickness. When fit, he rejoined his regiment and went into action at Mouquet Farm in France.[46] The terrible conditions in this sector of the front, which was bitterly contested from July to September 1916, were later described by Charles Bean, the official historian, as follows:

> [T]he flayed land, shell-hole bordering shell-hole, corpses of young men lying against the trench walls or in shell-holes; some – except for the dust settling on them – seeming to sleep; others torn in half; others rotting, swollen, and discoloured … the air fetid with their stench or at times pungent with the chemical reek of high explosive; the troops of both sides – always in desperate need of sleep – working or fighting by night and living by day in niches scooped in the trench side – dangerous places perilously shaken with the crashing thump of each heavy shell whose burst might all too easily shovel on top of their occupants.[47]

Here Burgess suffered gunshot wounds to the head and chest. After being evacuated to England for treatment, he returned to his unit, where he was again wounded in action with shrapnel wounds to the face and right loin. After a further spell of hospital rehabilitation, Burgess was once more returned to active service and suffered another gunshot wound to the left foot.[48]

William Allan Irwin deserves particular recognition as a highly decorated Australian Aboriginal soldier of the war. He suffered wounds on three separate occasions, to the right buttock, torso, arm, thigh and back. But it was for distinguished gallantry and devotion to duty during stalled operations at Road Wood near Mont St Quentin on 31 August 1918, that he is remembered:

> Single handed and in the face of extremely heavy fire Private Irwin rushed three separate machine gun posts and captured the three guns and crews. It was while rushing a fourth that he was severely wounded. On his irresistible dash and magnificent gallantry this man materially assisted our advance through this strongly held and defended wood; and by his daring actions he greatly inspired the whole of his company.[49]

Irwin would be recognised with the Distinguished Conduct Medal. He fought alongside the Victoria Cross recipient George Cartwright, who had also stormed a machine gun nest under heavy fire. Most notably, Irwin is the only Aboriginal soldier to gain a place in Bean's twelve-volume *The Official History of Australia in the War of 1914–1918*. Bean describes Irwin as 'an Australian half-caste, [who] after attacking like Cartwright, was mortally wounded'.[50] Irwin would die of his wounds the following day, 1 September 1918.

Ewan Rose, a Sydney-based horse breaker, also established an impressive military record. He was promoted to corporal, having been employed as a scout and courier. On many occasions, Rose carried important messages through heavy artillery barrages. He took part in the battle of Broodseinde Ridge, one of the most successful engagements of the battle of Third Ypres in Belgium in October 1917. Rose was in charge of a 'gun taken forward with an advancing infantry party and did excellent work':

> he was in charge of a party of 6 in a gun position when 3 were killed and the remainder buried by an enemy shell, though considerably shaken himself he refused assistance and succeeded in extricating his comrades though under heavy fire all the time. He absolutely refused to leave the position until relieved. His courage and cheerfulness at a very telling time period was an inspiration to all under his command.[51]

Corporal Rose was awarded the Belgian Croix de Guerre for his bravery.

Lance Corporal Harry Thorpe too established a long record of surviving the direst of circumstances in some of the most fiercely contested battles. Wounded at Pozières in 1916 with a gunshot wound to the leg, he suffered a further gunshot wound to the shoulder at Bullecourt in 1917. He also suffered shellshock. Thorpe was conspicuous for his courage and leadership near Ypres in October 1917. He displayed great 'courage and initiative in mopping up enemy dugouts and pill boxes …' And he handled his men with 'great skill and materially assisted his company commander. By his splendid example and disregard of all danger he inspired those under him.'[52] Thorpe ran out of luck on 9 August 1918 at Lihones Wood, France. A stretcher bearer found him shot in the stomach. He died shortly after. Thorpe was buried with his fellow Aboriginal friend and soldier William Rawlings, who was killed on the same day in the process of winning the Military Medal for bravery. They are both interred at the Heath Military Cemetery in Harbonnières. Sadly, back in Australia Thorpe's family and community were subject to 'exceptionally slanderous statements … made to the effect that this soldier saw no fighting and died of disease'. There was pressure mounting on Aboriginal land holdings within Thorpe's community and it appears that some white residents had sought to discredit his memory. The RSL of Lakes Entrance made reply that 'Thorpe is a full blooded black and to our knowledge had a fine record & died I believe of wounds.'[53]

Like many soldiers Aboriginal men established deep friendships amongst their fellow soldiers. Thomas Lewis was killed during the attack on Pozières on 24 July 1916: one soldier, H. Clarke, recalled that 'I was told by the burying party that he had been buried just behind the lines … Lewis was very tall, dark aged 21, and was a great pal of mine.' Lewis was killed along with two other men when a shell exploded in their front-line trench: a witness, C Lutton, stated that 'I knew the soldier well, as he was in the same section. He came from Redfern' and had a dark complexion. Another observer reported 'I was within three yards of him when he was killed in a trench which we had taken from the Germans three days before at Pozieres [sic]. He was buried all but his head. … He was black in the face and quite dead.'[54]

The aftermath

One of the tragedies of the Great War was the condition that became known as 'shellshock'. Many men carried deep mental scars of the horrific carnage they had witnessed at close quarters and there was little help or understanding of the condition at the time. The men suffering from 'shellshock' often carried it for the remainder of their lives, living out their own personal hell. Geoffrey Blainey recently reflected on this unforeseen and misunderstood condition:

> A malady called 'shell shock' was increasingly experienced after the battle of Pozieres in 1916, but most of the medical officers on the battle field were not trained to detect mental illness. When soldiers were rattled by the noise, the sight of friends killed, or their own deep fear, they might express openly their distress, but as a result they could be condemned as shirkers or cowards by their own officers. To respond or pander to them was viewed as lowering morale at a time when morale was vital. It was not realized that the time to tackle trauma was immediately. When shell shocked soldiers did enter mental hospitals, most doctors did not know how to treat them. Sleep, a healthy diet and maybe a week in bed were often prescribed. This proved a feeble recipe for mental health.[55]

Alfred Frederick Bolton of Forster in New South Wales was one of many Aboriginal men to suffer the impact of shellshock. Examining Bolton's record, I tremble at the thought of his experiences. He was wounded at Gallipoli in 1915 with a bayonet wound to the knee, and then wounded again in 1916 in the heavy fighting of the offensive at the Somme. These life-threatening moments clearly had more than a physical impact. When recovering from his Gallipoli wound an unsettled Bolton broke out of the hospital in

Malta and was given five days' detention. After a gunshot wound to the head in France and while recovering in England, he went Absent Without Leave (AWOL); he was given 168 hours' detention and forfeited seven days' pay. He subsequently contracted influenza and is recorded as returning to Australia in 1917 suffering from 'shell shock'.[56]

Back home shellshock, if left unchecked, ruined many lives; not just those of the soldiers, but those closest to them, such as wives, children and family.[57] Many men would find returning to a normal life a difficult proposition. Some descended into alcohol abuse to overcome the pain they carried. A number cut themselves off from families and lost themselves as loners in the cities. This was the case with a number of returning Indigenous servicemen who did not return back to their communities and families. Some men invented a protective cloak about their identity. Alexander Stanley from Ballina stated both his parents were dead and that his father was an American Negro and his mother a white woman: 'I have lived all my life with white people,' he explained, and said there was no need to return home as he had no friends there.[58] Leanne Holt reflects that these experiences continued into the Second World War; her grandfather's war experiences 'seemed to cause distance between himself and his family … he lost touch with his family at Karauh'.[59] This may have been necessitated by the increased levels of control being exerted over Aboriginal lives by the state government Protection Boards. Aboriginal land and farms were being revoked. Aboriginal children were being taken from their families and institutionalised and the level of government interference over Aboriginal lives stifled any initiative or enterprise.

Another, perhaps unexpected, outcome of the war was the fact that a number of Aboriginal soldiers married British women and eventually brought their brides back to Australia. This was clearly a break from a long-ingrained taboo that prevented the likelihood of such unions taking place in Australia. Dick Johnson from the south coast of New South Wales had lost both his first wife and child before enlisting in 1916 at the age of 32. He was married a second time to Scottish woman Thomesina Douglas in Edinburgh in 1919. George Morley was wounded twice in Egypt and France, lost an eye and married his English sweetheart before returning to Australia. Ngarrindjeri man Hurtle Muckray was a member of the Australian Light Horse who enlisted in late 1914 and left a late-night note for his mother on the kitchen table: 'Going to the dardinells [sic] tonight don't worry goodbye Mother, Hurtle.'[60] He served in Gallipoli and in the battle of Romani, in the Sinai. Later, Muckray (by now another sufferer of shellshock) would marry a white British woman. Harry Murray of Dubbo also married his English girlfriend in the seaside town of Torquay. Gordon Charles Naley had been wounded in the hip in France, captured and interned in a prisoner-of-war camp at Limburg, Germany. On his release, he married English girl, Cecelia Marsh of Fulham, in London in 1919.

Unfortunately, there is nothing in the military records to reveal how these and other mixed marriages fared into the future. Were they accepted by the white community on their return to Australia? Were they accepted within Aboriginal communities and families? It clearly would not have been an easy path to tread for either party of such unions. Some records provide a glimpse of the difficulties they might have faced. An article in the *Adelaide News* in 1925 stated that the majority of Australians would condone intermarriage between a British person and someone from Sweden, Spain or Greece, but they would oppose such unions when 'it came to a Persian, an Indian or an Australian nigger'.[61] Many Aboriginal men and their white wives 'withdrew into social obscurity' in the face of the patriarchal power structures and opposition within Australian society.[62]

One member of the Ngarrindjeri Muckray family in South

Australia, George Muckray, also married a white woman. Historian Graham Jenkins could only speculate on Muckray's wife needing 'a great amount of courage ... There was every likelihood that such a wife would be despised and rejected by the European community – including her own family – and never really accepted by the Ngarrindjeri community'.[63] But as a counter-story, we do know that Dick Johnson and his wife Thomesina remained happily married until the end of their days; Johnson will figure prominently in chapter 6 on early Aboriginal political activism.

This chapter has highlighted some of the varied and intriguing aspects of Indigenous experiences during the First World War. The personal stories embedded within the archival record enhance our understanding of the Aboriginal soldiers' experiences on the frontline and the difficulties they faced in coming home. Within these records, Aboriginal soldiers' letters and records are tinged with humour and sadness. These records also reveal some significant patterns. All the men who enlisted stated they were employed. Two-thirds of these men came from or enlisted in the rural and country regions. One of the most surprising findings was that the majority of Aboriginal men volunteered to serve in the war before military restrictions on Indigenous enlistment were relaxed in May 1917. Many Aboriginal Diggers, then, were connected to country, self-supporting and eager to be a part of the broader Australian commitment to the war effort. Privileging Indigenous voices embedded in the Great War enriches and deepens our understandings of Australian history and the savage injustice of the Aboriginal experience.

5

The home front in the First World War

Samuel Furphy

'[W]hat little rations I get from the Board
is not the worth of my dear only son's life.'
– *Bessie Rawlings*

In 1936 Angus & Robertson published volume XI of the *Official History of Australia in the War of 1914–1918*. Written by a professor of history at the University of Melbourne, Ernest Scott, and subtitled *Australia During the War*, it was the only volume in the series of 12 to deal with the Australian home front.[1] A notable feature of Scott's account was that in nearly 900 pages it contained no mention of Aboriginal or Torres Strait Islander people. Given its date of publication, the omission is not surprising: the 1930s were the height of what anthropologist WEH Stanner later called 'the Great Australian Silence', when Indigenous people were absent from most national historical writing.[2] More recent scholarship has been less blinkered, but the general historiography on Australia's home front from 1914 to 1918 has often struggled to integrate Aboriginal perspectives.[3] Most recently, volume 4 of Oxford University Press's *Centenary History of Australia and the Great War* (2015), subtitled *The War at Home*, includes a three-page section on 'Aborigines and the War', but much of it discusses frontier wars and Indigenous recruitment, rather than the home front.[4]

The life experiences of Aboriginal people on the home front are, of course, not absent from the wider historical record. Within the field of Aboriginal history, which has flourished in Australia since the 1970s, several valuable state-based studies cover wartime experiences in the context of broader narratives.[5] Some recent journal articles also explore home front experiences more explicitly.[6] And yet the historiographies of mainstream and Aboriginal experiences of the home front have developed in parallel, so there is an opportunity for researchers to bring these two strands into a more sophisticated conversation.

Joan Beaumont has described the Australian home front as 'an essential part of the national experience of war'.[7] She and other historians emphasise the crucial contribution to the national war effort of Australians who remained at home, while also highlighting the broader economic, political and social consequences of the war for the nation. Aboriginal people are, of course, a part of this national story. The First World War affected Aboriginal employment and the development of regimes for Aboriginal 'protection'. Aboriginal people contributed to fundraising and patriotic campaigns, and their encounters with repatriation and soldier settlement schemes in the aftermath of war deserve attention. In exploring these themes, I aim to consider when and how Aboriginal experiences were typical or distinctive compared to those of other Australians, and to highlight the diversity of Aboriginal experiences.

Indigenous employment

The effects of the First World War on Indigenous employment varied considerably, both temporally and spatially, with fluctuating employment for Aboriginal people in the south-east, but more consistently high employment in Queensland and Western Australia. After the declaration of war in August 1914, mining companies in Australia reduced their workforces as key export markets became enemies; the wool and building industries also slumped. By the end of 1914 the percentage of trade union members who were unemployed almost doubled, to 11 per cent, and, as Peter Yule argues, 'overall unemployment was probably significantly higher'.[8] Inevitably, such conditions affected Aboriginal people, notably in New South Wales, where administrators expressed a fear in 1914 'that large numbers of aborigines will be thrown out of employment'.[9] Unemployment was compounded by the drought of 1914–15, prompting the New South Wales Aborigines Protection Board to declare that 'numbers of men who had been expelled from Reserves for misconduct, &c. were allowed to return temporarily in order that no hardship would result'.[10] In time, however, the rising wartime demand for rural labour prompted the board to order all 'half-castes' over the age of 18 to leave government stations and camps.[11]

In South Australia, the Chief Protector reported in 1915 that a combination of drought and war had caused both high unemployment for Aboriginal people and 'a considerable rise in the prices of goods required for the aborigines'.[12] The resultant financial instability led the South Australian government to take direct control of the Aboriginal missions at Point Pearce and Point McLeay (Raukkan), which led to more coercive policies by the end of the war. However, as the war progressed, employment opportunities increased. On the west coast of South Australia, a bumper harvest in 1916 created a labour shortage that lured many Aboriginal men away from the Koonibba Mission, near Ceduna.[13] Several men from Point McLeay found work in the construction of the Hindmarsh Valley reservoir. In 1917 the Chief Protector reported that 'able-bodied natives can obtain (if they wish) abundance of employment at a good rate of wage … particularly on the stations in the Far North'.[14] Yet, in some instances, these opportunities were temporary. When white labourers returned to the west coast in 1919, Aboriginal people moved back to Koonibba as their employment opportunities dried up.[15]

Fluctuating employment for Aboriginal people was not the experience in all Australian states. The Chief Protector in Queensland, JW Bleakley, reported a keen demand 'for all classes of aboriginal labour' in both 1914 and 1915.[16] However, Aboriginal people in that state felt the economic impact of the war in other ways, as blanket distribution was curtailed and rising prices affected rations provided on missions.[17] Nor were Aboriginal labourers always welcomed; in November 1916 the Queensland government restricted the use of Aboriginal labour on sugar cane fields following accusations that growers were using them as strike-breakers.[18] Moreover, high employment did not guarantee decent labour conditions. In 1918 Bleakley reported that the poor treatment of Aboriginal labourers by some employers would 'convey the impression that he is regarded more as a part of the stock or working plant than as a human being'.[19] Consistent wartime employment in Queensland reflects the historically stronger reliance on Aboriginal labour in that state, especially in the pastoral industry.[20] Similar factors were influential in Western Australia where a flourishing wartime pastoral industry, combined with the absence of white labourers, led to a greater prevalence of cash employment for Aboriginal workers. In this context, the number of Aboriginal people registered for welfare dropped by more than three-quarters between 1914 and 1918.[21]

Aboriginal administration

The availability or lack of employment for Aboriginal people shaped their ability to assert a level of independence from missions, or from government agencies charged with their 'protection'. The significance of this dynamic was heightened by the fact that the First World War coincided with a period of increasing control by state governments over Aboriginal peoples. This was particularly evident in Victoria, where the *Aborigines Act* of 1915, followed by a series of regulations in 1916, expanded the coercive powers of the Board for Protection of Aborigines. Richard Broome has noted the irony of this coincidence: 'as Aboriginal servicemen fought for "freedom from tyranny" at Gallipoli and then in France, the board increasingly controlled the lives of their families back home'.[22] A key aspect of the Victorian board's policy was its 'concentration' plan, which entailed relocating all those Aboriginal people for whom the board still claimed responsibility to a single government reserve. The board selected the Lake Tyers station in eastern Victoria for this purpose, prompting protests from Aboriginal people who did not wish to be relocated.[23]

A similar situation existed in New South Wales following the *Aborigines Protection (Amendment) Act* in 1918, which authorised the Aborigines Protection Board to remove Aboriginal people of 'lighter caste' from government reserves. In 1921 the board reported that 'the process of gradually eliminating quadroons and octoroons [from the reserves] is being quietly carried on'.[24] These policies were not purely coincidental to the war, as the closure of reserves (or at least a reduction in their size) was explicitly linked with making land available for returned soldier settlement schemes. Moreover, the general climate of hysteria and intolerance generated by the war, which led to strict censorship and the erosion of civil liberties for many groups, may have contributed to intensified controls over Aboriginal Australians.

The hardening of Aboriginal policy during the First World War was evident in other ways, and a particularly potent issue was the removal of children. In New South Wales, station managers and police were granted summary powers in 1915 to remove Aboriginal children, the Protection Board having complained that it was often hard to prove 'neglect' in the courts.[25] The New South Wales Colonial Secretary had observed (apparently without irony) that 'if the aboriginal child happens to be decently clad or apparently looked after, it is very difficult to show that the half-caste or aboriginal child is actually in a neglected condition'.[26] As Heather Goodall has argued, these new powers enabled the removal of 1427 Aboriginal children in New South Wales between 1912 and 1938, from an Aboriginal population of between 7000 and 10 000.[27]

In South Australia, child removal policies were also advanced during the war, despite the opinion expressed by the Ngarrindjeri man Matthew Kropinyeri to a 1913 Royal Commission that 'to be subjected to complete alienation from our children is to say the least an unequalled act of injustice'.[28] Having taken control of the missions at Point Pearce and Point McLeay, Chief Protector William Garnet South proposed in 1918 that children should be transferred to a central school near Adelaide at age seven and later placed in indentured service with 'reputable persons'. His plan was enshrined in legislation in 1923, but met with strong opposition, including by a delegation to parliament led by Edward Kropinyeri (Matthew's brother). The first removal under the scheme – the infant daughter of a young mother, Priscilla Karpany – ignited a public controversy, especially as Priscilla's brothers, George and William Karpany, were war veterans. Priscilla's mother drew the attention of the Adelaide press to her sons' service and remarked: 'Is there to be one law for the white people, and another for the black?' Following this controversy, the Act was suspended, but as Robert Foster has argued, child removals continued under earlier legislation, and South's scheme was eventually incorporated into the *Aborigines Act* of 1934.[29]

The First World War also coincided with increasing government intervention in more remote Aboriginal communities. In 1911 the Commonwealth government had taken control of the

Northern Territory from South Australia, resulting in more rigid control of Aboriginal people's lives.[30] The historian Anna Haebich has described it as a shift from 'pacification and dispersal' to 'protection through authoritarian control'.[31] This more interventionist approach was evident in the creation of two new Aboriginal institutions on the eve of the war – the Kahlin compound in Darwin and the Bungalow in Alice Springs – which focused especially on so-called 'half-caste' Aboriginal children. Towards the end of the war, the territory administrator, John Gilruth, defended as necessary a new ordinance for the discipline of Aboriginal labour.[32] Wartime conditions also shaped the assimilationist ideas of the new administration. The Chief Inspector of Aborigines, JT Beckett, remarked in his 1915 report that a military life promised an honourable future for Aboriginal men.[33] He also spruiked his plan to place young Aboriginal people 'in useful and protective avocations'; he proposed that boys might breed and train horses for war purposes while girls might form 'a fine mobile Red Cross Corps'.[34] Although there is no evidence that Beckett implemented this policy, it was an idea that presaged the extensive use of Aboriginal labour for military purposes in northern Australia during the Second World War (see chapter 8).

In Western Australia the war coincided with the establishment of the Carrolup and Moore River native settlements (1915 and 1918 respectively), decisions motivated in part by concerns of white Western Australians at the rising population of Aboriginal people on the fringes of rural towns. In 1919 the Chief Protector, AO Neville, confidently described the new system as an interesting 'sociological experiment' with substantial benefits for Aboriginal people.[35] These institutions became synonymous with the Stolen Generations of Aboriginal children.

Aboriginal Australians and imperial loyalty

The restrictive conditions of state-based Aborigines Acts presumably provided a strong motivation for Aboriginal men to escape discrimination by enlisting for military service. It is perhaps harder to account for the patriotic attitudes of those Aboriginal people who remained at home and continued to live under such conditions, but among whom expressions of loyalty were undoubtedly common. The historian Raymond Evans has observed that communities across Queensland 'from wealthy graziers to institutionalised Aborigines' responded enthusiastically to fundraising campaigns early in the war.[36] For example, people from the Barambah (later Cherbourg) Aboriginal Settlement contributed to fundraising events, including the annual 'Patriotic Day' celebrations at Wondai. According to the *Brisbane Courier*, the celebrations on 30 August 1915 featured 'a squad of aboriginals' who gave demonstrations of boomerang and spear throwing.[37] Later in the year the Barambah community organised a fete involving native sports which raised more than £16 for the Queensland patriotic funds.[38]

These were not isolated examples. In April 1915 the *Bathurst Times* reported that 'thirty aboriginals in full war paint held a corroboree at Copmanhurst', raising £15 for the Belgian Fund.[39] At the Cummeragunja Reserve in southern New South Wales, the 1915 Empire Day celebrations featured patriotic singing and flag-waving during the day, followed by a concert which raised money for a patriotic fund through the New South Wales Department of Education.[40] Similar events occurred elsewhere in the state, such as at Wallaga Lake on the south coast, where Aboriginal pupils sang patriotic hymns 'as earnestly as ever' as part of a successful fundraising event.[41]

Donations of money and useful articles to the Red Cross were also common. On 7 April 1915, the *Sydney Mail* reported that

Aboriginal people from the Mount Olive settlement near Singleton, New South Wales, had responded to an appeal for 'walking-sticks for convalescent soldiers' by sending 'a batch of sticks'.[42] Aboriginal people at the Cabbage Tree Island settlement near Grafton made a similar effort, while students from the Cootamundra Girls' Home contributed 'a number of garments to the local Red Cross Society as their donation for Belgian Day'.[43] In Queensland, Indigenous children contributed items to the 'Aboriginal Court' at the Brisbane Exhibition in 1916. The Chief Protector reported that children from the Weipa mission had donated their prize money to the Red Cross. He also praised the work of two Torres Strait Islander children from the Thursday Island Aboriginal School: 'A very fine recruiting poster in the shape of a crayon map of the Dardanelles, decorated with patriotic emblems and portraits of the leading generals, &c., is worthy of special mention.'[44]

These various expressions of loyal support for the war effort raise important questions regarding agency, especially as many of the examples cited in newspapers or in the reports of white bureaucrats involved Aboriginal children. Students at the Cootamundra Girls' School were surely aware that they were expected to support patriotic projects when instructed to do so by white staff. We might also question whether Barambah people freely offered their services as performers or were directed to do so by the settlement's superintendent. However, many of the communities which displayed conspicuous loyalty (such as Barambah) were those from which large numbers of Aboriginal people enlisted.[45] This surely provided a strong motivation for those at home to support wartime fundraising, especially as the money raised often funded 'comforts' for the soldiers themselves after they were deployed to the battlefront. Reports of Aboriginal loyalty by white officials might also be viewed as exaggerated or oversimplified in the interests of wartime propaganda. Aboriginal enlistment was occasionally used to shame white men into enlisting, and reports of Aboriginal loyalty on the home front implicitly supported this mood.[46]

The complexity surrounding Aboriginal agency and imperial loyalty was addressed in a more nuanced way by the journalist reporting on the Cummeragunja celebrations for Empire Day in 1915. He or she made a revealing observation: 'Cummeragunjians may grumble – do grumble – and, in this, prove that they have been with Britons whose boast it is that they are privileged to grumble.'[47] The reporter identified an ambivalence at the heart of Aboriginal wartime patriotism, implying that support for the war was tempered by disquiet at the living conditions of Aboriginal people, and their inferior status as British subjects. It is likely that Aboriginal loyalty on the home front, like Aboriginal enlistment, was partly motivated by an expectation that demonstrating good citizenship might result in better treatment for Aboriginal people as citizens. Certainly, this expectation was made explicit by Aboriginal activists after the war (see chapter 6).

Motivations for loyalty are complex and difficult to discern 100 years later, but as Newman, Lawrence and Scarlett have argued, Aboriginal involvement in fundraising does indicate 'a level of awareness of the war itself' and a willingness 'to engage at some level with the war effort'.[48] A keen awareness of hostilities in Europe was evident among the Ngarrindjeri people in South Australia from the very beginning of the war. In August 1914 Matthew Kropinyeri told an Adelaide journalist, 'it is a great pity that Great Britain has been drawn into the struggle', before recounting the critical opinions of senior men at Point McLeay regarding British military tactics during the Boer War.[49] The strong engagement of the Point McLeay community with the First World War is also evident in the very high rates of enlistment among Ngarrindjeri men.[50] In some communities, a pervasive interest in the events of the war opened the eyes of Aboriginal people to a wider world. Jimmie Barker (born in 1900) grew up in the Aboriginal community at Brewarrina, New South Wales, and later recalled:

> We knew little about what was happening overseas, but everyone was talking about it. Suddenly it made a difference to us. People bought newspapers and there was more knowledge of world events. Even school children became aware of other places and of the importance of such occurrences as the sinking of the *Emden* and the fighting at Gallipoli.[51]

Not all Aboriginal people lived on missions or reserves, and some were prominent in the home front activities of the wider community. At Port Lincoln in South Australia, the colourful local Aboriginal personality 'Black Fanny' posed in 1916 for a photograph before a large blue ensign with servicemen. When a British naval officer visited Port Lincoln after the war, he 'was boldly accosted by the spectacular figure of Black Fannie [sic] … all decked in red, white, and blue'.[52]

Homecomings

With hundreds of Aboriginal men serving overseas, Aboriginal communities shared in the nationwide anxiety over the safety of family members. Rose Carter from Point McLeay wrote regularly to the Red Cross Information Bureau in Adelaide requesting news of her son Roland, especially after he was taken prisoner in Germany in 1917. Having heard nothing from him for months, she wrote on 23 October 1918 that she was 'very anxious to hear from him or anything concerning him'. The Red Cross explained that the mail was erratic and she was 'unduly anxious', but on 10 January 1919, reported that Roland had arrived in England as an exchanged prisoner.[53]

The return of soldiers to Australia was thus a source of both relief and celebration. In August 1919 Matthew Kropinyeri wrote that Point McLeay residents enthusiastically anticipated the return of enlisted men: 'the bustle of preparation seems to pervade the mission, and the triumphant emblems of the Allies are to be seen rising and falling languidly to the gentle breeze even at the humblest abodes'. Kropinyeri commended the soldiers' service to 'king and country' and insisted that 'none are more cordially welcomed than these sons of Australia'.[54]

Celebrations like those held at Point McLeay were common in Aboriginal communities around Australia, just as they were in non-Indigenous communities. When Charlie Bird and George Bennett returned in 1919 to the Euraba mission in northern New South Wales, there was a 'splendid gathering' which included 'an old-time tribal feast', traditional music, and a patriotic song performed by Bennett's daughter Grace Waters.[55] Grace's son Len later served as a fighter pilot during the Second World War.[56] Similarly, a fete was held at the Terry Hie Hie reserve, south of Moree, to welcome home Walter Duncan and Jack Stacey who after 'three years away in Egypt and Palestine' had returned 'in health and athletic activity'. The newspaper report of their homecoming featured alongside several others noting welcome parades for non-Indigenous soldiers.[57]

In some Aboriginal communities, notably in Queensland, the excitement surrounding soldiers returning home was diminished by the devastating effects of the Spanish influenza pandemic. In May and June of 1919 almost the entire community at the Barambah Aboriginal Settlement contracted the virus. The Chief Protector, JW Bleakley, reported more than 600 cases and 87 deaths. During the initial outbreak, many people 'took to the bush' to escape the virus and were thus remote from medical assistance. The protector unfairly attributed these deaths to 'sheer superstitious fright', overlooking the fact that Aboriginal people were more vulnerable to influenza due to substandard housing. An outbreak at the Taroom Settlement followed soon afterwards, with 200 cases and 31 deaths, including the settlement's superintendent, who directed medical operations from his bedroom window. Various other regions in Queensland were badly affected. At the end of 1919, the Chief Protector estimated that 298 Aboriginal people had died, and in 1920 the virus spread to camps on remote Cape York, where there were 32 more deaths.[58] Mortality rates were lower in other states, notably Western Australia, where Chief Protector Neville enforced a rigid program of quarantine and vaccination at the Carrolup Aboriginal Reserve. Only four Aboriginal people died in the southern region of the state. This was an unlikely benefit of Neville's authoritarian paternalism, the protector rebuffing criticism by some white Western Australians who saw Aboriginal people as the carriers of the disease.[59]

Repatriation

While many Aboriginal communities avoided the influenza pandemic, most Aboriginal soldiers returned to discriminatory conditions at home. Racist government policies remained, to which was added inequality in the administration of support schemes for returned soldiers or for the families of those killed in action. In 1919 the comptroller of the Commonwealth government's Department of Repatriation, David John Gilbert, responded to uncertainty regarding the eligibility of Aboriginal veterans for repatriation benefits, insisting that 'nothing in the Aborigines Act[s] denies the right to such aboriginals of the full use and enjoyment of any benefits granted to him to [by] the Department'. Clem Lloyd and Jacqueline Rees have noted, however, the 'dearth of evidence' as to how Gilbert's 'reasonably enlightened policy' was applied, observing that there were 'sporadic complaints about discrimination against Aboriginal war veterans throughout the 1920s and 1930s'.[60] Recent research by Andrea Gerrard and Kristyn Harman suggests that Aboriginal veterans in Tasmania were able to access the pensions and support to which they were entitled; but further research, using the recently released repatriation files held by the National Archives of Australia, is required to assess whether fair treatment by the Department of Repatriation was common throughout Australia.[61]

In other contexts, discrimination against returned Aboriginal soldiers and their families is clear. The annual reports of Queensland's protector of Aborigines reveal the extent to which his department attempted to control the income of Aboriginal veterans. As soon as Aboriginal men were accepted into the AIF, the department had moved 'to extend its protection to the dependents [sic] of such men by controlling the military allotments of such as were wards of the Department'.[62] In subsequent reports, Protector Bleakley trumpeted the success of his scheme, which he painted in entirely benevolent terms, describing the 'pleasant surprise' of veterans that 'their military pay had been saved for them' and that their 'womenfolk had been well cared for'.[63] His view was not shared by Esme Fisher, whose husband Frank served in the 11th Light Horse. She had complained about limited access to her husband's military pay: 'I used to draw at the Murgon Post Office, and Mr Bleakley has taken it to Brisbane without my consent.'[64] In October 1917, Frank had clearly directed that a portion of his pay be directed to his wife at Murgon, so the protector's interference was both unwelcome and unnecessary.[65]

The paternalism inherent in Bleakley's policy was made clear in 1919, when he criticised the military authorities who 'for some inexplicable reason' had provided reserve pay directly to discharged Aboriginal soldiers.[66] After the war Bleakley's department managed to take control of War Gratuity Bonds paid to returned soldiers (this was a one-off payment distinct from any pension entitlements). Frank Morris, who had also served in the 11th Light Horse, held an exemption certificate, which should have ensured no interference in the payment of his gratuity. Nonetheless, the local Aboriginal protector was asked a range of questions about Morris's ability to manage money.[67] For Aboriginal veterans still subject to the Aborigines Act, wages and entitlements were paid into trust accounts, the administration of which has been the subject of ongoing controversy. There is evidence to suggest that in some instances quarantined monies were not paid out.[68]

Aboriginal women in Victoria were subject to similar interference, including the families of William Rawlings and Harry Thorpe, both Military Medal winners who were killed in action. In 1918, the Board for Protection of Aborigines requested that the Department of Defence quarantine the military allotments of serving Aboriginal soldiers to prevent alleged misuse by the soldiers' dependants. While Rawlings was serving with distinction on the Western Front, the payment of his allotment to his mother, Bessie, was suspended, prompting the local Guardian of Aborigines to complain that Bessie 'never spends one shilling foolishly'. Bessie herself wrote that 'what little rations I get from the Board is not the worth of my dear only son's life of which he has gone to give up for king & freedom'. The board subsequently recommended Bessie's payments be restored, but the requirement that she justify the use of her son's military pay was surely unique to Aboriginal people.[69] After the war, Harry Thorpe's widow, Julia, experienced similarly unwelcome interference when the military pension due to her son was suspended, while her suitability as guardian of the child was determined. The manager of the Lake Tyers reserve, where Julia resided – without rations or other assistance – wrote to the protection board protesting this 'serious wrong', describing Julia as 'a woman of very good character' and 'the best and most suitable guardian for her fatherless child'.[70]

Soldier settlement

Arguably the most sensitive issue for returned Indigenous soldiers was the administration of soldier settlement schemes, which promoted closer settlement by leasing small allotments of subdivided rural land to returned soldiers. These schemes were notable for the high failure rates of soldiers who were undercapitalised, or settled on land that was of marginal quality or insufficient acreage to be viable.[71] However, for Aboriginal people soldier settlement was controversial for other reasons, including the low rate of successful applications by Aboriginal veterans, and the extensive use of Aboriginal reserve land for the scheme.

Andrea Gerrard has shown that nine Tasmanian Aboriginal veterans successfully applied for soldier settlement blocks.[72] For these veterans there might have been benefits in not being recognised as 'Aboriginal'. But Tasmania is the exception to the general rule that Aboriginal soldiers rarely benefited from these schemes. On the mainland, two Aboriginal soldier settlers have been prominent in the literature: George Kennedy was granted a 17 000-acre (7000-hectare) block near Ivanhoe, New South Wales, which he lost after five years due to drought and under-capitalisation; in Victoria, Percy Pepper successfully applied for a block at Koo Wee Rup in 1918, but struggled to make it viable before losing his farm in 1924.[73] Paradoxically, these men are the success stories, because for most Aboriginal veterans the scheme was simply out of reach.

In a recent study, Bruce Scates and Melanie Oppenheimer concluded that Aboriginal veterans were technically eligible for soldier settlement, but found 'every impediment placed in their way'.[74] Their survey of more than 7000 loan applications to the soldier settlement scheme in New South Wales identified only four Aboriginal veterans, including George Kennedy. The three other men all faced overt discrimination against their claims. Although Albert

Beulah was granted a soldier settlement block near Forbes, his application for a loan to develop the land was rejected by an inspector: 'This case is unsatisfactory … the holder is a black man … altogether the wrong sort of man.' Beulah's own detailed account of his requirements in his application bely the racist conclusion of the inspector, but with no financial support he had little choice but to abandon his farm. Thomas Abdullah's application for a dairy property at Casino and a £300 advance was supported by a local land board, but rejected by the inspector for the district, who described Abdullah as 'a half caste, lazy, irresponsible and untrustworthy'. A bureaucrat in Sydney subsequently censured the local board for supporting Abdullah's application. George Kapeen did not receive a soldier settlement block, but was permitted to farm a small plot on the Cabbage Tree Island Aboriginal reserve, at the manager's discretion and on condition of good conduct. When he applied for a modest loan through the soldier settlement scheme, the protection board was unsupportive and the Lands Department rejected his application.[75]

The result of these prejudices was that very few Aboriginal veterans became soldier settlers. In addition to Kennedy, Pepper and Beulah, Philippa Scarlett has identified two other Aboriginal soldier settlers after the First World War: Clifford Wilson, from Point McLeay in South Australia, and Archie Murphy, a former tracker with the New South Wales police.[76] To these can be added Frederick Smith, an Aboriginal veteran who was granted a lease through Western Australia's closer settlement scheme; he succeeded in his application despite the extreme views of AO Neville that it was 'useless granting farms to Aborigines as they made few improvements and simply wanted land in order that they may feel they possess it'.[77]

Discrimination against Aboriginal veterans in soldier settlement schemes is only half the story. In some states soldier settlement is notorious as a major cause of a 'second dispossession' of Aboriginal reserve land. In New South Wales, the *Closer Settlement Act* of 1905 created pressure to annex Aboriginal reserve land for white settlers. While this was resisted for many years, the emotive appeal of soldier settlement eventually proved irresistible. In 1926, for example, 1410 acres (570 hectares) of the Warangesda Aboriginal Reserve was allocated to soldier settlement, after which many residents moved to an un-official camp on the Murrumbidgee River, near Narrandera.[78] There were similar effects in Victoria, where the soldier settlement scheme encouraged the Board for Protection of Aborigines to pursue its broader policy of closing reserves. In 1921, for example, it advised the Victorian government to sell the Lake Condah Mission (near Heywood) to the closer settlement board.[79]

In 1925 the Aboriginal activist John Egan reminded authorities that 'these Mission Stations have all given their loved ones to serve in the Great War. The writer has lost a brother (killed in action) over there; a family near Heywood gave five sons.'[80] Although four of the Lovett brothers from Heywood enlisted again in the Second World War, none of them benefited from the soldier settlement scheme when the Lake Condah Mission was eventually broken up after the Second World War (see chapter 9). The injustices of soldier settlement thus became a key motivation for Aboriginal activism.

It is clear then that while certain Aboriginal experiences in wartime, such as increased employment opportunities and involvement in fundraising, were broadly similar to those of other Australians, the discriminatory policies under which Aboriginal people lived, and to which Aboriginal servicemen returned, were unique. The creation of new Aboriginal institutions and the introduction of more coercive laws that coincided with the First World War profoundly affected the lives of Aboriginal people at a time when around 1000 Aboriginal soldiers were serving their country. Moreover, after the war, neither Aboriginal military service nor loyalty at home resulted in significant advances in Aboriginal rights. In 1928 an Aboriginal veteran from South Australia, John Eustace Bews, explained the impact of this injustice on Aboriginal people: 'we feel humiliated to know that we are still looked upon as a servile cringing race'.[81] These factors motivated Aboriginal activists who had lived through the war, and who rose to prominence in the interwar years. The experience and legacy of the war for Aboriginal people was thus both complex and enduring.

Note: Parts of this chapter were previously published in Samuel Furphy, 'Aboriginal Australians and the Home Front,' in *Australians and the First World War: Local-Global Connections and Contexts*, Kate Ariotti and James Bennett (eds), Palgrave, 2017, pp. 143–64.

6

The rise of the modern Aboriginal political movement, 1924–39

John Maynard

'There was no colour bar in the trenches.'
– *Douglas Grant*

One of the most important outcomes of the First World War for Aboriginal Australians was the rise of a united, well-organised Aboriginal political movement. During the 1920s and 1930s a number of Aboriginal political organisations were formed, with varying degrees of success and longevity, in New South Wales, Victoria, South Australia, Western Australia and the Northern Territory. This political activism was galvanised by the increasing control of Australian state governments over Aboriginal lives, particularly evident in the separation of Aboriginal children from their families, the revoking of independent Aboriginal farming land, and the confiscation of Aboriginal belongings and property. Significantly, many individuals connected to the Aboriginal political revolt were returned soldiers who became disillusioned as they realised that their sacrifices and service overseas had failed to deliver recognition equal to that of white soldiers. They witnessed the increased hardship of and pressure on their families and communities; and many of these battle-hardened and worldly-wise men were now in the city, a recognised fertile ground for radicalisation.

The war years

The fight for recognition and justice began in the war years, as Jessica Horton's study of Gunditjmara men, James Arden and Richard King of the Lake Condah Reserve in Victoria, reveals.[1] Although both men enlisted for the AIF, they did not see fighting overseas. King died only two months after enlisting, 'in the Ballarat training camp of "influenza with heart failure". James Arden, too, fell ill and suffered in a military camp for seven months with meningitis before returning to Lake Condah.'[2] After being discharged from military service, Arden quickly became disillusioned by the attempts of the mission manager, William Galbraith, to withhold his military pension. The manager cast him as a 'trouble maker' and a 'bad example' for the other reserve residents. Arden was not a man to step away from a fight and would prove a 'fierce defender of his rights'. Arden wrote to the Victorian Board for the Protection of Aborigines, defiantly answering Galbraith's efforts to divert his military pension to the board:

> I beg to say that I cannot see my way clear to hand my money over to the Board, I think I deserve the money I am getting no one knows the pains and sufferings I underwent [with] the Meningitis.[3]

Arden eventually took steps to leave Lake Condah and dispel any perception that he relied on board support. He and his family rented a house nearby in Dunmore West.[4] He retained his pension and defiant stance, labelling both Galbraith and his wife as not fit to manage an Aboriginal reserve as 'they are to [sic] fond of drink'.[5]

As chapter 5 showed, the government in Victoria at this time was intent on breaking up the more independent Aboriginal reserves and forcing their residents to transfer to Lake Tyers under a 'concentration scheme'.[6] However, Charles Lovett, six of whose sons had enlisted, spoke 'on behalf of the half-caste soldiers in the District. He urged that the reserve be kept for half-caste returned soldiers.'[7] As Horton has argued, 'Aboriginal grassroots political activism … fuelled the political agitation of the 1920s and 1930s.'[8]

A gathering storm of global discontent

The Aboriginal soldiers' story did not appear in a vacuum. Dissent in Australia mirrored a global surge of anti-colonialism and a cry for self-determination. The foundations of British colonial power had been seriously shaken by the First World War, with uprisings in India, Egypt and Ireland. Russia had meanwhile experienced a radical revolution in which the Communist Bolsheviks, who came to power in November 1917, promised workers an inclusive future of equality across classes. In the United States meanwhile, a young Jamaican radical, Marcus Garvey (1887–1940) rose to prominence after the war, inspiring black people with a message of race pride, economic salvation and 'black nationalism'. Garvey was blessed with persuasive and inspirational oratorical skills and his impact at this volatile moment in world affairs would be far reaching.

At Garvey's meetings in Harlem, New York, the voice of international black dissent was raised:

> You are asked to go and fight the Germans who had done you no wrong. You were told to give the Germans hell, while they were giving you hell over here, and while you were giving the Germans hell, they were giving your mothers, sisters and sons hell in Mississippi, Georgia and Alabama.[9]

In an interview in the United States Garvey was cutting in his assessment:

> During the World War nations were vying with each other in proclaiming lofty concepts of humanity ... Now that the war is over we find those same nations making every effort by word and deed to convince us that their blatant professions were just meaningless platitudes never intended to apply to earth's darker millions.[10]

Garvey's message gained alarmist newspaper coverage in Australia. The Melbourne *Argus*, for example, highlighted his view of the unjust treatment of returned black soldiers: '[T]he voteless Negroe was conscripted with the rest in 1917 and went to fight into a war of which he knew little [and] for a country which denied him his full rights of citizenship.'[11] For any returned Aboriginal soldiers who read this coverage Garvey's message would have touched a raw wound. Their efforts too had gone unrecognised, and, upon returning to Australia, they had to fight to protect their land, children and families from government assault. Aboriginal veterans could not vote in Commonwealth elections (though they could vote in some state elections) and were not recognised as citizens by a country they had gone overseas to protect.

Their situation had many parallels with that of returned Indigenous soldiers in other colonised countries. In the United States the Hualapai (Arizona) veteran of the Great War, Fred Mahone, recognised the dire situation facing Native American people and described them as being 'ruled like slaves'.[12] He 'returned to the reservation alone after the war, mobilised the Hualapai, and used his education to secure Indian rights'.[13] In the United States, as in Canada, much of the agitation was over land and the failure of governments to treat their returned Indigenous soldiers on an equal footing with white soldiers. The First Nations veteran, Francis Pegahmagabow, had served on the Western Front for a long period and was a three-time Military Medal winner. However, on his repatriation when he sought to apply for a farming loan under the newly adopted Canadian *Soldier Settlement Act*, he was repeatedly rebuffed. In another Canadian incident, First Nations land owners were forcibly removed from their land, which was handed over to returning white soldiers. One First Nations man took matters into his own hands when told his land had been reserved for ex-servicemen, as the press reported:

> Canadian court officials who attempted to evict the squatter barely escaped with their lives. The Indians exhibit an ancient deed, which purports to give them complete rights over the reservation.[14]

The Iroquois were so incensed they sent a delegation of chiefs to England to see the king. But the Secretary of State for the Colonies, Winston Churchill, intervened and informed the chiefs this was a matter 'wholly for the Canadian government to settle'.[15] Having travelled a great distance in hope of support, the First Nations delegation were dismissed without even getting close to their so-called 'Sovereign Protector'.

These grievances of Indigenous soldiers in Canada and the United States mirrored those of Aboriginal veterans in Australia. For example, Mick Flick had enlisted as a 23-year-old in 1916 and served as a machine gunner on the Western Front. On his return home he found that 'he was not such a respected soldier as the white man'.[16] He was 'effectively blocked by local lands boards from gaining land through the "Soldier Settlement" scheme'.[17] Adding to his anger, his six children and 21 other Aboriginal children were refused entry to the local school in Collarenebri, NSW. The sad irony of this educational lockout was that the protection board then threatened to remove Flick's children because they were not being educated. Mick Flick would carry a burning resentment over his family's treatment and his unrecognised contribution to the war effort.[18]

New South Wales State Archive records reveal that some Aboriginal soldiers who fought overseas returned to find that their children had been removed from their wives' care.[19] As Heather Goodall has said in relation to New South Wales: 'Systematically and ruthlessly 1427 children were removed from their families between 1912 and 1938' and that 'half of the apparently secure land of the reserves [was] gone, with Aboriginal farmers evicted by force and in mid-crop'.[20]

As Aboriginal people saw it, the authorities were not protecting them, but persecuting them. It was a national 'horror story' and in September 1921, William Harris of Western Australia vented his frustration in the press:

> The Aborigines have always had a rough time owing to the absurd regulations that are forced on them by the Aborigines Protection Society ... I do not know how they are treated in the other states of the Commonwealth, but I do know that in Western Australia the [A]borigines never had a fair deal. I am prepared to prove this at any time.[21]

Weeks later his brother James Harris added weight to the response, declaring:

> Some of our number took part in the great war [sic] and made the supreme sacrifice, while others have returned to find that they are no nearer getting a fair deal. We haven't got a vote in the country, nor a voice in the framing of the laws that govern us.[22]

Five years later William Harris would establish the Native Union, a short-lived, but very important, Aboriginal political organisation in Western Australia. In 1928 he would lead a deputation of this Union to meet with the state Premier Philip Collier. In this meeting Harris stated that Aboriginal people wanted to 'live up to the white man's standard, but in order to be able to do this we should be exempted from the Aborigines Act, and allowed to live our lives in our own way'.[23]

The growing attacks on Aboriginal independence were another factor inspiring Aboriginal political revolt. As Peggy Brock has put it, Aboriginal people were opposed to living 'parasitically off the Australian public'. Rather, they were a 'people who [were] forever on the move in search of work'.[24] Despite the impact of harsher government policies, the enterprise and initiative of Aboriginal people and communities continued into the 1920s. At a meeting of the Australian Aboriginal Progressive Association in 1927 with over 200 Aboriginal people in attendance, only 'half a dozen' of them were receiving government help: 'The others were working; timber-getting, scrub clearing, and other rural employments. In most cases earning the basic wage.' White missionary and Aboriginal rights supporter Elizabeth McKenzie Hatton also repudiated in the press claims that Aboriginal people would not work: 'she had been in close touch with the people, and those she knew all worked, the women as well as the men'.[25]

'No Man's Land': The Aboriginal fight for land

The inspiration and influence of Garveyism on Aboriginal activists of the time was significant.[26] Aboriginal activists, including Fred Maynard and Tom Lacey, joined Garvey's United Negro Improvement Association (UNIA) and a branch was established in Sydney in 1920. This operated until 1924 when the Aboriginal members of the organisation broke away to form the Australian Aboriginal Progressive Association (AAPA). This was the country's first politically organised, united Aboriginal activist group, having, at its height, 13 branches, four sub-branches and more than 600 members in New South Wales. Many members of this early Aboriginal political movement, including prominent office bearers Dick Johnson, Ben Rountree and Edward Walker, were returned soldiers.

The AAPA promoted the concept of a pan-Aboriginal identity and a national agenda for improving Aboriginal social and economic conditions, including the call for enough land for every Aboriginal family in the country. On 31 March 1928, Ben Rountree, secretary of the AAPA, wrote to the Commonwealth Government Royal Commission on the Constitution:

> We heartily endorse the views of the commission now sitting at Canberra and pledge ourselves to stand solid behind the commission for the emancipation of the whole of our conditions and people throughout Australia … our unswerving loyalty is with you in the fight for the federalizing of the whole of Aboriginal affairs and the abolition of state control.[27]

While Maynard referenced the 'loyalty, fidelity, and bravery' of Aboriginal servicemen in the Great War he was also a member of the Waterside Workers Union, who had vociferously opposed and helped defeat the 1916 and 1917 referenda for conscription for overseas service.[28] Of greater significance to Maynard was the fact that a catastrophic war had taken place on the Australian continent:

> That the European people by the arts of war destroyed our more ancient civilization is freely admitted and that by their vices and diseases our people have been decimated is also

> patent, but neither of these facts are evidence of superiority. Quite the contrary is the case ... The members of [the AAPA] have also noted the strenuous efforts of the Trade Union leaders to attain the conditions which existed in our country at the time of invasion by Europeans – the men only worked when necessary – we called no man 'Master' and we had no king.[29]

Maynard also bluntly expressed Aboriginal land claims to the New South Wales Premier Jack Lang: 'the Australian [Aboriginal] people are the original owners of the land and have a prior right over all other people in this respect'.[30]

As chapter 5 has shown, the grab of Aboriginal land had accelerated dramatically during and after the First World War with the introduction of the soldier settlement scheme.[31] Not only were former reserve lands handed over to white soldiers with no recompense for decades of labour by Aboriginal people; but when some Aboriginal soldiers applied to the resettlement scheme they were informed it did not apply to them.[32] At Karuah in New South Wales, a racist complaint printed in the local press in 1923 reveals the ingrained sentiment of many in the wider white community:

> The residence of Aborigines on allotments is detrimental to white settlement ... It is not much encouragement for returned men who want allotments near Karuah to have to live alongside blacks, and to be classed socially the same as them.[33]

Yet there was some non-Indigenous support of the Aboriginal community at Karuah and their contribution to the Great War. TE Colebrook, President of the Australian Aborigines Mission, declared:

> Dark men, many of them went to the front, as well as white men, some lost their lives in defence of the King and country, and some returned bearing the brand of brave soldiers of the King.[34]

The mounting pressure applied to Karuah was replicated in many other areas where Aboriginal people held land. In 1917 in Victoria, Aboriginal man John Egan was driven to write to the press to expose the dire and unjust circumstances under which Aboriginal land was being broken up by the protection board and the residents deported. The land at Lake Condah was then to be handed over to returning white soldiers:

> Apparently, these gentlemen have come to the conclusion that, being blacks, our likes and dislikes are a matter of total indifference to them, that being blacks, we have not the same feelings of sentiment as regards our homes as the white man, therefore we must be treated as savages.[35]

Egan called upon returning veterans to recognise the Aboriginal plight and that Aboriginal men had served alongside of them on the battlefield:

> I am sure the returned heroes, the men who made their country's name ring with the mighty deeds in France and Gallipoli, would not thank those in authority for their future homes if they were aware of the fact that in providing these homes the poor blacks had to be first forcibly ejected … I would like to draw your attention to the fact that each of these Mission Stations has given men to swell the ranks … No less than 24 men enlisted from Lake Condah Mission Station … Two of them have just paid to the Kaiser's account with their lives. From all parts coloured lads have answered the great call. On the face of this alone it

> seems hard that while these lads are doing their best to uphold the traditions of the Empire, their relatives and friends cannot be shown a little fairness. If this is not a sample of the Prussian touch, then I would like to know what is.[36]

The battle for Lake Condah Mission would be a long drawn-out fight.[37] Four years later a protection board member delivered a predictable, callous comment in the press:

> The time of sentimentality in matters leading to the development of the State has passed, and it is considered that better use can be made of the land, which is practically lying idle, by throwing it open to returned soldiers.[38]

At Cummeragunja the 'Aboriginal occupants fought for their land and lifestyle. When they were issued with expulsion orders after long drawn out court battles they resisted and refused to be moved':

> At times there was literally hand to hand fighting over land, farms and children, with Board managers and, less frequently, Aborigines themselves firing guns. The resistance was so strong at Cumeragunja [sic] that police were stationed there for three months early in 1922, after a decade of persistent and severe disturbances. By that time, many of the station's residents had been dispersed.[39]

It appears that Aboriginal economic success, independence and well-being was to be sacrificed. Vocal and staunch advocate of Aboriginal people, Elizabeth McKenzie Hatton, revealed 'the land is being sold and they are finding themselves on the roadsides, or any corner of "no man's land [sic]," where they, in their hapless lot find themselves, homeless, disheartened, and resentful of the injustice which is being meted out to them'.[40] One Anne F Bon, in a letter to the editor of the Melbourne *Argus*, wrote:

> It grieves me to see the blacks driven from the homes they loved so dearly, but as that seems inevitable, let us see that justice is done to the returned soldiers, some of whom were halfcastes … Surely our returned soldiers merit every consideration at our hands seeing that they so bravely defended the Empire in her hour of need.[41]

In South Australia a number of Aboriginal writers wrote to the press to voice their discontent at increased control, surveillance and pressure on Aboriginal land. Albert Bews, a veteran of the Western Front, was caustic in his appraisal of government actions that classed Aboriginal people as 'little children':

> The deceptive policy miscalled 'Protection' does not protect, and its continued practice spells destruction … There have been [A]borigines who have nobly responded to our Empires 'call to arms' overseas. Many have paid the supreme sacrifice … I respectfully ask should not this Act be abolished at the next sitting of Parliament thereby allowing us to be independent citizens?[42]

Another South Australian Aboriginal man, George Rankine, was 'convinced that the natives in the southern parts of the state, on mission stations and so on, are fully aware of the facts, and that Aboriginal Protectors, Superintendents and other officials connected with the mission stations are no longer wanted'.[43]

The agitation in South Australia was responsible for the establishment in 1928 of the Australian Aboriginal Association (AAA). Its rallying message was 'all Aboriginals should join this association and have a voice'.[44] A branch was established at Point Pearce and the organisation had an active membership across the state of over a hundred members.[45] In late June its membership was part of a delegation that met with Senator Alexander McLachlan, an honorary minister in the Commonwealth government of Stanley Bruce, requesting that '64,000 acres [26 000 hectares] on Eyre's Peninsula' be reserved for Aboriginal people. This reserve was to be 'placed in charge of educated Aboriginal people where they should be given a chance on land of their own, free from the interference of white people, to work out their own destiny on their own lines'.[46] The Aboriginal plea was ignored.

Standing by comrades from the trenches

Some returned white soldiers who had fought alongside Aboriginal men in the trenches of Gallipoli and the Western Front were appalled by the wider society's treatment of Aboriginal people. James Bennett of the 15th AIF Battalion, could not contain his outrage when reading in the press that a conference of the Returned Sailor's and Soldier's Imperial League of Australia (RSSILA) in Cairns had raised the possibility of requesting the government to remove Aboriginal children from a local school. Bennett was quoted in *The Cairns Post* as saying: 'I consider as a returned soldier and a white man that they have as much right to be in that school as the white children. The Schools are there for all Australian children, whether black, white or brindle.' During the war Aboriginal servicemen 'did their duty, wounded four or five times in action':

> I have stood shoulder to shoulder with half-castes in Hell's Pit, on Quinn's Post, and seen them die like the grandest of white men … So please be fair and have a little bit of human feeling. Hoping there will be no more stunts of that kind with the R.S.S.I.L.A.[47]

Another white veteran in Queensland was equally angered in 1920 by a government-initiated removal of Aboriginal families from their land:

> Yes, we heard of the Germans deporting Belgians to Germany, but here we have a more brutal thing taking place … to send him away by force, say, 100 miles to a mission would be like deporting us to China. A black-fellow dearly loves the place where he was born.[48]

Aboriginal ex-servicemen themselves certainly believed they had earned the rights and privileges that were available to all other members of society. This included the simple right to enter hotels and drink alcohol. A letter to the Adelaide *Register* from Point Pearce argued in July 1915 that while Aboriginal men:

> [W]ore the King's uniform, on active service abroad, they were quite eligible to have as much liquor as they cared to consume. The law here gives the police officers almost unlimited power, over the poor, unfortunate "aboriginal". The time has arrived when they no longer need the protection of the State but would do far better if they were on the same level as their fellow comrades.[49]

The tragedy of Douglas Grant

One Aboriginal ex-serviceman whose story reveals the difficult adjustments required after the war was Douglas Grant. His life was the stuff a Hollywood film director could only dream of. As a young 'full-blood' baby he was 'saved' by the chief taxidermist of the Australian Museum in Sydney, Robert Grant, after Douglas's family was 'killed by a punitive expedition of white settlers and native police, apparently launched from the colonial outpost of Cairns'.[50]

Grant and his wife legally adopted the boy and raised him on equal footing with their other children. Living in Annandale, Douglas received a good education and later qualified as a draftsman and woolclasser. During the First World War, he followed several of his workmates and volunteered for the army in 1915. After enlistment, he sat the 'Sergeants examination successfully, his previous training with the Cadet movement being of a great advantage'. It was noted that he was 'a wonderfully accurate rifle shot, and at the Rutherford Military encampment just before leaving Australia, hit the "running man" 30 times with consecutive shots at 1,000 yards'.[51] When he was about to leave Australia for overseas active service Grant was discharged because of regulations preventing Aborigines leaving the country without government approval. Yet, manifesting the same ingenuity of many other Aboriginal men, he managed to quietly re-enlist and finally embarked for France in August 1916 to join the 13th Battalion.[52] He was wounded in the first battle of Bullecourt in April 1917, and then captured by the Germans. He would spend the rest of the war as a prisoner of war and became an exotic curiosity for German doctors, scientists and anthropologists. The Germans recognised Grant as a well-educated leader with great organisational and administrative abilities. He was also nominated by other prisoners to act and speak on their behalf, becoming president of the British Help Committee and organising the distribution of Red Cross food parcels, comforts and medical supplies for many Indigenous prisoners.[53] One of the German scientists described him 'as an unmistakable figure' and noted that the other prisoners afforded him great respect for 'his honesty, his quick mind, and because he was aggressively Australian'.[54]

On his return to Australia, Grant returned to his position as a draftsman with Mort's Dock & Engineering Company in Sydney. However, despite his 'enjoying a degree of celebrity as a war hero', Grant was unsettled by his wartime experiences and headed to

Lithgow.[55] Here he took a position in a small arms factory and became active within the local community. According to a report in *The Sun* newspaper in Sydney, he was 'immensely popular'.[56] He became the secretary of the Lithgow Returned Soldiers League and conducted a weekly 'Diggers Session' on the commercial radio station.[57] It was while in Lithgow that Grant began to speak out on issues facing Aboriginal people, including the notorious 1928 Coniston Massacre in the Northern Territory. In February 1929 he was quoted in the press as saying:

> The shooting of 31 [A]borigines in Central Australia is damning in the extreme. It shows the utter lack of the law and order and protection that is theirs by law of the same government whose officers shot these unfortunate natives.[58]

He later declared that when his people 'called for justice, they are answered with the lash and the gun'.[59] Grant was again in the news when later in June 1929 he was incensed over the actions of a Condobolin football team drawing the 'colour-line' and refusing to play against an Aboriginal team in the local cup. Grant declared that the 'colour line was never drawn in the trenches'.[60]

Grant returned to Sydney in the early 1930s, where he descended into alcoholism. By the early 1930s the loss of his step-family left a hole in his life too difficult to fill. Despite having been, at one time, a friend of the likes of poet Perce Cowan and writer Henry Lawson, Grant found that acceptance in the wider community was now a thing of the past. At one point, he was a clerk at the Callan Park Mental Hospital, lived on site and designed a replica of Sydney Harbour Bridge as a memorial. Grant also put forward an official application to be considered as the architect of new cottages to be built for the Aboriginal community at La Perouse, contending that 'because he was an [A]borigine he knows and understands the needs of his people'.[61] He later lived at the Salvation Army Old Men's Quarters in Sydney and, after 1949, at La Perouse. His last decade was a lonely one until his death in 1951. It was a sad descent for such an outstanding man and soldier.

Activism in the 1930s

As Grant's story reveals, the activism inspired by the war continued well into the 1920s and beyond. The AAPA succeeded for a short time in slowing the removal of Aboriginal children from their families and the revoking of Aboriginal land. However, the AAPA disappeared from public view in 1928, and startling, recently uncovered material reveals that the New South Wales police played a major role in its break-up. A 1927 newspaper interview with my grandfather Fred Maynard indicates the level of intimidation he was subjected to. Maynard stated that:

> [H]e had been warned on many occasions that the doors of Long Bay [Gaol] were opening for him. He would cheerfully go to gaol for the remainder of his life, he declared, if, by so doing, he could make the people of Australia realise the truly frightful administration of the Aborigines Act.[62]

Evidence suggests that the AAPA was effectively broken up through the combined efforts of the New South Wales Protection Board, the missionaries and the police.[63] Aboriginal leader and activist, Bill Ferguson, would later recall that the AAPA was 'hounded out of existence by the police acting for the Board'.[64]

The AAPA left a lasting legacy as Aboriginal people were encouraged to step forward and voice demands on behalf of their people. The La Perouse Aboriginal community of Sydney refused to be moved off their land in 1928, stating forcefully:

> We, the undersigned [A]borigines of the La Perouse reserve, emphatically protest against our removal to any place. This is our heritage bestowed upon us: in these circumstances, we feel justified in refusing to leave.[65]

Tom Williams was another First World War veteran who sought freedom away from the control of the government, preferring to live his life at the Salt Pan Creek camp on the Georges River in Sydney. This camp was a hive of Aboriginal political activism. Here Williams 'socialised with his war mates and was an active member of the local RSL, becoming widely known among white returnees'.[66] He stated defiantly to his family 'that he would rather take them to live in a bag hut than go on to a mission with a manager standing over them!'[67]

The demise of the AAPA was not the end of organised Aboriginal protest. New organisations would form: the Victorian Australian Aborigines League in 1934; the Northern Territory Australian Half-Caste Progressive Association in the mid-1930s; and the New South Wales Aborigines Progressive Association (APA) in 1937. A rejuvenated movement in south-eastern Australia was led by a new wave of leaders that included William Cooper, Bill Ferguson, Jack Patten and Pearl Gibbs. In the most notable of their achievements these activists conducted the 'Day of Mourning' protest in Sydney on 26 January 1938, coinciding with the 150th anniversary of British colonisation. Jack Patten in his address as president of the APA targeted the hypocrisy of the national celebration:

> On this day the white people are rejoicing, but we, as Aborigines, have no reason to rejoice on Australia's 150th birthday. Our purpose in meeting today is to bring home to the white people of Australia the frightful conditions in which the native Aborigines of this continent live. This land belonged to our forefathers

> 150 years ago, but today we are pushed further into the background.[68]

In late 1938 Aboriginal activists, led by Cooper, also marched on the German embassy in Melbourne to protest against the ill-treatment of the Jewish people in Nazi Germany. They were one of the first groups in Australian to publicly speak out on this issue. In the press the Aboriginal activists noted the similarities with their own experience, stating 'the Jews like our people have suffered cruelty and exploitation as a national minority … We are a poor people, and few in number but in extending our sympathy to the Jewish race we also pledge ourselves to help them by all means in our power'.[69] The embassy, predictably, refused to meet the deputation.

The 1930s generation of leadership continued to draw attention to Aboriginal military service and the lack of any significant progress in the years since. In a letter to the editor of the Melbourne *Age* in 1933, Cooper argued: 'During the war many [A]borigines were among the first to offer for enlistment in the A.I.F. to protect the British Empire. Surely, then, it is our duty to protect the remainder of their race from inhuman treatment.'[70] Cooper was deeply affected by the loss of his son Dan during the First World War. When writing to the Minister for the Interior John McEwan in 1939, Cooper reminded him that despite Aboriginal sacrifices made during the war, the callous treatment of Aboriginal people continued:

> I am father of a soldier who gave his life for his King on the battlefield and thousands of coloured men enlisted in the A.I.F. They will doubtless do so again though on their return last time, that is those that survived, were pushed back to the bush to resume the status of [A]boriginals … We submit that to put us in the trenches, until we have something to fight for, is not right.[71]

It must have distressed Cooper to have lost his son defending a country that continued to persecute Aboriginal people. In a letter to Reverend William Morley, the Secretary of the Association for the Protection of Native Races, Cooper highlighted the injustice of Aboriginal military service:

> One of the greatest qualities ever shown in history was when at least one thousand Aborigines enlisted to take part in the World's War from 1914 to 1918 for the Protection of the British Empire for which they gave the supreme sacrifice and unfortunately received no better consideration for their valuable service at the war.[72]

With another war appearing on the horizon, Cooper continued to beat the drum of discontent over the neglect of Aboriginal conditions and reward for their service to their country. Writing to Prime Minister Joseph Lyons in 1938, Cooper could not be clearer in stating that the fault lay with state control: '[A]t least a thousand Aborigines were among the first to enlist in the defence of the British Empire in the 1914–1918 war and for which Empire they gave their lives. It was a thankless task for them.'[73]

Despite sharing an agenda of opposition to discrimination, there were disagreements about tactics among the Aboriginal leadership. Only a year after the famous 'Day of Mourning' protest in Sydney, Cooper took objection to Patten's on-air recommendations for the formation of Aboriginal regiments in the Army. Cooper was adamant that the past experiences after the First World War showed that participation in the armed services in the hope of changes in political and social status was futile: 'the [A]boriginal now has no status, no rights, no land … he has no country and nothing to fight for but the privilege of defending the land which was taken from him'.[74] Cooper also took issue with Patten's labelling missions and missionaries as 'our greatest enemies'.[75] Such divisions among Aboriginal leaders of the late 1930s were a stark reality during this very turbulent period globally. Patten, Ferguson and Cooper were at odds over the political directions and alliances needed to take Aboriginal demands forward: Patten leaning more to the right and having connections with radical nationalists, PR Stephensen and WB Miles; while Ferguson and Cooper were aligned with the trade union movement and Communist party.[76] Nevertheless, as Bain Attwood details, despite their differences Ferguson, Gibbs, Patten, Cooper and their supporters 'were united in their concern about the loss of civil rights, the growth in the Aborigines Protection Board's powers and the terrible conditions on its stations'.[77]

The Aboriginal political movement of the interwar period would be forced into hibernation through these divisions among the leadership. With the start of the Second World War too came the need to assist in the war effort, restricted mobility and the problems of providing for families. The interest of the media also waned with all attention focused on the war. It would not be until the vibrant 1960s that organised Aboriginal political protest would be revived (see chapter 13).

We are left today to recognise and remember the early Aboriginal freedom fighters who were prepared to step forward to challenge the tight government and police control over Aboriginal lives. It is amazing that this history lay forgotten for such a long period, erased from Australian history and memory. This chapter has examined the impact that military service in the First World War had on the rise of the modern Aboriginal political movement. This was only one of the catalysts for political action by Aboriginal soldiers, which arose through an accumulation of grievances that included the lack of recognition equal to that of white soldiers, Aboriginal land loss and the ongoing assaults against Aboriginal families. In the inter-war period Australian Aboriginal leaders were also influenced by international developments and the similarities of experience for Indigenous soldiers globally. Douglas Grant's sad tale reveals the flawed frailties of the assimilation project. No matter what qualifications an Aboriginal person attained, or the sacrifices they made in military service, acceptance in wider white Australia would prove the most difficult hurdle to achieve. Aboriginal people were not treated equally, fairly or with any respect and were widely described as a 'dying race'. The influential Daisy Bates, reflecting the mindset of the time, stated in the press without any compassion that the 'only good half-caste is a dead one'.[78] There was no thanks, reward or recognition for the Aboriginal soldiers who died in battle. The final word on the aftermath of Aboriginal military service in the First World War is perhaps best captured by Aboriginal veteran Tom Blackman in 1934: 'We were good men at war but looked down on now the war is over.'[79]

7

Australian Military Forces in the Second World War

Joan Beaumont and Tristan Moss

'[N]either necessary nor desirable.'
– *The Australian Defence Committee*

There were only 21 years – scarcely a generation – between the end of the First World War and the outbreak of war in Europe again in 1939. In these years little had changed in the systemic disadvantage of Indigenous Australians. Despite the service of around 1000 Indigenous men in the war of 1914–18 and the emergence of an Aboriginal activist movement in the interwar years, the discriminatory regimes of the Protection Acts and the denial of full citizenship had been further entrenched. Not surprisingly then, when war broke out again in September 1939, the same barriers to Aboriginal and Torres Strait Islander service in the defence forces which had prevailed in the First World War continued. Even though some Indigenous men managed to volunteer in the first months of the war, in 1940, the Australian authorities formally reaffirmed the First World War policy of restricting recruitment for the Australian Army to 'half-castes'. Nor, it seems, were any Indigenous people admitted to the Royal Australian Navy (RAN). Entry to the Royal Australian Air Force (RAAF) was more relaxed, however. Significant change came only in 1941–42 when Australia faced the threat of invasion by the Japanese. This national security crisis finally forced the military authorities to concede that Aboriginal and Torres Strait Islander people could play a valuable role in the defence of Australia's north. Not only were Indigenous people then used in a variety of non-combatant roles (see chapter 8) but specialist units were mobilised and trained to support defence operations. As a result the number of Indigenous people who served in the armed forces in the Second World War was nearly four times that of the First World War: some 3000–4000 Aboriginal and Torres Strait Islander people.[1] Many of these individuals benefited from the opportunity to gain new skills and experience and, in combat zones at least, they experienced life in a situation less burdened with the racism that was so deeply prevalent within Australian society.

Government enlistment policy 1939–41

The structure of Australia's defence forces during the Second World War was complex. In addition to the RAN and the RAAF, Australia fielded the Australian Military Forces (AMF), which were, in fact, two separate armies. The first of these, the 2nd Australian Imperial Force (AIF), was composed entirely of volunteers, as the 1st AIF had been in 1914–18. The second army was the Citizen Military Forces (CMF), made up of conscripts and members of the prewar militia who chose not to transfer to the AIF. From 1940 to 1945 the 2nd AIF was deployed to theatres of war across the globe, including North Africa, Greece and Crete, Syria, Malaya, Singapore, the Netherlands East Indies and the islands to Australia's north. The CMF meanwhile was used in defence only of Australian territories, although, in early 1943, the Labor government of John Curtin decided to extend the definition of Australian territories to include 'such other territories in the South-West Pacific area' as the governor-general proclaimed to be territories 'associated with the defence of Australia'.[2]

When war broke out in September 1939, there was some confusion as to whether Aboriginal and Torres Strait Islander people could serve in any of these defence forces. The *Defence Act* of 1909 had excluded from compulsory military service in peacetime anyone who was not 'substantially of European origin or descent' (see p. 39). Despite the record of Indigenous service in the First World War, this ruling remained unchanged in the 1920s. When the compulsory military service scheme was suspended in 1929, and enlistment to the militia became voluntary, an Australian Military Regulation and Order (AMR&O) number 177[1] of 1932 confirmed that no person could enlist unless he were substantially of European origin or descent.[3]

Hence there was no official support when in March 1938 the Australian Aborigines League (AAL) proposed to create an 'Aboriginal citizen corps' and enrol Aboriginal boys in cadet forces. When a similar plan was put to Prime Minister Joseph Lyons by the Aborigines Progressive Association (APA) in December 1938, the Minister for Defence, Geoffrey Street, soon stated that no person was to be enlisted to the militia unless he was substantially of European origin.[4] Possibly the government was deterred by Indigenous attempts to link their military service to the removal of entrenched discrimination, as William Cooper, the honorary secretary of the AAL, had already done (see pp. 131–32).

Despite the government's negative attitude, some Indigenous people did manage to join the AMF in the early months of the Second World War. Fifty 'part-Aborigines' were permitted to enlist in the militia of the 7th Military District, Darwin, while a month later the Labor Premier of Queensland, W Forgan Smith, offered Prime Minister Robert Menzies some 20 'half-caste men' from Cape Bedford mission in north Queensland 'to serve their country in any way Government wish them to do'.[5] In all, by December 1939 at least 22 Aboriginal Australians and Torres Strait Islanders had enlisted in the 2nd AIF and some soon left Australia with the 6th Division headed for the Middle East and London.[6] In April 1940, the man who would become one of the highest-profile Aboriginal veterans, Reginald Saunders, also enlisted.

At the same time some Aboriginal men joined the RAAF. The first (though he was not known to be Aboriginal at the time) was Pilot Officer David Paul. Later he would be shot down over the Aegean Sea in 1943, and, while a prisoner of the Germans, be awarded the Distinguished Flying Cross. Sergeant Len Waters would become the RAAF's first Aboriginal fighter pilot and served in the Netherlands East Indies (now Indonesia). In August 1945 Flight Sergeant Arnold Lockyer was shot down over Celebes (now Sulawesi), and was killed by his captors six days after Japan's surrender.[7]

Yet, if these Aboriginal and Torres Strait Islander Australians managed to volunteer, the door to the Army was soon closed. In early 1940 the War Cabinet asked the Defence Committee to report on the question of 'British subjects of non-European origin or descent', foreigners and aliens (that is, residents of enemy extraction) enlisting in the Australian services. This request was triggered by an American's attempt to join the RAAF, but beyond that, the presence of German nationals in the services was assumed to be a security threat.[8]

In response, the Defence Committee concluded on 15 February 1940 that it was 'undesirable in principle' to admit to the Australian defence forces either aliens or British subjects of non-European origin. Although a departure from this principle might be justified 'to provide for the special needs of the Services during the war', so far as the Army and the RAN were concerned, the admission of such persons was 'neither necessary nor desirable'. Only the RAAF was exempt. In view of the heavy commitments already made in late

1939 to provide air crew for the Empire Air Training Scheme, it was agreed that aliens and British subjects of non-European origin or descent should be allowed to enlist in this service at the discretion of the Air Board.[9]

This ruling was made, it seems, without Aboriginal and Torres Strait Islander men specifically in mind, but it soon encompassed them. In April and May 1940 the land war in Europe erupted with stunning German victories in Norway, the Netherlands, Belgium and France. With Britain 'standing alone' against Nazism, many Australians rushed to volunteer for the 2nd AIF: in June to August 1940 over 102 000 Australians enlisted as opposed to only 2344 in January to March 1940.[10] With this surge of interest in military service the military authorities clarified the status of Indigenous Australians. On 6 May 1940 they advised local commands that they should exclude 'British subjects of non-European origin or descent' from enlistment for the Army.[11] Then, in late May 1940, after clarification had been sought as to how to implement this instruction, the various military commands were advised that enlisting 'half-caste' Aboriginal people was 'not advisable'.[12] One instruction even ruled that only Indigenous Australians who were 'at least three-quarter-caste' were to be accepted.[13] It seems that this prohibition included Torres Strait Islanders as well as mainland Aboriginal Australians. This was despite the fact that Islanders were distinct from mainland Indigenous peoples and, although long administered alongside other Aboriginal groups in Queensland, had been recognised a separate people, under the *Torres Strait Islander Act* in 1939.[14]

There is little on the documentary record to suggest what influenced this policy decision. At times it was claimed that white soldiers would not tolerate Indigenous men in their ranks; or that Indigenous soldiers would be unable to cope with the climatic conditions of existing theatres of war.[15] More probably the military authorities, working within the dominant ideology of White Australia and facing no shortage of volunteers for the 2nd AIF, simply assumed that the precedents at the start of the First World War and the peacetime militia would apply in this new wartime situation.

In thinking thus, they seem to have expected that the decision to restrict Indigenous recruitment would be uncontentious. However, when reports began to spread about Indigenous men being rejected when they tried to enlist, various voices were raised in protest. On 13 June 1940 the secretary of the Aborigines Welfare Board, Sydney, complained to Victoria Barracks (where Eastern Command was based), about the rejection of a half-caste Aboriginal man who tried to enlist, Clarrie Combo. Citing the service of Aboriginal men in the First World War, the secretary noted that a considerable number of men 'of aboriginal blood', including Combo's brother, had already enlisted and were serving abroad with the AIF. Moreover, at his Board's stations the honour rolls listed 15 men who had served in the First World War, more than half of whom had died while on active service. Beyond this, the proposed policy of exclusion, the secretary argued, was at odds with the NSW state government's policy, which aimed at merging 'lighter castes into the general community'.[16] Meanwhile from Queensland the Director of Native Affairs wrote that, under that state's *Aboriginals Preservation and Protection Act* of 1939, those Aboriginal Australians not under the control of the Department of Native Affairs were entitled to full citizenship rights, including by implication the right to enlist in the armed forces.[17] On 7 July 1940 APA Burdeu, president of the Australian Aborigines League, also sought clarification from the prime minister as to why Aboriginal Australians were debarred from service in the AIF: the Aboriginal population, he claimed, 'is intensely loyal to the Empire and the volunteering of the native men is for this reason'.[18] Meanwhile the NSW Premier, Alexander Mair, wrote to Menzies on 23 July 1940 complaining about Aboriginal men being accepted by local recruiting officials but then rejected when they arrived in Sydney.[19] Finally, the Aborigines Progressive Association proposed on 8 July 1940 that Aboriginal Australians should form their own division, with only nurses and the officers training them being white.[20] This was impractical: the total Aboriginal population at that time was fewer than 70 000, of whom perhaps only between 30 and 40 per cent would have been men of an age suited to military service (18 to 45).[21] A division would have required at least 15 000 volunteers. In New Zealand, where the Māori population was just under 100 000, it proved possible to maintain only a Māori battalion in which some 3600 men of a total of 15 744 Māori volunteers served.[22]

Some of these arguments in favour of Indigenous service, it must be said, were couched in the language of assimilation and discrimination that informed government policy planning at this time. Burdeu, for example, on 30 June 1940 lobbied Prime Minister Menzies for assurances that 'immediate and full citizenship should be conferred on all aborigines accepted for service in the A.I.F. and that they retain this citizenship on their return to Australia'. But in his letter of 7 July he wrote:

> [Aboriginal soldiers] are capable, with good initiative, and I am informed by those training them that they will make excellent soldiers ... Of course we always discriminate between natives who are primitive or semi-civilised as apart from those who are civilised. For the latter we have always sought full citizenship, which now includes the right to fight for King and Empire.[23]

The superintendent of the Cherbourg Aboriginal Settlement, meanwhile, wrote to his parliamentarian (who forwarded his letter to the Minister for Defence, Geoffrey Street), that the local men who had tried to volunteer 'are of light colour, speak perfect English and are intelligent, with a state education up to usual standards. They are fine specimens of men, all play football or cricket, and no doubt could stand up to the rigors [sic] of training and climate'.[24]

Faced with these negative reactions – and some confusion about how to implement the 6 May directive – the Military Board clarified its position.[25] There would be no change to the regulations which prohibited personnel not substantially of European origin or descent from enlisting. There was no question of enlisting 'full-blooded' Aboriginal men in the future.[26] But it was not necessary to 'exclude half-caste aborigines when they are otherwise entirely suitable'.[27] In order to leave open the option of recruiting 'the better type of half-caste', medical authorities should determine whether or not a person with some Aboriginal blood was, or was not, 'substantially of European origin or descent', by considering the 'general suitability' of the applicant and the state laws at the place of enlistment.[28] As for those Aboriginal men who had already managed to enlist, they could remain in the AIF. This, it should be said, did not prevent some of the men from the missions at Lake Tyers in Victoria and Point McLeay in South Australia who had volunteered in 1940 being discharged in early 1941. This was an episode which fuelled a sense of grievance both at Lake Tyers and within the Aborigines' Uplift Society.[29]

Now confirmed, this policy of limiting eligibility to 'half-castes' would remain the 'essentially racist' framework for enlistment to the AMF for the rest of the war.[30] Occasional exceptions were made, such as the admission of the 'full blood' Robert McGuire whose case for admission to the AIF in 1941 was made by the Commissioner of Native Affairs in Western Australia, FI Bray. He argued successfully that McGuire held a Certificate of Exemption from the Native Administration Act: 'therefore he is not a native in law and … the colour ban does not apply in his case'.[31] But for the majority of Indigenous Australians the door to the Army and the

RAN remained closed. When the acute national security crisis of 1941–42 forced the military authorities to rethink their policies for defending the north, their response was not to open the door to the mainstream defence forces but rather to create discrete, temporary and auxiliary Indigenous units.

Indigenous units

In 1940–41 Australia's strategic environment deteriorated as the Japanese moved into French Indochina, while the United Kingdom, now forced to focus on defending the British Isles and defeating Axis forces in North Africa, failed to meet its promised commitments to the defence of Malaya and Singapore. With the north of Australia increasingly vulnerable, Australian military authorities began, with some reluctance, to see the value of raising specialist units from local Indigenous labour who had a deep knowledge of the local terrain. The first such unit, created in early 1940, was the Papuan Infantry Battalion (PIB). As its title indicates, this was not composed of Indigenous Australians; rather it was formed of Papuans, a people then under Australia's colonial rule. The PIB was intended to free up policemen in Papua, who were increasingly being used for military tasks beyond their remit, such as guarding key installations. When the Japanese then attacked Papua in mid-1942, the PIB saw action in the Kokoda campaign of July to November 1942, and was later joined by five New Guinea Infantry Battalions. These were grouped with the PIB under the aegis of the Pacific Islands Regiment (PIR). This served in all-bar-one of Australia's campaigns in Papua and New Guinea in 1943–45.[32]

At roughly the same time that the PIB was being raised, Australian authorities created units drawing on manpower from the Torres Strait Islands. The use of Islanders as soldiers was first suggested in December 1940, as a means of replacing or augmenting army personnel garrisoning the strategic waterway of the Torres Strait. Initially the AMF leadership was cautious. However, after liaising with the Protector of Aborigines in Queensland, the Deputy Chief of the General Staff concluded in January 1941 that 'Torres Strait Islanders are well suited to be trained for military service.'[33] Why he argued this is unclear. Perhaps it was because Torres Strait Islanders were already integrated into the local economy, working in the pearling industry, being employed as labourers, and in some cases serving as soldiers, with the garrison units then on the islands. Moreover, there was a practical need to replace white troops, particularly as the Torres Strait garrison, while important, was a drain on manpower that could be used elsewhere.

The creation of a Torres Strait Islander unit, initially a single company of infantry, was formally approved in May 1941.[34] Recruiting began in June, and by October 1941, 106 men had volunteered.[35] In March 1942, after the Japanese had conquered most of South-East Asia, further recruits were sought. The AMF enlisted Torres Strait Islanders from mainland Queensland to man shipping along the coasts of New Guinea. These men were deemed particularly useful given their knowledge of local waters. By early 1943 around 270 men were serving in the Water Transport Group.[36]

On the Torres Strait Islands themselves, an employment company of around 110 men was raised for use in constructing fortifications and other military projects. Although these men were intended to undertake non-combatant tasks and were not trained as infantry, they were formally enlisted in the AMF. In contrast, a third unit, a labour company of 160 Islanders, was a civilian labour unit whose men were not inducted into the armed forces.[37] This division between combat troops and labourers caused some dissatisfaction among the Torres Strait Islanders, who frequently requested to be 'proper soldiers'. More importantly for the AMF, this arrangement was inefficient, as the various Torres Strait units had different tasks and headquarters, while more than two-thirds of the men had not received military training.[38]

To remedy this situation Headquarters First Australian Army proposed in January 1943 that the three companies be amalgamated into a battalion. This, it was thought, would improve esprit de corps, enable central control and administration, and 'augment the infantry fighting strength' in the Torres Strait. This new structure required an additional 38 white officers and non-commissioned officers, but the 417 other ranks were drawn from Torres Strait Islanders already serving in the infantry and labour companies.[39] By the end of 1943 the Torres Strait Light Infantry Battalion (TSLI), along with the 5th Australian Machine Gun Battalion, formed the core of the defence of the Torres Strait Islands, supporting the static coastal artillery.[40] As the war moved further away from the Torres Strait, both units were used as a labour force, mainly on the docks. Seven Islanders were sent to Merauke in Dutch New Guinea, where they undertook patrols from the Australian base and some of their number were wounded.[41]

During 1943 Torres Strait Islanders became increasingly angry about their treatment. Unlike Aboriginal members of the 2nd AIF, who received the same pay and conditions as non-Aboriginal soldiers, Torres Strait Islanders serving in the Army remained under the *Torres Strait Islanders Act*.[42] The strictures that had applied before the war remained in force. Rates of pay for the TSLI had been set with reference to prewar living standards on the islands; by contrast, all white soldiers were paid the same, regardless of their socio-economic background.[43] Senior officers in the AMF, in fact, felt that it was easier administratively to pay all men the same, but it took into account the Queensland government's control over Islanders, arguing that 'if soldiers and their dependants are now placed in the position of receiving a much greater income than they are likely to earn after the war, they may be spoilt from the State point of view for times of peace'.[44] In December 1943, three companies went on strike over their pay. A number were punished, but by March 1944 pay was raised by the Commonwealth cabinet to two-thirds of the rate accorded white soldiers.[45]

Despite the success of the TSLI, no comparable Aboriginal unit was raised on mainland Australia. This was not for want of proposals. The anthropologist AP Elkin, who was a respected adviser to the federal government and served on the Aborigines Welfare Board of New South Wales, suggested to Prime Minister Curtin in April 1942 that a 'part-Aboriginal' battalion might be created or that Aboriginal men be incorporated into auxiliary units. However, the authorities were cautious about mobilising Aboriginal men even for irregular operations. Hence, when Major GD Mitchell, commander of a guerrilla warfare group in the Kimberley region, and a First World War veteran John Longmore, recommended to Curtin that a Native Auxiliary Corps of about 250 Aboriginal volunteers be raised in Australia's north-west, the proposal was stymied. Commissioner Bray and the General Officer Commanding 3 Australian Corps, General Gordon Bennett (recently and notoriously back in Australia after the fall of Singapore), both opposed it. Their reasons? The Kimberley 'native', they maintained, was wholly uneducated; his allegiance could be 'readily transferred with small gifts by an invading enemy'; he was likely to desert if asked to serve outside his own 'tribal area'; and he did not understand military discipline. Moreover, 'the issue of firearms to natives might lead to tribal warfare with consequent desertions and dislocation of labour in the district'. The latter point, Brian Willis argues, was critical. After considerable debate, powerful vested interests in the pastoral industry and the paternalistic grip of the Western Australia Native Affairs bureaucrats prevailed; and Bennett concluded that 'no useful purpose would be served' by raising an Aboriginal Auxiliary Corps.[46]

Yet while this proposal languished, a Northern Territory Special

Reconnaissance Unit (NTSRU) was successfully raised in the different conditions of Arnhem Land. When, in mid-1941, the AMF concluded the defence of northern Australia required independent units undertaking reconnaissance and raids, the officer responsible for these, Lieutenant Colonel WRJ Scott, became convinced of the value of recruiting Aboriginal men for the defence of Arnhem Land.[47] He formed this opinion after attending a lecture by another anthropologist, Lieutenant-Colonel Donald Thomson, who, having developed extensive experience with the Yolngu people of Arnhem Land, had recruited coast watchers in the Solomon Islands in 1940. Scott approached Thomson to lead what became the NTSRU.[48]

Thomson's plans for the NTSRU were to survey the Arnhem Land area, which was poorly mapped; to establish friendly relations with local people and assess the extent of Japanese influence among them (as described on pp. 156–57, it was believed that Aboriginal people were potentially disloyal); to provide protection for Darwin; to organise small fighting groups for patrolling and ambushing; and to establish a base of bushcraft knowledge from which to teach any independent companies that might be later deployed in the area.[49] The NTSRU would form the outer layer of Australia's defence in Arnhem Land, with larger and more conventional units closer to the centres of population and industry.[50] Arriving in Arnhem Land in February 1942, Thompson quickly recruited 50 Yolngu men, six Solomon Islanders, one Torres Strait Islander and several white non-commissioned officers.[51] Notably, the unit was not armed with rifles, since Thomson believed that this would risk the men being identified by the Japanese and then exposed to possible retaliation.[52] Instead, Aboriginal men were encouraged to carry spears. Thus armed, Thomson hoped, their guerrilla attacks, such as ambushing water parties and killing reconnaissance parties, would have a 'considerable' effect on morale, as the Japanese would face the prospect of 'having men constantly picked off by spears'.[53]

The NTSRU existed for a little over a year. In mid-1942 the North Australian Observer Unit (NAOU), was created with a similar role of patrolling the northern coastal areas, looking for signs of enemy activity. This unit consisted mainly of non-Aboriginal personnel (though they relied heavily on Aboriginal guides), and the speed with which it was raised after the opening of hostilities with Japan, Noah Riseman suggests, reflected the AMF's belief that Australia could only be defended by white troops.[54] As the war moved northward from the Australian coast in 1943, the NTSRU was disbanded. However, memories of its role survived among local communities; and in 2016 two Aboriginal men would attribute their decision to join the later NORFORCE to the inspiration provided by Thomson and the NTSRU.[55]

Meanwhile a further 35 Aboriginal men had been employed by the RAN in the so-called Snake Bay Patrol. Based on Melville Island near Darwin, this unit mounted patrols to detect and counter any Japanese infiltration of the island, assisted in the rescue of downed airmen and located sea mines. Unlike the NTSRU, the members of the patrol were trained to use small arms and automatic weapons.[56] Yet none of the men who served in this or the other irregular units was paid during the war, though they did receive rations. Only decades later was their service formally acknowledged with the receipt of pay and service medals.

Why did they serve?

What motivated Aboriginal and Torres Strait Islander Australians to serve in defence of the state which was the agent of their disadvantage? We do not know precisely. During the Second World War no attempts were made to survey Indigenous men about the reasons for their enlisting; and when historian John Barrett conducted an extensive survey of returned soldiers in the early 1980s, Indigenous

Australians were statistically underrepresented among his respondents.[57] Nonetheless it can be deduced from oral histories and family memories that Indigenous soldiers, like other Australians, chose to serve for a mix of reasons. Some saw military service as a way of escaping the economic and social constraints of their lives. Leonard Waters, who became the only known Australian Aboriginal fighter pilot of the Second World War, claimed that: 'When war broke out in '39 … I would have liked to have gone into aircrew straight away. I was obsessed with it … you know, it was the pioneering days of the air … I was always interested in motors too.'[58]

Athol Fred Lester, so his son John recalled in 2015, joined the Army because that was the only job he could get at that time.[59] Not only were Indigenous men the victims of systemic disadvantage, but unemployment remained high in the aftermath of the Great Depression. Other Indigenous volunteers recalled the influence of being part of a family or community with a tradition of military service. Reg Saunders, for example, was 'very conscious of the service of Aboriginal men during the First World War'.[60] He later recalled:

> My Dad was a soldier, and all my uncles and various cousins were soldiers, including my grandfather … There was three of us. Mum and Dad and my brother … We discussed the war; we took it quite seriously and because I was the eldest we decided that I was the one that was going to enter the war … I never fought for anybody but Australia … my loyalty was purely Australian. It was a sense of duty to the country.[61]

John Lovett, too, came from a family with a proud history of military service, though in 2015 he also recalled that his father may have gone to war 'so he could feed his family'.[62] Yet others seem to have volunteered due to a mix of peer pressure and patriotism. Charles Mene from Thursday Island enlisted on 15 December 1939 because 'some of the boys I know, they enlisted, and I thought, well, I might as well be in it too ... And I also wanted to fight for the country'.[63]

When northern Australia was under direct attack, fear of the Japanese may have provided an additional incentive to volunteer. Rosie Ware, when recalling in 2014 the service of her father, Elia Ware, a Torres Strait Islander, claimed that 'without them ... Japan would have invaded Australia'.[64] Or, as Aden Eades put it in 2015, 'Dad went willingly because he wanted to serve his country.'[65] Claude McDermott too would later say to his son, James, 'I needed to fight for my family, for my community and for Australia.'[66] Yet Alec Kruger, who enlisted after Pearl Harbor, said:

> We knew that the army was taking a lot of people and paying good money. We would be fighting for our country. People who had left to join the services were looked up to in Alice Springs. Even full descent Aboriginal people were getting paid real money and being employed to do army jobs ... I was ripe for a bit of real money and ruination.[67]

Finally, military service was seen by some Aboriginal activists as providing an opportunity to press their claims for political rights. Michael Sawtell of the Committee for Aboriginal Citizenship wrote to Prime Minister Menzies on 20 September 1939:

> Our committee does not wish in any way to hamper you & we are not hostile to the compulsory training, but as we are at war to uphold democracy, we do consider that democracy should begin at home in Australia.

There were, his Committee claimed, a few cases of Aboriginal veterans of the First World War who were not receiving the old age pension, while 'full-blood' women were being denied invalid pensions and maternity bonuses. 'We feel sure that good loyal Australian citizens do not wish to see their Aboriginal people, & those young men who are to defend our shores treated in such a poor manner.'[68] William Cooper added his voice to this complaint, arguing in December 1939 that the war was 'by reason of the tyranny over minorities and their cruel discriminating treatment. Australia cannot fight that cause in honesty, while still oppressing her minority though we know that no white person sees this.'[69]

Indigenous experiences of war

The experiences of those Aboriginal and Torres Strait Islander Australians who served in the formal defence forces were probably little different from those of other non-Aboriginal servicemen. On active service Indigenous Australians would have been integrated into military units where there were no racially determined constraints on how and where they were deployed. Many rose to non-commissioned officer rank within the Army, although only Saunders was promoted to commissioned rank.[70] Some Indigenous soldiers were among the more than 30 000 Australians taken as prisoners of war. Jim Brennan of Western Australia, for instance, was captured at the battle of El Alamein in 1942, and interned in Italy, before escaping and joining a partisan group. Other Indigenous men were captured with the 8th Division in Malaya and Singapore, and faced three-and-a-half years of privation under the Japanese.[71] Ron Ralph recalled that his uncle Arthur, came home 'like a rake … He had a little darkness in him.'[72] An Aboriginal man was also one of the last Australians to die in the Second World War. Flight Sergeant Arnold Lockyer parachuted from his damaged plane over the Celebes Islands, where he was executed, possibly by being buried alive by his Japanese captors, six days after the war ended.[73]

A common perception is that Aboriginal and Torres Strait Islander men encountered little racism within the defence forces. Historian Robert Hall concludes that the relationship between black and white men in uniform was 'remarkably free from racism'. This, he argues was the result of 'the psychology of the small group in battle, the nature of the military as a sub-culture and the presence of new models of behaviour'. While the higher command tended to retain a prejudiced view of Aboriginal and Islander people, 'the "normal Australian" was far more ready' to adopt new modes of behaviour.[74] It is a judgment that Aboriginal servicemen have confirmed. As Mene later said, 'I had no difficulty … getting on with the white soldiers. We were all in it [together].'[75] Saunders meanwhile recalled, 'I had a bit of reputation as a fighter. … So I didn't get very much cheek from anybody.' While he did note racism towards local Aboriginal Australians when training in North Queensland, he personally met none in the Army itself.[76]

These testimonies of personal experiences are powerful, but it is likely that the experiences of Indigenous servicemen were different when a unit was based in Australia rather than in a combat zone. At home their treatment would still have been shaped by the local protection regimes. Hence, Alexander Bell, an Aboriginal soldier in the artillery, testified to a court-martial in 1943 that he left his unit without permission because he was 'not given the same privileges as a white man when I proceed on leave. I go into a hotel with the white men whom I class as my cobbers in camp. We ask for a drink and they won't serve me.'[77] Similarly, John Ceissman from La Perouse went Absent Without Leave (AWOL) in 1944 after his corporal called him a 'dirty mongrel'.[78] Private Russell Amato went AWOL three times from three different units, because he 'couldn't stand' the other soldiers making derogatory remarks about Aboriginal people, particularly women, about whom the talk was sexual. In this court-martial in June 1943 Amato's defending officer reported: 'From previous instances where men of aboriginal blood have been before the Court, it appears that there is a certain element in the camps that brings up the colour bar against such men'.[79]

Moreover, systemic racism was evident in the way that Australian newspapers used racialised language when discussing Indigenous soldiers. Words such as 'abo' and 'half-caste' were commonplace, and rural newspapers were patronising in their descriptions of Indigenous servicemen. The *West Coast Sentinel*, in South Australia, for instance, contrasted the tall khaki-clad Australians with 'a little aboriginal', Sydney Cook, who excelled at drill despite having been 'discarded by his cannibalistic parents'.[80] Similarly, Aboriginal men who went AWOL were described as having gone 'walkabout'.[81]

Any judgment as to the impact of military service in the Second World War on Indigenous Australians must be qualified. On the one hand, the war saw little change in the military's traditional policies of discrimination, so far as eligibility for service in the defence forces was concerned. Only 'half-castes' were admitted to the Army at the discretion of local officials; and the creation of discrete Indigenous units to defend the north of Australia was a relatively short-lived and temporary response to the national crisis of 1942. So far as we can tell, the RAN was closed to Indigenous Australians. Only in the RAAF were there few formal constraints on Indigenous men enlisting, though those seeking admission were subject to the often rigorous skills testing demanded by the technical requirements of that force. Yet if there was little structural change within the defence forces, those Indigenous Australians who managed to enlist found new opportunities: the chance to live in an environment which was often free from the racism of home; the prospect, should they survive combat, of returning to civilian life with new experiences and skills; and above all, the possibility of fulfilling what has traditionally been seen as the core obligation of citizenship, risking their life in defence of the nation. In this, and in personal empowerment of those who served in the defence forces, and who worked in the labour units raised to defend Australia, the Second World War expedited both post-war activism and changes in Indigenous rights that were to come in subsequent decades.

8

Labour and surveillance in northern Australia, 1939–45

Geoffrey Gray

'Aboriginal people served Australia well.' – *AP Elkin*

During the wartime crisis of 1941–42 Aboriginal and Torres Strait Islander Australians were not only drawn into service in the Australian defence forces and the specialist units created to defend the north of the continent against Japanese attack; they were also employed for a range of auxiliary work supporting the national war effort and economy in the north. This occurred despite initial concern among government officials that Indigenous Australians, especially those living in remote areas beyond tight government control, might be potentially subversive and disloyal to the Australian war effort. These fears proved to be groundless, despite the many reasons that Indigenous Australians had to be disaffected. Ultimately Aboriginal and Torres Strait Islander Australians were drawn, willingly and unwillingly, into the general war effort in a variety of ways.

This chapter considers the work that was auxiliary to the main defence forces in the north of Australia: the changing attitudes of government officials; the conditions under which Indigenous labourers were employed; and the impact this wartime labour had on the wider conditions of employment for Indigenous workers. It asks how the Second World War served as a catalyst for change and the associated politicisation of Indigenous labour. In addressing these questions this chapter relies to a considerable degree on the observations, not of Indigenous Australians whose voice was often muted or ignored during these war years, but on those non-Indigenous 'experts' who observed and worked with them. Anthropology was an emerging discipline within Australia and the close knowledge of Indigenous societies that anthropologists had acquired in the interwar years was acknowledged by the Australian government to be an important source of advice and information about peoples who were only now seen to be a resource of value to Australia.

Issues of loyalty

In the racially structured society of Australia the problem of loyalty to the nation was bound to be complicated. When war broke out in September 1939, many in the military services, government circles and print media suspected that some Indigenous people might favour a victory by Australia's enemies. They were also perceived as likely to be easily influenced by both inside and outside agents. These concerns over Indigenous loyalty were linked to the assumed anti-British sentiments of German missionaries, Catholic and Lutheran especially. As enemy aliens, they were seen as a potential security threat, able to exercise a negative influence over Aboriginal residents on their missions.

Hence, in October 1940, German-born missionaries at Beagle Bay in Western Australia were interned, and in December 1941, the mission itself was taken over by Army intelligence.[1] Australian army chaplains were posted to Beagle Bay for the duration of the war. In April 1942, George Schwarz, the superintendent of the

Lutheran Cape Bedford (Hope Vale) mission in northern Queensland, was interned after accusations that he was anti-British and had been in touch with the Japanese. Once Schwarz was removed, the Aboriginal residents on the mission were forcibly evacuated to the Woorabinda reserve. Within months of their arrival at Woorabinda, almost a quarter of the community had died of disease, exposure to cold weather, and malnutrition.[2] Many of the men did heavy roadwork, while some of the women picked peanuts at Kingaroy. The survivors were not allowed to return to the new Hope Vale mission until several years after the war.[3]

The insistence on Indigenous loyalty, and the concomitant fear that Indigenous people might be disloyal, was a specific colonial preoccupation.[4] It was fundamentally different from the expectation that non-Indigenous Australians, including those immigrants who had been 'naturalised', would be unequivocally loyal to the nation and to the British Empire. Indigenous loyalty was not a litmus test of citizenship, which was denied Aboriginal and Torres Strait Islander peoples (see chapter 2), but of successful colonial relations and colonial governance. As the anthropologist Kenneth Eyre Read later commented in relation to Australia's colonial subjects in New Guinea (the Army's Directorate of Research and Civil Affairs had sent him to the Markham Valley, in New Guinea, to investigate 'the possibility that anti-British propaganda had been disseminated'), the concept of loyalty was inappropriate. The demand that New Guineans be loyal to Australia was, in his view, a longing for the implementation of 'our form of government' as well as a justification for colonial rule.[5]

The concern that Indigenous people might be disloyal inevitably became more acute when a Japanese invasion of the north of Australia seemed imminent in early 1942. In January, when the Japanese had already captured one of the strategic islands to Australia's north, New Britain, one Townsville observer advised the military authorities that Indigenous people could 'convey information by signalling in native fashion by fire, smoke and other means' to the Japanese.[6] At the highest levels of government, too, there was anxiety about the reliability of Indigenous Australians in regions under aerial attack from the Japanese. Prime Minister John Curtin wrote to Frank Forde, Minister for the Army, on 24 July 1942, noting that:

> Investigations disclose that natives and half-castes in [the north west of Western Australia] are definitely sympathetic to the enemy. If there was an invasion, it is considered that they would be prepared to help the enemy. It has been common talk among the natives that when the Japs come they would be boss.[7]

Curtin sought accurate information regarding 'the real attitude of the aborigines' from officers responsible for the 'protection and control of aborigines'. A Queensland security report of July 1942, entitled 'Japanese Activities Among the Aborigines', meanwhile stated that 'aboriginals have openly stated that the Japs told them that the country belonged to the blacks, had been stolen from them by the whites and that "bye bye" they [the Japs] would give it back to them'.[8]

War, then, caused the deep suppressed unease within white Australia over settlement and the dispossession of Aboriginal peoples to surface, leading to calls for tighter control of the original inhabitants. In north Queensland there were suggestions that should 'the aboriginals become treacherous they should be shot'.[9] Queensland government authorities also warned of the dangers inherent in Aboriginal mobility. Aboriginal station hands, especially drovers, had been travelling the stock routes for years and their natural affinity with 'country' gave them invaluable knowledge of

Queensland topography. This knowledge was understood to be of 'inestimable value to the enemy in an overland drive'.[10]

Despite these alarmist concerns about Aboriginal unreliability, there were others who saw the potential for Aboriginal people to be incorporated into the war effort. The Western Australian Commissioner for Native Affairs, Francis Bray, for example, did not share the view of the military authorities that 'full-blood natives' were a security threat. He claimed that they '[hate] the Japanese, and the half-caste [has] nothing in common with the Japanese'. Bray strategically omitted that there was a sizable mixed population, many of whom were of Japanese descent.[11] Nevertheless, 'both classes', Bray stated, would be 'more enthusiastic to our cause if we treated him as a human being'.[12] This plea was ignored. After Broome and Port Hedland were bombed in early and mid-1942, white residents responded with fears that Aboriginal people in the township and outlying areas were a security risk, a view which was reinforced by the Army when in early 1943 it planned to remove 'all nomadic, unemployed, aged and infirm natives from the North West coastal areas from Carnarvon to Derby, and for a distance inland of approximately 100 miles [160 kilometres]'.[13] Although this plan was not ultimately carried out, it highlighted how Aboriginal people were enmeshed in the often conflicting objectives of the Commissioner for Native Affairs, who tried to defend his authority over his charges, and the military authorities, who were anxious to exclude Aboriginal people from strategic locations.

Another person to see the potential rather than the threat of Indigenous peoples was AP Elkin. As professor of anthropology at the University of Sydney he had established a reputation within government circles as 'probably the foremost authority on the Australian Aboriginal'. In the words of the secretary to the Department of the Interior, JA Carrodus, he 'has been a good friend to this Department over the years and has assisted us on many occasions with advice'.[14] In April 1942 Elkin suggested to Prime Minister Curtin that anthropologists would be able to assist in reducing the danger of Aboriginal people sympathising with the Japanese. As he put it, 'unless they [Aborigines] were told to the contrary by [anthropologists] whom they understood and trusted [they] would not see why they should not guide and help the Japanese'.[15]

Importantly, Elkin also made the point that it was time to give the Aborigines a chance of helping their country, either in the fighting services or as auxiliaries in these services or in factories. The military authorities too, under the pressures of war, had come to the same conclusion, and (as the previous chapter showed) by mid-1942 were willing to incorporate Indigenous people into the war effort in a variety of ways. This included not just specialist military units, one of which was put under the command of another anthropologist with particular expertise with the Yolngu people of the north, Donald Thomson, but also labour units supporting the war effort.

Aboriginal labour

Even before the military began to mobilise Aboriginal labour, the war had brought about changes in Aboriginal employment in northern Australia. At the outbreak of war some 80 per cent of the total number of Aboriginal people employed in the Northern Territory were working in the pastoral industry.[16] As white pastoral workers left to serve in the war, Indigenous pastoral workers were able to assume different responsibilities.[17] The removal from pastoral stations of Chinese and Japanese station cooks, for example, opened up these occupations to Aboriginal people.[18] Jack Jangari became an overseer for Bovril, working between the Victoria River Downs head station and the outstations. It was a job 'defined as one for white men but, because of the war, it was given to Jack'. With three children and a wife to support, he demanded wages and when denied these, he moved to Wave Hill where he worked as a drover and 'camped out with the Afghans'. Unlike Aboriginal people, people of mixed ancestry like Jack had a few rights, 'one of which was to choose his place of residence'.[19]

Beyond the pastoral industry, the war brought about many other changes in Aboriginal employment. At the beginning of the war the flying boat base on Groote Eylandt (eastern Arnhem Land) was transformed from a civilian to an operational base, with the emergency airstrip at the mission station being expanded and a road built for heavy trucks, 40 miles (64 kilometres) long. All of this was done with Aboriginal labour. In northern Queensland large numbers of Aboriginal people were drawn into industries, including sugar. Here they received award wages for the first time.[20] Most importantly, the government became a major employer of Aboriginal men and women as the war effort focused on defending the north. Paddy Roe, born in 1912 at Roebuck station in the Kimberley, Western Australia, later recalled that he was brought into Broome for war-related work:

> I went working in the slaughteryard [sic] then. Slaughter man, slaughtering bullock meat for the army … I was never frightened for whatsaname – you know, if we get killed or not … bomb … machine-gun … anything like that. … one night they dropped about six or seven bombs but nothing went off. We was very lucky.[21]

Other Aboriginal men were employed by the Civil Construction Corps, which was created by the government in April 1942 to supply labour for constructing infrastructure, such as airfields, gun emplacements, barracks and roads. In this employment Aboriginal people were given the opportunity to acquire new skills, such as driving trucks and using heavy equipment.[22] Other Aboriginal men, such as David Mowaljarai from the Kimberley region, were employed by the RAN:

> We had to put our fingerstamps on some paper [he later recalled]. I could write of course. I had been to mission schools, but they didn't know that … they gave me the job of running around the coast with the barge, because I knew shoals and water there.[23]

The Army was accorded a 'supreme priority' in regard to people not already employed, while pastoralists and essential services within the civil administration had a lower claim.[24]

At the height of the war the number of Aboriginal people under direct control of the military in the Northern Territory was over a thousand men, women and children. Most were resident at the Native Affairs compounds along the main highway (now the Stuart Highway), Alice Springs, which became the administrative centre for the duration of the war, and various army camps on the main road. Others were attached to naval units and RAAF bases.[25] The Army's labour demands, incidentally, posed a labour shortage for the cattle industry.

The conditions under which Aboriginal men worked for the military forces in the Northern Territory were negotiated by the Administrator, CLA Abbott. His priority was the development of the north, and consequently having a cheap and compliant Aboriginal workforce. In the past he had overlooked the excesses of cattle stations, often questioning the veracity of complaints or reports by Aboriginal workers.[26] Now he was faced with the prospect of the defence forces disrupting the old social and economic order by paying wages, though less than the regular wage of non-Indigenous personnel, and providing improved conditions of employment. In

Table 8.1.
Numbers in Army compounds Northern Territory, 1944

Settlement	Men	Aged and infirm	'Lubras'*	Children	Total
Koolpinyah	75	11	33	6	125
Adelaide River	172	26	128	55	381
Pine Creek	54	7	45	16	122
Mataranka	141	38	118	38	335
Larrimah	47	0	19	8	74
Alice Springs	76	2	39	36	153

* Though used in the original source, 'lubra' is a particularly offensive term: see Liz Connor, 'The "Lubra" Type in Australian Imaginings of the Aboriginal Woman from 1836–1973', *Gender & History*, vol. 25, no. 2, 2013, pp. 230–51.

SOURCE FR Morris, Director of Native Personnel, NT Force, to HM Arrowsmith, CMS, 11 April 1944. Copy in Elkin Papers, 8/1/8/2, University of Sydney Archive.

addition, the armed forces, as had the pastoral employers, distributed clothing and provided a plate, knife, fork, spoon and mug.[27]

Information about the conditions under which Indigenous men and women worked at this time can be gleaned from the work of two anthropologists, Ronald and Catherine Berndt. In mid-1945, as the war was ending, on behalf of Vestey's, one of the largest foreign-owned cattle companies in the Northern Territory and Queensland, they investigated Army labour and the effect it might have on future employment in the cattle industry. The Berndts travelled to various military compounds, noting the numbers of people employed and describing their daily work. They reported that, unlike on the pastoral stations, where workers were given little time off, the normal working week was five-and-a-half days, and the working day, eight-and-a-half hours, including the lunch hour.[28] The receipt of a wage gave Aboriginal people 'a sense of independence and responsibility [that] was out of all proportion to the actual sums involved'. The Berndts went on to conclude that Aboriginal people who were being paid a wage 'took greater interest in their work, feeling they were receiving something tangible in return for their efforts', and that they had 'something to show' for their labour.[29] It was a conclusion that tracker Tommy Jingli Elliott confirmed many years later:

> Army bin bringem back money. Now we bin showem the wages then. All the time we bin work for clothes, tobacco, bread, beef. Army come through here, and bringem money, we bin look money.[30]

The Berndts further noted that not only was the old system of white control and management subverted by the payment of a wage but it also witnessed 'the gradual but steady breaking down of tribal boundaries'. This was also a consequence of wartime conditions, where people were 'obliged to live side by side within the confines of the settlements'. Nevertheless, the 'lure of tribal country was still strong'.[31]

Beyond this, the Berndts observed that housing for Aboriginal workers in the Army labour camps was properly constructed and medical services were both provided and used. The diet of Aboriginal employees was dramatically improved from that on cattle stations and included vegetables from the settlement gardens and fresh beef. Furthermore, this 'contributed … towards building up their resistance to disease'.[32] In summary, the Berndts believed that the Army was providing Indigenous people with working conditions and skills that would enable a more active and constructive incorporation into the economic and social life of the north.[33] Furthermore, their experiences in Army labour camps led them to assert that Indigenous people were able to adapt to changing conditions, contrary to a long-held belief that Aboriginal culture was static and an impediment to their ability to adapt to changed conditions.

The effect of wartime changes in the conditions of Indigenous workers were also noted by a meteorologist on Groote Eylandt in the early 1940s, Frederick Rose, who later became professor of anthropology at the Von Humboldt University in East Berlin. A dedicated (Stalinist) Marxist, Rose commented that local people working for the military received the same food and medical treatment as the white soldiers and airmen. They 'worked as equals with white servicemen ... from whom they learned something of proletarian solidarity. They also learnt that white men were not just policemen or missionaries but also human beings who laboured like themselves.' As Rose saw it, this 'bore fruit in the post war years'.[34]

However, the conclusions of anthropologists should be read keeping in mind they had engaged relations with Indigenous people, and elicited Indigenous viewpoints which they believed were best represented by them. Later research suggests that local people may have viewed their treatment differently. Not only were communities disrupted, especially by the forced evacuations of Indigenous peoples from the north of Australia (see chapter 9), but there were periods when people suffered food shortages, although it is unclear whether the military services were solely responsible for these.[35] It was also the practice of missions and cattle stations to retain Aboriginal 'wages' and pensions, initially the maternity allowance (including child allowance) and later the age pension.[36] The mission superintendent of Milingimbi Mission (Yurruwi), on the largest of the Crocodile Islands off Arnhem Land, explained in March 1943 that paying a wage 'would only be doing these primitive folk a dis-service if we in any way flooded them with things they do not need to know how to handle or have any need of, or, if by too generous pay they become able to support an increasing number of idle dependents [sic]'.[37] When local labourers were hired out to the RAAF by the Christian Missionary Society (CMS) mission and the local protector of Aborigines, Fred Gray, they did not see any of their pay.[38] The RAAF paid the wages directly to mission headquarters in Sydney, who provided any items requested by Aboriginal people, which were shipped from Sydney to Emerald River. Fred Gray also retained wages.[39] Such a paternalistic attitude only reinforced the notion that Aboriginal people were unable to manage money, and thus denied any possibility of economic independence.

Moreover, many of the opportunities opened by the imperatives of wartime closed in the post-war era. The performance of Indigenous peoples during the war was largely attributed to their supposed 'natural' aptitude for this type of work, rather than any ability to acquire knowledge and skills.[40] When faced with the possibility of having to pay wages after the war, pastoralists opportunistically dismissed the abilities of Aboriginal workers.[41] There were individual exceptions, but overall Indigenous peoples were described as lazy, incapable of taking responsibility, unreliable and needing constant supervision. Employers maintained further that Aboriginal peoples lacked the intelligence of 'whites' and were therefore not capable of work apart from seasonal mustering and of grasping the technical skills required for tasks such as windmill repair.[42]

Coastwatchers

The long coast of northern and north-western Australia posed huge strategic problems for Australian military planners in 1942. This led the Army (as chapter 7 has shown) to mobilise Indigenous men in the Torres Strait Islanders Infantry Battalion and the Northern Territory Special Reconnaissance Unit. The latter was under the command of Thomson, whose powers of persuasion were later recalled by a Yolngu elder, Mowarra Gamanbarr. In a 2000 documentary, *Thomson of Arnhem Land*, he recalled that Thomson warned them:

> 'If they [Japanese] win, this will be Japanese country, and our children won't have the chance to learn our culture.' Thomson said we had to combine with the white people. This was never done before. We all went to war, fighting for this country of ours.[43]

In a further effort to try and maintain surveillance along the vulnerable coastline of northern Australia the military authorities developed a string of watching posts and placed Aboriginal people as 'coastwatchers'. Tex Camfoo, for example, was employed 'watching the river so no submarine or anything comes up the Roper River'.[44] In contrast to those working in Army military or labour units, most Aboriginal people undertook these actions for little reward other than rations. Missionaries at Croker Island, Goulburn Island, Milingimbi, Yirrkala, and Groote Eylandt also worked as coastwatchers for Naval Intelligence, and were often supported by Aboriginal residents.[45] The 'Black Watch' was organised by Jack Murray, superintendent of Delissaville, to patrol the Cox Peninsula and north of Darwin, acting as coastwatchers and rescuing downed pilots.[46] Its personnel wore no uniforms and had no rifles. They were not enlisted or formally recognised by the Australian military services. Rarely were Indigenous coastwatchers singled out for recognition, although since 1994 they have been eligible for the Civilian Service Medal 1939–1945.

Some tales of manly bravery, however, have been told and retold. Among the stories that have become legendary is the capture of the first Japanese prisoner of war on Australian soil. Tiwi Islander Matthias Ulungura crept up behind the Japanese pilot, Hajime Toyoshima, who had crash landed: then 'He put his axe at his side and said, "Stick 'em up" to the Japanese, and then the Japanese put his two hands up'.[47] This dramatic incident is now commemorated by a bronze-sized statue of Ulungura on Bathurst Island. Another Tiwi Islander, Louis (Louie) Munkara, buried drowned sailors and is believed to have captured five Japanese airmen and rescued another three from the sea.[48] Further to the east, Yolngu were also rescuing allied pilots. Wandjuk Marika, the later Aboriginal leader and artist, who was then a 16-year-old, retold his and his companions' rescue of Clarence Sanford. The allied pilot suspected that they would betray him (if not kill and eat him). This was not an idle fear; Sanford had joked he was Japanese and Marika was unsure whether he was or not. If he had been, Marika would have killed him then and there.[49] Yet another notable coastwatcher was Charlie One Lampungmeiua. One of 39 Melville Islanders recruited for this work, he spoke Malay, Tiwi and English and was chosen to make secret trips by submarine to occupied Timor, 'to assist in landing small parties of allied troops and stores'.[50]

The Nackeroos: The 2/1 North Australia Observer Unit

Indigenous men also played a significant role to another unit created to protect northern Australia, the 2/1 North Australia Observer Unit (NAOU). Known colloquially as the 'Nackeroos', or 'Curtin's Cowboys', the NAOU was formed in mid-1942 to communicate information from observer stations and in particular aircraft sightings and naval and military movements. In establishing the NAOU, as military command at Victoria Barracks (Melbourne) had done when creating the Northern Territory Special Reconnaissance Unit (NTSRU), the authorities drew again on the expertise and knowledge of anthropologists, in this case, WEH Stanner.[51] Once formed, the unit's role was to provide early warning of a Japanese invasion and to form a guerrilla force in the event of such an attack. The men carried out horseback reconnaissance patrols and other work across the vast areas of northern Australia stretching from the Kimberley to the Gulf of Carpentaria. In such operations local Aboriginal knowledge of the land was an immense asset. At the peak of its strength the NAOU numbered around 550 men, with about 50 Aboriginal personnel attached as guides and labourers.[52] As the threat of invasion passed, the unit was reduced in strength and was finally disbanded in March 1945. A plaque installed in 1999 to commemorate the Nackeroos, at Timber Creek, Northern Territory, carries the words: 'Also in memory of aboriginal trackers who helped the nackeroos survive in this harsh environment. "[Y]ou always felt safe when you had an aborigine with you": Quote by NAOU from "A" Company.'[53]

The legacy of wartime labour

What was the legacy of the integration of Aboriginal labour into the war effort in the north? At the time it was recognised that this deployment had the potential to disrupt traditional communities. When Stanner and Thomson were consulted by the government in early 1943 about the use of Aboriginal labour, Thomson was of the opinion that 'any scheme to employ [nomadic] aboriginals … cannot be justified and that the removal of the men from reserves as suggested must inevitably break down native organisation and aggravate conditions that are now leading to the extinction of the aboriginal race'.[54] Stanner, on the other hand, suggested that mission stations, 'non-essential' pastoral stations, government 'aboriginal settlements', town encampments and 'all other out back centres' were suitable sources for Aboriginal labour: 'Natives involved can all be regarded as civilised or semi-civilised and therefore responsible to intelligent and fair control.' However, Aborigines who lived in inaccessible parts of the country, or were too scattered to concentrate, or too close to their 'nomadic mode of life to hold and work without ruining them', should be excluded.[55]

Anthropologists were torn between the excitement of recording changing conditions and harbouring a paternalistic desire to protect and help people who still lived a 'traditional' life from intensive large-scale intrusive contact.[56] However, the demand for labour by both the pastoral industry, and then the Army, was unrelenting. Labour movements resulting from the war thus threatened to accelerate 'de-tribalisation' (the term then used to describe the loss of cultural life and attachment to country) and to speed up change. This posed ethical and moral problems for officials and anthropologists alike. As we have seen, Ronald and Catherine Berndt provided information about working conditions to Vestey's, but they also directed them to explore two potential sources for labour: the shortly to be abandoned Army compounds, and 'bush natives'. Were they complicit in coercing Aboriginal people into working for pastoral interests that overall treated these workers as chattels?[57]

Clearly, in the eyes of white Australians it was the usefulness of Aboriginal labour to commerce and the war effort that was the main determinant of their value. Once the war ended many people were no longer of such value and were left to return to their pre-war life. Historian Peggy Brock describes it as tragedy:

> The search [for work] had the elements of a Greek tragic quest. Every time one obstacle was overcome, another rose in its place. These people are not hanging around towns aimlessly, they have positioned themselves purposefully and strategically to optimise their employment possibilities. Meanwhile police, missionaries and non-Aboriginal citizens try to prevent easy access to work and then accuse them of being lazy, dirty, immoral and worst of all, aimless wanderers.[58]

Yet if the impact of the war on Aboriginal communities was inherently deleterious, there is also some evidence that it contributed to a growing sense of Indigenous empowerment. One newspaper report begrudgingly said (albeit with the jarring racialised paternalism of the time) in November 1944:

> Lubras do general duties [at Adelaide River] … The same ten do not always arrive [at the barracks] because Millie might want to go 'walkabout,' so Nellie comes instead, but 'No 1 girl', 'Cpl' Dolly, always manages to produce ten aborigines. Dolly is proud of her two stripes … Like other lubras she wears AWAS [Australian Women's Army Service] issue khaki drill overalls, but the stripes may appear on either sleeve or on her chest. AWAS in the Northern Territory feel that they are really in a war zone.[59]

For Aboriginal men employed by the Army it was also positive to have their skills and knowledge of their country recognised. Wandjuk Marika, who was barely 15 at the time, recalled that when Thomson, who by then had known his father and others for just short of eight years and held people like Marika and Raiwalla in high regard, asked his father to 'show me where this [Japanese] is coming from … My father said "I know where to lead you, where to tell you".'[60]

In addition to such pride, the war also triggered collective action through which discontent among Indigenous workers, particularly on pastoral stations, found expression. This usually meant withdrawal of labour in walk-offs or brief strike action. Each such action was fraught as the response from the bosses, both Indigenous and non-Indigenous, was swift.[61] The workers were summarily taught their lesson or banished, and so cut off from the material things they had come to find almost indispensable. They served as examples, and warnings, to those who might be tempted to respond in the same way.[62]

Resistance was not the preserve of wartime. Before the war

Indigenous workers withdrawing their labour was spasmodic and localised; however, there was an awareness by government officials during the war of 'growing dissatisfaction … implicitly expressed' by people refusing to supply labour to some stations.[63] People were subtly withdrawing their labour in ways that were not confrontational. Furthermore, station managers found their workforce harder to control and discipline. TJ Quilty, manager of Coolibah Station, wrote to Prime Minister Curtin in 1943, explaining that the war had created a problem:

> At one time no Station manager would employ a boy from another station; each place had its batch of boys. Boys were let go for their 'walk-about' at the end of the season and returned about the end of March to start work. Now you never know if they will return. The result is, if a boy is spoken to a bit sharply, he walks off and gets a job on a place managed by a white blackfellow. This type of Manager cannot handle natives; the natives get the upper hand after a while, and are no use on any place.[64]

Withdrawing their labour was not merely a response by Indigenous Australians to having learned about better pay and conditions while working for the Army. Increasingly Indigenous people realised they could choose to work where it suited them, although many people preferred to remain on country. This was the nub of Quilty's complaint.[65]

Other forms of protest were less obvious to the white observer. Aboriginal protest, the Berndts reported, was often performed through ceremony, dance and song. These performances provided an 'outlet' in which people looked on the humorous side, 'mimicking the people who most of the time appear to have such power over them … showing that they are still, essentially, undefeated in spirit'.[66] These ceremonies and songs dealt with scenes and events which involved strain and friction, 'or behaviour that seemed … strange or illogical' to Indigenous people. As performances indicating dissatisfaction, they could be 'interpreted as the beginnings or the emergence of a limited form of protest or possibly a substitute for direct protest'.[67] They were 'a conventionalised kind of catharsis, a means of side stepping a direct confrontation in which Aborigines could not have hoped … to achieve any worthwhile results'.[68] Similar dances and ceremonies occurred on the Army compounds, usually a special event put on for visitors. Some were traditional songs and dances, others reflected current events.

Working for the armed services during the Second World War, then, gave Indigenous people a glimpse into what life might be once they returned to the pastoral stations, perhaps even emboldening them to take action. There was already evidence, which was given impetus by the war, of a certain restlessness, a growing dissatisfaction, on the stations caused by 'semi-educated natives and "half-castes" from mission stations' in Western Australia and Queensland passing through the cattle stations with droving plans. They had received 'some wages' for their work and talked about conditions in other areas where station employees received wages. These transient contacts resulted in people becoming dissatisfied with their conditions, 'more deeply conscious of differences in treatment between one station and another, as well as the individual personal differences that they have always recognized'.[69]

This new consciousness became starkly manifest when in May 1946 some 800 Aboriginal pastoral workers walked off about 25 sheep and cattle stations across the Pilbara in north-west Australia and from workplaces in Port Hedland and Marble Bar. In this, the longest industrial action in Australia's history, work on stations was paralysed. The historic importance of this event, which ultimately won significantly improved conditions for Aboriginal pastoral workers, was recognised in 2010 when four streets were named after the strike leaders (Clancy McKenna Crescent, Dooley Binbin Street, Peter Coppin Street and Don McLeod Lane) in the Canberra suburb of Bonner, itself named after the first Indigenous federal parliamentarian, Neville Bonner. In addition the strike has been remembered in two later documentaries and the memoirs of the Nyamal lawman, Peter Coppin.

It is difficult to ascertain a more direct connection with wartime experience and post-war political action, but it would be unwise to dismiss it. Direct service during the war, auxiliary labour and wider changes all subtly contributed to post-war activism challenging the status quo (see chapter 13). There was a push for change and the integration of Indigenous people into the economy and life of the north. New skills were acquired as a result of war work. There were calls to change the old regime from non-Aboriginal commentators, such as the Northern Territory 'bushman' Bill Harney, who had been patrol officer with the Northern Territory Native Affairs Branch. He wrote: 'Aborigines have proved their worth in the war. ... Their cry for a square deal must not be drowned in the post-war clamour'.[70]

Nevertheless, again on the negative side, the war disrupted Aboriginal people's lives and old traditions were challenged and broken down by the intensity of contact. Of those living in northern townships such as Broome, Port Hedland and Darwin which were bombed, some were killed, others injured. People were forcibly removed, sometimes coerced into work, while being paid little other than rations. Indigenous people in northern Australia were also placed under suspicion, their loyalty questioned. This distrust was used as a dubious justification for the imposition of a level of control and restriction on Aboriginal people that was more appropriate to 'enemy aliens'. It was disingenuous – a denial of fact – therefore of the Western Australian Commissioner for Native Affairs to declare as the war ended, 'At least the natives have not suffered the vicissitudes of the war. Many white people have suffered grievously by the war, but this is not so with the natives.'[71]

9

The Second World War home front

Samuel Furphy

'I shuddered at the bullets we were making,
but I enjoyed working the machines.'
– *Marge Tucker*

The Second World War had a profound impact on Indigenous Australians. Not only was the military participation of Aboriginal and Torres Strait Islander people more extensive than in the First World War, but the closeness of the Pacific theatre of war, and the greater military presence in Australia that flowed from this, resulted in a more transformative home front experience. Many Aboriginal and Torres Strait Islander people, especially women and children, were evacuated to southern Australia in 1942, while those who remained in the north found that the boundary between home front and war front was blurred. The war also created a myriad of employment opportunities for Aboriginal men and women, not only in auxiliary labour units in northern Australia (see chapter 8), but also in a range of industries elsewhere in Australia, including munitions manufacturing and agriculture. The American military presence in Australia was an important influence, especially given interactions between Aboriginal people and African-American soldiers. In many Indigenous communities, there was a subtle relationship between wartime patriotism and political activism. When the war ended, Aboriginal and Torres Strait Islander people were faced with challenges relating to the mental health of soldiers, the removal of veterans' children, and the operation of soldier settlement schemes. Together these form a rich and diverse range of Aboriginal and Torres Strait Islander home front experiences.

Evacuations from northern Australia

Following the Japanese attack on South-East Asia in early 1942, the home front became a war front across Australia's top end. In 1942–43 Japanese forces conducted at least 97 air raids across northern Australia. The most destructive was the first, the bombing of Darwin on 19 February 1942. In the preceding two months, all white women and children had been evacuated from Darwin to southern states, but Aboriginal people experienced these evacuations somewhat differently. As Regina Ganter has noted, 'there was much procrastination on safeguarding Aborigines in the north'.[1] Only mixed-race children from missions, and some from towns, were evacuated to South Australia and New South Wales. Meanwhile, the Australian Army relocated many Aboriginal people from coastal areas, especially around Darwin, to supervised inland camps. The motives for this move were mixed; concern for the safety of Aboriginal people was certainly evident, but anxieties that Aboriginal people would collaborate with the Japanese also played a role (see pp. 156–58). However, not all Aboriginal people left Darwin. William Jack Scully from Adelaide River enlisted on 28 February 1942 and served in the 29th Australian Employment Company. He was killed in action at Winnellie during an air raid on 20 June 1943.[2]

Among those Aboriginal people most affected by wartime evacuations were so-called 'half-caste' children at missions in the top end. On the eve of the war, the Commonwealth government had introduced a new policy to remove 'half-caste' children from the Bungalow in Alice Springs (an official institution originally established in 1915) and the Kahlin compound in Darwin (a reserve created in 1913), to remote missions.[3] One of the children affected by this policy was Claire Henty, who was taken from her Aboriginal mother to the Bungalow when she was about four years old. In 1941 she was among 95 children who undertook the long journey north to establish a Methodist mission on Croker Island in the Arafura Sea, arriving in November 1941. Henty later recalled: 'We'd hardly settled on the island when news of the Japanese attack on Pearl Harbor shocked the world.'[4]

The evacuation of Croker Island, 200 kilometres north-east of Darwin, was inescapable, owing to safety concerns and the difficulties of supplying the mission.[5] But it was not until 13 February 1942 that the wives and children of Methodist missionaries were ordered to leave the various missions in the north. Aboriginal children were to be evacuated later, a policy which enraged some of the white staff at Croker Island, who refused to leave. All the children were still on the island when Darwin was bombed. The mission staff knew it would be some time before boats would be available for evacuation; and so, as Henty recalls, 'the staff unpacked and we resumed school again'. The children and staff constructed a large cross from white-painted stones, to signify to planes flying overhead that Croker Island was a mission station, a project which increased the children's anxiety until they were finally evacuated on 8 April.[6]

The destinations to which Aboriginal people were evacuated from northern Australia were various. The Croker Island children were eventually housed at a Methodist complex in Otford, near Sydney.[7] Evacuations tended to be in a southerly direction, but as many as 350 Aboriginal people from Broome were evacuated further north to the Beagle Bay mission on the Dampier peninsula.

Furthermore, the Commissioner of Native Affairs rejected plans to evacuate the mission children south to Geraldton, citing concerns about the spread of leprosy.[8] Many women, children and some men from the Northern Territory were accommodated at the Balaklava Aboriginal Welfare Institution, north of Adelaide. William Scully's nephew, Boyd Scully, was six when he arrived there from Darwin; he later recalled that he found it cold and that all the Darwin people suffered diarrhoea.[9] Four-year-old Gordon Briscoe and his mother were evacuated from Alice Springs to Sydney in 1942, but they spent time at Balaklava in 1945. In his autobiography, Briscoe recalled it was 'a compound governed by the military ... surrounded by a four metre high fence patrolled by soldiers with rifles'.[10]

Not all Aboriginal people were evacuated to church- or government-run institutions. In 1942 Jane Christophersen travelled with her aunt from Darwin to Adelaide, where they were asked if they had relatives with whom they might stay. Her aunt's mother-in-law lived in Merbein, a small country town near Mildura in Victoria. Jane lived there for 18 months, and worked picking grapes, beans and asparagus. She later recalled encountering racism that she had not experienced in Darwin, with people avoiding her in the street, and a butcher refusing to serve her quality meats, only the 'flanks and shanks'.[11]

In some instances, when white mission staff were evacuated to southern Australia, Aboriginal people were left to a life of greater freedom and given a chance to revive cultural practices and connection with country. At the Forrest River Mission in Western Australia in 1942, nine-year-old Connie Nungulla McDonald took on the role of teacher's aide under an older Indigenous girl. In a memoir she later recalled being told by her tribal elders: 'You learnim all them wongalongs (children).'[12] She also learnt more about Oombulgurri practices, as the girls and boys were allowed the 'special privilege' of leaving the dormitories and visiting their people: 'we were taken on walkabouts where we were told about tribal law'.[13] Elsie Roughsey (Labumore) has recalled a similar experience at the Mornington Island mission off northern Queensland, when between 1942 and 1944 the missionaries 'left us by ourselves to face the enemies on our own'. Leaving the dormitories and returning to life with her parents was challenging at first: 'it was hard to start all over again, to get around and start learning to hunt for land and sea food'.[14]

Some Aboriginal people were not evacuated, but rather interned as enemy aliens, including several women in Broome who came under suspicion due to their Japanese husbands. Lydia Kanagae – 'a full-blooded Aboriginal native 47 years old' – had been married for 25 years when she was interned with her husband; his request that she be released so she could manage their shop was denied.[15] Elsewhere, families were broken up by internment policies; George Derschow, who was born in 1935, has recalled that his German-born father, Frank, who arrived in Australia in 1901 and was subsequently naturalised, was nonetheless interned during the Second World War (as he was in the First World War), leaving his Aboriginal mother, Ivy Swan, unable to support George and his many siblings.[16] On Thursday Island, many Japanese men with Torres Strait Islander wives were interned, and if their families were not also interned, they were subject to close surveillance.[17]

Living in a war zone

Aboriginal people who remained in northern Australia experienced the danger, and sometimes the tragedy, of living in a war zone. The Kalumburu (Drysdale River) Mission was established by Benedictines near the northern-most tip of Western Australia in 1931. In March 1940 the Australian government commissioned an airfield nearby, which was built quickly and cheaply by Aboriginal labourers, including women, and became an important RAAF refuelling and ammunition depot. With the outbreak of the Pacific War, Japanese reconnaissance planes became a frequent sight high above the mission.[18] In the diary of one of the missionaries, Father Eugene Perez, 27 September 1943 is described as 'a day of blood and mourning'. A reconnaissance plane passed overhead unnoticed at 9 a.m., followed half an hour later by sirens and the roar of approaching engines: 'Within a minute we were subjected to the deafening noise of the machine guns and cannons with shining bombs falling over the mission.'[19] Perez was conducting agricultural work with most of the mission residents, and when he returned to the mission he found destruction and desolation:

> The convent, garage and workshops were in flames. Pieces of bombs were everywhere. There was a fire in the monastery also, and I found a huge crater in the trench near the fowl yard. Looking into it I saw, at the bottom, Father Thomas [Gill] half buried. Digging with my hands I touched the head of little Dominic, next to Father and nearby the face of Veronica.[20]

Gill was the mission superintendent and his death was described by Western Australia's Native Commissioner, Francis Bray, as 'the supreme and most lamentable part of the attack'. According to the commissioner, Gill 'was valiantly protective to his charges in the last moments of his righteous life ... [when] a direct hit by a bomb killed him instantly together with a native woman and four children'.[21] While the commissioner did not think it necessary to name the Aboriginal victims in his annual report, they were certainly mourned by the missionaries, who buried them with Father Thomas in a common grave. Seventy years later the Kalumburu community unveiled a plaque which named all victims, including an Aboriginal mother, Veronica Cheinmora, and four children, Sylvester, Dominic, Benedict and Jeremy.

Like Kalumburu, the Methodist Overseas Mission's establishment on Milingimbi Island was the site of an RAAF refuelling base, with an airstrip built by Aboriginal mission residents between 1939 and 1942. Japanese aircraft attacked the mission and airstrip three times in 1943, resulting in the destruction of the church, the death of two Yolngu people, and injuries to three others.[22] The wreckage of RAAF planes hit during one raid have remained a feature of the Milingimbi landscape. In 2016 Ganygulpa Dhurrkay recalled playing on a rusty plane as a child: 'We used to sit and pretend we were passengers'.[23] Annie Lange, née Blitner, also remembers growing up in a landscape marked by the war. She recalls the stories of her father Gerry Blitner, who worked for the Air Force on Groote Island, and who later showed his children the sites of the old mission, the airstrip built by hand, the humpy he built to live in, and the bombs he defused.[24]

Torres Strait Islander people also lived their lives in a war zone. Most able-bodied men joined the Torres Strait Light Infantry Battalion, which was stationed on Thursday Island (see pp. 144–45). This meant that women and children were left vulnerable and isolated around the Torres Strait. The women on Thursday Island were evacuated to the mainland, where they were shocked by the racial prejudice they encountered, notably at the Cherbourg (formerly Barambah) Aboriginal Settlement in southern Queensland.[25] But communities elsewhere in the Torres Strait, including 3675 Islanders living on the 'outer islands', were not evacuated. The danger of their becoming a labour force in the event of a Japanese invasion concerned military personnel, but Queensland's Director of Native Affairs instructed that the Islanders should remain where they were.[26] Women on Yam Island lived off their gardens and fishing catch, as store boats rarely visited. They hid in caves when Japanese planes flew over. The dangers of the war were highlighted when a flaming Japanese plane crashed into the sea; when a woman spotted a Japanese submarine while fishing; and when a Japanese plane fired its machine guns at people on the beach.[27] Sorbie Ware lived at St Pauls on Moa Island and her daughter Rosie recalled reading that when sirens sounded for an air raid, everyone ran into the bush, where there were trenches.[28] As Rosie explained in 2014: 'The women were just vulnerable', because the men were elsewhere, 'defending Australia'.[29]

In northern Australia, Aboriginal children quickly learnt the dangers of enemy aircraft. In 2002 Doris Pilkington Garimara recalled learning from her aunts the dangers of aeroplanes and how 'the pilot or "Japani man" would shoot down at them'. On one occasion, when a plane flew overhead at Jigalong, Western Australia, Doris determinedly escorted her blind grandmother to shelter under 'thick acacia bushes and the tall wintamarra trees'.[30] In southern Australia, however, children were more likely to be sheltered from news of the war. Furley Gardner, who grew up on Cape Barren Island, later recalled:

> I think there were only about three families who had a wireless. It used to be that the menfolk would go and listen to the news and they would never come home and talk about it … They would run us outside: 'It's not for you to hear.'[31]

While most Aboriginal communities did not live with a day-to-day threat of attack, their lives were shaped in various ways by war conditions. In Alice Springs, for example, the white population increased from 400 to 6000 during the war, outnumbering Aboriginal people for the first time. In this context, as Anna Haebich explains, the 'enforced interdependence of a small frontier population' gave way to a social system based more on racial distinctions and segregation.[32] The war also resulted in the construction of an all-weather road between Alice Springs and Darwin, linking previously remote communities to the wider world. Buludja, a

Mangarrayi woman who lived at Elsey Station on the Roper River south of Katherine, observed in the late 1940s:

> All the time during the war we had lots of visitors. They came nearly every day, often slept at the homestead, and usually came to see our camp ... Our hardest work ... was to get enough things to sell the visitors.[33]

After the war the demand for better roads continued as remote pastoralists purchased cheap surplus trucks of American origin as an alternative to camels and donkeys. The anthropologist Frederick Rose later observed that these improvements in transport ended the isolation of Aboriginal communities in the remote south-west of the Northern Territory.[34]

Employment opportunities

Aboriginal and Torres Strait Islander people were employed in a wide range of industries during the Second World War, and their contribution to the wartime economy is often undervalued. In Queensland, for example, the state government actively recruited Aboriginal people to meet a labour shortage in agricultural industries, especially around harvest time. In 1942, for example, 100 men from Cherbourg travelled to Kingaroy for the peanut harvest, 120 'Palm Island boys' were sent to Ingham to work as cane cutters, 100 boys from Woorabinda travelled to Biloela to pick cotton, and 140 boys were recruited from Palm Island, Woorabinda and Yarrabah, to work for the Maize Board at Atherton. The Minister for Health and Home Affairs, Ned Hanlon, insisted that these Aboriginal labourers were motivated not only by financial gain but, given barriers to military service, their desire to contribute to the war effort: 'They cannot enlist in the armed forces, and they want to do their bit.'[35]

In Western Australia, Aboriginal people were similarly crucial as a source of labour in rural industries, but under conditions which the Commissioner of Native Affairs freely admitted amounted to a form of forced labour. In 1943, following complaints from farmers and pastoralists that Aboriginal people had been attracted elsewhere by better-paid employment, the Department of Native Affairs ordered Aboriginal people to remain in rural or pastoral work, and rejected permits for work in other industries unless they were war related.[36]

At Lake Tyers in Victoria, several men were granted permission to take jobs in Melbourne as labourers in glass and munitions manufacturing.[37] At Cummeragunja in southern New South Wales men worked in nearby charcoal burning businesses, including Alf Turner, who later recalled 'it was dirty work, but I enjoyed it'.[38] From the Koonibba Mission in South Australia Aboriginal people found work at the port near Ceduna, where the labour shortage ensured that their presence in a camp near town was tolerated.[39] In 1943 the Aborigines Protection Board in South Australia reported that Aboriginal people were engaged in work directly related to the war effort, such as munitions manufacture, but also worked 'on farms and orchards, in flax mills, and as domestics in hospitals and other institutions'. Some remote pastoral stations were staffed entirely by Aboriginal people.[40]

Employment of Aboriginal women

The Second World War resulted in a marked increase in workplace participation by Australian women, and Aboriginal women were no exception. In South Australia, Aboriginal women took on paid employment 'in dairies, vineyards, flax mills, and factories'.[41] In Queensland, 50 women from Cherbourg 'dug the greater part of the Murgon district potato crop' in 1943 and 1944.[42] Connie

Alberts from Lake Condah in Victoria found work at a munitions factory in Footscray, operating a machine cutting copper cases for bullets: 'Oh, I must have cut millions of them.'[43] She was joined there by several other Aboriginal women, including Marge Tucker, who later recalled: 'I shuddered at the bullets we were making, but I enjoyed working the machines.'[44] Gladys Elphick (whose son Tim Hughes was awarded a Military Medal in 1942) worked in munitions manufacture at the South Australian Railways' Islington workshops, where she won an award for a shop-floor invention.[45]

Many of these women were part of a significant migration of Aboriginal people to cities, where they found greater opportunities for work, but also greater freedom from discriminatory legislation. In Western Australia, Dot Collard and two of her sisters found work in Fremantle as domestic servants, where they got a taste of city life: 'We were far away from our camp days of going hungry, … [and] even though we were only maids in the families we were working for, they were our good friends and treated us as members of the family.'[46]

Aboriginal women also worked alongside white women in the Australian Women's Land Army (AWLA), which was created to address labour shortages in the farming sector. In June 1940 Brisbane's *Telegraph* described a group of women preparing for service in the AWLA: 'One of the most enthusiastic trainees to day was a tall aboriginal girl whose parents have a banana farm at Ingham: her dark face was glowing with enthusiasm in the service of her native Australia'.[47] It is unclear how many Aboriginal women joined the AWLA, but Jan (Kabarli) James records at least three Aboriginal members in Western Australia: Gloria Headland, Elizabeth Prosser and Rose Prior.[48] Martha Alley from Charters Towers, Queensland, also joined, as did Faith Bandler (née Mussing), who was of South Sea Islander descent, but a leading activist on Aboriginal issues.[49] Elvie Hutchison left her work as a domestic servant in Brisbane to join the AWLA in her forties; she enjoyed the experience and recalls encountering two other Aboriginal girls, including her friend Mavis Ford.[50] Historian Sue Hardisty also notes that several white AWLA members recalled instances of working alongside Aboriginal women who were outside the structure of the AWLA. One member remembered picking cherries near Young in New South Wales: 'Over the fence, across the next farm, of a morning, there'd be a large truck of Aboriginal people, women and children and some men.'[51]

Aboriginal women also found employment with the US Army, notably in Queensland. As a child Mabel Edmund helped her mother wash and iron clothes for American troops stationed near Rockhampton: 'We had no electricity, nor washing machine, she washed by hand and used two copper boilers. … I used to iron the dozens and dozens of handkerchiefs and big cotton underpants.'[52] For teenager Gladys Saunders, the Americans gave her the chance to serve when the Australian authorities would not. In 1943 she forged her birth certificate and identity papers and attempted to join the Women's Auxiliary Air Force in Townsville. When her deception was recognised, she went instead to a nearby recruiting centre for the United States Army and subsequently worked as a driver through the Women's National Emergency Legion. After the war she married Len Waters, the first Aboriginal fighter pilot.[53]

Aboriginal Australians and African-American GIs

The presence of American military personnel in Australia during the Second World War has long been recognised as an important aspect of the home front experience, with significant social and cultural impacts.[54] Approximately eight per cent of US servicemen stationed in Australia were African-American and stories of their interactions with Aboriginal people are common. According to Alice Nannup, soldiers attended dances and card games hosted by the Aboriginal community in Geraldton, Western Australia: 'it was only the black Americans that used to come because the white soldiers and airmen wouldn't mix with us'.[55] In Melbourne, African-American soldiers gravitated towards the growing Aboriginal community living in and around Fitzroy.[56]

Strong relationships between Aboriginal Australians and visiting African-Americans were sometimes built upon shared experiences of racial discrimination. David Potts and Annette Potts record instances of Aboriginal people physically defending African-American GIs if they were subject to racist taunts.[57] Similarly, African-American servicemen in Western Australia were often indignant at the racist treatment of their Aboriginal girlfriends, who had to 'run the gauntlet of the Pass System' to see them; as the Aboriginal writer Steve Kinnane has observed, their disbelief and the stand they sometimes took 'left a mark on the minds of those in the community who had long term visions of equality'.[58] Decades later the Aboriginal activist Len Watson wrote about the self-confidence derived from seeing African-American people 'with money in their hands; blacks who were confident and who stood up straight and looked you in the eye; blacks who were mechanics, bulldozer operators, truck drivers'.[59]

The presence of African-American soldiers caused considerable anxiety among white male officials regarding Aboriginal women's sexuality. In 1944 the Western Australian Commissioner of Native Affairs, Francis Bray, reported that due to concern regarding 'female misbehaviour during the presence of Allied coloured servicemen' his department had removed Aboriginal women and girls from Perth and Fremantle to settlements outside the city. He noted that girls regularly absconded from these settlements, and expressed regret that it was not possible to punish the servicemen, 'whose money resources seemed unlimited'.[60] The following year he reported the conviction of a 43-year-old white woman 'for the despicable offence of procuring native girls for negro servicemen of the United States'.[61] Bray's interventions reflected his broader concern about relationships between Aboriginal women and soldiers of any race. In 1942 he had urged the Australian Army to restrict 'soldiers intercourse with natives' by issuing 'orders warning troops against prejudicial conduct with natives and native women'.[62]

The attempts of bureaucrats like Bray to regulate the social activities of Aboriginal women were undermined, however, by the broader racial dilemma of how to entertain African-American troops, especially as the authorities knew that black GIs were often not tolerated at white dances. In Queensland, as Kay Saunders has shown, American authorities allowed, and even promoted, social interaction between Aboriginal people and African-American soldiers, notably by creating separate clubs, which Aboriginal women were encouraged to frequent. Sexual surveillance was part of the motive here, authorities believing it was better to regulate segregated dances than have black GIs go to brothels in South Brisbane, where Aboriginal women were known to be employed by African-American clients.[63]

Despite encouraging social interaction in some contexts, white authorities, both Australian and American, attempted to prevent marriages involving Aboriginal women. In 1943 the US consulate in Brisbane resisted a marriage between an American soldier and an Aboriginal girl who had claimed to be of Greek and Swedish ancestry. The consulate subsequently stressed the need to ensure proposed Australian brides had 'no coloured blood in her veins'; while the Queensland Department of Native Affairs directed that unions of American GIs with Aboriginal women should be avoided except in 'particularly extenuating circumstances'.[64] The legacy of wartime relationships between African-American men and Aboriginal women is the subject of a current research project which explores the lives of children born of such relationships, including

Don Carter, who was born in Townsville in 1943. Although his parents were married, 'neither parent could travel to the home country of the other in order to form a family to raise young Don'.[65]

Patriotism or activism?

As in 1914–18, Indigenous Australians were often engaged in the voluntary war effort in 1939–45. Torres Strait Islander women, for example, provided comforts through the Red Cross to their men serving in the Torres Strait Light Infantry Battalion; in 1943, Queensland's Director of Native Affairs described this as 'an excellent example of what organised efforts in this direction can attain'.[66] Similarly, Aboriginal children at the Cabbage Tree Island Settlement in northern New South Wales made pyjamas from material supplied by the Lismore branch of the Country Women's Association (CWA). In August 1942, the *Northern Star* reported that the children had used the off-cuts to make 'a nicely worked cot quilt' which the CWA displayed at its knitting depot.[67] Aboriginal people also raised money through entertainment, a notable example being the Cummeragunja Choir, which held concerts in aid of the war effort or the local Echuca District Hospital.[68]

However, such displays of loyalty and commitment to the war occurred within a context of more vocal activism than had been the case in the First World War. The rise of Aboriginal activism in the interwar period (see chapter 6) had reached a peak on the eve of the Second World War, when a congress of Aboriginal people in Sydney marked a 'National Day of Mourning' on 26 January 1938. Yet, this rising tide was disrupted by the outbreak of hostilities, a break well illustrated by the history of the Cummeragunja reserve. In February 1939 over a hundred of the residents abandoned the station in protest at their treatment by the manager. The 'walk-off' was inspired by a visit to the station by Jack Patten, an organiser of the 1938

'Day of Mourning,' who sent a telegram to the New South Wales premier citing 'intimidation, starvation, [and] victimisation' as the root cause of the protest.[69] The strike attracted considerable interest, with various groups calling for a proper inquiry into conditions on the station; but the outbreak of war quickly pushed the issue off the pages of the local newspaper, and the agenda papers of the premier.[70] Patten was given a suspended sentence for inciting the walk-off, then enlisted for military service in December 1939; he was injured while serving in the Middle East, then joined the Civil Construction Corps in the Northern Territory.[71] Several men from Cummeragunja also enlisted, while women contributed extensively to the war effort, knitting socks, jumpers, scarves and balaclavas for the troops.[72]

The example of Cummeragunja shows that patriotism and support for the war effort could co-exist with strongly held views about Aboriginal people's right to better treatment by state authorities. This is well illustrated in the life of Marge Tucker, who was born at Cummeragunja in 1904 and raised at the Moonaculla Mission at Deniliquin. In 1917, Tucker was taken to the Cootamundra Girls' Home, against her mother's wishes, to be trained for domestic service. Her experiences prompted a lifelong commitment to Aboriginal activism. With William Cooper and others, she was involved in the formation of the Australian Aborigines League in the early 1930s, and she helped organise the 1938 'Day of Mourning'. Following the Cummeragunja walk-off, she raised money for food and blankets for the protesters. During the war, while working at the munitions factory in Footscray, she turned her talents in new directions, as Alick Jackomos and Derek Fowell have explained: 'She organised Aboriginal friends into concert parties which raised money for the Red Cross, gave concerts for servicemen in repatriation hospitals and entertained the troops.'[73] Wartime patriotism of this kind, like war service itself, highlighted the injustice of racist laws, and was a powerful argument in favour of citizenship rights for Aboriginal people in the post-war period.

Homecomings

In the aftermath of war, Indigenous veterans (like all returned soldiers) were susceptible to physical and mental illness and the impact of this on their families was considerable. Arthur George Jarrett from Mullumbimby, New South Wales, enlisted in January 1942 and served overseas in Papua and Borneo. His daughter Kathryn later recalled him being a nice man, but also a violent man who told disturbing stories about his war experiences: 'every scar had a story to tell that went for at least an hour'. Jarrett hated Americans because of the loss of friends in incidents of friendly fire, and 'he couldn't get past the war'.[74] June Rose from Newcastle recalls that when her uncles, Bill and Joe Clarke, returned from the war they struggled to reintegrate: 'it used to play on their mind a bit, and so they started drinking.' Joe died in a car accident, while Bill became alienated from the community due to his mental health issues: 'Sometimes I think he thought he was back in the army, because he'd be hiding behind a telegraph pole, or he made out he had a gun'. His wife and two children had to leave him and it was a very distressing experience for the whole Clarke family.[75] Marge Tucker's marriage was also a casualty of the war. She later recalled:

> The young men who went away, those that came home again, all needed such love and care, only to find wives who didn't know how to respond to their many needs and moods. Many drifted apart like we did.[76]

Aboriginal families were also broken up by government officials during the war, and some Aboriginal veterans returned to discover their children had been removed to institutions. These included men from the Kickett family in Western Australia, whose children had been placed in the Carrolup Native Settlement. In response, they 'marched into the Superintendent's office in full army uniform and carrying their army issue rifles and demanded the return of their children at gunpoint'.[77] But not all Aboriginal soldiers were able to retrieve their children. Cecil Bowden, who was born at Erambie Mission, near Cowra, recalled in 2014 that he and his ten siblings were removed to various institutions during the war after their mother died. Cecil was one of the younger children and was sent first to Bomaderry Aboriginal Children's Home and then to Kinchela Boys Home. Bowden recalled that 'in the homes, they constantly told us we had no parents'. He also grew up thinking he had only one brother and one sister. It was only as an adult that he learnt that his father, Cecil Coe, was a veteran of the First World War and had attempted to collect his children from the homes after their mother's death, but had been told never to come back. Decades later, Bowden remained angry at his treatment by the New South Wales government, and contrasted his father's war service with his own membership of the Stolen Generations.[78]

Soldier settlement

After the Second World War, land settlement schemes in various states once again saw returned soldiers placed on rural properties, but rarely did Aboriginal veterans benefit. An exception was the Military Medal winner Tim Hughes, who became a soldier-settler in 1953 when he leased a 987-acre (400-hectare) block at Conmurra, South Australia. He ran a dairy herd, before switching to sheep and training as a woolclasser. He was moderately successful over a 22-year stay at the property.[79] In contrast, Jack Quayle from Wilcannia, who had served in Papua and New Guinea, was the recipient of marginal land under the New South Wales scheme; his son Gerald later recalled: 'They gave my father five acres [2 hectares] of nothing. They gave him five acres on a flood plain. You can't grow nothing on it, you can't even build a house on it.'[80]

Jack Coyne from Western Australia enlisted in 1942 and served in New Guinea, but was unable to take advantage of land settlement schemes like other soldiers from his district. His uncle Syd worked for the Land Army, also supervising Italian-Australian internees on farms in the south of the state. After the war Jack Coyne and his brothers Noel, Dave, Fred and Clarry were involved in land clearing: Lester Coyne, remembers hearing his father and his uncles talking about this work, and wondering why they had not received an allocation of land themselves; the conversations were not heated, but curious.[81] Aden Eades and Eliza Woods have similar recollections of their father, Frederick Eades, who worked on a cargo ship and building airstrips in the Pilbara before enlisting in 1942 and serving in Borneo. After the war he did paid work for friends from his battalion on their farms, which was difficult for him as he did not own land himself.[82]

In Victoria, moves to carve up the Lake Condah mission for soldier settlement, which had been proposed during the First World War, finally came to fruition, despite opposition from the Portland Shire Council. In July 1944 the local press reported that one councillor had argued 'there was no shortage of land for this purpose', while another described the neglect of Aboriginal people at Condah as a disgrace.[83] The matter was raised again at a council meeting in 1949, but by this time the reserve had been subdivided and applications sought.[84] Despite making applications, no Gunditjmara war veterans received soldier settlement blocks.[85] John Lovett recalls that his father, Herb Lovett, who had served in both world wars, applied for a block at Lake Condah: 'He didn't receive a reply, he didn't get a block of land, and he was back to being black.'[86]

Aboriginal and Torres Strait Islander people's experiences of the home front during the Second World War were highly diverse. For some there was greater freedom or opportunity, while for others there was increased surveillance or government interference in their lives. Experiences also differed according to location. Indigenous people in northern Australia were subject to the threat of invasion, to bombings and evacuations; the war also focused the attention of military and government authorities on previously remote regions, resulting in rapid development and social transformation. Life on the home front in southern Australia was different in character, but the war still had a profound effect, notably in terms of employment opportunities. Indigenous people's contributions to the war effort, at home and abroad, also bolstered the growing calls for Aboriginal citizenship rights, and inspired a new generation of activists.

10

Opening the military door, 1945–65

Noah Riseman

'No trouble. Made a lot of good mates. No trouble.
We was young, you muck around …
yeah, good life, Army life.'
– *Len Ogilvie*

The Second World War offered new opportunities for many Aboriginal and Torres Strait Islander Australians, but the coming of peace represented a return to the status quo of inequality. Assimilation policies became standard practice across all states and territories. Child removal continued and even accelerated, as state Aboriginal welfare boards (renamed from their earlier incarnations as Protection Boards) adopted policies reflecting the resolution of the 1951 Native Welfare Meeting of Commonwealth and State Ministers: 'Assimilation means, in practical terms that, in the course of time, it is expected that all persons of aboriginal blood or mixed blood in Australia will live like other white Australians do.'[1] It would not be until the 1960s that the country witnessed the beginning of significant changes for Indigenous rights.

However, the two decades after the Second World War did

witness gradual changes in policies governing the military service of Aboriginal and Torres Strait Islander Australians. Initially, as the active hostilities ended, their role in a changing defence force was uncertain. Very quickly the end of the war saw the re-imposition of rules barring persons 'not substantially of European origin or descent'. Yet by 1948, under significant pressure from the RSL and public figures like the Aboriginal Lieutenant Reginald Saunders, the Army, and then later the Navy and Air Force, updated their regulations to permit Indigenous enlistment on a case-by-case basis. Consequently, there was a small number of Aboriginal and Torres Strait Islander men who served in the Malayan Emergency (1950–60) and the Korean War (1950–53).

One of the main drivers of change was the introduction of national service in 1951 and its reintroduction in 1964. The *National Service Act* explicitly did not require Aboriginal people to register, yet the accompanying regulations and debates over the complex meanings of Aboriginality left many men still liable. For those Aboriginal and Torres Strait Islander men and women navigating these complex policies, one thing was constant: once in the armed forces, the sense of equality that their forebears generally experienced in the two world wars continued. This chapter examines all of these themes through the lens of change and continuity: how changing Defence regulations gradually aligned their policies with the lived experience of interracial equality within the forces.

Service in the British Commonwealth Occupation Force

After Japan's formal surrender on 2 September 1945 the Allied forces, under American leadership, made plans for the country's occupation. Australia agreed to contribute to the multinational British Commonwealth Occupation Force (BCOF), which operated from

1946 until 1952. About 16000 Australians, the majority of them from the Army, were among the 45000 BCOF members drawn from across the British Commonwealth.[2] Only a small number of Aboriginal men were among these ranks, their numbers limited primarily because the Labor government of Ben Chifley (1945–49) was determined to reimpose the colour bar that had been relaxed during wartime hostilities. Frank Forde, the Minister for the Army, decreed: 'Aboriginal members of the Australian Military Forces gave splendid service during the war, but most of them cannot conform to the standard laid down for the Japan force.'[3] Consequently, only those Aboriginal men who were already in Japan as a result of serving in the 2nd AIF, or those few who again slipped through the colour net, served in BCOF.

Only snippets of information about these Aboriginal and Torres Strait Islander men are available. Among these Aboriginal soldiers was Donald Edward Waters, known as Jimmy, brother of the first Aboriginal RAAF pilot, Len Waters. Jimmy enlisted in Warwick, Queensland, at the same time as Len, and served with BCOF for 18 months. Len once reported that Jimmy 'had a ball' in Japan, but according to Len's widow, Gladys, he returned traumatised from his overall war experience. Gladys also recalled in 2014 that Jimmy was not paid for part of his Second World War and BCOF service. When his wife, Ruby, found out years later, she sued the government and was awarded back-pay for Jimmy's service.[4] Photographs in the Australian War Memorial reinforce Len Waters' observations about Jimmy's and other Aboriginal men's positive experience of serving in Japan. They show Aboriginal men casually mixing with their mates and even participating in inter-service athletics competitions. An Army Public Relations short film in the late 1940s entitled 'BCOF on Parade' showed an Aboriginal soldier participating in Bren gun training and practice.[5]

One of the few recorded Aboriginal oral histories about BCOF comes from Kenneth Colbung, who reflected when being interviewed by the ABC in 2004:

> And then I saw that what had happened to the civilian population there and how they would cower down. I could really reflect ... how those people were feeling. It wasn't the civilian population, it was the military that moved in and caused all the atrocities that were around. And, of course, the civilians had to take the brunt of it.[6]

Another member of BCOF, Torres Strait Islander Charles Mene, did not recall any problems signing up for BCOF. Mene said he wanted to see Japan because:

> [We'd] been fighting them, and I thought I'd better go up and see what the place is like ... We used to go up to Tokyo to do the guards around the area. That was our duty. And then after a time, we would come back again to the Battalion area.[7]

Changing attitudes within Australia

While only a small number of Aboriginal and Torres Strait Islander men served in Japan, the military's reimposed colour bar was facing a challenge in Australia. Indigenous and non-Indigenous veterans alike wrote to newspapers in 1946 praising Indigenous efforts in the Second World War and calling for the armed forces to admit Aboriginal men. The most high-profile of Aboriginal ex-servicemen, Saunders, featured prominently in this campaign, even participating in rallies against the exclusion of Aboriginal men from BCOF.[8] In March 1946 he described the colour bar as 'a very narrow-minded and ignorant attitude taken by both the Army and Government officials'.[9] The RSL was generally silent at the Commonwealth level on the question of ongoing Defence regulations banning Indigenous service, but there were some local branches that challenged the ban.[10] In November 1951 the Victorian RSL even suggested an all-Aboriginal unit, commanded by Saunders, to lift Aboriginal people's national prestige.[11]

In 1947 the Army became a permanent regular force for the first time in Australian history. In response to public and RSL pressure the Army became the first service to reconsider its position and, at last, in 1948 lifted the colour bar that had formally been in place since the *Defence Act* of 1909. Order 177 removed the reference to recruits needing to be 'substantially of European origin or descent', theoretically opening the door to Aboriginal and Torres Strait Islander soldiers on a regular, rather than the hitherto exceptional, basis. Even so, Army officials were worried about the prospect of substantial Aboriginal enlistments for three prejudicial reasons:

1. 'Command: Given the ability, there would be no reason why an aborigine should not rise to NCO or WO rank and thus be in a position to command over white troops. This may not be desirable';
2. They would have access to liquor; and
3. Barracks would be integrated.[12]

Consequently, the Regular Army determined that they would allow Aboriginal (and presumably Torres Strait Islander) people to sign up on a case-by-case basis, after an interview and approval from the senior administrative officer of the Command of Military District.[13] The Navy and Air Force continued to exclude Indigenous enlistments until 1951, when amendments to the *Defence Act* repealed the earlier section which had exempted those 'not substantially of European origin or descent' from compulsory call-up in peacetime.[14]

These particular changes to the *Defence Act* were not related to Indigenous rights, but rather were tied to another defence reform: the re-introduction of national service. In 1951 the coalition government of Robert Menzies introduced the *National Service Act*, requiring Australian men aged 18 to partake in 176 days of military training. Since the government wanted national service to apply to immigrants, including non-Europeans, it needed to amend the *Defence Act* to repeal the clauses exempting persons of 'non-European origin or descent'.[15] Yet while these amendments, and the consequential Air Force and Navy policy reforms, ended the legal barriers to Indigenous enlistment, the *National Service Act* set up a new obstructive framework. Conscious that amending the *Defence Act* would open the door to Indigenous service, the Cabinet decided to exempt 'aboriginal natives' from compulsory national service under section 18 of the *National Service Act 1951*. This was a practical decision, as the racial discourse of the time principally considered 'real' Aboriginal people to be those of 'full blood' who were living in remote areas.[16]

Despite the exemption in the Act, an unknown number of Aboriginal and Torres Strait Islander men did serve, both during this first period of national service, from 1951 to 1959, and in its second incarnation, from 1964 to 1972. Some served because they were unaware of their exemption; some volunteered; and others who were of mixed descent sometimes did not fit within the *National Service Regulations*' definition of Aboriginality, which focused primarily on so-called 'full bloods'. Chapter 11 explains in more detail the problematic aspects of the *National Service Regulations*' definition of Aboriginality, particularly in relation to Aboriginal men of mixed descent.

Indigenous men called to register for national service included, for instance, Torres Strait Islander Eddie Koiki Mabo. When summoned, he told his local member of parliament that he did not want to serve. The member found out that Mabo was exempt and he 'never heard anything from them afterwards'.[17] Victorian Koorie man Noel Tovey, meanwhile, was excited when he received the letter summoning him for national service, as it represented an opportunity to reinvent his identity. He later said of the experience: 'No one laughed or called me a poof or Choc or Darkie ... the great thing about our group was that, even though we all came from totally different backgrounds, once in uniform we were all the same.'[18] He further stated that:

> [W]earing the uniform filled me with pride and self-esteem and that I was even considering joining the Air Force permanently. In six months, I thought that I had been well equipped for the rest of my life and that I was on the right track. I would never have to answer to anybody about colour, background or indeed anything again.[19]

Tovey's comments in 2004, relishing his military service for the equality it provided, echoed with those of earlier generations of Aboriginal servicemen.

Malayan Emergency and Korean War

As the global order changed after the Second World War, Australia's geopolitical and military strategy, too, changed. With the coming of the Cold War and decolonisation in Asia, Australia's strategic planners progressively assumed that the United States would primarily maintain security in the Asia-Pacific.[20] Yet strategic links to the traditional ally, the United Kingdom (UK), continued. In 1950 Australia became involved in two conflicts that symbolised these dual fidelities.

The Malayan Emergency (1950–60) was a commitment in

support of the UK, the colonial power in Malaya. Australia contributed RAAF personnel and, later, ground troops to intermittent operations suppressing a Communist insurgency.[21] At least 15 Aboriginal men served in this conflict, two of whom were killed in action: Cecil Anderson and Cedric Charles Ingra. Anderson was shot by a hidden sniper at close range. Though mortally wounded, he still managed to return fire and cover his patrol until the enemy retreated. For his bravery under fire, Anderson was posthumously mentioned in despatches.[22] However, most of the men who served in Malaya had little, if any, confrontation with the enemy. Charles Mene recalled in 1995:

> I did lots of patrols but when I went we never come across any enemy. We were in the jungle, patrolling, yes, but we never come across any of the enemy. We were in the jungle for a fortnight sometimes, but we didn't come across the terrorists.[23]

The Malayan Emergency formally ended in 1960, though Australian troops continued to operate in the country until 1963. Australia still retains an RAAF base at Butterworth as part of the Five Power Defence Arrangements (UK, Australia, New Zealand, Malaysia and Singapore) signed in 1971.

The fighting in the Korean War (1950–53), in contrast, lasted only three years but entailed widespread destruction and fighting. In response to the North Korean invasion of South Korea in late June 1950, the United Nations (UN) Security Council passed a resolution authorising the use of force to repel the attack and restore peace and security to the area. The UN coalition, led by the United States, quickly incorporated Australian forces already in Japan: the RAAF, the Royal Australian Navy, and finally the 3RAR (3rd Battalion Royal Australian Regiment). The battalion was brought up to strength by raising K-Force, made up of volunteers who agreed to serve a three-year period in the Army, including a year in Korea. By 1953 over 17 000 Australians had served in the Korean War.[24] The Aboriginal and Torres Strait Islander membership of this force was small: at least 36 men have been identified by the Australian War Memorial. Among them were poet Cec Fisher, actor Stephen Dodd, Second World War and Malaya veteran Charles Mene, Eugene and Charles Lovett (continuing the family's long tradition of military service), Reg Saunders and activists Kenneth Brindle and Kenneth Colbung.

A few oral history interviews were recorded before most of these veterans passed away, and all speakers commented on the harsh environmental and fighting conditions in Korea. The country has great extremes of climate, with temperatures in the winter falling to minus 17 degrees Celsius in mountainous regions. When interviewed for ABC radio in 1998, Ned Egglestone recalled that the Australian Army's equipment had been run down and was not appropriate for the icy conditions in Korea. Like many other soldiers, he had never seen snow before; let alone was he prepared to fight in it. He remembered:

> It was rugged [pauses], very very cold, your rifle – sometimes you could put your hand on the butt, on the steel, so it would stick. And your feet, and your ears and that. Ohhh … and then your trench in the ground, that would get pretty snow bound.[25]

Pat Owen's 1991 recollections revolved around the intersections between the bleak climatic and fighting conditions:

> We were on the 38th Parallel near what we called the Valley of Death. Nobody could bury their dead. The valley separated us and the Chinese. If you were killed in a valley they had to leave your body there. Even at night they put flares up and you would

> get caught. There was thousands of bodies, all decomposing. The winter preserved them but in the summer, when the bodies were swollen and the wind was blowing our way, they were on the nose.[26]

Veterans' memories of combat contribute further to a picture of Korea as a traumatising experience. Len Ogilvie was a machine-gun carrier who was injured and nearly died in an ambush on 5 November 1950. He recalled when speaking to this author in 2015:

> They didn't give us that final order to move. I got out the trench to look where my mates were and they were gone. I was wounded and my mate was killed. I was behind enemy lines all night until they pick me up the following morning, straight out of there.[27]

Ned Egglestone was part of the Battle of Kapyong on 22–25 April 1951, the most significant battle for Australian troops in Korea. He remembered that the Australians and Turks (serving in the Turkish Brigade) had to cancel their planned Anzac Day celebrations.[28] Pat Owen meanwhile said of Korea: 'I've never known anything like the war, being a young bloke you don't really know what you're in for. We were lucky we had veterans from the Second World War, so we had good instructors.'[29] Kenneth Colbung also recalled the psychological challenges and war trauma more than 50 years later:

> I saw some pretty heavy duty fighting, but as a soldier you don't talk about it, you just get drunk. In a time of war you survive by putting the bad things to one side and trying not to think about them. That's why alcohol becomes important.[30]

Besides the hard fighting and conditions, the other prominent memory among Aboriginal veterans was their interactions with the

Korean people and the tragic circumstances in which these people found themselves. As Colbung remembered it, the soldiers had to flatten mud huts as they advanced across Korea, but as they proceeded, people were scattered and crops were left unattended. Notwithstanding the danger, civilians would come behind the soldiers on the front lines to pick up brass shells to sell. Colbung also witnessed extreme poverty in Korea, including a camp of 5000 displaced children under the Salvation Army's care; they were barely coping with their limited resources. Even 46 years after the war, Colbung could distinctly remember the smell of rotting, burning flesh.[31] Children also featured in some of the stories about Korea that Reg Saunders told his family. His daughter Glenda Humes recounted in 2014 an incident in which her father and his men came across an empty house with a crying baby on the floor, covered in rags. As the commanding officer, Saunders was responsible for figuring out how to look after the baby, an awkward situation until he could find someone suitable. Saunders also told a story about seeing a little girl who reminded him of Glenda. The girl was fleeing artillery which Saunders' company was firing on her village; as Glenda told it:

> He said, 'I was watching her run with the binoculars, and I was saying, "You got to make this, make it." And she didn't.' And I think it was those types of things that really affected Dad much more than the Second World War did because there were children involved. And he was always really special around children, and it certainly changed him so that when he came back, my mother and their relationship wasn't able to withstand that trauma of Korea, I think. And for a lot of people, for those veterans, it was a different experience. They didn't talk about the trouble that they had sleeping and the nightmares.[32]

The trauma and silences that Humes described partly contributed to Korea's popular status as 'The Forgotten War'. Its short duration, the smaller commitment of Australian troops, the war's stalemate ending and its positioning between the Second World War and the Vietnam War have all perpetuated the conflict's lesser status in public memory. So, too, has its status as a UN-sanctioned intervention, dubbed a 'police action' in the United States. Egglestone believed there was little public interest when the soldiers returned (though histories show that there were indeed welcome home parades). Egglestone maintained that the RSL was not interested at all in veterans of the war in Korea, which was one reason so many joined the Korean Veterans Association of Australia.[33] Saunders was involved with the association's activities, as was his daughter. Some of Saunders' words are even inscribed on a specially dedicated wall of the North Bondi War Memorial and a plaque in the Australian War Memorial commemorating the battle of Kapyong, Korea: 'At last I felt like an ANZAC and I imagine there were 600 others like me.'

It is not surprising that Saunders' words are part of the Korean War memorial, as men who served under him remembered him as a commander who cared about their wellbeing. Humes said in 2014, 'It was really great to be able to meet people who served with Dad – it was always how proud they were to serve with him.'[34] The respect Saunders commanded within the forces was echoed by the RSL, who led an unsuccessful push in 1953 to send Saunders to London as part of Australia's official contingent to the coronation of Queen Elizabeth II. The Victorian RSL executive pointed to Māori representation in New Zealand's contingent, arguing 'that it is important to Australia that overseas countries should be given an assurance that the "natives" are represented'.[35] The proposition was a marker of Saunders' high standing within the Victorian veterans' community, as well as his public position as a 'successful' Aboriginal man. In the 1950s, the media and government departments also included Saunders among a pantheon of Aboriginal 'celebrities', such as Albert Namatjira and Harold Blair, who were being touted as models of assimilation.[36] Yet, despite his high profile and respect within the veterans' community, Saunders struggled to find steady employment in civilian life and still battled racism. Colbung similarly told stories of discrimination after Korea, even while he was still serving in the Army. He was at an Adelaide pub with some Army mates and the publican would not serve him. When he complained to a policeman, the response was: 'He's in his rights not to serve you. That's the law. He can serve all of you, except him.' Colbung and his mates went to another pub that would serve him, but only after they 'smashed the other place up a bit'.[37]

New opportunities

There is no indication in the archival record as to when Australian military authorities ended the practice of requiring Indigenous recruits to have interviews with senior military officers. However, it is clear that gradually, through the 1950s, joining the armed forces became an employment opportunity for Indigenous people.

Aboriginal and Torres Strait Islander women were part of this process, joining the newly constituted Women's Royal Australian Air Force (1950), Women's Royal Australian Naval Service (re-formed 1951), Women's Royal Australian Army Corps (1951) and the respective nursing corps. Many of these women seem to have enlisted as a means to escape domestic service or because the armed forces provided steady employment not available in civilian life.[38] Mabel Quakawoot, for instance, was working as a domestic servant for a former RAAF pilot. She recalled in 2011:

> He was the one who gave me the incentive, and he said, 'You have enough brains to join the Air Force.' [I] thought it was quite funny. But it was really great because they believed in me, even though I didn't believe in what I was doing. And I put in an application to join and I had to have an aptitude test, and I passed my aptitude test, and so I was in the Air Force [1957–62].[39]

Although the thought of joining the Air Force had not originally occurred to Quakawoot, she actually came from a family with a tradition of military service; her sister later joined the women's services and her brother enlisted in the Army and served in Vietnam. Doris Follent joined the Army Nursing Corps in 1963, again as part of a family tradition; her father had served in the First World War and her brother was in the Navy.[40]

While the women's services provided a significant opportunity for Aboriginal and Torres Strait Islander women, their numbers were still small. Thelma Weston recalled in 2014:

> I think I was the only Black nurse in that time period [early to mid-1950s] in the Army Nursing Corps. And I don't know – people used to ask me where I was from all the time. I'd say, from the Torres Strait Islands, see a lot of people didn't know where the Torres Strait Islands were. And I think that they thought I was French.[41]

Yet, by the late 1960s, the women's services were gaining wider recognition as a possible career opportunity for Indigenous women. The New South Wales Aborigines Welfare Board monthly magazine *Dawn* even featured a two-thirds page advertisement about career opportunities in the women's services.[42] This was one of many *Dawn* features about the military. Indeed, throughout its publication history in the 1950s and 1960s, *Dawn* included stories about

Aboriginal men training in the services, receiving awards for their service, and preparing to go to war in Vietnam. Aboriginal servicemen twice featured on *Dawn*'s cover: in March 1955 it was a photo of Citizen Military Forces member, Cecil Donovan, while the February 1962 issue carried a picture of Private Keith Walsh, with his seven children, commanding officer and the Minister for the Army, all seeing him off to Malaya. *Dawn* even carried advertisements about job opportunities in the armed forces. As a publication specifically designed to promote assimilation to New South Wales' Aboriginal population, *Dawn* gave a prominence to the military and Aboriginal service across the magazine's history from 1952 to 1969, which suggests that the board saw military service as aligning with its assimilation agenda.

Many members of the Stolen Generations also joined the military in the 1950s and 1960s. These Aboriginal men and women who had been forcibly removed from their parents were often raised in institutions where they had only limited education and job opportunities. In 2015 Len Ogilvie speculated as to the motives of many Stolen Generations members who joined the armed forces: 'A better life. Where else can you get a job that's everything supplied? And your money, in your pocket, is your pocket money – you're saving … I didn't join the Army for King and Country, I can tell you that!'[43] Sue Gordon explained in 2015 that she and the men from Sister Kate's Home in Perth, who served in the military regularly, attend commemorative services together. They consider themselves as family and even wear the medals of the deceased. Gordon related that Korean War veteran, Andy Sanford, once said: 'We grew up as brothers and sisters, so we're entitled to wear them.'[44]

In other jurisdictions, signing up may have required the approval of the welfare board, or other guardians, if the Aboriginal person were still a ward of the state. David Cook, for instance, was a member of the Stolen Generations who had lived at the notorious Kinchela Boys Home before being fostered out. He joined the Australian Navy in 1962, but did not adjust well to the lifestyle. According to his oral history interview in 2010, there was a particular officer who did not like him because he was Aboriginal.[45] His welfare file, though, contains letters from the Navy addressed to the New South Wales Aborigines Welfare Board, indicating that he was having disciplinary problems.[46] Regardless of the real reason for his discharge, it is significant that the Navy was corresponding with the Aborigines Welfare Board about the problems their 'ward' was having. Cook left the Navy after a few months and then enlisted in the Army; on his application for enlistment, the guardian's signature is from the 'Supt of Aborigines Welfare Board, GPO Sydney'.[47] Cook fitted in well in the Army. Indeed, for many of the Stolen Generations men and women who joined the military, the discipline instilled in them at the institutions prepared them well.[48] The pattern of Stolen Generations survivors joining up would continue into the Vietnam era and beyond.

The Indonesian Confrontation

In the early 1960s Aboriginal and Torres Strait Islander servicemen were deployed overseas again, this time to Malaysia. Conflict arose with Indonesia in 1963 when the creation of the Federation of Malaysia (Malaya, Borneo, Sarawak and Singapore) was taken by Indonesia's President Sukarno to represent a British attempt to maintain its colonial rule in the region. At the request of both the British and Malaysian governments, Australia sent a battalion to Borneo in January 1965. Australian troops rotated through Borneo until the end of the so-called Confrontation in August 1966.

Geoff Shaw was one of the Aboriginal men who served in Borneo, and when interviewed in 2015 he vividly remembered the jungle and high treetops with orangutans.[49] Reuben Chadburn likewise recalled night-time jungle exercises: 'the tigers used to circle us of a night. You could hear them and smell them.' Troops would take anti-malaria tablets every day because 'the mosquitos would come in clouds'.[50] Dave Cook was a member of the Royal Australian Engineers, who were tasked with building a road for the British supply lines. His best memory of Borneo, recalled in 2010, was playing against the visiting British Lions Rugby League Team, which passed through on its way to tour Australia: 'It was a pretty close game because they couldn't handle the heat, coming from England. It was a friendly but it was pretty hard. So I played against the British Lions. That's one thing a lot of people can't say.'[51]

While Confrontation involved no large-scale battles, there were long patrols on both sides of the border between Borneo and Indonesia. Torres Strait Islander Mial Bingarape maintained later that his background and knowledge, hunting in the bush, prepared him well for such patrols, priming him to sense problems in the jungle.

> So there've been times, three or four times we've gone in and I've looked at the area. I was called forward by my forward scout, looked at the area and I could sense – oh what I – I look at it, ideal ambush site: 'I'm not going to put my boys through there.'… If I change direction and traverse, he [platoon commander] always says, 'There's got to be a reason for this. Bing wouldn't do that.'

However, patrols could result in contacts, and bring casualties. Bingarape also remembered when he lost a close mate, Vince Vella. Just before Vella went out on patrol, they had been talking about their families catching up in Australia after their tour. On the patrol, a scout suspected something and called Vella forward to check it out. When the forward scout stepped aside, he tripped a wire, blowing both himself and Vella to bits. This particular loss still weighed heavily on Bingarape in 2014.[52]

Bingarape's story is also of interest because, like many Torres Strait Islanders, he had Malay heritage. His biological and adopted fathers were both Indonesian, and his older siblings were raised in Indonesia. Bingarape did not even think about the potentially tragic implications of this familial connection until he received a letter from his older sister telling him that two of his brothers were in the Indonesian Army. He later said:

> It's a case of firing the first shot and hope for the best. Pray to God that you've done the right thing, you know. Oh [sighs], it was [long pause] [sighs] – it saddened me, really. Oh. I come to find out also [long pause] – yeah, they were on the other side patrolling. My elder brother was – he's two years ahead of me. He was a lieutenant in the Indonesian intelligence.

Another way that Bingarape's multicultural upbringing contributed to his Army work was his language skills: he could speak Kalau Lagau Ya, Torres Strait Creole and Malay. Often the patrol commander would send Bingarape to communicate with local village head men.[53]

The experiences in Malaysia were in many ways a prelude to the next major chapter in Australia's military history, Vietnam. Although the casualty and fatality figures were low (only 23 Australian deaths), there were many other commonalities: assisting a fledgling postcolonial nation's defence, long patrols in the jungle, humid and harsh environmental conditions, a hidden enemy, major cultural differences with the locals, separate facilities among coalition partners, and lots of downtime at the base characterised by excessive boozing and misbehaviour. By the mid-1960s, there were no longer debates over whether or not Aboriginal and Torres Strait

Islander people could volunteer for the military (though the matter of national service was another story). In fact, many of the Aboriginal and Torres Strait Islander men who served in Borneo and Malaysia would also be sent to Vietnam. Their stories continue in the next chapter.

6.1 Marcus Garvey, August 1924. Garvey's pan-African philosophy, which sought to bring about economic empowerment of the African diaspora, became known as 'Garveyism'.
Source: George Grantham Bain Collection, Library of Congress LC-USZ61-1854

6.2 Portrait of Douglas Grant with his replica of the Sydney Harbour Bridge in Callan Park, 1940. Grant designed the war memorial to honour his fallen comrades in the Great War.
Source: SLNSW a4447079

6.3 Son of prominent Aboriginal activist William Cooper,
Private Daniel Cooper was killed in action on 20 September 1917 in Belgium.
Source: AIATSIS JACKAMOS.A12.BW-N05339_21

7.1 *Above* Aboriginal recruits from the Lake Tyers region the day after their arrival at Caulfield Military Camp, Melbourne. They all enlisted on 27 June 1940 and served with the 2/23rd Battalion, only to be discharged in 1941.
Source: AWM P01066.001

7.2 *Right* Aboriginal digger in the 2nd AIF Victor Blanco asks a policewoman to direct him while on leave in London. In civilian life Blanco was a pearl diver from Thursday Island.
Source: AWM 002420

7.3 Lieutenant CV Matters, Company Commander of C Company, and Warrant Officer RH Crane, inspecting members of the Torres Strait Light Infantry Battalion, Thursday Island, 29 October 1945.

Source: AWM 119170

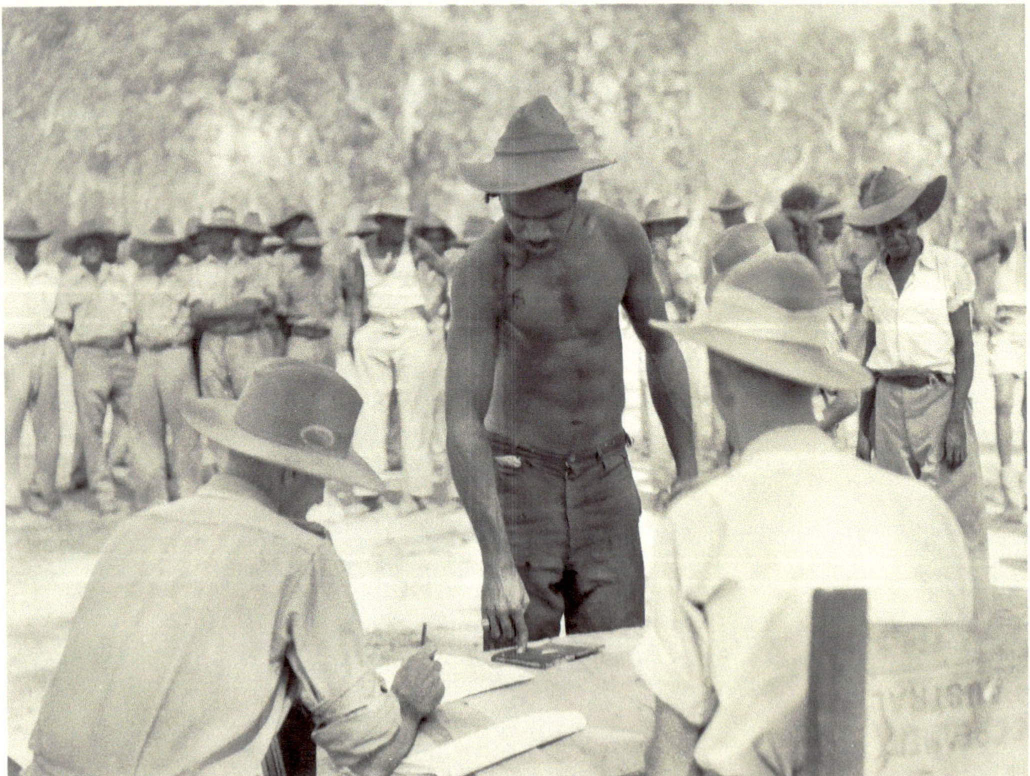

8.1 *Top left* To provide fresh meat to Allied soldiers, the Army established its own slaughter yards in the Northern Territory. Aboriginal labour was used to bring the cattle to the slaughter yards from widely spread areas. Stockmen (L–R) Bobby, Paddy and 12-year-old John Buckley were photographed in the north-west of Australia in February 1943, while driving cattle towards the slaughter yards.

Source: AWM 014291

8.2 *Below left* An Aboriginal employee in Katherine in the Northern Territory signing for his pay in September 1943. It was common practice in Army compounds for Aboriginal workers to sign for their wages with their fingerprints.

Source: AWM 057361

8.3 *Above* Members of the 69th Australian Women's Army Service, Adelaide River, Northern Territory, September 1944. Reported as the AWAS's 'No. 1 girl' in Adelaide River in the *West Australian* newspaper in 1944, Corporal Dolly is in the front row, second from the left.

Source: AWM 069186

9.1 Children from the Alice Springs area standing on a Spencer Street railway station platform in Melbourne on 3 June 1942. They were awaiting a train to take them to a Church Missionary Society evacuee camp in the Blue Mountains of New South Wales.

Source: AWM 136298

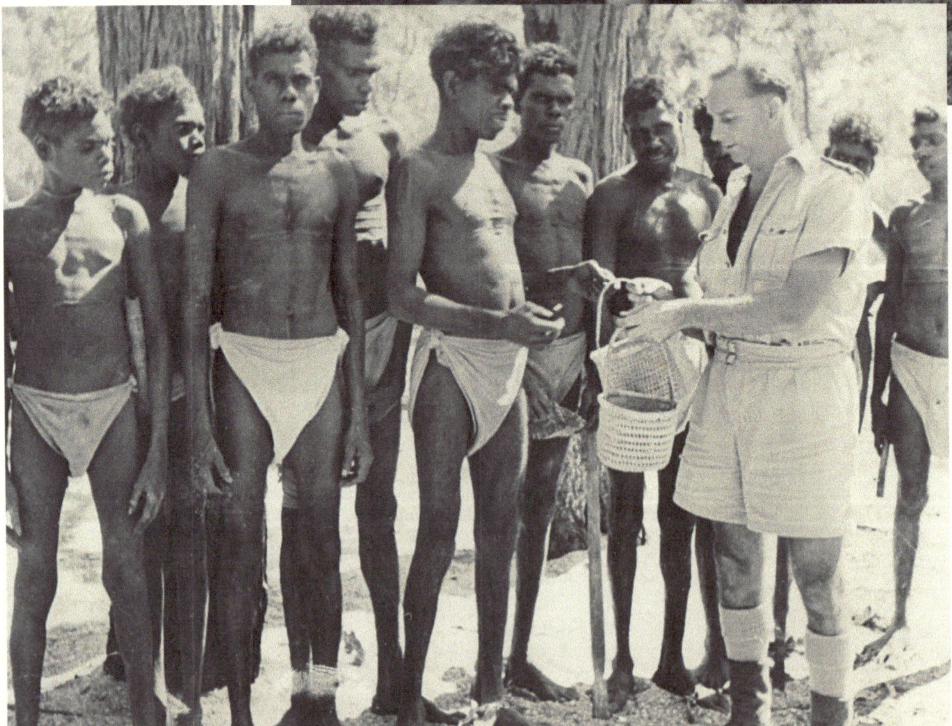

9.2 *Left* Flying Officer JC Reilly purchasing souvenirs near a north Western Australian outpost, September 1943. Reilly paid the Aboriginal man in tobacco.

Source: AWM 015667

9.3 *Above* Group portrait of Aboriginal women and girls knitting socks, jumpers and balaclavas for the war effort at Cummeragunja, NSW. Identified, left to right, back row: Merle Morgan, June Morgan, Weeny Charles, Amy Briggs, Valda McGee, Edna Walker, Sheila Charles, Joan Charles, Elsie Cooper, Midge Walsh, Florry Walker. Front row: Joyce Atkinson, Clare Charles, Alma Charles, Ada Cooper, Nelly Davis?, Elizabeth Morgan, Lauraine Charles, Greta Cooper, Violet Charles, Wynnie Walker, Hilda Walker, Georgina Atkinson, Lydia Morgan, Reta Cooper, Maggie Weston.

Source: AWM P01562.001

10.1 Aboriginal serviceman Private SKJ 'Len' Lenoy attempts to clear the bar in a pole vault competition. He is participating in a British Commonwealth Occupation Force (BCOF) interzone athletics meeting, at Anzac Park, Kure, Japan. He was later killed in action on 24 April 1951 at the Battle of Kapyong in the Korean War. He had also served in the Second World War.

Source: AWM HOBJ0707

10.2 Four members of the Salvage Unit of the Australian component of the British Commonwealth Occupation Force. Left to right: back row: Ned Egglestone and 'Tiny' Taylor and front row: Jim Coxhead and 'Snowy' Dickson. The soldiers are brandishing bundles of banknotes with which they have just been paid.

Source: AWM P01795.001, donated by N Egglestone

10.3 Four members of 1 Platoon, A Company, 3rd Battalion, The Royal Australian Regiment (3RAR), about to move off from a secure area after taking a break during a patrol near the Kalimantan–Sarawak border, Borneo. The section commander, Bingarape (standing) has just given the section's forward scout Private McGrath a compass bearing and the general direction to follow.

Source: AWM P00944.06

11.1 *Above* Sapper Clement William 'Bill' Coolburra gouges a fighting pit from the earth at a jungle camp during Operation Roundhouse, a search-and-destroy mission against the Viet Cong. Coolburra served with the Third Field Troop, Royal Australian Engineers, based at Bien Hoa, Vietnam.
Source: AWM BLA/66/0109/VN/

11.2 *Left* Yon Ivanovic cutting Des Mayo's hair in Nui Dat, Vietnam, outside their accommodation in 1968.
Source: Des Mayo

11.3 George Anderson (third from left) remembered of his time serving in Vietnam that 'there was no time for segregation'.

Source: George Anderson

11

The Vietnam War

Noah Riseman

> 'There was a lot of things that were done that shouldn't be done and all that business, but when you're there and that, you've got to put that out of your mind and all that business to stay alive and the idea is to keep one another alive and look after one another.'
>
> – *Roy Mundine*

The Vietnam War was one of Australia's longest and most divisive conflicts, and Aboriginal and Torres Strait Islander people were as involved as non-Indigenous people were. Australia sent its first group of 30 military advisers to South Vietnam in 1962, as the Australian Army Training Team Vietnam. A major escalation of Australia's commitment came in June 1965 when, at the request of the US government, Australia sent the 1st Battalion, Royal Australian Regiment (1RAR) to support the US 173rd Airborne Brigade. In March 1966 Australia moved its enlarged Vietnam taskforce to the newly constructed Nui Dat base in Phuoc Tuy Province, southwest of Saigon. It was here that the majority of Australian soldiers served, although medical units and smaller contingents of RAAF and Navy personnel were based in the coastal town of Vung Tau. This town would also be the site of Australian soldiers' rest and convalescence leave and the accompanying drinking, brawls and sexual encounters with local women (not to mention with other American and Australian men). As the United States (US) slowly withdrew its forces under the auspices of Vietnamisation, so too did Australia begin to draw down its troops from late 1970. The final Australians left Nui Dat in November 1971, and the last combat troops withdrew by December 1972. Throughout this entire period, 1962 to 1973, nearly 60 000 Australians served in Vietnam; there were over 3000 wounded and 521 killed in action.[1]

At least 300 Aboriginal and Torres Strait Islander men were among the ranks of Australia's personnel in Vietnam. This is a gendered history because, notwithstanding visiting Aboriginal performers such as the Sapphires, there have been no identified Aboriginal or Torres Strait Islander women among the 43 members of the Royal Australian Army Nursing Corps in Vietnam. In contrast to earlier conflicts where the Aboriginal voice was largely unrecorded, for the Vietnam War there is still a rich oral history from survivors, so I have drawn heavily on interviews conducted as part of the Yarn Ups or recorded for other projects on the history of Indigenous military service. Indeed, 28 of the Yarn Ups were with Vietnam veterans, nine were with family members of deceased veterans, and for a previous study (2010–13) I interviewed an additional nine Indigenous Vietnam veterans and the sister of a deceased veteran. The reliability of memory is a regular challenge for oral historians, particularly when examining memories of conflicts such as the Vietnam War which are clouded in myth. In my analysis I am therefore cautious to discuss not only what the veterans remember, but also *why* they attach particular meanings to their memories – including those which may be (re)constructed, deriving from the dominant mythology of the war and its aftermath.

Those Indigenous servicemen's experiences form a rich history, including: their motivations to serve; their experiences in Vietnam;

their interactions with the Americans; and their homecomings. The war left many legacies for the individuals who served: not only their difficulties in adjusting to civilian life and in suffering Post Traumatic Stress Disorder (PTSD); but also the opportunities military service afforded them. The actual experience of the Vietnam War for Indigenous veterans was not dissimilar to that recalled by non-Indigenous men. This is a testament both to the equality instilled in the armed forces, and also the power of the dominant narrative of the Vietnam War to shape veterans' memories.[2] Even so, both the pre-war and post-war narratives of Aboriginal and Torres Strait Islander men address matters such as encountering racism and undertaking leadership roles in Indigenous affairs, thus producing a distinctly Aboriginal and Torres Strait Islander veterans' experience within the wider dominant narrative of Vietnam veterans' trauma.

Upbringings and enlistments

The majority of Vietnam servicemen were born either during or shortly after the Second World War. This was the assimilation era, a period characterised by segregated facilities, racial vilification and child removal. As in earlier conflicts, there were numerous Aboriginal servicemen in Vietnam who were members of the Stolen Generations and who joined the military for the stability and discipline it provided.[3] The service records of over 100 Indigenous Vietnam veterans identified by the Australian War Memorial indicate that the most common education level was 'reasonable primary', usually meaning they had left school by year seven. Most listed their professions as 'labourer', whether in the railroads, farms, meatworks or other industries. Most of these jobs were seasonal or casual, and often Indigenous men received lower rates of pay or had part of their wages quarantined as part of the Stolen Wages.[4] In this social environment, the armed forces provided steady employment, a decent wage and, as many interviews affirm, an 'escape' from the challenges of daily life. Frank Mallard was working on a farm in Yuna, Western Australia, and 'joined the Army because it was offering a better pay system than what I was getting. I was working, doing a man's job at fifteen and getting paid a boy's wage, so I thought joining the Army would've been the best thing to do.'[5] Claude Malone similarly stated in 2014 that 'It was hard for me to get a job, me being an Aboriginal, back in the late '60s and early '70s, so I joined the Army then.'[6] Other men enlisted for the sense of adventure or out of a sense of duty. Fenton D'Antoine said in 2015 that his brother Gordon volunteered to go to Vietnam because his mates were going, and he saw it as his duty to join them.[7]

For men who were living 'under the act' in more restrictive jurisdictions, enlisting was not so straightforward. Boys who were still under 18 sometimes required the permission of the Welfare Board, rather than their parents, to enlist. For 17-year-old Phil Prosser, the protection legislation in Western Australia required the local welfare officer to sign his enlistment form. As he described it in 2000:

> So here was this bombastic, drunken idiot that came out of the Hotel with alcoholic fumes breathing all over us. And he signed the approval on the bonnet of a car in the main street of Northam, Fitzgerald Street, Northam. And my father also signed it as a witness to my signature, not as the approving male, or the adult, but as a witness to my signature and to this particular person's signature.[8]

Bill Coolburra confronted similar challenges because he was resident on Palm Island, Queensland. According to his widow, Edna, in 2014: 'When he was sixteen, he [Bill] asked them [chief protector] if he could go to the Townsville show because you had to get permission … so they gave him permission, and he went to the Townsville show, but then he ran away to some foster parents … From there he met a friend, and they ended up going into the Army.'[9]

National service

Other Aboriginal and Torres Strait Islander men served in Vietnam as national servicemen, although their relationship with the national service regime was complicated. The specific wording of the *National Service Act 1964* exempted 'aboriginal natives of Australia, as defined by the regulations, other than a class of aboriginal natives as so defined that is specified in the regulations'.[10] However, the Department of Labour and National Service indicated that it was only from *compulsory* national service that Aboriginal men were exempt; they could still *volunteer*. Department representatives also highlighted the *National Service Regulations*, where the complex definition of Aboriginality did not apply to all men of mixed descent. Regulation 18 defined an Aboriginal person as:

> (a) a full-blooded aboriginal native of Australia;
> (b) a person who is a half-caste aboriginal native of Australia or has an admixture of aboriginal blood greater than a half-caste; or
> (c) a person who has an admixture of aboriginal blood and lives as an aboriginal native or amongst aborigines.[11]

Even though Aboriginal and Torres Strait Islander men were not obliged to register for national service, almost a quarter of the Aboriginal and Torres Strait Islanders who served in Vietnam were national servicemen. Though this is a lower percentage than in the Australian forces as a whole – one-third were national servicemen – it still reflects a significant number of Indigenous people doing national service. There are several reasons for this – one of course being the confusing regulations classifying some Aboriginal men as non-Indigenous. Also, some men who identify as Aboriginal under current definitions may not have identified as such during the Vietnam War era, whether because they did not know they were Aboriginal or did not meet state or Commonwealth definitions. Some men were never told that they were exempt from national service. Des Mayo was working on the railways in north Queensland, where he received a message that he had to register for the national service ballot. He returned to Darwin to register and, as he put it in 2015, national service was: 'the only lottery I ever won'.[12]

Other men, when they learned they could opt out, chose to serve anyway. David Nean stated in 2014: 'I had a chance not to go, because I worked on the railway and because I was Aboriginal Dad sat me down one day and said, "It's up to you, son. I'm proud of you any way".'[13] Les Kropinyeri indicates that the government made no differentiation based on race when his number was called. He went for a medical examination along with 19 other non-Aboriginal men and, standing in their jocks and socks, he was informed by the doctor that as an Aboriginal man he could be exempted from call-up. He replied that as the marble did not differentiate between Aboriginal and non-Aboriginal, and as he had come this far, he would continue with the journey.[14] Other men voluntarily signed up for national service. For Alec Illin, interestingly, it was his mother who tried to stop him from signing up in 1965 because she feared he would be sent to Vietnam – which did happen.[15] In 2015 George Anderson recalled going to Rockhampton and being told he did not have to register because he was Aboriginal: 'So I said, "Hold on mate. I might be black but I'm still Australian! I want to put my name down!" And bugger me dead it came up!'[16] Eventually the definition of Aboriginality's openness to interpretation would lead to legal problems for Aboriginal people and tricky public relations for the government.

Combat

Like non-Indigenous veterans, many Aboriginal and Torres Strait Islander ex-servicemen are uncomfortable talking about their experience of war. Perhaps Geoff Shaw best summarised the sentiments of many of the veterans in a 2015 interview: 'I don't like to tell you … the itty gritty side of war. The lighter side, yeah – I can tell you a lot of [the] funny side of war.'[17] While veterans' reticence at times makes it difficult to write a historical narrative of their Vietnam experiences, the reticence itself is also telling about how these men have (re)constructed their memories.[18]

Aboriginal veterans who were willing to share their memories in interviews spoke of the challenges fighting a guerrilla war: the patrols, the difficult jungle conditions and the psychological dimensions of not knowing who or where the enemy was. Among the 108 men who fought in Australia's most famous battle in Vietnam, the battle of Long Tan on 18 August 1966, five have been identified as Aboriginal: Thomas 'Buddy' Lea, Vic Simon, Jeffrey Duroux, Dennis Graham and Brian Hornung. Vic Simon described the battle in 2013:

> First off we had a contact and then we moved up in sort of like an open box and unfortunately 11 Platoon they sort of walked into the ambush. They copped it pretty bad and then we sort of went in to help them out and that's when it's all started: just there for three hours' solid fighting in the rain and pouring down rain. And the artillery was very good even though they landed pretty close to us but they sort of saved our lives.[19]

After the battle, authorities discerned that the 108 Australians had fought an entire Viet Cong regiment of around 1500–2000. Given the incredible odds, Buddy Lea reflected: 'How we all did not get killed, I will never know to this day. 18 of our men got killed; 24 of us, including myself, got wounded.'[20]

The challenges of fighting a guerrilla enemy feature in veterans' recollections of combat. In 2015 Des Mayo described one time when his patrol came across a bucket system of Viet Cong booby traps, and shots were fired on his patrol. They called in the artillery to fire on the area. In this instance, American jets flew in and carpet bombed the area. The Australians had to hide from them, even suffering casualties from the friendly fire.[21] In 2014 Roy Mundine described another incident which left him permanently wounded:

> Well we were going down into a bunker system and we come in there and that and we moved forward to check the area and I stepped on a mine or hit the side of a mine that went off and it blew us up, blew me up and blew me leg off.[22]

The majority of Indigenous troops in Vietnam – approximately 60 per cent – served in the infantry. This was more likely to do with their education levels rather than officials determining Indigenous people to be more racially 'suited' to front-line combat. The next most common corps membership, constituting approximately 12 per cent of Indigenous soldiers, was the Royal Australian Engineers; smaller numbers served in specialised corps such as Signals. American scholars have found significant evidence that many commanders viewed Native American soldiers as a martial race who were 'natural' soldiers. The martial race construct influenced many commanders to send Native Americans as forward scouts because they could supposedly sense the enemy, or had better eyesight.[23] In Australia, only two Indigenous interviewees hinted at similar sentiments; David Nean speculated in 2014: 'I reckon over there they looked up to you more because they thought you was better qualified for fight in the bush and that.'[24] Edna Coolburra also said in 2014, 'Every time they were looking for a forward scout, they would pick Bill.'[25] None of the other interviewees implied that race played any role in Aboriginal and Torres Strait Islander soldiers' assignments.

Men who served in the RAAF and the RAN had different experiences from the infantry. Of the 260 Indigenous Vietnam veterans identified by the Australian War Memorial in 2010, 19 were Navy. Many sailors were involved in transporting servicemen to Vietnam from Australia and patrols off the North Vietnamese coast. Clarence Williams recalled in 2015 an incident in Vung Tau Harbour when a turbo generator blew in the aft engine room. While he was not hurt at the time, he stated: 'what I remember about it was all the asbestos falling like a cloud, like a snowstorm'.[26] The RAAF had the fewest Indigenous members and the smallest Australian force in Vietnam – only five identified by the Australian War Memorial in 2010. Rob Bryant was an airframe fitter who served with 9 Squadron in Vung Tau for 12 months from April 1970 to 1971. He remembered two other Aboriginal RAAF members working in maintenance roles in Vung Tau during that period.[27]

Social relations in Vietnam

The hub of Australian life in Phuoc Tuy province was the base at Nui Dat. Located in the rubber and banana plantations, it was often muddy and wet, given the tropical climate. As Glenn James recalled in 2001:

> The living quarters in Nui Dat were sandbags and tents, a canvas tent over the top to four corners and then after some time they were renewed with corrugated iron, tropical hut type accommodation, at this time with no sandbags around them and quite often the enemy would fire into those.[28]

Notwithstanding such dangers, there was a comforting sense of safety when returning to Nui Dat from patrols. Several men spoke of the boozer, and others remembered the outdoor theatre, movies and visiting performers such as Col Joye and Little Pattie.

Like the entire Australian military, Nui Dat was integrated, and in later interviews Aboriginal and Torres Strait Islander veterans recalled that they did not experience racism. As Geoff Shaw said in 2015: 'I don't know where they get the perception of this racism … the only colour that everybody knew was green – their uniform.'[29] George Anderson remembered serving in Vietnam with three other Murri men, and he said in 2014 that there was no time for segregation.[30] All of the veterans interviewed emphasised the mateship and sense of brotherhood, which endured for years after the war. Bill Coolburra, for example, was so close to George 'Snowy' Wilson that they were nicknamed twins – ironically – since Coolburra was very dark, while Wilson was so white that he looked like an albino. When Prime Minister Harold Holt visited Vietnam in 1966, he wanted to meet the twins. As Coolburra's widow Edna told the story in 2014, Holt asked Wilson:

> 'Well where's your other twin brother?' He looked at him, he said – he just killed himself laughing. He said, 'My twin brother is out on the frontline doing some sort of job there; that's where I should be, with him.' And he said, 'Didn't he want to come?' And he explained to him, he said, 'No, my brother is a full-blooded Aboriginal … and his name is Bill Coolburra!'[31]

While interviewed veterans were unanimous about active service in Vietnam being free of prejudice, there were some who recalled racism during training in Australia. Usually it took the form of taunts or epithets such as 'black bastard'. Sometimes it was other trainees who made these statements, and on other occasions, drill sergeants. George Bostock and John Schnaars said that when faced with taunts, they confronted the offenders; Bostock said in 2010: 'I copped no shit; the racist remark, bang [a punch].'[32] Claude Malone said in 2014 that he would say, 'If you don't like it, then lump it!' and then fight the 'rednecks'.[33]

Interestingly, several Indigenous ex-servicemen reported witnessing racism among the American forces.[34] Frank Mallard remembered in 2010, 'But they did treat their Hispanics and their Negroes with contempt. They were always calling them by name and whatever; there was always some sort of a fight going on within their ranks and we found it difficult to understand that.'[35] However, the Aboriginal and Torres Strait Islander troops themselves were not targets of American racism. Coolburra befriended African-American and Native American soldiers; in 2014 his wife said that the African-Americans asked, 'How come you come from Australia when they're all white?' He would answer that the African-Americans were brought to the US as slaves, and similarly the Aboriginal people were treated as slaves in Australia. He also talked to Native American soldiers, saying: 'You know when the British came there and took your land? Well that's the way they came to Australia and took our land away from us.'[36]

For rest and convalescence, Australian soldiers went to Vung Tau – a site of excessive drinking, fighting and engaging in sexual relations. Interestingly, scholarly texts about Australia's Vietnam War mostly gloss over the behaviour in Vung Tau, though it does receive minor attention in some popular histories.[37] Most interviewees were similarly reticent to talk about Vung Tau, as best indicated by Frank Mallard's witty comment in 2015: 'Never got into any mischief at all. I was a good boy.'[38] Several service records have charge reports of going AWOL, and a few have reports of soldiers clashing with local people. In 2015 Des Mayo remembered one night at the Grand Hotel when a few mates got into a fight with some Vietnamese people. They grabbed Mayo, and as he remembered:

> We're all getting into it, knocking these people left and right the next thing the old police come along and start rattling off their machine-guns. So hands on heads and knees on the floor, and you're still getting rocked until the MPs come and they picked us up and took us back to camp.[39]

A staggering omission from almost all interviewees' discussions about Vung Tau is references to relationships with Vietnamese women. One exception is David Nean's 2014 allusion: 'Worst ones [Vietnamese] were the girls. You couldn't trust the girls. You know what I'm talking about. They had terrible ideas of, you know, terrible [pause] ways of getting at people. [pause] I won't go into it, but they were the worst of them all, the ones you couldn't trust, especially if you going with them.'[40] These allusions, combined with the wider knowledge base of Australians in Vietnam, suggest that Aboriginal and Torres Strait Islander men, too, were participating in the sex trade in Vung Tau. If so, it is likely that they were among the large percentage of troops who contracted venereal diseases.[41]

The anti-war movement at home

As news of advances by the North Vietnamese army and the Viet Cong, such as the 1968 Tet Offensive, and US atrocities, such as the My Lai massacre and the use of napalm, filled the Australian press, the anti-war movement within Australia grew substantially. By the time of the First Moratorium in May 1970, the anti-war movement was drawing members from across the spectrum of Australian society: mothers, the New Left, unionists, students, religious figures and members of the professional and middle class. Aboriginal and Torres Strait Islander people, too, were involved in the anti-war movement. In 2013 the unionist Kevin Cook recollected marching against the Vietnam War with the Builders Labourers Federation.[42] Patricia O'Shane recalled in 1993 being heavily involved in both the anti–Vietnam War movement and Aboriginal civil rights causes while she was a law student.[43] Yet Margaret Culbong, whose brother Len served in Vietnam, indicated in 2015 that while she was personally anti-war, she and many Aboriginal communities did not get involved in the protest movement: 'It didn't affect me in that much way, and I think that the same applied to most of the Aboriginal community because that was their fight. They were the invaders, they were the ones who had to go and fight. We're still fighting for our country.'[44]

One significant difference between the American and Australian anti-war movements is that in the US, the Black Power, Red Power and Chicano movements all took up opposition to the Vietnam War as part of their mantras. Yet, in Australia there is little evidence of the Black Power Movement becoming involved in the anti-war movement. Instead, Black Power activists were primarily focused on issues such as land rights, police abuse and the living conditions of urban and remote Aboriginal communities.[45] Another difference from the US is that Aboriginal and Torres Strait Islander veterans themselves, unlike black and Native American veterans, played little if any role in the anti-war movement. Indeed, like non-Indigenous veterans, many of the Indigenous ex-servicemen interviewed blamed the anti-war movement for Australia and the US losing the war.

There was, however, almost a convergence of Indigenous and anti-war issues around the issue of national service. In the early 1970s, the Department of Labour and National Service continued to adhere to its confusing definition of Aboriginality. These problematic regulations proved untenable in 1971, when two

Aboriginal men were convicted for failing to register for national service. Drawing on essentialist ideas of Aboriginality, the magistrates determined in both cases that the fact that the men lived in houses, dressed in modern clothes, owned a car and spoke English meant that they were not living as Aboriginal people.[46] The cases caused outrage in the press, with numerous op-eds and letters condemning the criteria by which the magistrates were judging Aboriginality. It was likely that the timing of the two verdicts, in December 1971, and June 1972 respectively, prevented the issue of Aboriginal people and national service from continuing to have traction. They were delivered just before and during the Aboriginal Tent Embassy protest, which garnered much more media attention. Moreover, by December 1972 the staged withdrawal of Australian troops from Vietnam was nearly completed. When Gough Whitlam's Labor government was elected, it soon repealed the *National Service Act* – although the final clause exempting Aboriginal men from compulsory call-up in a time of war remained in the *Defence Act* until amendments in 1992.[47]

Homecomings

It is a common trope of the memory of the Vietnam War that the anti-war movement made veterans' transition to civilian life even more difficult. This was echoed in the Aboriginal and Torres Strait Islander ex-servicemen's interviews, reflecting their hatred for the movement. As James Tang Wei put it in 2015: 'Why should we have to put up with stuff like that [name-calling]? We were only doing what we were told to do. It's our job. It's not that we wanted to go there. It's something that we had to do, whether we liked it or not.'[48] In 2014 David Nean remembered anti-war protesters disrupting his welcome home march in Sydney in 1968: 'You had those protesters, you know, like throwing eggs in front of you –

rotten eggs and rotten tomatoes and things like that. That hurt us a bit.'[49] George Anderson also recalled a march in the city of Adelaide, claiming in 2014 that he was hit in the side of the head by a potato thrown by an anti-war protester.[50]

Ray Minniecon relates a story about how his brother Joseph reacted to anti-war protesters:

> He done four tours in Vietnam. And when he came back, I don't know if this is the reason behind it, but they were marching in the streets of Sydney here, at that time when all this anti-Vietnam protests were on. And this white woman came out there and poured a whole bucket of white paint all over him [laughter] … First thing he did, he went back and signed up and went back to Vietnam.[51]

This story is actually about anti-war protester Nadine Jensen disrupting 1RAR's welcome home parade in June 1966, and it was Minniecon's commander whom the protester smeared with red paint and turpentine. Historians such as Ann Curthoys and Chris Dixon have written about how many Vietnam veterans have unconsciously taken this particular story and (re)constructed their own memories around it. Essentially, the story has become so dominant that it has become part of many servicemen's own memories, and as such there is a strong mythology and collective memory of hostile encounters with the anti-war movement.[52] Few testimonies explicitly recalled a positive welcome home parade; Ray Orchard said: 'We marched through Sydney and everybody said hooray.'[53]

(Re)constructed memories and mythologies permeate other aspects of the dominant Vietnam War narrative. Several veterans talk about returning home at night and being told to change immediately into civilian clothes so that they would not be targeted by anti-war protesters. However, as author Mark Dapin points out, planes returned at night, not to avoid protesters, but for operational reasons. Nor is there any evidence of anti-war protesters at Sydney Airport.[54] Yet, veterans' testimonies tend to dwell on reconstructed memories of confrontational protesters and the supposed mistreatment they received at their homecomings. Such examples align with Alistair Thomson's research about First World War veterans reconstructing their own memories of war to fit a collective memory of war and their return from it.[55]

Another common, though not unanimous, memory of homecoming for Indigenous veterans is that they were not welcomed in RSL branches. In some instances they were rejected for being Vietnam veterans, and in others for being Indigenous, so it is sometimes hard to separate those two intersecting identities for Indigenous veterans. A dominant narrative of Vietnam veterans' return is that the local RSLs rejected them on the grounds that Vietnam was not a real war. In 2015 Geoff Shaw remembered one Second World War veteran telling him it could not have been a real war because there was no frontline.[56] In 2014 Eric Law attributed the RSL hostility more to the fact that Australia lost the Vietnam War, and the RSLs did not want Vietnam veterans to be present as a reminder.[57] Over time there was generational change at the RSLs, and nowadays most RSL leadership consists of Vietnam veterans.

In other interviews, it was Aboriginal or Torres Strait Islander veterans' race which barred them from entering the RSLs. In 2014 Edna Coolburra told the following tale about Bill:

> They went drinking at a pub place in the RSL. He had one drink with his mates and then, because of his colour, 'Oh, you're not allowed in here.' He said, 'Why? Why not? I fought beside my friends.' They all said, 'Yeah. He fought beside us. He our friend, drink with us.' 'No. No blackfella allowed in here. No blackfella allowed in any pub.'[58]

Dave Cook, George Anderson and Phil Prosser related similar stories. Cook stated in 2010:

> They wouldn't let me into their RSL [Karuah, NSW] because I was Aboriginal. This was in the early '70s. And they said, 'No way! You can't come in here!' I said, 'Mate, I'm a fucking returned serviceman!' I was with a policeman, as a matter of fact. Still they said, 'You can come in; he can't.' So, we just all went up to the local hotel and drank there and came back home.[59]

This treatment was not universal. The RSL is often mistaken for a monolithic organisation, when in reality it is a highly devolved institution with most local branches setting their own rules about admission.

The racism that many Indigenous veterans experienced within the RSL echoed across civilian society. In Western Australia and Queensland, for instance, there were still restrictions on Aboriginal movement and alcohol consumption (repealed in 1971 in Western Australia). Indigenous veterans endured police harassment. In 2015 Des Mayo remembered when he bought a new car and was pulled over 15 times by police over a four-month period. On the 15th occasion, he asked the cop: 'Isn't a black man allowed to own a new car?' He also said to the cop, '"I've been in Vietnam, mate, and Malaya … You were probably swimming around looking for a home while I was out there fighting." And they don't like that comment.'[60]

A common element among Indigenous and non-Indigenous veterans' experiences was suffering Post Traumatic Stress Disorder (PTSD) upon their return. Many interviews reference alcohol abuse, while alcohol-related charges are listed in numerous service records of Indigenous men who remained in the Army. James Tang Wei stated in 2015: 'When you're young, you get drunk and just hide everything through grog and stuff like that. And as you get older, it comes back and then, you know, you just think, "Holy hell, all these blokes." And then you get a bit angry again – you know, like a lot of anger, a lot of hurt.'[61] In 2000 Phil Prosser talked about recurring nightmares that he suffered for years: 'I used to have nightmares of him [Vietnamese boy] and me walking down the road when suddenly the ground would open up and he'd fall in. I'd grab him by the arm and try to pull him out but the next thing he'd turn into a North Vietnamese soldier who was pointing a gun at my head.'[62]

Tang Wei's mental health deteriorated to the point that he contemplated suicide. He confessed to mood swings and thoughts like: 'Maybe I should just run off the road and hit the tree. You know, I thought about it a couple of times, you know … and the only thing that kept me going was the grannies [grandkids]'.[63] Another discussion of suicidal ideation came from Des Mayo. He recalled in 2015:

> I tried once to do meself in. Having a few beers, and the shotgun upstairs, and I walked up … just cocked it and, luckily me brother-in-law was there run up, and knocked me arse over head got me gun and then it took me a while, I stayed away from home for about three months.[64]

Not all veterans experienced PTSD right away, but even if it were decades later, almost all veterans interviewed as part of the Serving Our Country project did claim to have had mental health problems related to their war service.

PTSD symptoms affected not only the veterans, but their families as well. Dave Cook admitted in 2010: 'It felt like I had been in the bush looking for anything you can shoot and twenty-four hours later I was sitting in my lounge in Green Valley with two screaming kids and a missus that I didn't know whether I was in love with or not. And it was the kids that I couldn't handle. The change was so horrific; I just couldn't handle it'.[65] Robyn Kropinyeri remembered in 2015 that when her husband, Les, used to drink, he would get aggressive (though never violent), and Robyn would send the children away.[66]

The psychological care of Vietnam veterans was, and continues to be, contentious. It was not until the early 1980s that the term PTSD entered psychological and popular discourse. In 1983 the Hawke Labor government established a *Royal Commission on the Use and Effects of Chemical Agents on Australian Personnel in Vietnam*. Among its findings in 1985 were reports that, contrary to popular opinion, the majority of veterans were not suffering behavioural problems, criminality or alcoholism often associated with PTSD. Moreover, the Royal Commission concluded that chemicals used in Vietnam, including Agent Orange, were not responsible for veterans' ill-health.[67] Yet, the Royal Commission and subsequent health studies – including a comprehensive Department of Veterans' Affairs (DVA) survey in 1998 – have still indicated higher rates of mental health problems and cancers among Vietnam veterans.[68]

There were several reasons why veterans did not receive adequate psychological care. Sometimes it was the veterans' own pride or hesitancy to seek help which prolonged their and their family's suffering. Victor Slockee said in 2015, that for him, it was support groups with other veterans that helped him through his PTSD as well as with advice to apply for pensions.[69] Des Mayo only sought psychiatric assistance around 1989, after some of his veteran mates quizzed him about his mental health and told him he needed help. They filled out the DVA forms for him and he was then sent to a few doctors and psychiatrists.[70] Michael Markham said in 2015 that the DVA was 'excellent' at referring him to appropriate services, and he had no problems with them because he filled out the right paperwork.[71]

Most interviewees, though, criticised the DVA (formerly Department of Repatriation), especially in the early post-Vietnam years. Often the doctors would prescribe medications which only temporarily reduced PTSD symptoms or did not work. By the mid- to late 1980s, particularly owing to the activism of the Vietnam Veterans' Association of Australia, there were more psychologists and counsellors trained to work with veterans suffering PTSD. New approaches to therapy were also helpful in supporting family members. Robyn Kropinyeri said in 2015 that it was when her husband, Les, invited her to accompany him to counselling that she began to understand what he was going through and how they could support each other. She talked about courses and family workshops for partners which have been more-effective forms of therapy.[72]

Notwithstanding Michael Markham's comment about needing to fill out the right paperwork, several veterans testified to there being a large number of forms, boards, tribunals and appeals processes before they secured pensions or coverage for medical ailments. Most claimed that neither the military, nor the DVA, provided adequate assistance to transition back to civilian life. An extreme example of the maladjustment came from Geoff Shaw. When he returned to Alice Springs, he could not find a job and became homeless. He stated in 2015: 'From 1970 to '73, I was in skid row. You know what skid row is? Yeah, like down in the riverbed drinking plonk and so on. Then I went up at Katherine looking for work, and so on, skid row there, living in the long grass, no accommodation whatsoever, and trying to find work there.' Shaw moved back to Alice Springs and worked at the Tangentyere Council. He applied for a disability pension when he started seeing a psychiatrist in 1991. He was in and out of hospitals, having regular meetings and diagnoses with psychiatrists and other doctors before he was finally awarded a disability pension. As he put it: 'And, Christ, I'd been to Malaya and Borneo, two tours of Vietnam, and they took seven years to realise that, you know, that I'm a bit messed up in the brain.'[73]

Despite the findings of the Royal Commission, several veterans also claim to have suffered significant health problems as a result of Agent Orange. In 2014 Laurel Williams said of her Uncle Ross: 'He had to have a really massive operation on his stomach, and he said then, you know, that he was – that was a result of part of the Agent Orange thing'.[74] Some of the most interesting allegations of Agent Orange health problems came from Claude Malone: 'I suffer from a skin disease. They don't want to know about that. It's the American government, they don't want to … veterans getting it.' Malone's skin disease is so severe that he needs to wear mittens on his hands.[75] The Navy also used lead-based paints and ships had asbestos on them, so James Tang Wei said that he was terrified about what sorts of health problems he and others might develop.[76]

While over the years veterans eventually received their entitlements, there remain perceived shortcomings. Les Kropinyeri lamented cutbacks within DVA counselling services which have disadvantaged veterans in country areas.[77] Patrick Mills discussed a 25-year battle to receive his medal entitlements. It was resolved when another veteran took down Mills' information and wrote a letter to the Queen which then filtered through the governor-general down to the DVA. Mills stated in 2014: 'When I got the medal, just walked away and got around, just chuck it in the bush. I said forget it. Until today. I haven't got it.'[78] Admittedly, Mills' story is an outlier because most Indigenous Vietnam veterans have indeed received their medals, but it is an indicator of the sense of grievance many have faced interacting with the DVA bureaucracy.

Legacies

Importantly, many Aboriginal and Torres Strait Islander veterans have overcome the challenges of PTSD. They have not only functioned in Australian society, but in many cases have gone on to hold significant leadership positions. Two themes are prevalent among veterans' memories about their experience of war: learning leadership skills to relate to whitefellas, and ongoing mateship. Some men continued in the armed forces through the 1970s and 1980s and even into the 1990s. Buddy Lea served for 33 years total; Frank Mallard served until the 1990s, and even after retiring in 1993 he went to Croatia and Bosnia as a reservist working with the United Nations Peacekeeping force. Roy Mundine had joined the Army in 1958 and served until 1995. In recognition of his long service and role as a mentor, in 2015 Chief of Army Lieutenant-General David Morrison appointed Mundine the Army's inaugural Indigenous Elder.[79]

Many other Australian Indigenous Vietnam veterans partook in other community leadership roles later in life, some of which are discussed in chapter 13. George Bostock years later became a playwright and an actor and was a consultant in the 2014–15 productions of *Black Diggers*. He has also been a member of Queensland's Murri Court, which brings Elders into the judicial process to find appropriate non-gaol sentences for young Aboriginal offenders charged with particular crimes. Michael Markham has served on nine boards of several Aboriginal organisations and as president of the Northern Territory branch of the Vietnam Veterans' Association of Australia. John Kinsela represented Australia as a wrestler at the 1972 Munich Olympics – in fact he had competed in 1968 before going to Vietnam – and now works in New South Wales' circle sentencing at the Mt Druitt Justice Group. Glenn James became a VFL umpire and was the first Aboriginal person to umpire an AFL-VFL Grand Final in 1984. Geoff Shaw returned to Alice Springs in 1972–73, helped to set up the local Aboriginal medical service and did work for legal aid; in 1974 he began working on the Tangentyere Council until about the year 2000. He, like several of these veterans, credited his Army experience as preparing him for such leadership roles because of the mateship, camaraderie and discipline that it instilled.[80] Vietnam veterans have also been at the forefront of efforts to organise and honour Indigenous military service in Australia, playing key roles in groups such as Honouring Indigenous War Graves (see p. 332).

The mateship generated during war has offered emotional and psychological support to veterans over the years. Reflecting a common trope, in 2014 Ray Minniecon said of his brother Sonny: 'He holds a lot of that stuff in, and the only time that he spoke about those matters is when he's with other Vietnam vets.'[81] To return to the tale of 'twins' Bill Coolburra and Snowy Wilson: by 2001 Coolburra was suffering severe renal problems. When he was in South Australia for a unit reunion, he told Snowy about his illness. His wife, Edna, said in 2014 what happened next: 'That's when I told Snowy that, "Oh, Bill need a new kidney – you know, another kidney or else I'll lose him." And he said, "Oh, what? Why didn't you tell me that early part." I said, "Well I didn't, you know, think …" That's where he said, "Nah. I'm gonna give my brother one of my kidneys." Which he done.' The families went to Brisbane together for the operations, which were successful.[82]

It is hard to balance the legacies of mateship and leadership skills against the mental and physical scars that Indigenous Vietnam veterans have carried. All veterans say that war is a terrible thing that should be avoided. Some interviews also acknowledge the suffering of the Vietnamese people, whom Roy Mundine described in 2014 as 'In a no-win situation probably like a lot of civilian communities that get caught in the meat in the sandwich and that.'[83] Des Mayo's reflections on Australia's costs of the war seem a fitting conclusion:

> What were we over there for, you know, really? 'Cos the French tried to kick 'em out, and how many people have tried to kick

'em out and it didn't eventuate? And we weren't really threatened like the Japanese. It was just the political backyard, you know, sort of thing. 'Cos we lost a lot of young lives over there, you know – their early 20s, also a couple of 17, 18 year olds. We didn't have to go if we didn't wanna but, you know, adventure.[84]

12

Servicewomen

Allison Cadzow

'We were there doing a job as well.' – *Gaye Doolan*

The experiences of Aboriginal and Torres Strait Islander women serving in the defence forces during the Second World War and later decades are not widely known or analysed, either in histories of Australia's defence forces or more recent works on Indigenous people's military service. Noah Riseman's work is an exception. He has argued that from the 1940s to the 1960s, defence service represented an escape from policies which restricted educational and employment opportunities for Aboriginal and Torres Strait Islander women, beyond domestic service. Joining the armed services enabled them to carve out an 'alternative path' for themselves.[1] This chapter builds upon the work of Riseman and Richard Trembath, using insights from Yarn Ups and other oral histories of Aboriginal and Torres Strait Islander women who served in the separate women's services, to examine their participation in the defence forces – their motivations, working lives and perspectives.[2] It also considers the impacts service had on their lives and communities.

There is a range of reasons why Aboriginal and Torres Strait Islander women's defence service is not well known. The first is sheer numbers. Fewer women than men have served in the

Australian defence forces over the twentieth century, and for many decades, women were unable to enlist in the mainstream services. Additionally, much of the literature on women in the military gives little explicit acknowledgment to the service of Aboriginal and Torres Strait Islander women, giving the impression that servicewomen were white, as does much of the Australian literature on war brides and intimacy.[3] Nor do these works consider how the servicewomen's experiences and engagement were, in part, 'the product of intersecting patterns of racism and sexism' as explained by African-American lawyer and academic Kimberlé Crenshaw. Her intersectionality theory illuminates how different forms of discrimination – such as gender and race (class, sexuality and colonialism could also be added) interact in specific ways in the lives of women of colour. They are not lived as discrete, 'one or the other' dimensions, but simultaneously and need to be understood as such.[4] Lastly, the autobiographical boom of the 1980s and 1990s, especially among Aboriginal women telling their life stories, has not produced many accounts of Aboriginal women's service, though some are now in process. Men's stories of active service and battle still loom large and tend to overshadow the women's accounts.

With limited information from memoirs and service records, oral histories are a key means to understanding the experiences of Indigenous servicewomen, as noted in Riseman's work and Grace Poulin's publication on Aboriginal servicewomen in Canada.[5] The reflections of these servicewomen provide more than 'content'. Rather, they reveal the women's interpretations of their own histories. As Larissa Behrendt, Eualeyai-Kamilaroi lawyer, academic and writer has argued: 'Oral history acknowledges the real experience of Aboriginal women that has not been recorded and allows for an expression of experience in a way that is reflective of our culture at the same time.'[6]

The two world wars

Aboriginal women were given no opportunity to play a role in the Australian defence forces during the First World War, when women were marginalised from anything but the patriotic war effort. The Australian government refused to create any women's auxiliaries forces and the only unit in which women could serve at the battlefront was the Australian Army Nursing Service.[7] Aboriginal women, however, were excluded from the nursing profession. Philippa Scarlett's research has uncovered the remarkable Marion Leane, a Sydney Aboriginal woman who studied nursing in the United States and joined the Canadian services, but she did not serve with the Australian forces.[8]

During the Second World War, women had the opportunity to do valuable work in auxiliary forces. As the national security situation deteriorated, the Australian government created the Australian Women's Army Service (AWAS), 1941–1947; the Women's Auxiliary Australian Air Force (WAAAF), 1941–1947; and the Women's Royal Australian Naval Service (WRANS), 1942–1947. Auxiliary forces were established to 'free up' men for active service, by employing women in onshore roles, such as clerical and communications work. Although many in authority opposed women's participation in the defence sphere, arguing that military service was a masculine profession which conflicted with women's nurturing/homemaking roles, the histories of Shirley Fenton Huie, Joyce Thomson, Ann Howard, Patsy Adam-Smith, Jan Bassett, Janette Bomford and others have shown that the women's services did important work in communications, transport, health care and other roles.[9] However, what is not obvious from these historians' work is that Aboriginal women participated.

Thirty-four Aboriginal and/or Torres Strait Islander women are known to have served during the Second World War in the WAAAF and AWAS. One Aboriginal woman served in the WRANS: Margaret Mills, from Katanning, Western Australia, who was a cook and seamstress.[10] It is likely there were more women who have not been identified. Sometimes there is little more than a service record which is not explicit about heritage or background. These records were often ambiguous about recruits' backgrounds, with some listing the women's complexions as 'dark', 'olive' or 'medium', which could also mean they had non-Aboriginal heritage. In some cases recruits were separated from knowledge of their own heritage, such as Rosina Parfitt from Western Australia, who listed her birthplace as 'unknown'. Linda Nhill (née Lester), from Granite Downs, South Australia, a Sick Quarters Attendant with nursing experience, left the space for her place of birth blank. Nhill's daughter noted later that she lived at the Colebrook Home.[11] In several of these cases, women were removed from their families by welfare authorities and were part of the Stolen Generations. Combining knowledge from Aboriginal and Torres Strait Islander family histories, oral histories and service records research has played a significant role in identifying more servicewomen.

The records of servicewomen in the Second World War do often provide information on their previous employment. Most had worked in small or regional towns as domestics or cooks, or doing other home duties, with a few having been machinist factory workers or waitresses. There were also nurses with practical experience, if not official qualifications. Some took the application very seriously. Florence Stewart from Lake Boga in Victoria was described by her great-niece Alana Garwood in 2015 as 'a very strong woman'.[12] When Stewart joined the AWAS in 1943, she submitted references from previous employers praising her work as a cook, and a character reference stating that her family were 'well respected in the district'.[13] Helen McDonald from Colac, Victoria, who also joined the AWAS in 1943, and served in the catering corps, included references from a Methodist minister and an employer who said she was 'a trusted servant'.[14] Respectability was an issue all the women's services struggled with.[15] While women were celebrated for doing the work of men, their femininity was also heavily emphasised. For many Aboriginal women joining up, underlining their respectability in the eyes of white communities and employers was a practice they were accustomed to. It reveals an attempt to counter racialised representations and an anticipation of potential prejudice among recruiters.

Most women were employed with AWAS and the WAAAF, rather than WRANS, during the Second World War. Their roles were listed as: mess assistants, telegraphists, and communications, radio and clerical workers. Others served in the nursing corps. These occupations accorded with the services' initial intentions to place women into familiar gendered roles. Yet, some women took the opportunity to do something different, seeking technical roles and experience. Betty Pike (née Ray) from Perth, who joined the WAAAF in 1943, chose flight mechanic as her desired 'mustering', while Dorothy Nicholls from Walgett, New South Wales, who joined the AWAS in 1943, became a dispatch rider, carrying military documents and messages.[16] Some women undertook additional training and sought promotions. Winifred Iselin from Brisbane joined the AWAS as an 'unqualified nurse' and was promoted to sergeant. She was recommended for future employment as a non-commissioned officer (NCO) in Barracks.[17] Ivy Bell, from Moora, Western Australia had 17 years' experience as a cook; after joining the WAAAF in 1941 she was promoted from corporal to sergeant.[18]

Motives for joining

Glimpses of why women sought employment in the services can be found in these service records. However, a much richer history can be gleaned from oral histories. Some of their reasons for enlisting were relatively straightforward. Ella Thompson from Morawa in Western Australia joined the AWAS for financial reasons. Her sister Pat Kopusar (née Thompson), said in 2015 that there were few jobs available at the time and being the eldest in the family, Ella was responsible for contributing to the family income.[19] Other oral histories reveal struggles and tangled back stories. Pike's file shows that she joined the WAAAF in 1943, when she was underage. On exploring her accounts and oral history with Noah Riseman in 2011, the reason she decided to join becomes clearer. Pike revealed that once she turned 16 she was no longer allowed to stay at Graceville Salvation Army home and went to stay with her aunt and uncle. After disclosing her new-found knowledge of her Aboriginality to her relatives, she had to move on yet again; her uncle feared that the Department of Native Affairs, Western Australia would increase surveillance of his family and that he might lose his job. Pike needed somewhere to live and though underage decided, 'I'll go and join up in the Air Force … I loved aeroplanes and flying was pretty new.'[20] Pike then trained as a mechanic in Perth and Melbourne, and worked in Geraldton, Western Australia, and Bairnsdale, Victoria, checking and fixing plane engines. She said that she was fearful of her true age being 'found out' the entire time.[21]

One of the better known servicewomen is Kathleen Ruska, later known as poet Kath Walker, then as Oodgeroo Noonuccal. She had grown up on Stradbroke Island with her family before travelling to the mainland (Brisbane) to work as a domestic. Her brothers Eddie and Eric enlisted and became prisoners of war when Singapore fell in February 1942.[22] This weighed heavily upon her and, being opposed to fascism, she felt she needed to do something as the war came closer to Australian shores. Noonuccal had other motivations too. Having worked as a domestic for a mere two shillings and sixpence a week since she was 13, she desired education, training and better work opportunities. Aboriginal men and women often had limited access to schools and were taught a less challenging curriculum, geared to manual or domestic work. In rural New South Wales, for example, white townspeople pushed to exclude Aboriginal children from public schools. Though Aboriginal communities fought this, the outcome was often sub-standard schooling for their children at reserve schools.[23] As Noonuccal explained:

> [One of the reasons] I joined the army was it was the only way I could learn … I would be allowed to learn. And I thought, after the war, if I am still alive I'll be able to take the 'dimwits' course and it was the only way Aboriginals could learn extra education at that time.[24]

In the AWAS she became a telegraphist/radio operator and was promoted to lance corporal.[25] She completed a stenographer course, as well as shorthand, typing and bookkeeping, seizing educational opportunities as did other Aboriginal service people who she knew.

Noonuccal's oral history interview with historian Robert Hall suggests that her military experience was an education in several ways; unlike in domestic work, she was treated equally in the AWAS, experienced camaraderie with non-Aboriginal women, and according to the *Tribune*, 'taught white girls'.[26] Her AWAS service altered her world view:

> I joined the Australian Women's Army which really opened my eyes to the injustices suffered by Aboriginals. I'd always known, of course, but the war made people more equal in a way, and I got a taste of not being just a maid in a white man's house.[27]

She became more politically involved and outspoken on service-related issues and equal rights for Aboriginal people, becoming a prominent activist (see chapter 13).

Noonuccal was not alone in having a desire for something more. The WAAAF application of Alice McDonald (née Lovett), from Hamilton, Victoria, contained a revealing recruiter's annotation: 'is tired of housework'.[28] McDonald had worked as a domestic/child minder in Brighton. She became a mess woman at Nhill flight training school, and later recalled what the precise routine involved: from setting tables, to how the dishes were washed and the jam tins set for the meals of men returning from nightshift flights.[29] Such work sounds domestic and repetitive, much like her previous employment. Yet, working for the WAAAF had some key differences. There was adult company, it was less isolating and the pay was better. McDonald rejected a promotion in Queensland to work in a Footscray munitions factory with her friends including Marjorie (Marge) Tucker.[30] McDonald gleefully related a story about banking her final Army payout, irrespective of her husband's wishes, foregrounding her independent decision making:

> I just said to Claude 'You wheel the baby and I'll just race into the bank.' He said 'No, no, don't bank it all, don't bank it all.' I was in the door before he could leave the baby. I went in and I banked the money and I wouldn't give it to him, he couldn't get it out and he was going crook.[31]

However, there were challenges living in the women's barracks on the RAAF base and returning from her night shifts:

> Sometimes the men were a bit rough. They were drunk before they finished work and you've got to be very careful. I had to go across to my barracks in the dark and oh there was men waiting

> in the laundry, just along from where you go into the dining rooms. I was a bit scared. They waited around to see if they could coax you out.[32]

Jean Williamson (née Stewart) from Melbourne, worked in a box factory and as a boot jacker before joining the WAAAF in mid-1945.[33] Williamson also found aspects of service life to be confronting, especially the lack of privacy in the bathrooms at the Point Cook RAAF base. Later when she worked at the Heidelberg Repatriation Hospital in Melbourne, she had to wash male patients, a task which, as a steward, she felt unprepared for. She recalled that she had been attracted to the WAAAF as her friends were joining and because she liked the outfit: 'The uniform! Big time! It was big time to be in the Air Force, to be one of the girls.'[34] Williamson's recollection points to how the uniform was understood by some servicewomen to convey an authority otherwise not readily available to them, and was also associated with a sense of belonging.

Williamson was the youngest WAAAF at the time, and friendships, dances and romance feature in her oral history. She met her future husband, RAAF serviceman Noel, at a dance. She left the WAAAF to marry him in 1946 and they were still married (and dancing) until he passed away 69 years later. Williamson was unaware of her Aboriginal background before and during her service and, being fair-complexioned, she did not recall being treated differently. Since learning of her Taungurung heritage, she has embraced it and attends family reunions and sits on numerous Aboriginal advisory bodies. This contrasts sharply with Pike's experience. For Pike, showing awareness of her background was 'dangerous', and 'passing' as best she could was a strategic necessity until many years after service.[35] Aboriginal women on the home front also carefully foregrounded particular aspects of their identity during the Second

World War and after, especially to avoid protection regimes, as Karen Hughes has shown.[36]

Service in the post-war decades

After the Second World War the women's auxiliary services were disbanded but then revived: the Women's Royal Australian Air Force, WRAAF (1951–1977), Women's Royal Australian Naval Service, WRANS (1951–1985), Women's Royal Australian Army Corps, WRAAC (1951–1984) and Royal Australian Army Nursing Corps, RAANC (1951–). These services were reconstituted partly because there were fewer men enlisting in the defence forces, and Cold War engagements and fear of another total war put demands on the number of servicemen. Despite doing the same work as the men, these women were mostly paid two-thirds of the male wage (some later had increases to a three-quarter wage).

Some 36 Aboriginal and Torres Strait Islander women are known to have served in these services. They often listed clerk and typist as previous occupations, though several still listed domestic work. Many of the women served as stewards, others worked in communications and nursing. Again, most came from country or regional towns. More women joined the WRANS in this period. In the 1960s, *The Dawn*, a New South Wales Aborigines Welfare Board magazine, promoted service employment for women as part of its pro-assimilation position. The magazine featured photographs of Val Close and Marj Tripp in their WRANS uniforms. Val Close (née Brown) from Woodenbong Reserve was depicted as an achiever, having passed her school exams, completed a typist's course in Sydney, and working as a clerk. She stated that she was used to discipline from her family and had adjusted well to Navy life since joining up in 1964.[37]

Of the 11 ex-servicewomen interviewed in 2014–16, most had

served in the 1960s and 1970s (see chapter 10 also). These women emphasised that they did not see active combat. Revealingly, some of the women came to Yarn Ups to speak about male relatives who had served, not their own service. It was only through discussion that their service was mentioned, and they were encouraged to speak about their experiences. They often shifted the focus to discussing the recognition of others who served, or used humour to deflect attention from themselves. For example, Pattie Lees (née Janke) shared her own experiences, but paid tribute to Fran Loban from Thursday Island, who served from 1966 to 1970 and helped her to adjust to life in the WRANS.[38] Tracey Hoffman (née Cannard), from Cairns who joined the Navy in 1985, discussed her children's defence service achievements nearly as much as her own.[39] Phrases such as 'it was only for a few years' downplayed the significance of their work, a common feature of women's oral histories.[40] That they *did* speak of their defence service is a powerful statement nonetheless. As Kathleen Ryan stated of interviewing US ex-servicewomen: 'through telling the stories, the women are saying they and their work mattered'.[41]

The reasons these women gave for their joining up were diverse and multifaceted. For some it was a way of fulfilling a childhood ambition, such as working on planes, as highlighted in the cases of Linda Albert and Elizabeth Pike. Many were inspired by their families' service history. Marjorie (Marj) Tripp, a Ramindjeri woman who grew up in McLaren Vale and Goolwa, South Australia, joined the WRANS in 1963 because her cousin Daryl Sumner had joined the Navy:

> We were like Danny de Vito and Arnie Schwarzenegger [in the movie *Twins*], we were! I was the big girl and he was the little boy, he's the blue-eyed blond and I'm the black fella. But we were brought up like brother and sister, me and him. We were both

> taken, well ... I was left, when I was a baby, left in a home. And he had to go when his mother decided she didn't need any kids. So we were always close, always, and that sort of made me go.[42]

Numerous members of Tripp's family had served in the two world wars. Even so, she had to seek the permission of the Protector of Aborigines to enlist.[43] Family history also influenced Gaye Doolan's (née Holt) joining, as she knew her Aboriginal father, Tasman Holt, had served in the Second World War. A Palawa woman from Launceston, Doolan worked in Communications in the WRANS from 1968 to 1972, having joined at the age of 17. She chose the WRANS, she said facetiously, 'for all the right reasons – the uniform!'. Exceeding her father's limited expectations of her was another reason. His words, 'you are just a girl, you don't need an education', stung Doolan and she was determined to prove him wrong.[44]

A distinctive reason some Aboriginal women joined up was their desire to escape the influences of Aboriginal welfare authorities or institutional care. Welfare boards had a great deal of influence over people's lives. They could remove Aboriginal children from their families, determine whom people could marry, restrict their movements, turn people off reserve land and compel Aboriginal people into exploitative labour (especially in Western Australia and Queensland).[45] For Pattie Lees from Cairns, who joined the WRANS in 1967 aged 18 and became a steward, the services were a means of extricating herself from 'protection'. She had been removed from her Murray Islander mother as a child, as had her other siblings, and placed in a Townsville orphanage. She was then made a ward of the state and confined to notorious Palm Island – a reserve where Aboriginal people were exiled, punished, and subjected to violence and oppressive conditions – with her brother. Later, she ran away to find her mother and then joined up.[46] Sue

Gordon (née Giller), a Ngoonooru Wajarri woman from near Meekatharra, Western Australia, was also taken from her mother as a child and sent to Sister Kate's Home in Perth. She joined the WRAAC in 1961, and worked in signals as a cipher operator, receiving top secret code during the 1962 Cuban Missile Crisis.[47] She regarded the services as a means of seeking and finding shelter after being taken away:

> When I was removed … I don't have a memory of it at all: that was post-traumatic stress. And he [her psychologist] found that a lot of the Stolen Generation people went through similar things and unless they spoke to somebody about it, they just carried it … and the way we joined the services, was not for patriotic reasons. I went because they were going to give me accommodation and pay me, and [Pattie] you were escaping Palm Island. So … there were a lot of women who went into the army for those reasons … And they found this safe haven.[48]

Lees also described the services as a 'sanctuary'. For both Lees and Gordon, joining the services was also an economic necessity because once they turned 18, the homes in which they had been placed as children would no longer shelter them. They had been told that they had no family (although in both cases they had been removed from them), so turning to relations for support was not an option. For Gordon, employment with the WRAAC provided 'a stable job', while Lees said that she also wanted work, and she was intrigued by an advertisement in the *Australian Post*, which said: 'Come and join the Navy, see the world'.[49]

Joining up was primarily a financial decision for Thelma Weston (née Williams), who had been evacuated from Mer Island to Cairns during the Second World War, then to Brisbane. She had left school to support her family, but went to night school to improve her prospects, and was accepted into the Brisbane General nursing course in 1952. She resigned to care for her ill mother and younger brothers, but once her mother recovered Weston had to find a job, so she joined the RAANC in 1954. She recalled in 2016 that: 'I loved being in the Army, but I don't think I was that patriotic. It was just a job … I thought will I go back to nursing. But all my friends had moved on.'[50] Weston trained in Queenscliff and Healesville in Victoria, then worked at Yeronga in Brisbane, looking after military patients including soldiers and national servicemen. To her knowledge she was the only Torres Strait Islander nurse in the RAANC at the time. Weston remembered the camaraderie as a high point of her service: 'all the girls, the comradeship in there … you didn't like the sergeants and the officers'.[51] After years of working in nursing homes, as a nurse's aide and raising her family in Perth, she qualified as an Aboriginal and Torres Strait Islander health worker, a career she continues at the time of writing.

New opportunities

The services also offered the chance to develop skills and travel. Eileen McHughes (née Kropinyeri) from Murray Bridge, South Australia joined the WRAAC in 1959. She had grown up at Three Mile Camp with her family, and later worked as a domestic, then at a roadhouse, at Tailem Bend. She wanted an education and reflected:

> I really wanted to be a truck driver … But I enjoyed it because I like meeting people and getting their views on things and I also got to go to places like Geelong and Queenscliff, in Victoria, and to Mosman Heights, in Sydney. It gave me the chance to have a look about the country where maybe I wouldn't have done if I hadn't been in the army.[52]

Gaining work and life skills was an aspect of their service that these women valued highly. For example, Linda Albert, a Yidinji/Girramay/Wujul Wujul/Kuku-Yalingi/Guugu-Yimithir and South Sea Islander woman from Babinda, Queensland, who served in the WRAAF from 1965 to 1975, said she had previously found mathematics challenging. She marvelled at how she ended up doing bookkeeping and wage management for large numbers of RAAF employees.[53] Albert was promoted to sergeant and said that being in the WRAAF 'opened up a lot of doors' for her.[54] Gordon and others mentioned how the services taught them discipline. Tripp said the Navy 'taught me how to do things right', while also developing her independence and good decision making.[55] These skills helped the women to operate successfully in higher education, government, health and community work after leaving the services. Several of them continue to be important community leaders in areas such as aged care, commemoration, education and health; they are highly regarded within their communities for this work and their mentoring.[56] Tripp received an Order of Australia Medal (OAM) for her services towards recognition of Aboriginal and Torres Strait Islander servicemen and women. Gordon became a magistrate and has led numerous inquiries, while Lees received an AM for services to the Mt Isa Indigenous community, and others like Doris Follent (aka Sue Bellear) received the Centenary Medal and NAIDOC awards (see chapter 13 also).

These women recalled that they became more confident, valuing themselves, their skills and their potential as a result of their time in service: as Riseman and Trembath have noted, it enhanced the women's leadership abilities.[57] Lees recalled in 2014 that being in the WRANS 'helped build her', gave her resilience, and a strong sense of purpose.[58] For Doolan, it was a time of learning to live independently, flatting 'on shore' in Sydney with a female Navy friend, her first experience of living away from home. She recalled they made signal flag curtains and held weekend gatherings, creating some sense of an unregimented 'normal life'.[59]

Defence service was cast as a central part of these women's transition from being young or naive to more worldly. For those who had lived in the country, it was often their first taste of city life. Albert recalled there were opportunities to enjoy city entertainment with the other 'girls', such as going to the Silver Spade Room in Kings Cross:

> Even to this day, I can see Shirley Bassey there. This is when she released her song 'Hey Big Spender' … Absolutely blew me away … We used to go to the RSL at Richmond, I saw Sandy Scott, Col Joye … And it was just a different time in life. And you always dressed up.[60]

Whether recalling unwitting encounters with drug dealers in Sydney, or cluelessly strolling in white shoes that sex workers wore to signal their availability to kerb crawlers in St Kilda, these women often represented themselves as being 'green behind the ears'. Their oral histories are coming-of-age stories, moving from girlhood to womanhood, a time of relative freedom and independence before marriage and children.[61]

Personal relationships

For many of the women their service time also meant encountering more diverse sexual possibilities than they had been aware of. They were cautioned about lesbians and were told not to share or sit on each other's beds.[62] As Gordon later recalled:

> [I] joined as an 18 year old, I knew nothing about the world. When we first went out to Watsonia, another worldly corporal

> pointed out 'the lesbians', never be on my own with any of those two. I didn't even know what a lesbian was![63]

Lesbian relationships were not widely discussed, and since the term was rarely used, many women were surprised by it.[64] Gordon indicated that within the WRAAC lesbianism was tacitly acknowledged as a fact of service life, with few punitive consequences. By contrast, Doolan recalled that in her first four weeks at the WRANS, women were dismissed for being 'discovered' as same-sex attracted.[65] As historian Ruth Ford has argued, the services were faced with a dilemma: by mentioning lesbianism as something to guard against, they publicised its existence, even as they were seeking to stamp it out.[66] Sex education was a revelation for some of the women too, with graphic images of venereal diseases shown in presentations, and later being the cause of much laughter among themselves.

Several women mentioned that they provided emotional support and guidance to higher ranked servicemen. Gordon explained it as 'another role that women in service had … that you walked in to'.[67] Gendered perceptions of women as empathetic listeners were associated with their service. For example, Lees became an unofficial counsellor to her boss:

> I virtually saved his marriage, I was his confidante, I told him how to look after his kids. When he'd had a fight with his wife, I'd tell him send her a box of chocolates, I used to tell him how to live.[68]

Doolan found that she was uniquely placed to assist a male pen-pal friend who had seen some 'awful' things when serving, including the 1969 HMAS *Melbourne* and USS *Frank E Evans* collision, resulting in 74 deaths. She recalled:

> He debriefed by beginning to talk to me, and having somebody he could write to … Somebody in civvy street wouldn't understand those sorts of things. He couldn't talk to somebody at home about it. His mates he could probably … sometimes the females in the services were someone … who understood them.[69]

The emotional work that these women did has not been recognised, but they identified it as an important contribution that they had made. It is significant that these recollections of emotional work emerged in group discussion, rather than individual interviews, suggesting that opportunities for collective reflection are important in triggering storytelling.[70]

Even as they helped others, these women bore an emotional cost. This was especially so when they received news of relatives and acquaintances serving in Vietnam, and injured men began to return. Doris Follent from Chinderah, New South Wales, who had worked as a nurse for ten years before joining the Army Nursing Corps in 1963, alluded to challenges she faced at work, including seeing the first Australian Vietnam serviceman 'only about 19', die in an Australian hospital. While she said she did not get close to patients and that work was business, she left the service soon after that incident.[71]

Marriage and pregnancy emerged as a frequent topic in these women's oral histories. Several had to leave because they were marrying, a requirement of all women in the Navy and Army services until 1968, and 1969 for the Air Force. Until 1973, pregnancy meant certain dismissal. Doolan recalled women being 'out in 24 hours or less' once pregnancy was discovered. Demonstrating that you were *not* pregnant took considerable time and energy too. Tripp recalled conspicuously 'parading up and down the street [in Victor Harbor] in my uniform' every couple of days, to prove to the town gossips that she was not pregnant. She located this episode within her experiences of racism in Victor Harbor, which she described as 'a wicked place'. Her family had to live on the outskirts of town, were falsely presumed to have stolen goods, and her father was hassled by police for 'consorting'.[72] Tripp was subjected to extra surveillance as an Aboriginal woman and had to contend with prevailing assumptions about Indigenous women's sexual availability and being stereotyped as 'Jezebels' who sought 'trouble'.[73] Yet even more strikingly, her memories demonstrated how she used her agency to take charge of the situation; as she said, to 'show them!'. Doolan recalled that the attitudes of some naval personnel were sexist and negative, considering that 'we were there doing a job as well'. Some male officers referred to the WRANS as 'dogs', and the women's accommodation blocks as 'the kennels'.[74]

Racism

Racism was also present during the women's service. Although many of the women interviewed said they did not personally experience racism within the services, and were treated equally, they witnessed colleagues who did so. Gordon recalled racist insults being used against her colleague Irene, who retaliated verbally.[75] Gordon gravitated to Irene and 'Lofty', an Aboriginal serviceman, as a 'protective mechanism'.[76] Her account of dealing with racism is narrated as a story of sticking together.[77] Albert, as the only Aboriginal woman in her WRAAF unit, recalled being stared at, treated as a novelty and being made to feel different. Her younger brothers in the Army were refused drinks in hotels, but she was not. Rather, people were surprised that she had rank and she felt they underestimated her because of her background. She drew strength from her knowledge of her family's service history, especially the words of her father, Eddie Albert, who served in the Second World War: 'I fought for this country.'[78]

In Aboriginal ex-servicemen's oral histories and memoirs, being excluded from a bar or RSL clubs features frequently. These were masculine spaces until 1965, when women were finally allowed to drink in the public bar rather than the 'ladies lounge'. Women gathered elsewhere, such as at movie theatres, and their stories reflect this gendered and racialised geography. As historian Maria Nugent has argued, segregation at cinemas appears frequently in Aboriginal women's autobiographies, cinemas serving as a site for pushing for changes in race relations and dramatising them too.[79]

Cecilia Stanley-Taylor, who identifies as South Sea Islander and Indigenous Australian, came from Bowen, Queensland, to join the WRAAF, working in the officers' mess as a 'glorified waitress'. She recalled witnessing blatant racism in civilian Melbourne when a WRAAF and RAAF group went to the movies and her friend Janette was refused entry:

> She wasn't dark, she was whiter than me and yet she wasn't allowed in. And I said 'They can't do that to you!' … I went up to the counter and I said 'Hey you let me in, and you won't let her in, what's the difference?' And they said 'Oh no she's Aboriginal' … And I said 'Well, I can't go in either, so give me my money back' … Before long everyone came back out and they were all white … We all asked for our money back and we decided we'd just go into town till the bus came back for us.[80]

She recalled too that Janette was subjected to racism within the WRAAF itself. When Stanley-Taylor was transferred back to Townsville, some officers were racist towards her and other service-people. Others, however, treated her well. Her stories of racism were focused around achieving acceptance of Indigenous peoples in the services:

> I would always go to … the ones that were ostracised and support them and then a lot of the non-Indigenous would come across and support them as well … We were the first ones and they weren't used to having us, as part of their groups … But once we got in, we made it known that we was there! [laughs].[81]

Like Albert, Stanley-Taylor mentioned that some southerners had primitivist ideas about people from the north, presuming they lived in grass huts and wandered about naked. Even so, the depth of racism in northern Australia was mentioned by many female interviewees from the north as something they became more acutely aware of *after* their service in southern cities, suggesting they found southern cities more accepting.[82]

The ADF: A postscript

From 1977, the WRAAF was disbanded, followed by the WRAAC and WRANS in the mid-1980s, and women joined the mainstream Australian Defence Force. Equal pay was introduced from 1979, and women could marry and remain employed. The *Sex Discrimination Act 1984* and associated policy changes ultimately saw more roles and career paths opened to women, including deployment from 1990 and combat from 2016.[83] Aboriginal identity was increasingly being celebrated and valued more highly in the ADF (see chapter 15). Issues remain with the acceptance of women as equals, evident in sexual harassment cases and relatively low numbers of women serving. Much has changed, though. Just some of those changes and opportunities for travel, a career, family and pride in identity are evident in Tracey Hoffman's story. She joined the Navy in 1985 as a communicator, then had a family. She worked as an Army nursing officer in 2005 and transferred to the Navy in 2006. During her career, Hoffman worked with an international team on the US Navy ship *Mercy* in Indonesia. She has also been a platoon commander with Indigenous pre-recruitment programs. In 2014, approaching retirement, she reflected on the assets she brought to her career:

> I loved my sea time … and I think I did very well at it, just the camaraderie … the sharing of something that's totally unique. Not only am I a female in the Defence force, I'm also … an older mother and an Indigenous woman as well. So I've got all these extras to bring and I just made the most of it.[84]

From oral histories and other resources we can recover the formerly obscured history of Aboriginal and Torres Strait Islander women's involvement in the Defence forces. Their efforts to escape state control, to explore opportunities and develop life and workplace skills were prominent in their narratives about their time in the services. Less widely acknowledged skills, such as unofficial counselling roles, were also identified as important contributions they had made, especially to male colleagues and managers. Restrictive policies which meant marriage was the end of their career opportunities in the forces curtailed some of their momentum, though many women used the skills and contacts they had developed to serve their communities, as a 'service after the services', in health, recognition of military service, education and other fields. More recently, changing policies on marriage, pregnancy and sex discrimination have widened the opportunities available to women, though challenges remain. Their powerful accounts of their service enrich the history of Aboriginal and Torres Strait Islander people and Defence history, and their work and commitment continue to be a source of cultural pride for themselves and their communities.

12.1 Ella Thompson, AWAS servicewoman, c.1944–45.
Source: Pat Kopusar

12.2 Jean Williamson, WAAAF, with Noel Williamson, RAAF, in their winter uniforms, taken at a Melbourne garden, c.1945–46.
Source: Jean Williamson

12.3 *Above* Gaye Doolan, in her WRANS uniform c.1968–72.

Source: Gaye Doolan

13.1 *Top right* FCAATSI delegation meeting with Prime Minister Menzies in September 1963. Left to right: Kath Walker (Oodgeroo Noonuccal); Ted Penney; Gordon Bryant, MP; Elia Ware; Sir Robert Menzies, Prime Minister; Unknown; Joe McGinness, President of FCAATSI, shaking hands with the Prime Minister; Pastor Doug Nicholls.

Source: Fairfax Media

13.2 *Below right* Korean veteran Ken Colbung meeting with Malcom Fraser.

Source: AIATSIS COLBUNG.K08.BW-N03946_32

13.3 Rob Riley, in his capacity as chair of the National Aboriginal Conference, conducting a press conference at Parliament House, Canberra, 16 August 1984.

Source: Fairfax Media, image courtesy of ACT Heritage Library

HOLDINGS
HANDOUT
MENTALITY
LABOUR LIES on
HERITAGE
LEGISLATION
CLYD
is
CONNING
ABORIGINES

14.1 Members of NORFORCE demonstrate patrolling skills in remote Arnhem Land in 2005 for visiting members of the Defence Sub-Committee of the Australian Parliament's Joint Standing Committee on Foreign Affairs, Defence and Trade.
Source: Commonwealth of Australia, Department of Defence, 2005_S1398_08

Patricia

14.2 *Top left* Sergeant Tommy Munyarryun (right) indicates areas of historical significance to other members of Arnhem Squadron, NORFORCE, at Caledon Bay, Northern Territory, during a study tour in September 2014.

Source: Commonwealth of Australia, Department of Defence, 20140916adf8526959_201

14.3 *Left* Patricia Gibson undergoes live-fire training on the F88 Austeyr rifle under the watchful eye of Corporal James Woods of the North-West Mobile Force at the marksmanship training range at Robertson Barracks, Darwin, on 3 March 2016.

Source: Commonwealth of Australia, Department of Defence, 20160303ran8484535_001

15.1 *Above* Aboriginal soldier Private Graeme M ('Brownie') Brown on foot patrol in the streets of Baidoa, Somalia. Private Brown was a member of 2 Platoon, A Company, 1st Battalion, 1RAR, serving with the Australian contingent to the UNITAF.

Source: AWM P01735.401

H.M.A.S. CERBERUS

15.2 Commodore Justin Jones CSC, RAN (centre) with the graduating recruits of the Defence Indigenous Development Program at HMAS Cairns, Queensland, 15 December 2015.
Source: Commonwealth of Australia 2015, image number S20163289

15.3 Australian Army soldier Corporal Mark Rudledge is welcomed to country by Aboriginal traditional owners from the Daly River region, Northern Territory, where a three-week survival exercise for Australian, Chinese and US military, called Exercise Kowari, was held in 2015.

Source: Commonwealth of Australia 2015, image number S20152378

16.1 Korean War veteran and Aboriginal activist Ken Colbung, and his stepson Robert Ridgeway, laying wreaths at Hyde Park War Memorial, Sydney, in 1969.
Source: AIATSIS COLBUNG.K15.BW-N05704_10

16.2 Lieutenant TC Derrick (right) shaking hands with Lieutenant RW Saunders, as they congratulate each other following their successful graduation from the Officer's Cadet Training Unit at Seymour, Victoria. This image was used in the Australian government's 'Australia Remembers' campaign.

Source: AWM 083166

16.3 Dancers from the Bangarra Dance Company perform in front of Tony Albert's Yininmadyemi sculpture, featuring marble and steel bullets, during the launch of the memorial for Aboriginal and Torres Strait Islander servicemen and women in Hyde Park, Sydney, 31 March 2015.

Source: AAP, photograph by Mick Tsikas

13

Ex-service activism after 1945

Noah Riseman

'He [Len Culbong] went overseas to fight for his country, and he came back and he was still fighting for his country, for recognition of his people and for social justice and things like that.'
– *Margaret Culbong*

It is a story threaded through this book: Indigenous men and women joining the armed forces, protecting Australia at home and abroad, being treated in many instances as equals, and then returning to civilian life to face racial prejudice. It was not just individual incidents of racism that these ex-service personnel confronted. Until the 1970s (and the 1980s in Queensland), various state and Commonwealth jurisdictions continued to restrict aspects of Indigenous people's lives, such as access to wages, permission to drink alcohol and freedom of movement. For instance, it was illegal to serve alcohol to Aboriginal people in Western Australia until 1972; in Queensland 'assisted Aborigines' could be denied equal wages and the right to own property until 1971, and the *Aborigines Act 1971* continued to allow district officers to manage Aboriginal people's property in certain situations as well as require permits to enter reserves. In 2000 Western Australian Vietnam veteran Phil Prosser told two stories about the contrasting treatment he received in military and civilian life. The first is from early in his Army career, when a mate invited him to have a drink:

> Walking up to the canteen, as you walk through the front door, to the right was what we referred to as the wet canteen, the bar, and to the left was the dry canteen. And of course it was just an automatic reaction, as I walked in I went to go left. This guy grabbed me by the arm, and he said, 'Hey come on, in here.' He says, 'You're allowed in here now.' He says, 'Those bastards can't touch you anymore.'[1]

In the second story Prosser was out of uniform at the Hotel Manly in Sydney with some Army mates:

> And the steward came up to take orders … he turned to me and the guy said, 'I'm sorry; I can't serve this gentleman because he's Aboriginal.' And of course they became pretty upset, the guys. They said, 'But he's in the Army. You've got to serve him.' He said, 'I'm sorry but we can't.' So he refused to serve me.[2]

Not surprisingly, veterans such as Prosser were angered at returning to such inequality, and after 1945 many ex-service personnel played an active role fighting for Aboriginal and Torres Strait Islander civil rights. They were aptly suited among Indigenous Australians to become activists for several reasons. Not only had service in the armed forces given them a glimpse of equality, challenging notions of discrimination inherent in Australian society; but defending Australia and its supposed values of democracy and freedom also empowered Indigenous service personnel to fight for those very principles in their everyday lives. Moreover, while in the defence forces Aboriginal men and women were exposed to white bureaucracy and learned to work with(in) such frameworks. Whether through their military employment or through repatriation schemes, Indigenous service personnel also acquired new professional and educational skills that they could apply in their post-service lives.

There is a significant difference in how military service linked with activism during the post-war era when compared to the interwar years. As chapter 6 discussed, First World War veterans and the families of deceased Aboriginal servicemen cited their honourable military service as one of the reasons Aboriginal people should be granted equal citizenship rights. In the post–Second World War era, military service did not feature so heavily in Indigenous claims to rights. In the 1950s and 1960s, the arguments for equal citizenship rights were primarily grounded in international discourses of human rights and drew heavily on strategies and rhetoric from the African-American civil rights movement.[3] Since the 1970s, arguments for Indigenous rights have centred around the language of self-determination, while still appealing to global human rights discourse. Although military service was not prevalent among post-war activists' arguments, there was a link through the individual ex-servicemen and women who became involved in these causes for Indigenous advancement. It is those biographical experiences that drive this chapter.

Of course, not all Indigenous ex-service personnel became activists, and many who were involved in projects to advance the interests of Indigenous communities would shun the term 'activist' because of its associations with radicalism and protest. Yet, a significant number of ex-service personnel, whether upon their discharge or later in life, became strong advocates for their communities. This chapter will explore the many faces of Aboriginal and Torres Strait Islander activism and advocacy in the post–Second World War era. The early years tended to be state and national in focus, with veterans from the Second World War and Korea involved in organisations affiliated with the Federal Council for the Advancement of Aborigines and Torres Strait Islanders (FCAATSI) and being at the forefront of campaigns such as the 1967 referendum. During the land rights and Black Power struggles between the referendum and the 1972 election of the Whitlam Labor government, ex-service personnel played a less prominent national role and were still focused on state issues. With the rise of Indigenous self-management and new bureaucracies during the Whitlam (1972–75) and Fraser (1975–83) governments, Indigenous ex-service personnel became more involved in the management and leadership of Indigenous organisations at grassroots and state levels, pursuing projects designed to address specific aspects of Indigenous disadvantage.

Indigenous veterans' activism, 1945–67

Generally it was not until the 1950s that Indigenous veterans of the Second World War began to organise for civil rights battles, but in the previous decade they found support from some non-Indigenous allies. The RSL, often viewed as a bastion of Australian conservatism, was one high-profile organisation that largely (though not wholly) pushed for Indigenous veterans to have equal citizenship rights. In 1946, the RSL's annual congress passed a resolution that stated: 'the Commonwealth Government be requested to grant the franchise to Aboriginal ex-servicemen'.[4] Ultimately, amendments to the *Commonwealth Electoral Act 1949* granted Aboriginal or Torres Strait Islander current and former servicepeople the right to vote in federal elections.

In the 1950s numerous Aboriginal and Torres Strait Islander organisations emerged in urban and regional areas, usually in centres with growing Indigenous populations. Second World War veterans were at the forefront of many of these organisations. For instance, Joe McGinness had enlisted in the Army and served in South

Australia, Victoria and Borneo. After the war he worked on Thursday Island before settling in Cairns, where he became involved in the union movement. In 1958 McGinness became the founding secretary of the Cairns Aborigines and Torres Strait Islanders Advancement League, along with other veterans such as Torres Strait Light Infantry Battalion member Elia Ware. This organisation challenged the state government's mistreatment of Indigenous people in far north Queensland, taking up cases of missionary and police brutality. Importantly, the Cairns League worked with white allies and strove to make connections with similar-minded organisations within Australia and overseas.[5]

Other organisations in Queensland with veterans at the helm were the Queensland Council for the Advancement of Aborigines and Torres Strait Islanders (QCAATSI) and the One People of Australia League (OPAL). Oodgeroo Noonuccal, formerly known as Kath Walker, was a QCAATSI leader and consistently credited her Second World War service as changing the direction of her life. She remembered the Australian Women's Army Service as an overwhelmingly egalitarian experience: '[In] the army, I was accepted as one of them and none of the girls I trained with cared whether I was black, blue or purple. For the first time in my life I felt equal to other human beings.'[6] Noonuccal took advantage of repatriation courses offered to ex-servicemen and women – one of the few tertiary education schemes available to Indigenous Australians.[7]

After the war Noonuccal moved to Brisbane and settled in what was, until then, a white neighbourhood, where she encountered casual racism. In the 1950s she joined the Communist Party of Australia because it was the only political party that included equal rights for Aboriginal people in its platform. However, she quickly decided she did not like their modus operandi and groupthink, so she shifted her involvement towards new

Queensland Indigenous rights organisations. In 1958 she joined the QCAATSI and by 1960 she was elected the organisation's secretary.[8] QCAATSI was the Queensland affiliate of the newly formed Federal Council for the Advancement of Aborigines and Torres Strait Islanders (FCAATSI) and therefore was involved in much of the groundwork for federal campaigns such as the 1967 referendum. But as a Queensland organisation, QCAATSI was also focused on state issues, such as the ongoing discrimination segregating Indigenous Australians and controlling them on reserves through legislation such as the *Queensland Aborigines Preservation and Protection Act*.

Another Second World War veteran who became a QCAATSI leader was Lambert ('Stan') McBride. His daughter, Linda McBride-Yuke, recalled in 2009 that he joined the Army for two reasons: 'It was guaranteed income, and he did honestly feel like he wanted to defend his country and contribute to the defence of it. So it's twofold: it was for purely economic reasons of a steady income; and also getting a trade.' McBride served in Townsville in the Transportation Corps, where he learned to drive Army trucks, and also worked as a carpenter on military construction projects such as building bridges and roads.[9] After the war McBride and his wife May settled in Brisbane, where he continued to work as a bridge carpenter. As an early Aboriginal family to settle in Brisbane post-1945, the McBrides were shielded from the most restrictive aspects of protection legislation. Lambert was someone whom newly arrived Murris summoned for help, and gradually he became involved in organising the community. The McBrides were both active in OPAL and then QCAATSI in the 1960s, Lambert serving as QCAATSI president for much of the decade, while May was the publicity officer.[10] Their daughter Linda explained:

> They'd be lobbying, mainly for that Queensland Act to be dismantled, but other kinds of issues on the side were Aboriginal education, Aboriginal employment, deaths in custody, housing: all that stuff that Aboriginal people had to fight tooth and nail to get because they were second-class citizens.[11]

Second World War veterans in other states, who were similarly focused on local and state issues, included Douglas Nicholls (Victoria) and Bert Groves (NSW). Both of these men represented links between the pre- and post-war activists. Nicholls had grown up on the Cummeragunja Reserve on the New South Wales side of the Murray River, before being forced out to fend for himself at age 14 under rules set by the New South Wales *Aborigines Protection Act 1909*. Nicholls found success in sport as a runner, then as a boxer, and finally as an Australian Rules footballer, playing for Fitzroy in Melbourne. In the late 1930s he became active in Fitzroy's growing Aboriginal community and William Cooper's Australian Aborigines' League, even attending the 1938 Day of Mourning protest in Sydney. Interestingly, even though the *Defence Act* released Aboriginal people from compulsory national service, Nicholls did not ask for an exemption when he received a notice from the Citizen Military Forces in June 1941. Nicholls' time in the Army was short-lived, however; in 1942 the police requested his discharge so that he could return to Fitzroy and ease racial tensions among the white community and the rapidly growing Aboriginal population, as well as African-American servicemen.[12]

After the war, Nicholls became ordained as a minister and set up the Gore Street Mission to preach to and support Fitzroy's Aboriginal community. In addition to his charity work, he protested against the Woomera Rocket Range tests on Aboriginal land and the abuses perpetrated against Victorian Koories by the Aborigines Protection Board (reconstituted as the Welfare Board in 1957). In

1957 Nicholls was one of two Aboriginal people appointed to the Welfare Board, and in the same year he co-founded the Victorian Aborigines Advancement League. That organisation focused on Victorian Aboriginal issues, such as protesting against the planned closure of Lake Tyers Reserve in 1963 (an issue over which Nicholls resigned from the Aborigines Welfare Board).[13]

Bert Groves had briefly been involved in William Ferguson's Aborigines Progressive Association in the late 1930s. He enlisted in the AIF in April 1943 and served in Australia for almost two years before being discharged in January 1945, with the official reason listed as 'there being no suitable vacancy in which his services could be employed'.[14] At the war's end Groves moved to Sydney and continued his involvement in the Aborigines Progressive Association, chairing meetings and organising social dances which doubled as fundraisers for the newly formed Redfern All-Blacks Rugby Club. Groves was involved in other Sydney campaigns, such as the small-scale protests against the rocket testing in the Western Desert (1946–47). In 1947 Groves became secretary of the Sydney branch of the now interstate Australian Aborigines' League, and in 1956 was elected inaugural president of the newly formed Aboriginal-Australian Fellowship.[15] Though this organisation challenged discrimination at the New South Wales state level, it also became actively involved in the organisation of FCAATSI and the national campaign for the 1967 referendum.[16]

The formation of FCAATSI in 1958 marked a turning point towards coordinated national activism. In 1961 Joe McGinness became FCAATSI's president, a position which he held until the organisation was discontinued in 1973. Other veterans, such as Oodgeroo Noonuccal and Lambert McBride, held leadership roles in state chapters such as the aforementioned QCAATSI. In its first decade FCAATSI campaigned for changes to Commonwealth legislation relating to social security, pastoral workers' wages, voting rights and Aboriginal health. FCAATSI also challenged assimilation policies, instead advocating for the integration of Indigenous Australians. While the distinction is subtle, 'integration' signified allowing Indigenous people to participate in all aspects of Australian society as equals, while not sacrificing their own cultural practices.[17] FCAATSI directed most of its energy towards securing a referendum to amend two sections of the Commonwealth constitution: firstly, to repeal section 127, which forbade governments including Aboriginal people in the census for population statistics; and secondly, to remove a clause in section 51 which forbade the Commonwealth from making laws relating to Aboriginal people.[18]

The abovementioned Aboriginal and Torres Strait Islander veterans were some of the highest profile activists lobbying for the 1967 referendum. Indeed, at one September 1963 meeting of FCAATSI delegates and Prime Minister Robert Menzies, four of the six Aboriginal and Torres Strait Islander representatives were Second World War veterans: Oodgeroo Noonuccal, Doug Nicholls, Joe McGinness and Elia Ware. South Sea Islander FCAATSI secretary Faith Bandler – herself an ex-member of the Australian Women's Land Army – in 1989 recalled an anecdote from that meeting:

> When the meeting ended we all showed signs of relief and began to relax as the Prime Minister offered drinks. He turned to Kath Walker and asked her what she would like to drink; whether she preferred whiskey or some other alcoholic beverage. Kath told the Prime Minister that if he had made that offer to her in Queensland, he would have been gaoled. Shock clouded Menzies' face and when he had regained composure he told Kath that he 'was the boss around here' and proceeded to pour her a drink. I believe that was the turning point – the incident caused him to give the situation of Aborigines more thought.[19]

When the referendum was scheduled for May 1967, FCAATSI activists swung into action to encourage a Yes vote. Linda McBride-Yuke was young at the time, but she remembered her father Lambert, working tirelessly:

> He'd be going back and forth from Brisbane to Queensland, Brisbane to Queensland. Mum stayed at home a lot of the time because us kids were small, but some of the records show that they travelled in their own car, at their own cost. They'd do fundraising to get petrol so that they could go to all the different communities except for missions because they wouldn't have been allowed on the missions, because you need a permit from the white superintendent. Enrolling and encouraging them to vote, and leaving them with some PR thing about [what] you need to get enrol[led], who you need to vote for; we need your support.[20]

The 1967 referendum campaign also attracted service personnel from the post-war era. Korea veteran Ken Colbung was still in the Army at the time, but campaigned with the Aboriginal community at La Perouse in Sydney. He recalled in 2007: 'We used to go out in our civvies and protest. We weren't supposed to mix politics with Army life, and if they'd caught us, they'd have run us in, but we never did get caught.'[21] The 1967 referendum passed with 90.77 per cent of Australians voting yes – the highest Yes vote ever recorded in a federal referendum.

Indigenous ex-servicemen and women's activism 1967–80

After the 1967 referendum, the Commonwealth government had the power to pass legislation relating to Aboriginal and Torres Strait Islander people, but rarely did it exercise that power. Many of the veteran-activists therefore continued their work in FCAATSI and state organisations, pushing for the repeal of extant discriminatory legislation. As with the campaigns leading up to the 1967 referendum, this work entailed building coalitions with non-Indigenous organisations such as unions, and religious and community groups. It also was a conservative form of activism, in that much of the work entailed lobbying activities rather than civil disobedience: petitions, holding public meetings, door-knocking and at times peaceful demonstrations.

As problems continued with poor Indigenous health, low levels of educational achievement and police brutality in custody, a younger generation of activists grew frustrated with the lack of progress in Indigenous affairs. This new wave of activism tended to be urban-based and more radical, and derived its inspiration from the United States Black Power movement. These activists were not afraid of police confrontations and significant tensions developed, particularly in places like Redfern in Sydney.

The event for which Black Power is most famous is the 1972 Aboriginal Tent Embassy protest in Canberra. Frustrated with the Commonwealth government's obstinate refusal to grant Aboriginal land rights, a group of activists travelled to the lawn outside Parliament House (now the Old Parliament) and pitched a beach umbrella with the name 'Aboriginal Embassy'. For almost six months they gathered national and international attention as the Tent Embassy became a lightning rod for Indigenous rights protesters. Members of the referendum movement joined this protest, including Faith Bandler and Doug Nicholls, who were captured in the footage of police violently breaking up the embassy protest in July 1972.[22]

Oodgeroo Noonuccal is one of the few persons with a record of military service who was involved in some of the other protests associated with the Black Power movement. While not a Black Power activist per se, in 1969 she joined the newly formed Brisbane

Aboriginal and Islanders Tribal Council. She was part of a growing movement within FCAATSI and its constituent groups to hand control over to Aboriginal people. When white members of QCAATSI objected to such propositions and even claimed 'We've made Kath Walker what she is', Noonuccal walked out and subsequently led the push for Aboriginal control of the Federal Council.[23] She also participated in a 1970 protest against the re-enactment of Captain Cook's 1770 arrival at Botany Bay. She remarked at that protest:

> No, I don't think we're rejecting modern white Australia. What we're doing is trying to wake them up out of their modern apathetic attitudes. Because we know how serious is the health of the race of the people – of the Aboriginal and Island people – and we are a race that could be wiped out unless the Australian public charges the government with the responsibility of doing something for the Aboriginal people.[24]

Noonuccal's son, Denis, was a founding member of the Brisbane chapter of the Australian Black Panther Party. Later in the 1970s Noonuccal became involved in the World Council of Churches, promoting Aboriginal rights and culture around the world. She also founded Moongalba on her traditional land of North Stradbroke Island in 1971, as a place for teaching culture to Indigenous and non-Indigenous students. In the 1980s Noonuccal continued to be involved in movements such as opposing nuclear power and campaigning for Aboriginal land rights. While she did reduce her activism due to aging and ill-health, she was still involved in the Bicentenary protests, in 1987 returning her MBE (which had been awarded in 1970) and changing her name to Oodgeroo Noonuccal.[25]

In Victoria, Second World War veteran Stewart Murray underwent a similar journey to Noonuccal's. Murray was a founding member of the Victorian Aborigines Advancement League in 1957, taking on various leadership roles including the presidency during the 1960s. In 1969 he served for two months as one of six members of the Aboriginal Affairs Advisory Council to the Victorian Department of Aboriginal Affairs. He resigned in protest, stating that 'the advisory council has no real power and the aboriginals who serve on it will be placed in a position where they will be under the State government's thumb'.[26] The Victorian Aborigines Advancement League had its own Black Power split in late 1969 when many Aboriginal members, including Murray, pushed non-Indigenous members out of leadership positions. Murray was also president of the Victorian Tribal Council, a precursor to the National Tribal Council formed as a breakaway Indigenous-only group from FCAATSI in 1970. Like Noonuccal, Murray participated in a protest against the bicentenary of Captain Cook's landing in 1970, wearing a red headband 'to depict blood' and lamenting how few Australians knew 'the raw deal we are getting on our land'.[27]

Korean War veteran Ken Colbung also became involved in the 1970s protest movements. After leaving the Army in 1969, he briefly worked as a field officer in Charles Perkins' Foundation for Aboriginal Affairs.[28] In that capacity Colbung was exposed to the burgeoning Black Power movement, before he returned to Perth and joined the Western Australian Aboriginal struggle. Colbung became the manager for Perth's Aboriginal Advancement Council, whose work focused on lobbying for policy change while also focusing on improving housing for Aboriginal residents.[29] In a 1972 interview with the ABC, Colbung criticised state and federal governments for hiring Aboriginal people as 'stooges for a political dictatorship'.[30] After confronting police at a few protests, Colbung tried to set up a Black Power base in Western Australia but found that the local Aboriginal people feared the term. He recalled in 2004:

> When you'd say 'Aboriginal Motivation Group', they'd say, 'Well, what the hell is that?' But if you say 'black power', everybody stood up in their seats. And the Aboriginal people said, 'Like hell, we're not gonna be that. We're not gonna get killed.' 'Cause a lot of Aboriginal people were frightened that white people would gang up and kill them if they set up that black power.[31]

It was Colbung's mother who inspired him to return to a vision of black and white working together.[32] He left the Aboriginal Advancement Council, but continued to work with unions, while demonstrating for policy changes for Noongar access to social services. He also retained a more militant approach to his activism. At a meeting about the 1980 land rights protest at Noonkanbah, Colbung stated:

> Well, we'll be as militant as we're required to be. If people wish to push us to the state that we've got to be desperately militant, well this is what we'll have to be. But this is not what's brought about, now, by the people concerned with starting this thing. Their militancy is going to be passive.[33]

He also invoked his military service to justify his logic when he declared:

> My immediate reaction as a soldier of some nineteen years and a reactionary in the rights movement for preservation of civil rights was one immediate thought: What can we do with this? Can we start now using firearms in order to create the necessary saner thinking that's required?[34]

However, not all Aboriginal community members or activists appreciated Colbung's confrontational approach, and in 1979 members voted to dismiss him as chair of a board of management because his presence would 'not do the Aboriginal movement any good in West Australia'.[35] In the 1980s Colbung became involved in the Western Australian Aboriginal Lands Trust and in 1984 was the first Aboriginal Chair of AIATSIS.[36] In 1997, he famously travelled to the United Kingdom while Prime Minister John Howard was there to enlist his support for returning the Noongar resistance fighter Yagan's remains to Australia.[37]

Other ex-servicemen and women also went through a transformation in the 1970s, leaving behind the Black Power militancy while still emphasising Indigenous empowerment. Gerry Bostock served in the Army for nine years before moving to Sydney in 1970, where he became involved in Redfern activism and the land rights movement. He and his brother Lester began writing short sketches and programs to publicise Aboriginal causes. They helped to found Black Theatre in 1972, while Gerry continued to work as a playwright until his death in 2014.[38] Ken Brindle was a Korean War veteran heavily involved in Redfern's Aboriginal community in the 1960s and 1970s. He once said of his Army service: 'for the first time in my life white people were treating me as an equal. It made me realise that aborigines don't have to be inferior.'[39] Brindle joined the Aboriginal-Australian Fellowship in 1961 and was especially active in challenging police brutality in Redfern.[40] He was also active in the Redfern All-Blacks and then New South Wales state secretary of FCAATSI from 1967 to 1971.[41] In the 1970s Brindle continued to work at the Redfern grassroots, helping to establish Aboriginal hostels and serving as trustee of the Aboriginal Children's Advancement Society.[42] These sorts of local Indigenous organisations would become the principal site of advocacy for ex-service personnel after the Whitlam Labor government was elected in December 1972.

Leadership and advocacy

During the Whitlam years the Commonwealth implemented a raft of Indigenous-related initiatives including: upgrading the Office of Aboriginal Affairs into a Department of Aboriginal Affairs; instigating the Woodward Land Rights Commission, which would frame the *Aboriginal Land Rights (Northern Territory) Act* in 1976; passing the *Racial Discrimination Act* in 1975; and founding the National Aboriginal Consultative Committee (NACC) – rebadged as the National Aboriginal Conference by the Fraser government in 1977 – as a forum for Indigenous input into government decision making. The Commonwealth also introduced self-management policies, providing direct funding to Aboriginal service-delivery organisations in areas such as health, legal assistance and housing.

Some of those to work within these new bureaucracies and organisations had been 1967 referendum activists. Lambert McBride worked for Aboriginal Hostels across Brisbane;[43] while Stewart Murray, who had been so determined to assert Aboriginal leadership in Victorian organisations, continued as the Victorian Aborigines Advancement League's liaison officer from 1970. He worked directly with Aboriginal families advising on court mediation, family counselling and community consultation. Murray became Director of the League in 1972 and adopted a more conciliatory, pragmatic approach to working with the Victorian Department of Aboriginal Affairs. He was a co-founder of Victoria's Aboriginal Legal Service in 1972 and in 1974–75 worked as a senior liaison officer with the Victorian Department of Aboriginal Affairs. After stepping down as Director of the League, he became involved in other local projects including: establishing an Aboriginal youth hostel in Swan Hill; then being on the board of Victorian Aboriginal Hostels; establishing the Victorian Aboriginal Funeral Service; serving on the Victorian Aboriginal Land

Council; and being administrator of Dandenong and District Aboriginal Cooperative Ltd.[44]

Serving as leaders of government-funded or supported organisations did not necessarily mean that these leaders left government policies unchallenged. Len Culbong had been raised in a family that had an activist streak. This upbringing instilled in Len a sense of social justice, which would guide his career both during and after the Army.[45] When serving in Vietnam, according to his sister, Margaret, he was troubled by the killing of Vietnamese women and children.[46] Len returned to Western Australia, where the experience of being rejected at the Narrogin RSL further radicalised him.[47] As Margaret said in 2015, Len 'took up the fight on the streets of Perth'. He also worked at the Aboriginal Legal Service, at one stage even as chief executive officer, fighting for 'a fair and just system'.[48] After the death in custody of John Pat in Roebourne in 1983, Len became involved in Black Action Group and the Committee to Defend Black Rights. He worked with activists in other states to document deaths in custody and toured nationally, as well as marching on the streets, until the Commonwealth government set up the *Royal Commission into Aboriginal Deaths in Custody*.[49] His daughter Nicole recalled in 2015: 'My earliest memories of my father would be always protesting and always being on Dad's shoulders – flags, and this proud feeling just being there and standing up.'[50]

Another Western Australian leader, Rob Riley, had a tumultuous childhood as a member of the Stolen Generations, being raised at Sister Kate's Home in Perth, where he suffered abuse. He joined the Army in 1973, serving for three years in the Armoured Personnel division and rising to the rank of sergeant. He wrote of this experience in 1987: 'In the Army … there was a system that everybody, no matter who it was, has to put up with, conform to', but the system was capable of change.[51] He began a long career at the Western Australia Aboriginal Legal Service as a field officer in 1979 and within six months was in charge of the organisation's field operations. Throughout the 1980s he was an active leader protesting against Western Australian state government issues affecting Aboriginal people, including police brutality, deaths in custody and land rights. Riley was elected to the National Aboriginal Conference in 1981 and became its chair in 1984. In this position he launched a powerful public attack against Prime Minister Bob Hawke for betraying Aboriginal people over national land rights. After the Hawke government abolished the conference in 1985, Riley continued to work in Aboriginal affairs, including working on the Northern Land Council; acting as adviser to Commonwealth Minister for Aboriginal Affairs Gerry Hand, working on projects such as setting up the *Royal Commission into Aboriginal Deaths in Custody* and the Aboriginal and Torres Strait Islander Commission (ATSIC); heading the WA Aboriginal Legal Service (1990–92); and forming part of the team negotiating with the Keating Labor government to establish the *Native Title Act 1993*.[52] Riley's biographer Quentin Beresford suggests that it was Riley's time in the Army that taught him how to harness 'this negative energy into a positive fight to end the kinds of injustice to which he had been exposed'.[53]

Most other Aboriginal and Torres Strait Islander ex-service personnel who worked in Indigenous organisations were less radical or outspoken in their criticisms of the government, but still credited their military experience as central to developing their skills. Vietnam veteran Graham Atkinson completed arts and social work courses after leaving the Army. He then worked in the Victorian Department of Aboriginal Affairs, the Victorian Aboriginal Child Care Agency, and as regional director of the Aboriginal Development Commission for Victoria and Tasmania. Atkinson said, 'I'd like to highlight my involvement in Aboriginal affairs because I think it all started through my experience in the Army. It was

Vietnam which forced me to become more aware of the social and political issues facing Aboriginal people.'[54] Phil Prosser worked with the Aboriginal Visitors Scheme since its founding in 1988. Initiated as a result of the *Royal Commission into Aboriginal Deaths in Custody*, the program sends visitors to local prisons and police lock-ups to provide counselling to Western Australian Aboriginal prisoners. Prosser has also coordinated diversity training programs for police recruits. Linking his Army service with these professional opportunities, Prosser stated in 2000: 'Well it [Army] gave me the chance that I'd been looking for. A polite way to do things and to prepare me for later stages of my life ... I was able to further my education.'[55]

One of the most prominent Indigenous ex-servicewomen is Sue Gordon, who served in the WRAAC from 1961 to 1963. After a series of other professional roles, in 1969 Gordon began a long career working in Indigenous affairs – first in the Pilbara region with organisations representing the Iergamadu people, then for the welfare department and then for the Commonwealth Employment Service in Port Hedland. In the 1980s she took on more prominent state and national roles, including with the Aboriginal Employment Committee, managing the Aboriginal Development Commission in Port Hedland, and as commissioner of Aboriginal Affairs – the first Aboriginal person to head a Western Australian government department. In 1988 she became the first Aboriginal magistrate of the new Western Australian Children's Court. For the next eight years, while working as a magistrate, Gordon completed a law degree part-time at the University of Western Australia. She also sat on national bodies including the National Committee on Violence, chaired the Western Australia Inquiry into Response by Government Agencies to Complaints of Family Violence and Child Abuse in Aboriginal Communities, and headed the Howard government's short-lived National Indigenous Council (2004–08). Her most high-profile national position was as the chair of the Northern

Territory Emergency Response Taskforce (colloquially known as the Intervention) in 2008. She attributed the discipline instilled in her through her upbringing at Sister Kate's Home and her three years in the Army as what prepared her for these significant roles.[56]

Other Aboriginal and Torres Strait Islander ex-service personnel have been involved in Indigenous social advancement through the private sector. Vietnam veteran Bob Blair worked for the Central Queensland Aboriginal Corporation for Training and Resources, providing training to several Aboriginal organisations in Central Queensland. In 1988 Blair was appointed the inaugural CEO of the Dreamtime Cultural Centre in Rockhampton. Since opening in 1988, the Dreamtime Cultural Centre has employed numerous Indigenous and non-Indigenous staff, worked with Indigenous contracting services such as catering outfits and has expanded to include a conference centre and hotel. Blair has also been the Deputy Chairperson of Indigenous Business Australia and has worked with the ADF to assist in Indigenous recruitment. In 2010 Bob Blair attributed his management skills and style to his Army training, remarking: 'there's no doubt in my mind, whatsoever, without my Army background, this place wouldn't be where it is today'.[57]

What these later examples have in common with each other and many pre-1967 activists is a conservative, reformist approach to Indigenous affairs. Rather than challenging the very structures of the Australian government, they were more inclined to work within the existing framework, seeking reforms to support Indigenous communities. It is perhaps not surprising that those with backgrounds in the military – a conservative, hierarchically structured institution – would be drawn to more orderly, organisational approaches to Indigenous advocacy rather than civil disobedience or radical protest. What is less clear, though, is if the military influenced their approaches to Indigenous advancement, or if the military attracted people with an anti-radical mindset.

Ex-service personnel have played leadership roles in other non-profit organisations and statutory bodies including the South Australia Aboriginal Prisoners and Offenders Support Services Incorporated; South Australia Commissioner for Aboriginal Engagement; Tangentyere Council (Alice Springs); ATSIC; Mt Isa Aboriginal and Torres Strait Islander Legal Services; Brothers' Act of Random Kindness (BARK – a Townsville social enterprise employing Indigenous parolees); Murri Courts; Port Curtis Coral Coast Corporation; Wabubadda Aboriginal Corporation in the Atherton Tablelands; Western Australia Aboriginal Medical Services; Canberra Aboriginal Health Services; and ACT Reconciliation.[58] Just the diversity of these organisations demonstrates the numerous ways that Indigenous ex-service personnel have continued to serve their communities.

14

North-West Mobile Force

Allison Cadzow

'Green: you are in the army of NORFORCE. Green: you are all brothers and sisters, you're working together.' – *Tommy Munyarryun*

Regional Force Surveillance Units (RFSUs), in particular the North-West Mobile Force (NORFORCE), have often been represented in media and regimental histories as shining examples of the success of the Australian Defence Force (ADF) in its relationships with Aboriginal and Torres Strait Islander communities. Established in 1981, NORFORCE was followed by the Pilbara Regiment in 1982 and the Far North Queensland Regiment (FNQR) in 1985. Like the specialist units created during the Second World War to defend Australia's north, these units have also drawn upon Aboriginal people's knowledge of country and communities in performing surveillance and reconnaissance. While some histories of NORFORCE discuss this role of Aboriginal reservists, they tend to focus on the voices and perspectives of NORFORCE leadership. The exception is Noah Riseman and Richard Trembath's study of Aboriginal and Torres Strait Islander defence service after 1945.[1] While it is important to acknowledge that non-Indigenous leaders have shaped these units' focus and direction, this chapter concentrates on the perspectives of Aboriginal participants in NORFORCE, the first and largest of the RFSUs. It draws upon nine oral histories with NORFORCE members who were in Darwin for the Freedom of Entry parade in August 2016. They came from communities in Arnhem Land, the Tiwi Islands and near Katherine; some had 20 years of experience in NORFORCE, while others were more recent recruits. The chapter also analyses interviews conducted earlier in Derby, Western Australia and with an ex-member from Cherbourg, Queensland, as well as media and written sources. It focuses on what being part of NORFORCE has meant for Aboriginal and Torres Strait Islander recruits, past and present, from the first training sessions of 1981 onwards.

Regional Force Surveillance Units

RFSUs were formed in the 1980s amid concerns within the Department of Defence that the far north of Australia needed a stronger military presence. In 1969, during the Vietnam War, the United States had announced the Nixon Doctrine (also known as the Guam Doctrine), which declared that although the United States would assist in defending its allies, each ally was ultimately in charge of its own security. Australian defence policy increasingly focused not just on South-East Asia, but on being able to defend the 'frontline' of Australia.[2] As Riseman and Trembath have noted, the former governor-general Michael Jeffery was a key proponent of the doctrine of northern surveillance and played a crucial role in establishing NORFORCE. When Jeffery became the first director of Special Action Forces in 1979, he set about developing the northern Australia surveillance scheme, which gave rise to the creation of the RFSUs.[3] The influence of earlier units created during the Second World War, such as the Northern Territory Special Reconnaissance Unit (NTSRU) and the North Australian Observer Unit

(NAOU), on the development of northern surveillance was significant, especially in demonstrating the value of relying on Aboriginal people's knowledge and labour.[4]

Today the RFSUs are responsible for surveilling an enormous and diverse area, from Broome in the west, to Gove in the north-east and down to Alice Springs. The terrain includes desert, mountain ranges and a long coastline. The tropical environment is subject to cyclones and wet/dry seasons. NORFORCE guards an astonishingly large area of 1.8 million square kilometres. The Pilbara Regiment is responsible for an area spanning 1.3 million square kilometres from Port Hedland to Carnarvon in Western Australia, and operates from Karratha and Port Hedland. The FNQR carries out reconnaissance and surveillance of 640 000 square kilometres from north Queensland to the Torres Strait and west to the Northern Territory border. It is based in Townsville with training held in Cairns and as a journalist noted in 2009, its personnel regard themselves as historically connected to the coastwatchers of the Second World War.[5]

The RFSUs consist of both Indigenous and non-Indigenous members; most of the Indigenous personnel are reservists. An estimated 60 per cent of NORFORCE are Indigenous, which includes several squadrons: Central, Arnhem and the Kimberley, with another unit and headquarters in Darwin.[6] The Pilbara Regiment has a lower participation rate for Aboriginal people, perhaps because the employment generated by the mining boom has proved more appealing.[7] Riseman and Trembath indicate that historical tensions and suspicions between Aboriginal people and non-Aboriginal authorities, and a smaller Aboriginal population, have also been contributing factors.[8] Torres Strait Islanders and members of the communities throughout Cape York and the Gulf Country make up approximately 30 per cent of the 51st Battalion, FNQR.[9]

The Indigenous reservists undertake training courses in handling weapons, field exercises, survival skills, observation and evading detection on country.[10] They serve 50 to 100 paid days a year, with some flexibility to allow them to return home for funerals and cultural business. The value of local knowledge held by Indigenous members of NORFORCE, particularly of challenging arid and tropical environments, is often emphasised as a vital contribution to ADF operations. Trevor Tough's history of the Kimberley Squadron quotes several current and former Commanding Officers who recalled that the close connections between Indigenous NORFORCE members and their communities meant that they can cover vast areas which the ADF cannot consistently patrol.[11]

More recently NORFORCE has been involved in surveilling drug smuggling, unauthorised boat arrivals, and landings at old airstrips as well as 'border control'. NORFORCE personnel were also involved in the ADF's delivery of the controversial Northern Territory National Emergency Response (NTER), commonly referred to as the 'Intervention'. A suite of measures aimed at protecting Aboriginal children in remote communities from sexual abuse, the NTER required the suspension of the *Racial Discrimination Act* to implement income management, removal of the permit system granting access to Aboriginal land, and mandatory health checks, all of which took place without consulting the Aboriginal communities affected.[12]

'Little bit of history there': NORFORCE and memories of past service

While RFSUs are a relatively recent development within the ADF, Aboriginal people with family histories of service have deeper roots to their involvement in defending country. Arnhem Land, in the north-east corner of the Northern Territory, is an area where colonisers attempted to settle much later than they did in the temperate south-east of the continent. Some communities have managed to remain on or near country, though not always consistently due to the impacts of colonialism, such as the missions established in the 1920s and 1930s, and land uses such as pastoralism and mining. In some cases, Yolngu have returned to country as part of the outstation movement from the early 1970s, which anthropologists Frances and Howard Morphy see as part of 'a continuing process of adjustment by Yolngu to the process of colonial encapsulation'.[13] Yolngu people's earlier trade with Macassans (which involved asserting resource control and negotiating trade and coastal landings by strangers) and stories of warrior leaders such as those who assisted the NAOU in the Second World War have also contributed to Yolngu people's enduring sense of maintaining and defending their country over a long period of time.

Histories of community and family service during the Second World War have also stimulated interest in NORFORCE. Linda Joshua, quoted in an article in 2000, stated that she joined to honour her grandfather, Joshua a guide with the 'Nackeroos' (NAOU). She said: 'I wanted to be like my grandfather. He was a very strong man who fought for his own people, for his rights.'[14] Tommy Munyarryun is from Yirrkala and Dhalinybuy outstation in east Arnhem Land, but lives in Ramingining, and was living there when he joined NORFORCE in 1991. A former Community Development Employment Programs (CDEP) supervisor and police aide, Munyarryun joined because members of his family had told him about how they had defended the east coast of Arnhem Land with the Nackeroos in wartime:

> I had joined to the NORFORCE because I'm interested, because my family tribe was in the World War Two in Nackeroos time, which you've probably heard of Binydjarrpuma, which is Wangurri clan leader. Also there was Bulawarra, who was Wangurri clan. So that interests me to join in the NORFORCE.[15]

As Munyarryun vividly expressed it, they operated 'as an eye to see what's coming in, going out, and to report back to the base ... the Aboriginal eyes was in the front line'.[16] Patrick Freddy Puruntatameri, an artist from Melville Island (Tiwi Islands), whose carvings and sculptures are held by Australian galleries and museums, has been in NORFORCE for 20 years. Puruntatameri also has strong family connections to the Second World War.[17] His grandfather was Matthais Ulungarra, who captured the first Japanese prisoner of war on Australian land, recently commemorated with a statue on Bathurst Island (see p. 167).[18] Puruntatameri recalled that:

> [S]ometime my family, tell story about that, his story, and sometime they show us that place where it happened ... That's why I'm proud to wear this uniform, you know. Little bit of history there.[19]

Warrk'Mattjun Gaykamangu, a Gupapuynu man from Milingimbi, who joined NORFORCE in 2008, explained that Milingimbi mission, established by the Methodist missionary society in 1923, was the site of an airstrip and an RAAF base during wartime. He said that 'Milingimbi has a big history fighting the war.'[20] It was attacked by Japanese forces in 1943 and two Yolngu men were killed. Plane wreckage remains are still visible there today. Gaykamangu recalled that finding the book *Donald Thomson in Arnhem Land*, and reading about the warriors who had fought in tribal wars being brought together by Thomson to defend Australia, made him keen to join NORFORCE.[21]

More recent military service has aroused several recruits' interest in NORFORCE. Benjamin Gurruwiwi from Galiwin'ku (Elcho Island), Northern Territory, mentioned in a 2016 interview that his father, an important role model for him, was a member of NORFORCE in the early 1980s.[22] Older ex-NORFORCE men from

Elcho, such as Derrick Gumbula, encouraged younger community members, such as Gurruwiwi, to join up, telling them that it was well-paid work, and that they would get to meet lots of people and make friends. NORFORCE benefits from the impression members make when they return to their communities, in uniform, as an unofficial form of recruitment.

'We all know that country': Respect and access

The first training course for Aboriginal recruits run by NORFORCE was held over two weeks in 1981 at Kimbolton homestead in the Kimberley, north-east of Derby, Western Australia. More than 30 Aboriginal people from Darwin, Broome, Kununurra, Croker Island and elsewhere attended the course, which was designed to train recruits, involve Aboriginal people in northern Australian defence, and promote the exchange of bush skills and ideas between Aboriginal members and the Army.[23] Elders from Kalumburu and Mowanjum were involved in the program too, visiting part of the way through the training.[24]

Ashley Oobagooma, a Worrorra man from Derby, enlisted in NORFORCE and completed the first training with other men from Mowanjum community, Western Australia. Mowanjum, a community of more than 380 people outside of Derby, was formed in 1956, after Worrorra, Wunambal and Ngarinyin speakers were forced to leave their lands. Living in remote areas which were unappealing to pastoralists or the pearling industry, they had initially experienced relatively little government interference. Inland, though, Ngarinyin survivors of frontier conflict were working on pastoral stations, near or on country. After the Second World War, as assimilation and centralisation became more influential and funding dried up, leaders decided the best response would be to form their own community.[25] Gibson Barunga was also born in Derby. A mechanic and house builder, he recalled joining NORFORCE with other Mowanjum men: Eddie Bear, Morris and Alfred Umbagai, Alfonse Buck, James Barunga and Oobagooma.[26] Oobagooma said they were curious about NORFORCE: 'we all talked to each other, let's give it a go. Might see different faces, places, you know.'[27]

Country featured powerfully in Oobagooma's reflections on NORFORCE: looking after it, teaching people about it and learning new skills in relation to it. He learned about firing M60s, using M203 grenade launchers, map navigation (also taught in Katherine and Maningrida) and camouflage. It was an opportunity for the Mowanjum men to teach non-Aboriginal people, such as the Warrant Officer (WO), their bush skills, especially finding food on country. Oobagooma had spent lots of time in the Kimbolton and Oobagooma station area before Defence took it over, and had been taught survival skills by his grandparents and parents:

> I kept everything, sort of like a brain map, and when it came to that situation, [I was] just trying to share something back to the defence. They was showing us how to survive out in the bush, but we knew all that. We shared both [white man knowledge and traditional knowledge].[28]

Oobagooma emphasised that their fathers had warned them before leaving for exercises at Galiwin'ku in the Northern Territory that they were to maintain their law and be careful and respectful as they moved around someone else's country. When they came across totems during night navigation exercises on Galiwin'ku they re-navigated their route around them, because they were not from this area and did not want to touch or disturb them. They simultaneously showed respect for elders' knowledge and place, devising a way of moving through country that was different from typical Defence operations.

The importance of caring for country and acting in an appropriate way while serving with NORFORCE is clear in Oobagooma's telling of the story of Dunbi (native Owl). For Ashley Oobagooma and his people in the Kimberley, Dunbi is a powerful Wandjina ancestral creator spirit being, who formed country, everything associated with it (animals, seasons, weather) and provided Law. A 'public' version of the story of Dunbi involves children tormenting the owl, plucking out his feathers and teasing him. Other powerful Wandjina spirit beings created a catastrophic storm and flood to punish the children and their families for their disrespect and cruelty towards Dunbi. Only a boy and girl survived to create a new population who learned the lessons of their ancestors and instituted sacred laws that respected the owl and other creatures.[29] In 2015 Oobagooma told an evocative version of the continuing relevance and spiritual power of Dunbi that was in evidence when he was on NORFORCE exercises in his own country near Kimbolton Defence Reserve, and the old pastoral station where his ancestors had worked:[30]

> One day we finished the exercise. This one Sergeant, he found a native owl, in our society we call him Dunbi.
>
> He said, 'Hey boys, look here … what do you guys call that?'
>
> 'He's Dunbi. We respect nature, we respect everything.'
>
> 'Oh come on boys, let's see now.' [He motions grabbing from above.]
>
> He wanted to play with it, which he did. I think he was a bit off … [Gestures 'not right in the head'.]
>
> When we look back we can see big dark clouds … right at Kimbolton homestead. Where we were firing the guns at the rifle range, we had not one drop. Then we can feel the breeze blowing. The dark cloud, it stood only one place that was at the homestead … By the time we finished firing the rifles, we were racing back,

> we can feel the wind blowing. As soon as we got into camp, we can see our tents right up the hillsides, the poles of the tents were bent, our bunks … everything was soaked wet.
>
> Then we all turn around and look at Sergeant –
>
> 'See Sir you shouldn't play with that owl.'
>
> 'I bloody know now for next time.'
>
> That's what he said.
>
> 'I believe you boys.'
>
> 'See what has happened. This is Wandjina country, Unguud country.'
>
> I think he got transferred to another place.[31]

WO Reg Davies' diary of this event contrasts with Oobagooma's account. Where Oobagooma focused on respect and the importance of valuing Aboriginal knowledge, the WO recorded it merely as 'a freak storm … a mini cyclone' which damaged tents, equipment and clothes.[32] These divergent accounts reveal different ways of relating to country and the depth of knowledge Aboriginal people bring to their roles in RFSUs. Oobagooma noted that he has a lot of respect for country, that it was central to his service practices and his life philosophy: 'You have to respect the country, like you respect yourself.'[33]

While Defence has been conscious of the need for RFSUs to show respect for country and its owners, relationships between Defence and communities have not always been untroubled. In 1991 Rhys Jones and Betty Meehan noted that seeking permission for access to country, by land council negotiations or permits, had been handled constructively by the ADF and NORFORCE.[34] Yet differing degrees of control by Aboriginal people over their country has a strong influence on these relationships. In areas controlled by the Commonwealth for Defence purposes, restrictions on Aboriginal and other people's access applies. For example, Kimbolton, a former pastoral station, which was transferred to the ADF in the mid-1970s, is the ancestral land of Oobagooma's family, and gaining access continues to be difficult for Oobagooma and his relations.[35] As he recalled in 2015:

> That's where my great, great grandparents had been living … for a long, long time … The old fellas and the old ladies they didn't know about this. The Commonwealth government seen that place it was 'vacant' and a reserve, but they put it as crown land … So if you're going to pass through that place, you have to ring Larrakeyah Barracks [Darwin], just to go through. We [Worrorra people] all know that country. We know where the Wandjina paintings are, all the living waters. It's a shame that we have to go by their rules today.[36]

Oobagooma visited the area on Fridays after school with his cousin brother, Donny Woolagoodja. Old burial grounds are located there, and Oobagooma buried his father and younger brother there. He said his family wanted to 'make it back to homeland', but Defence has kept them waiting and waiting.

Others with greater access to and say over their country have emphasised that NORFORCE was a means of getting out on country and being able to look after it. Gaykamangu said that being in NORFORCE is positive for him as a Yolngu person:

> For us being on country just feels right. We see things that can't be seen … Some of the country back home it's sort of like protected, sacred sites. We are the ones that look after that country.[37]

Participating in NORFORCE can support Yolngu to reassert their custodianship of country and serve as a way to maintain some continuity with caring for country roles practised over a much longer history.

'I run the show': Leadership

For Sergeant Munyarryun, who has served in NORFORCE for 20 years, mostly in Arnhem Squadron, joining NORFORCE has been a new way of manifesting leadership and reinforcing his existing community leadership role.[38] Rising through the ranks to gain his stripes has enhanced his standing, complementing his leadership in his Yolngu community. He was following in the footsteps of his father, a community leader who handed over to him before he passed away:

> I … look after my community at Dhalinybuy [outstation], I run the show. I'm there. Whatever they ask me, for any support, my family I give them support. Apart from that I … show my leadership in the Army as a Sergeant. I play a role in the Army to teach the Indigenous boys what I have learnt during my past when I was with the Army.[39]

This echoes aspects of *ganma*, a Yolngu philosophy of 'two way' or 'both ways' in education, music and art, whereby Western and Yolngu ideas and practices are used together, without diminishing either. Bakamana Yunupingu and Helen Watson have explained that *ganma*, which has multiple meanings, recognises 'the separateness of fresh water and salt water knowledge even where they meet and mix … a relationship in which two opposed patterns of ideas complement, interact and relate to one another, but never lose their distinctiveness as separate and opposed parts of one whole'.[40] That said, the Army has done less accommodating than Aboriginal community members who have joined up. There have been some changes in training and adjustments made to enable people to join, such as bridging courses to help people meet the minimum entry standards, 'flexibility' around criminal background checks for lesser offences as minors, and mentoring.[41] Yet as Debbie Hohaia explained in her doctoral research on Indigenous knowledge in the Defence services, efforts to increase participation without changing organisational structures, power dynamics, curricula and language use in training are insufficient.[42] Still, as Munyarryun's case shows, NORFORCE authority and rank have been incorporated into Yolngu worlds and given meaning. A turning point for him was noticing the officers with stripes during his NORFORCE service: he thought 'I want to be like them.' He now has three stripes as a sergeant, though he found some of the commander courses difficult as he had to navigate language differences; Yolngu Matha is his first language, but much of his training took place in English. It is a challenge many Indigenous recruits to NORFORCE face. Munyarryun said of making the transition from a community context to a Defence one: 'it's very hard, to go from one world to another world'.[43] As a senior Indigenous soldier he has taken on the responsibility and leadership role of assisting and supporting young Yolngu recruits, translating unfamiliar instructions, terms and ideas into Yolngu Matha.[44]

However, being in NORFORCE can also be seen as a way for younger people to take on leadership roles in their communities. When Gaykamangu returns to community, he said the older people showed him respect for what he does, and being a young leader in the community he is someone to look up to. He said he always shows the old people the same respect that they give him. Likewise, Jonah Thingle from Ngukurr, south-east of Katherine, who has been in NORFORCE for nine years, and worked as an assistant teacher in his community for six of those years, said the teachers always tell the kids to 'look up' to him.[45] NORFORCE recruits have often previously held responsible positions within their own communities. They are sometimes selected by elders to join, and their status increases by being part of NORFORCE.[46]

Language differences are not the only difficulty recruits have faced. Many of those interviewed found the physical aspects of training to be demanding (as did other recruits), such as early rising, running, carrying packs and marching, though they also expressed pride in their hard-won fitness and discipline. For others being homesick for country and family were hurdles they overcame.

NORFORCE and the Intervention

One of the more fraught aspects of Indigenous service has been the use of NORFORCE to support the government-initiated NTER, also known as the 'Intervention', from June 2007 to October 2008. This policy meant that NORFORCE, which had a good reputation in many communities, became tainted by association. Munyarryun found that he was placed in the awkward position of explaining the Intervention to several communities, such as Elcho, Ramingining and Milingimbi; he felt caught between government directives and community concerns and anxieties. He stated that some Indigenous people in the communities thought that NORFORCE was collecting information on them; however, its role as part of Operation Outreach was supportive and logistic, ensuring the delivery of beds, water, food, transport and tents. Munyarryun said of the time: 'our community thought we were baddies for helping them [the Intervention]'.[47]

Munyarrun's reflections upon the Intervention elsewhere in the interview indicated that it was neither well planned, nor clearly explained to NORFORCE members or the communities. Little had changed two years after it began, and government money soon ran out. As he explained it:

> Everyone lifted up their eyebrows 'What was it all about?' Some police [were] bought into our community. It was not the change that we wanted, it was the government, what they wanted to put into our community.[48]

Gaykamangu was not part of delivering the Intervention, but he remembered Munyarryun speaking, saying they were not 'against them'. He too remembered the confusion it caused for his community in Milingimbi, and that it brought about a 'feeling of being helpless'.[49]

In contrast, Richard Narwirr, who was born in Darwin, but grew up on Goulburn Island, and then Croker Island, was involved with the Intervention in Alice Springs for a month; he said that he felt good about doing such work and was favourably received. He saw the Intervention as an opportunity to learn about other communities, and enjoyed driving people to see doctors and back home again. Significantly, unlike Munyarryan, he was not put in the pos-ition of having to explain what was happening to his own community. Puruntatameri recalled that people were asking why bring it to the islands, why not leave it 'over there' on the mainland?[50] Perspectives on the Intervention from communities and within NORFORCE itself, then, are diverse and situationally specific. It remains an uneasy and uncomfortable topic.

'We teach them': Skills and knowledge

For Aboriginal members of the RFSUs, training has been an opportunity for them to show a different kind of leadership, by sharing their knowledge of country and bush skills with non-Indigenous NORFORCE members. NORFORCE, as WO Reg Davies noted during the first training period in the 1980s, was unusual: 'his "traditional" skills are relevant, that his aboriginality [sic] is *for the first time in his life* an asset in the interaction between cultures'.[51] Over

30 years later, there are still too few opportunities, aside from work in tourism, art, country-based programs and in national parks and Indigenous Protected Areas as rangers, for Aboriginal and Torres Strait Islander people to be recognised and paid for demonstrating such knowledge. A position of relative authority, and the associated respect that comes with having their knowledge valued, have benefits for the soldiers' self-esteem and identity.[52] This is reiterated in a NORFORCE member's comment in Hohaia's research, which has noted that Aboriginal members realised, '"I know more than them", where it's usually always the other way around … there's a transfer of knowledge (from Indigenous to non-Indigenous).'[53]

Puruntatameri and his best friend from his Darwin schooldays, Narwirr, explained that they were instructors rather than students in the survival course in NORFORCE. They taught other NORFORCE members their skills, and were recognised as authorities about living on country:

> They get us … to come in and teach all the boys from Darwin, how to find water, how to fish when you got no fishing line, how to survive, how to get good tucker when you are out bush, how to make fire in our traditional way. What tree is good to eat, and what's poison … it's all about survival. We teach them how to get oyster, crab, mushroom.[54]

Gurruwiwi emphasised that knowing the seasons and how to shop in the 'bush supermarket' was crucial. Just as vital was passing on this knowledge he and other NORFORCE members had gained from the older generation to their children and grandchildren.[55] In this way NORFORCE reinforces the value of this knowledge and spurs on efforts to pass it on for the future.

NORFORCE Majors I Barnes and John Lotu emphasised that this knowledge was not innate, or about having 'sharper than average eyes'; rather it was grounded in observation from living in particular country. Aboriginal people in many northern areas are trained by their community from childhood to be observant, to know what the level of water should be in a waterhole at that time of year, how many people had used it and so on.[56] Using such knowledge and involving community in keeping watch serves to create a broader surveillance network across an area of operations otherwise monitored intermittently by federal agencies or the ADF.[57]

Aside from sharing existing knowledge and drawing strength and pride from it, NORFORCE members valued gaining new skills and opportunities to learn. Puruntatameri said he joined up partly because he wanted to 'get out from the community, and try to learn something different … and maybe when we do our training, go back home and teach the locals'.[58] Knowledge is taken and used beyond its immediate and obvious individual context and shared with community.

'Different countries': Travel and kin connection

Being part of NORFORCE also allows Aboriginal members a way of maintaining and expanding a network across communities, widening family relationships and building extended community. Several NORFORCE members mentioned this as something they valued. Narwirr said that he enjoyed going to different communities and outstations that they had never been to before. When they went back home they told people about the places they had seen. Puruntatameri said they otherwise rarely have the opportunity to travel, as Centrelink pay is minimal, but with the Army the travel is included. The impact extends beyond individuals into community, as they learn from this and are brought into an extended network. For Thingle, being in NORFORCE has enabled him to travel to places like Broome, and learn further afield: 'I go to Warrk's country. You get to visit different countries, places, family, different bush tucker, learn from them what you can eat.'[59] Oobagooma noted of his training that getting to meet others and being welcomed onto their country in the 'proper' way was an important and memorable part of his NORFORCE service:

> Black fella/black fella get together like that. We had a good time, they took us fishing, meeting their family … Those fellas from Elcho Island, they introduced us to their mob.[60]

Sergeant Elgan Leedie, a Wakka Wakka and Lama Lama man from Cherbourg, Queensland, a former regular Army member, joined NORFORCE in 2006 after his discharge, serving for 14 years. He said he enjoyed his service with NORFORCE, especially the reconnaissance missions, coastal surveillance, living off the land and especially meeting local Indigenous people.[61] He valued 'being given a skin name by the soldiers and their families … I can go anywhere in the Top End from Croker Island, Goulburn, Bathurst Island and down as far as Port Keats, Daly River, I'm welcome back any time'.[62] He also saw NORFORCE as assisting young people to reinforce their cultural connections, noting that 'By taking them out, surviving on the land, Norforce [sic] is assisting these young blokes in the north keep their identity.'[63]

'We all green skin, that's what they call us'

Many of those interviewed in the Serving Our Country project used the term 'family' to explain relationships within NORFORCE. NORFORCE has adopted terms like family and kin, drawing upon meaningful cultural frameworks for community members. Other parallels can be seen to exist between Army culture and aspects of Aboriginal cultures: ceremonies, rituals, and group identity being privileged over individualism, although this downplays some major differences too.[64]

NORFORCE has adopted the concept of 'skin' groups and totems from Aboriginal culture to work with Aboriginal communities.[65] The camouflage uniform is known as the 'green skin' – 'skin' referring to the practice of classifying kin according to skin name. As Gurruwiwi explained of Yolngu culture, 'everyone we connect through our language … and we ask them "Do you know this person?" Then we ask relationship to each other, but mainly it's our skin name and who we related to, then talk to them. That's our main … duty.'[66]

Leedie, speaking of his experiences in the Army more broadly, including serving with the 2nd/4th battalion RAR, said he formed strong bonds with the other 11 Aboriginal members. They all knew where each person was from and could 'place' them. 'We were very close, us blackfellas in the defence force.'[67] Close relationships were also formed with non-Aboriginal soldiers, and many of them value the connections they have formed with Aboriginal NORFORCE members and their families.

Former CO Richard Parker explained how 'skin' is used by NORFORCE as a way of understanding the squadron. He said: 'The green skin of NORFORCE is something they understand in their culture. They come together, we form our own group, the green skin group. It's a very effective way of doing business.'[68] In 2000 the journalist David Hancock noted that a WO providing weapons training to recruits used the term consistently: 'I am green skin, you are green skin. The green skin is paying you and taking care of you. We of the green skin always protect our country.'[69] Recognition of the significant role that kinship, relationships of exchange (particularly giving and receiving in order to create relationships and the concept of 'looking after'), and ancestrally created country play in Indigenous life worlds means that NORFORCE's use of these key ideas is very astute.[70]

Munyarryun regarded NORFORCE participation in family terms, as 'brothers and sisters working together', while Puruntatameri expressed his understanding of coming together as one family in NORFORCE, by broadening family relationships through service:

> Once you got the [touches his uniform] cams, you got brothers and sisters, family there. Then when they go back home, we might get a chance to go out there, and get a bit closer, that's where we make good friends. Probably start up family like that, family here, family there.[71]

The expansion of family relationships was valued by others too. Gaykamangu indicated that while NORFORCE personnel may come from different communities, when they get to know each other an important and lasting connection is made. If he is stranded in Roper, or Nhulunbuy, or Groote, or Elcho, he knows there is someone there to help him: 'That's part of who we are as a family, you know.'[72] Participating in NORFORCE clearly helps Indigenous people create a wider network, develop relationships with other communities and sustain them.

'To do something with my life': Employment

In the remote north and north-west, where there are limited options for paid work, Defence has become a key employer, along with other land and sea ranger programs.[73] RFSUs have offered some community members a degree of financial security and in some cases a career pathway. Patricia Gibson recently joined NORFORCE after being employed by Ranger and Working on Country programs in Maningrida, Northern Territory. An Army visit to Maningrida, and seeing a program on television about NORFORCE, motivated her to join.[74] Gaykamangu had worked before joining up, but said that in the Army he felt he was 'providing something for the kids, putting food on the table. That's something.'[75] NORFORCE service can also be regarded as supportive of 'home' communities too. For others, such as Oobagooma and Thingle, it was their first experience of paid employment.[76] Elders such as Johnny Wilson from the Tiwi Islands see NORFORCE as important in helping younger community members learn skills, be employed and defeat boredom.[77] For others it has been a way to find more purpose and focus in their lives. Gaykamangu, recalled joining NORFORCE wanting to 'do something' with his life in 2001 after the birth of his youngest child, having rejected it as an option previously:

> I just look into her eyes, my youngest daughter … deep into her eyes, looking at her soul and just saying … I should change my life around … I was on a crooked path, and when she came, she changed everything for me.[78]

NORFORCE evidently provides a structure within which significant personal growth and change can manifest for some members.

The RFSUs, particularly NORFORCE, have provided situations where Aboriginal and Torres Strait Islander people, especially in northern Australia, have both found and made opportunities for themselves. Oral histories with serving and ex-service members make clear the role NORFORCE has played in providing an economic opportunity for employment on country. The development of new skills and the sharing of skills and knowledge of country with peers, and leadership were also emphasised. Several interviewees' knowledge of their relatives' work with Nackeroos and other units in the Second World War were noted as a motivation for joining up, and they saw continuities with their current roles in

NORFORCE. The chance to expand kin networks and grow family connections were mentioned as significant. While many positive aspects were emphasised, awkward associations with the Intervention, language difficulties and struggles to regain access to ancestral land now managed by Defence indicate that politics and historical entanglements with colonialism still beset NORFORCE's relationships with some communities. Nonetheless, NORFORCE remains unique in engaging Aboriginal and Torres Strait Islander people and valuing their knowledge and skills in a contemporary context, as is seen in Defence's working with translations of concepts such as skin and family. Defence broadly, as well as other Australian agencies, could learn much from this grounded form of inclusiveness and exchange.

15

The Australian Defence Force, 1990s to 2017

Shannyn Palmer

'If you can hang your hat on anything it's military service and Aboriginal men and women have answered the call.' – *Ricky Morris*

During the 1990s the Australian Defence Force (ADF) underwent significant change, implementing a range of policies and initiatives to create a more inclusive workplace. Recruitment and retention within the ADF had emerged as a problem that needed addressing; at the same time, the Australian government was establishing a program of national reconciliation between Indigenous and other Australians. This included measures intended to attract more Aboriginal and Torres Strait Islander recruits to the armed forces.

Simultaneously, the military operations the ADF undertook in the last decades of the twentieth century diverged significantly from earlier armed conflicts. Yet, the remembered experiences of Aboriginal and Torres Strait Islander service personnel who served in peacekeeping operations such as Somalia, Rwanda and East Timor in the 1990s, and the later military interventions in Iraq and Afghanistan, are strikingly similar to those who served in earlier wars. While the psychological trauma resulting from service emerges as a strong theme, Aboriginal and Torres Strait Islander oral histories also speak positively of their experiences while serving in the ADF. They evoke a sense of camaraderie that resonates with the stories of mateship and equality that have recurred in Indigenous memories of war and military service throughout the twentieth century. In some instances, Aboriginal and Torres Strait Islander memories of serving throughout this period illuminate the gradual changes taking place within the ADF. However, there is also a tension in many Indigenous memories between the lived experience of being treated as an equal in the ADF and the presence of an implicit structural racism. This highlights the inherent complexity of analysing themes such as 'mateship' and 'race' in the armed services. Although the ADF has implemented a range of access and equity initiatives, statistical progress has been modest. Nevertheless, Aboriginal and Torres Strait Islander oral histories of service provide a nuanced perspective on the changing relationship between Indigenous people and the ADF, illuminating the significant cultural shifts taking place.

It is difficult to obtain information regarding Indigenous participation rates within the ADF during its first two decades as an amalgamated entity (the three previously discrete services were combined in 1976). Historian Robert Hall notes that while Aboriginal and Torres Strait Islander people were overrepresented in the Regional Force Surveillance Units (RFSUs), by 1992 they were represented within the ADF as a whole 'in accordance with their representation within the community'. However, Hall does not say what this percentage was, and given the very little information available, it is impossible to verify whether this was the case. Military historian David Horner writes that in the early 1990s there were significantly higher numbers of Aboriginal and Torres Strait Islander people within the military than other minority groups and that this was the result of raising the RFSUs.[1]

From 1987 onwards the period of 'relative inactivity' for the

ADF began to change. At the beginning of 1987 the ADF had only 13 personnel involved in national peacekeeping operations. However, within two years the so-called 'peacekeeping revival', caused by political developments at the global and local levels, most notably the end of the Cold War, resulted in the ADF being deployed in a number of peacekeeping operations.[2] Such peacekeeping commitments meant that ADF personnel units were 'to a greater or lesser extent, almost continually on operations' throughout the 1990s.[3] The 1991 Gulf War suggested that the bipolar divisions of the Cold War were over, and that the world's major powers could work together in pursuit of international peace and stability. Yet, as historians Owen Hartley and Rachel Utley have argued, that early enthusiasm waned quickly as '[t]he very difficult problems of "peacekeeping" in theatres such as Somalia, Rwanda and the former Yugoslavia, where there was precious little peace to keep', problematised understandings and attitudes towards such undertakings.[4]

Aboriginal and Torres Strait Islander people were among those deployed to 'peacekeeping' missions throughout the 1990s, and their memories of their experiences serve to complicate the distinctions between war and peace. Between January and May 1993 Australia deployed 990 personnel to Somalia as part of the United Task Force in Somalia (UNITAF).[5] Torres Strait Islander Chris Townson was among the infantry troops who served with the First Battalion of the Royal Australian Regiment (1RAR) in Somalia. In an interview recorded for the Serving Our Country project in 2015, Townson recalled that it was 'hot as' in Baidoa where the Australian battalion group were based and that while the Americans were patrolling in vehicles, the Australian soldiers were carrying out patrols on foot, in 40 plus degrees Celsius, while carrying lots of heavy ammunition. Townson said that there was no food, or law and order, in Somalia and that the Australian soldiers' mission was to work with the non-government organisations (NGOs) and help to restore order in Baidoa and the surrounding region.[6] As well as the difficult conditions, Townson's recollections of his time serving in Somalia included several dangerous encounters with Somali bandits, the discovery of shallow graves containing the bodies of Somalis who had died from starvation and violence, and the smell of the dead, which Townson said is something he 'will never forget'.[7] After all he witnessed in Somalia, and 'what they'd done' there, the experience changed Townson's way of thinking 'in regards to everything'. He said that it was when he and the other Australian soldiers got back to Australia that 'things started to change':

> It was just things in your brain. In the end you can't, you can't slow down … 'cos you're used to things happening. You can't get tired, you can't get drunk, you're on a fuse and anyone says anything wrong and you want to do something bad and you're trained to do it … Because of that I needed more. I was hungry for more patrols, hungry for dead bodies, hungry to kill someone … a lot of other fellas were like that.[8]

Townson left the Army in 1994 with a Totally and Permanently Incapacitated (TPI) pension owing to the Post Traumatic Stress Disorder he suffered upon his return from Somalia. About ten years later Townson said that he went to Cape York, where his family lived, and as he described it, he 'went back to culture'. Townson said that this 'brought him back' and that now he does not like violence, or weapons and all the things he used to do, 'he's reversed'.[9]

The blurred boundary between peace and war and the profound psychological impact of so-called peacekeeping operations has also been described by Robert Syron, a Biripi and Worimi man from Sydney. Syron served in Rwanda as part of the Australian team sent to provide medical support to the United Nations Assistance Mission in Rwanda (UNAMIR). In August 1994 an Australian contingent of 308 personnel was deployed to Rwanda, which had been ravaged by civil war and ethnic violence, resulting in between 200 000 and 800 000 people being reported missing or dead.[10] Syron recalled that when he got off the plane in Rwanda the first thing he noticed 'was the smell of decaying bodies'. His oral history, recorded in 2013 as part of the City of Sydney Oral History Program, recalled the violence inflicted by the Hutu-led Rwandan government upon the Tutsi and politically moderate Hutu in confronting detail: bodies being chopped up and hundreds of bodies floating down the rivers with 'their heads cut off and their legs cut off and their arms'.[11] Remembering a reconnaissance mission he took with his section commander, Syron said 'and I think in three hundred kilometres there wasn't a patch of road where there wasn't a dead body on the side of the road with bits and pieces cut off it'. Describing the scene of a surgeon crying while operating on a victim of a village massacre, Syron said 'so even the surgeons weren't immune to the effect and to the emotional torment, you could say, of those experiences over there. It was crazy'. Syron discharged from the Army when he returned. He said of his return to his trade as a butcher:

> [Y]ou can imagine standing there in a butcher shop and chopping up meat all day and I just kept thinking about the things that I'd seen in Africa and it just kept triggering all those things and I just went downhill from there and I kind of just fell into this deep, dark, hole.[12]

Syron said that it took the government ten years to recognise that the experience in Rwanda 'wasn't peacekeeping' and that this acknowledgment of the 'warlike' nature of the situation 'was recognition for what we did over there and what really happened'.[13]

Some 5700 Australians served in East Timor in 1999 as part

of the International Force for East Timor (INTERFET), an 11 000 strong, 22-nation coalition, led by Australian Major General Peter Cosgrove and sanctioned as part of a UN resolution aimed at ending the violence that had consumed the country. This was arguably Australia's most significant military commitment throughout the 1990s, and as Australia provided the leading component of the force, Horner wrote that East Timor was the biggest test of the ADF's capacity since its inception.[14] Gunditjmara man Ricky Morris was posted to East Timor as part of INTERFET. He described active service as 'surreal'. He was later posted to Afghanistan in 2008–09 as part of the ongoing Australian military involvement in that country, which commenced in 2001 as part of the US-led International Coalition against Terrorism, also known as the 'war on terror'.[15] Morris recalled that he was 'wound tight' while in Afghanistan because 'you just don't know if you're going to cop it or not'. Morris left the Army upon returning to Australia and said that returning to civilian life was difficult and that 'he went into a bit of a hole'.[16]

As with earlier 'peacekeeping' operations in Somalia and Rwanda, Aboriginal and Torres Strait Islander people who served in later military operations in Afghanistan and Iraq during 2003–09 recounted experiencing shock upon returning to Australia and suffering the psychological legacies of serving in theatres of violence.[17] The Iraq War commenced in 2003 with a US-led coalition that sought to invade Iraq and locate and destroy the Weapons of Mass Destruction supposedly held by the regime of Saddam Hussein. Dennis Smallwood served in East Timor and twice in Iraq. He described the situation in Iraq as more complex than Timor and said that there was more chance of death and injury, and that it was difficult to tell who the enemy was. Like Morris, he said that the 'real battle' started when he got out of the Army. He too experienced problems with alcohol and said that he drank and took drugs to block out his memories of Iraq. Like Chris Townson, Smallwood also said that speaking with the uncles and his community was an important part of his healing process and that a spiritual connection with country had significantly influenced his recovery from his mental health problems.[18]

Mateship and race in the Australian Defence Force

Despite the psychological impact of service, Townson, Syron, Morris and Smallwood all spoke positively of their general experiences in the ADF. Townson said of his time training at Singleton that it was a 'grunt factory' – a slang term for infantry – and that he 'loved that place'. He was happy and proud of his service, despite what happened in, and after, Somalia.[19] Syron said that he loved being in the Army because he got to travel. He also 'loved the mateship and the brotherhood within the infantry battalion'.[20] Both Townson's and Syron's memories of service affirm the thread running throughout, and tying together, many of the chapters in this volume – that Indigenous people did not experience discrimination in the armed services.

Although, to his knowledge, he was the only Indigenous man at Kapooka at the time he enlisted, Townson said that he did not encounter many instances of discrimination. Syron recalled that he did, but only once and for a very short time: some young 'skinheads' joined his battalion and 'started talking about how they were going to bash the blacks within the battalion'. Syron described himself as a 'lighter shade of Aboriginal person' and decided to 'drop a bomb on them' by telling them 'well, you know, I'm actually an Aboriginal person'. He said there were 'quite a lot of Indigenous people within the battalion at that time' and 'it was the white boys that sorted out the skinheads and they were pulled back into line straight away and never, ever spoke about bashing blacks again'.[21]

Histories of Aboriginal and Torres Strait Islander military service that have emerged in recent decades, particularly those that have drawn upon oral histories as source material, have revealed common themes of mateship and equality across a broad range of Indigenous memories of service.[22] Townson's and Syron's memories quoted above also affirm this narrative of a camaraderie among mates, regardless of race. However, as Philippa Scarlett's research into Aboriginal service in the First World War demonstrates, the 'mateship' paradigm needs to be scrutinised more closely.[23] Without seeking to undermine or question Aboriginal and Torres Strait Islander experience, memories of mateship and equality should be approached in a more nuanced way, to try and illuminate the complexities of friendships and narratives of equality as they relate to military structures. As earlier chapters have shown, at various points throughout the twentieth century, the military used prevailing racial ideas and categories to exempt people deemed to be Aboriginal from military service. In the contemporary context, Aboriginal and Torres Strait Islander peoples are still under-represented, particularly within the senior ranks of the ADF. And yet, despite this, the armed forces appear to have given Indigenous Australians opportunities to participate in an organisational culture where racial distinction is rarely or never experienced as overtly harmful.[24] Further research into contemporary Aboriginal and Torres Strait Islander experiences of military service, in conjunction with those of their non-Indigenous counterparts, might help to shed some light on narratives of mateship and family, and perhaps point to the ways in which these narratives reflect less upon racial equality in the armed services, and more on the 'uniformity' and the sacrifice of the self for the state upon which military service hinges.

There is a tension in Aboriginal memories between experiences of 'mateship' and an implicit structural racism in the defence forces. Although the oral histories throughout this book tend not to emphasise overt racism, it lurks in the background, or at the peripheries of these memories, and therein lies the rub. Many people who were interviewed for the Serving Our Country project recalled being one of very few Indigenous people in their unit. Ricky Morris joined the Army Reserves in 1990 and the Regular Army in 1995. To his knowledge there was one other Aboriginal man, who was his cousin, and a Torres Strait Islander in his Reserve unit. Despite being in a very small minority, Morris said that racism was not a problem within his unit: 'mateship comes into play in the unit; you're accepted for who you are not what you are I guess and if you were a bludger, you were a bludger. It doesn't matter if you were black, white or brindle, everyone's gotta pull their weight.'[25] Dennis Smallwood joined the Army in 1998 and recalls that in his basic training platoon of about 60 people there were 'probably about three darkfellas that joined' and that he was the only Indigenous man during infantry training at Singleton. Despite this, when asked if he experienced racism Smallwood said that 'there was no time for backlashes or belittling … in infantry you've got to learn to be as one unit, so you're on an equal platform'. Nevertheless, Smallwood did say that he did 'hear racial remarks' and that some soldiers 'do try and get at you or taunt you'. However, he also said that he believed that in the late 1990s there was a lot more respect for Aboriginal soldiers serving then, as opposed to in Vietnam or the First or Second world wars. Moreover, by the time he served there was recourse to higher authorities when this happened, and incidents were identified and 'squashed on the head straight away'.[26] Morris too, recalled an incident of racism while conducting reconnaissance near Lake Tyers mission, when non-Indigenous soldiers made racial remarks. He and his cousin, who was a corporal at the time, used the chain of command to address this: 'it was one of the points where we took the challenge as Aboriginal men, we took the challenge to go up the chain and to make sure they were held accountable for their comments'.[27]

As Riseman and Trembath's research into Aboriginal and Torres Strait Islander military service since 1945 has shown, the issue of racism in the military throughout this period is complex. The memories of the ex-service personnel they interviewed 'varied dramatically, with some suggesting that they experienced no racism whatsoever, while others perceived that racism was widespread'.[28] Despite such variation, Riseman and Trembath's extensive oral history research led them to conclude that Indigenous ADF members in the 1980s and 1990s perceived more racism than those who served in the 1950s to 1970s and that racism 'was usually in the form of taunts or name-calling'. They further argue that there were diverse factors that underpinned this 'recent history of racism in the ADF … such [as] branch of service, combat versus peacetime work and skin colour of those personnel targeted for racial abuse', and that public opinion, polarised around Indigenous affairs in the 1990s, influenced these factors.[29] However, they also note that while reports of racial discrimination in the ADF after the 1970s were more prevalent in their research, in that same period servicemen and women 'have been more assertive in their condemnations of prejudice'.[30] Smallwood's and Morris's memories (opposite) testify to this more assertive response to incidents of racism. Furthermore, it is arguable that Smallwood's observation – that there was more respect for Aboriginal and Torres Strait Islander soldiers by the 1990s – is reflective of broader policy shifts taking place and the changing relationships between the ADF and Aboriginal and Torres Strait Islander people at the time.

Towards positive discrimination

The ADF sought to raise Indigenous participation rates in the early 1990s. Two important contexts shaped this shift from a long history of institutionalised exclusion towards policies aimed at including more Indigenous people within the ADF. First, from the mid-1980s, recruitment and retention emerged as significant problems for the ADF. Second, the Australian state instituted a policy of 'reconciliation' with Indigenous Australians in 1991.

Horner argued in 2001 that a fundamental shift in the values of Australian society meant that the armed forces found it increasingly difficult to recruit young people. A number of reasons were advanced for the declining appeal of a military career, such as young people having no memory of Australia's involvement in armed conflict, the changing career expectations of young people who no longer sought out a 'job for life', the increasingly demanding selection criteria as the ADF became more technologically sophisticated, and the concentration of defence assets and personnel in the north of Australia, which resulted in few alternative postings in the more populous southern states.[31] Retaining personnel also emerged as a challenge. Horner notes that these problems worked to 'persuade Defence personnel planners that they needed to access all the talent available in the community and to make the ADF an attractive employer for all able and qualified young Australians' – in other words, the ADF could no longer continue to draw almost exclusively from its traditional narrow pool of white Australian men.[32]

At around the same time that the ADF was confronting these problems in recruitment and retention, the Australian government instigated an official program of national reconciliation between Aboriginal and Torres Strait Islander peoples and other Australians. The 1990s witnessed Australian, New Zealand and Canadian governments all publicly acknowledging that Indigenous people in these settler societies 'had suffered historical injustices and that they deserved redress in the form of symbolic acts and the redistribution of social and economic goods'.[33] In 1991 the Australian parliament passed the *Council for Reconciliation Act*, the preamble of which legislated the need for a formal process of reconciliation, to atone for the dispossession and dispersal of Aboriginal and Torres Strait Islander people from their traditional lands by addressing Indigenous disadvantage and aspirations.[34] In this context the formal discrimination against and exclusion of Aboriginal and Torres Strait Islander peoples practised by the armed forces throughout much of the twentieth century was no longer tenable.

In this context the Department of Defence began implementing a range of measures to raise Indigenous participation. In 1993 the ADF commissioned a study into ethnic participation in the armed forces, focusing on people from non-English-speaking backgrounds and Indigenous people. It was the first Defence-commissioned report into race and ethnicity.[35] While the report found that some military norms clashed with Aboriginal and Torres Strait Islander priorities, such as the emphasis on discipline and punctuality, as well as requiring separation from family for long periods, it also identified the pride that Indigenous communities had in their histories of previous military service, noting strong support for the ADF among Indigenous communities.[36]

Despite this report's recommendations for changes to recruitment practices that would reflect a more multicultural Australia, Riseman and Trembath note that in the short term, 'there was little action on the recommendations for targeted recruitment of Indigenous Australians'.[37] It was not until the end of the 1990s that the ADF officially began to implement initiatives akin to those recommended in the 1993 report. The Workplace Equity and Diversity Plan 1998–2001, and the Indigenous Staff Recruitment and Career Development Action Plan 1999–2003, were established to promote greater diversity within Defence (both the military and the Australian Public Service) through employing Aboriginal and Torres Strait Islander peoples.[38] Ricky Morris was at the frontline of these changes. As he recalled it in 2015, in 1997 the ADF introduced the 'Indigenous Participation Program', which, as its title suggests, was aimed at increasing Indigenous participation across the three services. The ADF called for Aboriginal and Torres Strait Islander servicemen and women to accompany recruiters to Indigenous communities. Morris, who was a plumber and gasfitter in the Royal Australian Engineers (RAE) at the time, expressed his interest. He saw his role in the Indigenous recruitment program as an 'icebreaker' in Aboriginal communities, noting that the sergeants and corporals who made up the rest of the tri-service recruitment team had had little prior contact with Aboriginal people and were noticeably nervous going into communities. He said that he 'broke the ice' and helped them to 'get down to community level'. Morris worked with the ADF Indigenous recruitment program during the period 1997–2000. At the same time, in his role with the RAE, he was a part of the ATSIC/Army Community Assistance Program (AACAP). AACAP was a cooperative initiative between the Aboriginal and Torres Strait Islander Commission (ATSIC), the Australian Army and the Department of Health and Family Services (DHFS), designed to assist in delivering housing and infrastructure capital works to remote Aboriginal communities. AACAP delivered its first round of projects during 1997–2000, and Army construction elements such as the RAE completed 65 per cent of the work.[39] Morris said that the role of the AACAP program was to develop infrastructure in the communities, and work with and 'train up the local Indigenous population'; the program, he said, provided a 'skills transfer' opportunity. During that time Morris also observed 'a lot of cross-cultural experiences', noting that many soldiers he served with had never worked with Indigenous people and 'wouldn't have given them the time of day … Once they worked in those spaces the relationships and bonds formed and it was really good to see that space open up.'[40]

Reconciliation Australia, the peak national body for reconciliation, was established at the end of the Council for Reconciliation's term (and the end of the official reconciliation process itself) in 2001, and launched Reconciliation Action Plans (RAPs) as an initiative in 2006. RAPs were designed to 'provide a framework for organisations to realise their vision for reconciliation'. In 2007 the first Defence Reconciliation Action Plan 2007–09 (DRAP) was drafted.[41]

In 2007 Aboriginal and Torres Strait Islander personnel represented 1.4 per cent of the permanent workforce in the ADF and 1.8 per cent of the active reserve, considerably below their percentage of the Australian population, which in 2006 had been estimated to be 2.5 per cent.[42] The ADF implemented its Indigenous Employment Strategy 2007–17 (IES) to complement the first RAP and sought to strengthen the ADF's engagement with Indigenous Australians.[43] On 1 July 2008 the Department of Defence established the Directorate of Indigenous Affairs (DIA), which centralised the leadership of Indigenous affairs across the ADF and APS. In a 2014 interview the then head of DIA, Lisa Phelps, noted that there were two 'genesis areas' that led to the establishment of the DIA: the ADF was 'starting to think about the diversity of the organisation' and realised it 'could no longer rely on the traditional pool of applicants'; the timing also 'coincided with a government-led change in focus with the official apology by [Prime Minister] Kevin Rudd in 2008'. This was made to Australia's Indigenous peoples, particularly to the Stolen Generations, whose lives had been blighted by past government policies of forced child removal.[44] It seems that, as with the modest initiatives undertaken in the 1990s, the mix of recruitment and retention issues and government-initiated reconciliation influenced this next wave of official policy.[45]

These specific programs to encourage Indigenous recruitment and development in the ADF came after a decade in which the reconciliation agenda had clearly shifted with the change in government. The Coalition government of John Howard (1996–2007) had openly sought to discredit the 'politics of symbolism' and an Indigenous rights-based version of reconciliation, in favour of a 'practical reconciliation agenda' that the conservative side of politics promoted as a means of addressing areas of socio-economic disadvantage.[46] When the Rudd government (2007–10) came to power, however, a wider commitment to 'close the gap' between Indigenous peoples and other Australians generated the Indigenous Pre-Recruitment Courses (IPRC) in 2008 and the Defence Indigenous Development Program (DIDP) within Defence in 2009. The IPRC was designed to help Aboriginal and Torres Strait Islander people interested in a military career with the skills to assist them in applying. It covered numeracy and English literacy, aptitude, confidence building, motivation and discipline, first aid, communication and training in the skills needed to live away from home. The IPRC was originally administered by the DIA and ran from 2008 until 2016. At the time of writing, a new IPRC, run by the individual services, was being trialled. The DIDP meanwhile began as a five-month bridging course for entry in NORFORCE, which was then extended to a whole-of-government initiative to give Indigenous people from remote communities the opportunity to acquire skills they could transfer back to their communities.[47]

The Defence Indigenous Employment Strategy 2011–2017 (IES) adopted an objective of 2.7 per cent Aboriginal and Torres Strait Islander representation in the total Defence workforce (both ADF and APS) by 2015, to reflect the overall proportion of Indigenous people in the wider Australian population. The Defence RAP of 2015–2018 also adopted the same target. The DIA has indicated that the census figures show that, as of 1 January 2017, the number of Aboriginal and Torres Strait Islander people in the Permanent ADF and Active Reserves were both sitting at 2 per cent.[48] While this represents a modest improvement on the 2007 figures of 1.4 and 1.8 per cent respectively, in 2017 these figures still fall significantly short of targets that were set to be achieved by 2015. In the most recent Defence RAP 2015–2018 it was noted that while Defence has made progress in the commitment to Indigenous Affairs, as a key government contributor and major employer, there was 'still a long way to go in achieving reconciliation and meeting the Government's employment and procurement targets designed to contribute to reconciliation'.[49]

The changing nature of the relationship between Aboriginal and Torres Strait Islander peoples and the ADF cannot be achieved, nor reflected, in participation rates alone and cultural change within the Defence organisation has also been consciously encouraged. The ADF has created a formal network of Indigenous Liaison Officers who provide support to Defence units and seek to broaden cultural understanding and facilitate greater engagement with local Indigenous communities.[50] The Air Force and Army have appointed ex-service personnel to act as Service Indigenous Elders; Uncle Harry Allie was appointed the Air Force Elder from 2012 and Uncle Roy Mundine the inaugural Army Elder in 2015. The role of Indigenous Elder, as the Australian Army sees it, is to represent serving and ex-service Indigenous personnel, to advise the Army's senior leadership and to participate in events of Indigenous significance such as NAIDOC Week and Reconciliation Week.[51] In another initiative, a Defence Cultural Awareness Indigenous Learning Framework was implemented in 2015. A key element of the 2010–2014 Defence Reconciliation Action Plan, the framework is focused on ensuring all Defence employees have a better understanding of the culture, history and traditions of Aboriginal and Torres Strait Islander people. It offers an online e-learning course which provides a basic introduction to Indigenous culture.[52]

The Department of Defence and the ADF have their own cultures and the DIA recognises that having Indigenous people work with Defence in any capacity makes a 'huge contribution to culture change', affecting the Defence workforce's view of wider Australia, 'particularly Indigenous Australia'.[53] This sentiment was reflected by NORFORCE Warrant Officer Bob Terms in 2012:

> Before I joined NORFORCE, I wouldn't have sat in a foxhole with an Aboriginal and shared a cup of tea. Now I don't think twice about sharing a cup of tea with [the Indigenous soldiers], or giving them a smoke, and I'm honoured to be godparent to an Aboriginal girl. I guess I've stopped seeing them as a different class of person.[54]

Regimental commander Lieutenant-Colonel Christopher Goldston says that ADF members make 'some very deep personal connections' in northern Australia, which are highly valued in Indigenous culture. Goldston notes that communities in the north are 'used to a revolving door of people who fly in, promise the world and fly out, having delivered nothing'.[55] His observation reveals an understanding of some of the complexities of working with Indigenous people and communities, a knowledge of which would enable many policy makers and politicians in Canberra to meaningfully engage with Aboriginal and Torres Strait Islander Australians and bring about 'practical reconciliation'.

The importance of family and a proud history of service

Yorta Yorta man Steve Jones is the first known Aboriginal graduate of the Royal Military College in Duntroon. After graduating in 1977, he enjoyed a rewarding career including Officer Commanding 9 Transport Squadron and Commanding Officer of the Army School of Transport. Before retiring as a colonel he was promoted through the ranks from Major, to Commanding Officer and

Colonel following his appointment as the Defence Attaché to the Australian Mission to the UN in 2005. In an interview for the Serving Our Country project in 2016, he said that he thinks that Aboriginal culture fits well with the culture of the Army, particularly because both place the 'family' or the 'team' at the centre of everything. He says that, while the military college was a bit of a 'shock' to begin with, once he settled into the company he was assigned, he felt comfortable being a part of a team; this was the result of the culture he had been brought up in, which had a 'very strong sense of family'.[56]

It would seem that this commonality is not lost on Defence and that it has proved successful in encouraging and retaining Indigenous recruits. While the 1993 report into ethnic diversity in the ADF noted that the obligations and responsibilities of kinship clashed with military expectations, it would seem that the ADF has learned to embrace and utilise the concept of kin. All of the specific Indigenous programs involve cultural sessions designed to help Indigenous recruits navigate 'Walking in Two Worlds'. Delivered by a senior Indigenous warrant officer, the sessions inform potential recruits that when 'joining Defence, you're joining a family'. In 2014 the head of DIA noted that they spend 'quite some time' on this idea of recruits joining a Defence family and looking at how 'culture fits within Defence, its traditions and history'.[57]

Family looms large in Aboriginal and Torres Strait Islander memories of service. One of the strongest threads running through the oral histories discussed here, and those recorded for the Serving Our Country project more broadly, is a sense of pride among interviewees stemming from a family history of service. Ricky Morris's maternal grandfather was Frederick Amos Lovett, one of the five brothers from Lake Condah mission whose enlistment in the First World War began a history of service that has seen a member of the Lovett family serve in every major conflict from the First World

War through to Afghanistan. In his interview for Serving Our Country Morris said that he still encounters racism and it makes him 'wonder how far we've come … from WWI to now'. According to Morris 'we haven't moved too far in some spaces as Aboriginal people and if you can hang your hat on anything it's military service and Aboriginal men and women have answered the call'. Morris also said that when he encounters racism in his everyday life, and in his current cultural awareness training work, it is the proud history of Indigenous service that he uses to counteract racist assumptions and promote a deeper respect for Indigenous peoples.[58] Perhaps, as Morris's oral history suggests, an important defence against discrimination and racism within the ADF is to highlight this long history of service; a sentiment reflected on the ADF website in 2017, a section of which was titled 'A proud history' that recognised the century of service by Indigenous Australians protecting Australia and its interests.[59]

Modest statistical progress in Indigenous participation rates should not overshadow the progress the ADF has made in addressing over a century of discrimination against and exclusion of Indigenous people on racial grounds. Rather than a sudden change of heart, and explicit recognition of past wrongs on the part of the ADF, these shifts in policy and attitudes need to be understood in the context of changes in Australian society more broadly – primary among them the issues of recruitment and retention that emerged in the 1980s to challenge the ADF and the state-sanctioned program of reconciliation. While progress has been somewhat modest, it should be viewed with a long-term perspective; the kind of structural and cultural change to which the ADF has demonstrated commitment cannot be realised in the short term. Furthermore, given the disappointing statistics delivered in the 2016 Prime Minister's Closing the Gap report, the ADF's progress, particularly in the last decade since 2006, perhaps points to approaches that can bring about real and meaningful change in the move towards reconciliation.

16

Commemoration

Joan Beaumont

'ANZAC [was] a party to which they [had] not been invited.'
– *Frank Lampard*

For much of the twentieth century the military service of Indigenous Australians went unrecognised in national commemoration and remembrance. Since these men and women rarely formed a discrete cohort within the Australian defence forces, their service was simply subsumed into the wider rituals of public commemoration, such as Anzac Day. However, from the late 1980s on, there was a growing conviction in both community and official circles that the military service of Indigenous Australians needed to be recognised more explicitly; and with this came a plethora of new commemorative practices, created by Indigenous and non-Indigenous agents alike. In some instances these rituals combined traditional remembrance practices with Indigenous cultural forms to create new and inventive fusions. Yet, often this overdue recognition of Indigenous service was incorporated into the conservative narrative of Australia's wars, the Anzac legend. This mythic narrative of war has shown a remarkable capacity over the past century to adapt to changing social mores, but it remains essentially a narrative of white men defending a state which historically has dispossessed and discriminated against Indigenous people. There is therefore a tension between the desire of Aboriginal and Torres Strait Islander Australians for recognition within this dominant national narrative and their simultaneous aspiration that the 'frontier wars' between white settlers and Indigenous peoples should be recognised as part of the national history of conflict. It is a tension that remains unresolved at the time of writing.

The long silence, 1900–1980

For most of the twentieth century little effort was made at the national level to explicitly commemorate Indigenous military service. None of the Aboriginal trackers who served in the Boer War were honoured on the memorials to that conflict installed across Australia.[1] Then, when thousands of memorials were erected to commemorate the First World War a decade or so later, Aboriginal service was again subsumed within wider remembrance practices. Although Aboriginal names did appear on some memorials, 'you needed local knowledge to pick them', as historian Ken Inglis put it in 1998. In one rare instance, a memorial in Herberton, Queensland, the word 'Aboriginal' was listed after the name of one William Perrott.[2]

There were a few exceptions to this silence, almost all of them a result of Aboriginal agency. In 1925 the Ngarrindjeri community at Point McLeay (Raukkan) South Australia, funded a memorial stained-glass window in the mission church. As the Adelaide *News* reported:

> Ever since the war, when four of the 16 men they sent were killed, they have been collecting for the memorial, and when the great day arrived, their delight knew no bounds. By concerts and other means they raised more than £200 and procured a beautiful four-

> panelled memorial window on which was inscribed 'To the Glory of God and in sacred memory of our men who died for justice and freedom' and the names of the dead.[3]

Six years later, a replica of the Sydney Harbour Bridge was unveiled in the grounds of the Lilydale Repatriation Military Cottages, Callan Park, Sydney. Dedicated 'in proud memory of those who made the great sacrifice', this installation was created by First World War veteran Douglas Grant, whose story has been told in chapter 6. In his post-war life Grant had criticised the treatment of Aboriginal people, but he was also represented in the white press as a positive example of assimilation.[4] The New South Wales Governor, Sir Philip Game, then, unveiled his memorial, deeming it 'a reminder of fallen comrades and also … an inspiration to you all to do what you did during the four years of the war, and have been doing ever since – sticking it out in the good old Australian and British way'.[5]

At least three other memorials are known to have been erected by local communities in the 1930s: a memorial gateway to the Aboriginal residents of Walhallow station (Caroona mission), New South Wales, in 1934; a small obelisk on Flinders Island in the Bass Strait in 1936; and a stone memorial on Cape Barren Island, a place which had a predominantly Aboriginal population, of whom a significant number had volunteered for military service.[6] Meanwhile, on Palm Island, Queensland, the local community created in 1936 'a special dance of remembrance performed by warriors'.[7]

In these years *Reveille*, the magazine of the New South Wales Returned Sailor's and Soldier's Imperial League of Australia, initiated a semi-official attempt to remember Aboriginal service. In 1931 it launched an investigation to record the names of all Aboriginal men who had served in the First World War. After sending circulars to Aboriginal protectors, it published the lists of known men from New South Wales, Victoria and Queensland.[8] But this was a rare gesture of recognition on the part of non-Aboriginal Australians.

Little changed when it came time to remember military service in the Second World War. This silence owed something to a wider lack of enthusiasm for creating war memorials, since Australians now favoured more utilitarian ways of remembering their dead, ranging from community halls and gates to memorial parks and ovals. Where the names of the Second World War dead were recorded, they were often on existing memorials to the war of 1914–18. If any of these names happened to be Aboriginal, this could only be identified 'by someone who was looking for it'.[9]

Yet again there were exceptions at the initiative of Indigenous communities. In 1951 an honour board was unveiled at the Cherbourg Aboriginal Settlement in south-east Queensland commemorating 48 men who had served in the two world wars.[10] A Ngarrindjeri man from the Point McLeay mission, Gordon Rigney, laid a wreath of swan feathers at annual Anzac Day dawn services in Adelaide. In 1952 the Second World War veteran Reg Saunders spoke in Wagga Wagga at the Anzac Day march, while a band from the Mona Mona mission accompanied the Anzac Day service in Kuranda, Queensland. Meanwhile, a Korean War veteran Stephen Dodd led Adelaide's Anzac Day march for several years.[11] Then, in 1969, NAIDOC held a ceremony at Sydney's Anzac Day Memorial, Hyde Park, recognising Aboriginal service in the Second World War. Memories of that war were also progressively incorporated into the dances and songs of remote northern Indigenous communities.[12]

The memory 'boom'

Although (as chapter 10 has shown), there was some earlier recognition of Indigenous service in New South Wales, the Commonwealth government only began to play a significant role in commemorating this service when a remarkable resurgence in the memory of war occurred across the globe from the 1980s on. The reasons for this memory 'boom' are beyond the scope of this chapter to explore. Suffice to say that once begun, the memory boom owed its ongoing momentum in Australia to a symbiotic interaction between successive governments and their agencies, and diverse agents of a memory 'from below': the former invoking the memory of past wars for the purposes of legitimation and constructing a national identity, and the latter (so far as there is any consensus on this) being inspired by a mix of nationalist sentiment, an enthusiasm for genealogy, and a search for meaning and identity in a world where community and religion had been eroded by globalisation and secularism. All of this inspired a plethora of new commemorative activities, many of them instigated by the Australian government, but many also generated by previously marginalised groups seeking recognition for their 'forgotten' war service. As in many other countries, war memory became a critical tool in Australian identity politics.

In this context the demand for recognition of Indigenous military service gathered force. By the 1980s there was already a powerful movement of Aboriginal political activism, concerned with land rights, health issues, deaths in custody, the forcible removal of children, the mining of Aboriginal lands and the need for a treaty recognising Indigenous people's rights and prior occupation of the land. From the 1980s on a new generation of Aboriginal people also began to write their own history, interpreting it in their own way and reclaiming it from non-Indigenous historians and anthropologists.[13] The war memory boom added recognition of Aboriginal military service to this complex agenda.

The first initiatives in this more explicit commemoration of Indigenous service came, as in earlier decades, from individuals and local collectives. Early efforts were focused on the Anzac Day march, that annual parade which constitutes a powerful public performance of collective memory across the nation. In April 1985 some

15 Aboriginal ex-servicemen, forming the National Aboriginal and Islanders Ex-Services Association, attempted to march under their own banner in the Melbourne march. They met a mixed reaction. The Victorian President of the RSL, Bruce Ruxton, declared that: 'They cannot march alone ... This is the same whether they're black, white or brindle. The rules are the rules.'[14] Unable to reconcile diversity and difference with the traditional digger ideal, Ruxton believed that veterans had to choose between being Aboriginal *or* Australian, not claim a hyphenated identity of being Aboriginal *and* Australian.[15] The Anzac Day Memorial Council, however, was more divided, voting nine to four against allowing the Aboriginal group to march separately in Melbourne.[16] In the event, the group staged their own march, not down the traditional Anzac Day route, along St Kilda Road to the Shrine of Remembrance, but in the suburb of Northcote. Then later in the year, during NAIDOC Week, they staged an Aboriginal Memorial Service at the Shrine, where, much to Ruxton's dismay, the Aboriginal flag was raised.[17]

The Northcote Anzac Day march lasted only a matter of three years: the organisers concluded that the Second World War veterans were aging and that most Aboriginal veterans were content to march with their wider military units. However, in 1993 a group of about 50 Aboriginal people, under the leadership of the Kombumerri group, led an Anzac Day march on the Gold Coast, Queensland. Included in the marchers were the widow of Reg Saunders and the poet and ex-servicewoman-turned-activist Oodgeroo Noonuccal (formerly Kath Walker). Like the Northcote march, this did not become an annual event, but as Noah Riseman and Richard Trembath say, together these were 'a preview of Indigenous ex-service commemorations to come'.[18]

Meanwhile the bicentennial of Australian settlement in 1988 raised public sensitivities to the issue of Aboriginal dispossession and generated a number of new commemorative activities. The

National Aboriginal and Islander Ex-Services Association now applied for a grant to erect a memorial to Aboriginal people killed in war, and when this was rejected, they installed a simple memorial in front of the Aborigines Advancement League in Melbourne.[19] Reading of this in the press, a non-Aboriginal Canberra resident, Honor Thwaites, who had been awarded a grant to regenerate the bushland on Mt Ainslie, planted within walking distance of the Australian War Memorial a simple stone memorial inscribed 'Remembering the Aboriginal people who served in the Australian Forces'.[20] In 1988 Aboriginal curator and activist Djon Mundine organised a remarkable memorial consisting of 200 hollow log coffins (one for each year of European occupation). Created by artists from Ramingining in the Northern Territory and soon placed in the National Gallery, Canberra, this installation was not a traditional war memorial. Rather than honouring those who died in military service for the nation, it commemorated all the Indigenous people who, since 1788, lost their lives defending their land.

In the 1990s the Australian government and its agencies finally began to proactively recognise Indigenous military service. This acknowledgment came as part of an extraordinarily extensive program of war commemoration that the Labor government of Bob Hawke initiated (possibly in response to the controversy surrounding the bicentennial) and which governments of both political persuasions have maintained to this day.[21] A government-funded pilgrimage of veterans to Gallipoli in 1990, the 75th anniversary of the landing, is generally agreed to have marked the beginning of this massive investment in remembrance. It continued in 1992 with extensive coverage of the 50th anniversaries of the Second World War: especially the fall of Singapore and the Kokoda campaign. For Prime Minister Paul Keating, the Asia–Pacific war of 1941–45 was the moment when Australians shook off an anachronistic imperial dependence and unequivocally defended their national sovereignty.

Keating also championed Indigenous causes, delivering a clarion call for Reconciliation at Redfern, Sydney, in December 1992. 'Imagine if non-Aboriginal Australians had served their country in peace and war', he said, 'and were then ignored in history books.'[22] Yet when in 1993 Keating presided over the burial in the Australian War Memorial of an Unknown Soldier from the First World War, his now legendary eulogy failed to mention specifically Aboriginal and Torres Strait Islander Australians' service (though he did say that no one 'race', gender, religion or generation should be asserted above another). Nor, to the chagrin of some Aboriginal activists, was the Indigenous flag included in the standards raised around Canberra during the Unknown Soldier ceremony. 'Now we know the contribution of the Aboriginal soldiers [to the war]', said Alan Coe, 'but still they are not recognized and our flag does not fly.'[23]

However, in 1995 the Australian government engaged directly with the memory of Indigenous service when it launched its year-long commemoration of the end of the Second World War, 'Australia Remembers'. The vision of the Minister for Veterans' Affairs, Con Sciacca, who was an Italian immigrant, was a multicultural and inclusive one. Among the Australia Remembers posters, then, were images of Leonard Waters, the first Aboriginal RAAF pilot to earn his 'wings', and Reg Saunders, shaking hands with a white 'mate'. Moreover, when Keating spoke at the VP50 commemorations at Townsville, he said of Indigenous servicemen and women that 'even if the Australia of the 1940s was blind to their bravery and loyalty, we see it clearly now. And we acknowledge it now. It must not be forgotten.'[24]

Yet these first attempts to officially recognise Indigenous service, as Liz Reed has argued, were 'problematically contained within the non-Indigenous discourses of the nation'. Indigenous peoples were 'allowed in' to the Australia Remembers program but in ways that managed the national space through gestures of tolerance and inclusion. Moreover, the poster images of Indigenous personnel reflected what Marcia Langton has called an annoying paternalistic tendency to focus on the 'first Aborigine to …'. The Australia Remembers campaign also homogenised the Indigenous experience of the Second World War, giving little recognition to Torres Strait Islanders or Indigenous women. Even Keating's Townsville tribute to Indigenous personnel was positioned within a wider recognition of Pacific Island veterans and seemed to 'suggest a belief in Indigenous homogeneity'. Finally, Reed notes that the numbers of Aboriginal and Torres Strait Islander people participating in 'Australia Remembers' events were modest. Except for pressing their demands for recognition or compensation, they were 'mostly absent from the national remembering of their involvement'. Where they did participate, it was as members of their own wartime units rather than under their own flag.[25]

Converging remembrance?

This attempt to recognise Indigenous war service was therefore more of a 'top down' than a 'bottom up' exercise. But over the next two decades official and vernacular modes of remembering Indigenous military service converged. Naturally, there continued to be local initiatives that owed little to official support or tolerance (see Appendix 2, p. 360). Among them was a memorial at Whim Creek, in the Pilbara, to the five Lockyer brothers, who served with the 2nd AIF and RAAF during the Second World War, and only three of whom survived; and an innovative program called Honouring Indigenous War Graves, created in Western Australia by an Aboriginal Vietnam veteran, John Schnaars. From 2005 he installed remembrance plaques at the gravesites of deceased Aboriginal servicemen and women, while also constructing a wall of individual plaques. As Schnaars explains it:

> I believe it was the veterans who went away to war then, who had no rights in this country to vote or anything, and that it was those men and women, the few women that went away, that changed the course of history on the way Australia felt towards Aborigines.[26]

However, the majority of the Indigenous remembrance initiatives since the mid-1990s have involved accommodating and negotiating with official custodians of war memory. For example, in 2000 the recently formed Western Australian Aboriginal and Torres Strait Islander Veterans and Services Association approached the RSL for permission to march as a contingent in Perth's Anzac Day march. In contrast to Ruxton 15 years earlier, the RSL not only supported this proposal but invited the Indigenous veterans to lead the parade.[27] Similarly, in Victoria Koorie Elder Dot Peters worked with the Victorian RSL in 2006 to organise a ceremony at the Melbourne Shrine of Remembrance during National Reconciliation Week. Soon the Shrine itself developed a travelling exhibition, Indigenous Australians at War, which toured regional Victoria, and then the rest of Australia from late 2011 to 2015.[28]

Concurrently, a variety of cultural productions began to recognise Indigenous service. To mention only the most prominent: in 1999 the Queensland Theatre Company staged *The Sunshine Club*, a play which told the story of an Aboriginal serviceman challenging the racial divide on his return from the Second World War.[29] Two years later, in Queensland again, *Seems Like Yesterday* was launched with a mix of Indigenous, corporate and governmental support. This time the play was set in Vietnam, where a group of Australians have their sense of identity challenged by the arrival of an Aboriginal serviceman. The play's message (one that has become a dominant trope in Indigenous commemoration) was that race was irrelevant in small units facing combat: 'In Vietnam there were no blackfellas or whitefellas, we were all tarred with the same brush. Our colour was green.'[30] The ABC 2003 documentary, *The Forgotten*, meanwhile, voiced another increasingly common trope: of Aboriginal personnel taking pride in fighting and dying for Australia despite facing various prejudices and not being classed as citizens of the country.[31] The documentary's title also positioned Indigenous soldiers firmly within the wider politics of recognition where being 'forgotten' had become an almost essential sobriquet (other claimants to the title have included the veterans of the Korean and Vietnam wars, service nurses and civilian internees). Being forgotten was also one of the many themes explored in the powerful and critically acclaimed play *Black Diggers*, which marked the centenary of the First World War in 2014 by examining the Indigenous experience of wartime and post-war life.

Even more notable than these cultural productions was the appropriation of prominent public space for new memorials and rituals. Each of these involved a dynamic negotiation between Indigenous peoples and representatives of municipal and state governments. The initial inspiration for South Australia's Aboriginal and Torres Strait Islander War Memorial, for example, came from Aboriginal author Doreen Kartinyeri's *Ngarrindjeri Anzacs*, a 1996 publication which told the stories of the First World War service of 21 men from Raukkan and the Lower Murray in South Australia. This sensitised the local Indigenous community to the fact that 'ANZAC [was] a party to which they [had] not been invited'.[32] As Marj Tripp, Aboriginal Elder and the first known Aboriginal woman to become a member of the Women's Royal Australian Navy Service (1963–65), said in 2015:

> I never thought about all this stuff for a long, long time until about 2006 I was asked to take over as a chair person to organise a RAVSA [Register of Aboriginal Veterans of South Australia]

> type thing, about getting all the names of Aboriginal service people who were alive, or those that weren't ... lots and lots of information came forward through that. That was when we decided that we needed to do something about honouring our service people.[33]

In time, the then Minister for Aboriginal Affairs and Reconciliation, Jay Weatherill, made resources available from his department, and in 2007 a planning committee of mostly Indigenous ex-servicemen and women was established, with Tripp as the chair.[34] Although acutely conscious of the need not to lose control – to quote one of the drivers of the project, Frank Lampard, 'we did not want to be overrun' – the Indigenous leaders eventually accepted, in 2011, the need for support from Adelaide's political and business elite to raise some $1 million.[35] It took about seven years before the memorial was completed on Adelaide's Torrens Parade Ground, a site rich in colonial military history and significance for the Kaurna people. The memorial's dedication on 10 November 2013, by the then governor-general Quentin Bryce, spoke to the now high level of political support for Indigenous commemoration.

The Coloured Diggers march, meanwhile, had its origins in a relatively small Anzac Day church service conducted in 2006 in Redfern, a Sydney suburb with a significant Aboriginal community.[36] The following year this service was repeated and preceded by a march of 17 ex-servicemen and about 500 family members, friends and supporters.[37] Taking its name from a Second World War poem written by Sapper Bert Beros, the Coloured Diggers Project then grew, under the leadership of a local pastor, Ray Minniecon (two of whose brothers served in Vietnam) and the Babana Aboriginal Men's Fellowship. As it developed, an accommodation was reached with an initially suspicious RSL. The Coloured Diggers march was scheduled in the afternoon of Anzac Day, thus allowing

Indigenous servicemen and women to march with their own units in the main morning march. The broad political support for the march was soon evident in the attendance of state and federal politicians and military leaders, including the Lebanese-born Governor of New South Wales, Dame Marie Bashir (2001–14) and Lord Mayor Clover Moore (2004–). Since 2014 the City of Sydney has supported the march with $5000 in cash and in-kind support.[38]

The City of Sydney also played a key role in installing the most prominent of Indigenous war commemorations to date, the Yininmadyemi sculpture in Hyde Park, in 2015. Located close to Sydney's prime piece of memory real estate, the 1931 Anzac Memorial, where the 1969 Aboriginal ceremony had been held, this installation forms part of a wider Eora Journey project in which the Sydney City Council has undertaken a cultural mapping of Aboriginal and Torres Strait Islander heritage and history. Though the installation of a war memorial was a response to lobbying from the Coloured Diggers Project, it was not their preferred sculpture, 'Dancing with Strangers', that was selected.[39] This depicted a circle of Aboriginal dancers that service personnel could join on their return, but the committee of the Sydney City Council (on which there was Indigenous representation) opted for a more contemporary sculpture.[40] After a public competition which attracted about 30 entries, it commissioned a young Indigenous artist and official war artist with NORFORCE, Tony Albert, to produce the work.

'Riding the tiger' of national memory

The official embrace of Indigenous service from the 1990s onwards was most evident in the activities of the Australian War Memorial and the Department of Veterans' Affairs. For decades the Memorial had assumed that Indigenous service could be subsumed within the wider narrative of Australia's wars.[41] However, in the 1990s it too became aware of the need for a more distinctive recognition. In 1993 it launched an exhibition, 'Too Dark for the Light Horse'. This had been developed initially by an Indigenous employee of the Aboriginal and Torres Strait Islander Commission, David Huggonson, who had compiled photographs and documents depicting Aboriginal involvement in the Australian Army.[42] In later years the exhibition, now converted into an education resource with the support of the Department of Veterans' Affairs, toured nationally, showing at diverse locations ranging from the Parliamentary Library in Canberra to remote communities in the Northern Territory, Queensland, Western Australia and New South Wales.[43] Thereafter the Australian War Memorial, which was generously funded as the centenary of the First World War approached, went into something of a commemorative overdrive. In 2004 it endorsed the Anzac Day ceremony held by the Aboriginal and Torres Strait Islander Veterans and Services Association at the Mount Ainslie memorial, and in 2009 it appointed its first Indigenous Liaison Officer, Gary Oakley. A range of public education resources were developed: web pages about Indigenous service; tours with an Indigenous focus during Reconciliation Week; stories about Indigenous servicemen in the revamped First World War gallery; and Indigenous stories included in the daily Last Post ceremony, which was introduced in 2013. The Memorial, and its close partner in memory making, the Department of Veterans' Affairs (DVA), also worked with schools, assisted regional organisations in their commemorative programs, including the Aboriginal Art Program in Redfern; and became a partner in the Serving Our Country project funded by the Australian Research Council and based at the Australian National University.[44] The DVA meanwhile, in 2000, named its offices in Woden, ACT 'Lovett Tower', after the family from the Gunditjmara community in Victoria whose members have served in virtually every conflict of the twentieth century.

The centenary of the First World War intensified these efforts by the Memorial to recognise Indigenous service. The director, Brendan Nelson (2012–) commissioned a statue of a black and a white digger for the Memorial grounds, while the dawn service held on the centenary of the Gallipoli landing, 25 April 2015, opened with the evocative playing of a *yidaki* (didgeridoo) from the parapets of the Memorial. Remembrance Day later that year was marked by the naming of a gallery and courtyard after Reg Saunders. This was the first time the Memorial had named any space after any Australian.[45] Then in 2016 the Memorial opened a new exhibition, 'For Country, For Nation'. Developed in close consultation with Indigenous Elders and communities, this subtle exhibition allowed the story of Indigenous experiences of war, at home and abroad, to be told by Indigenous voices. It showcased traditional and contemporary Aboriginal and Torres Strait Islander weaponry and art, including work by Tony Albert; and although it was predictably focused on individual stories of war, the exhibition did not deny the discrimination and prejudice encountered by Indigenous peoples across the twentieth century.

It is noteworthy that all these official acts of recognition occurred at a time when there was a growing debate about whether the Australian War Memorial should also commemorate the 'frontier wars' between white settlers and Indigenous Australians. This issue was far from new, having been debated fiercely during the 'history wars' of the Howard government years, but it re-emerged in the lead-up to the centenary of the First World War.[46] Nelson's response was unequivocally negative. As he saw it, the story of frontier violence should be told – but not by the Memorial. The frontier wars, he claimed, were 'immensely complex and did not amount to war. There was not any occasion [he said in May 2015], that I'm aware where a colony specifically formed an army or a unit to go out and run a war with Indigenous Australians … after the British garrisons left, the violence where it was conducted, was conducted by colonial militia, mounted police militia and Indigenous militia.' Moreover, Nelson argued, today's serving Indigenous soldiers did not support frontier conflict being portrayed in the Memorial. The appropriate place for remembering frontier warfare was therefore the National Museum of Australia.[47] Nelson's historical interpretation, of course, is far from uncontested. But so long as he remains director, the War Memorial is unlikely to change its official position, though notably in 2017 it displayed a Rover Thomas painting of the Ruby Plains Massacre, so that visitors to the nearby 'For Country, For Nation' exhibition could 'ask questions about why the Aboriginal people wanted to fight'.[48]

It is too early to assess the value and impact of this incorporation of Indigenous service into the official memory of war. Clearly it is a significant gesture in the politics of recognition, providing Indigenous servicemen and women with a heightened visibility in Australia's narrative of war. But the Anzac legend was, and to a large degree remains, a story of white men. Moreover it is, to borrow historian Bruce Kapferer's phrase, both a legend of people and a myth of state – the very state that historically has been the agent of Indigenous dispossession, suffering and marginalisation.[49] Does Indigenous commemoration of the 'I was there too' kind then effectively deny Indigenous Australians a distinctive identity and silence more difficult narratives such as frontier wars? Can it be argued that incorporating Indigenous diggers into official remembrance is a form of cultural assimilation and that the active Indigenous involvement in this incorporation represents a form of 'state-conceded agency'?[50]

Such an argument is persuasive if we accept the theoretical position that settler colonies by definition cannot decolonise: that is, the 'invasion of colonising settler into Indigenous territories and life worlds is never reversed: colonial authority endures as a structure, and it does not abate or withdraw'.[51] According to one proponent of this view, Patrick Wolfe, the key characteristic of settler colonialism is the dual outcome of destruction and displacement, in which the logic is not necessarily a physical elimination but an 'erasure' or 'elimination'.[52] From this historiographical perspective, the integration of Indigenous service into the Anzac legend might be viewed as yet another episode where 'the structure of settler colonialism has … triumphed – either by erasing the Indigenous presence or by determining the forms of its survival'.[53]

However, there is an alternative interpretation. As historian Tim Rowse has argued, the 'elimination' paradigm is unhelpful. Firstly, it 'renders uninteresting … the recent empowerment of Indigenous Australians: the diversity of their remembered pasts and projected futures'.[54] Secondly, the notion of 'state-conceded agency' denies any Indigenous agency in the recent processes of remembrance. Perhaps, then, a more nuanced way of understanding the involvement of Indigenous peoples with remembrance projects of the state is as 'hyphenated histories' – a term which historian Miranda Johnson employs to describe processes whereby Indigenous peoples 'strategically engage settler institutions to further their own and their communities' goals'. Through this agency Indigenous peoples may 'enter institutions of the state, the national and global economic, and engage with diverse cultural forms by "indigenising" them to some extent'.[55]

Indigenising Anzac

This 'indigenising' of Anzac is evident in some recent remembrance practices which combine traditional Western rituals with Indigenous cultural forms to produce a new fusion. The South Australian Aboriginal and Torres Strait Islander War Memorial draws heavily on Indigenous imagery. Designed as a contemplative and reflective space, it has at its heart a half-circle representing people sitting at an Indigenous community gathering. A rainbow serpent, a creator ancestor in the Dreaming, is embedded in the slate pavers, while a stone topped by a coolamon provides a place for cleansing smoking ceremonies. Other boulders speak to Aboriginal people's connection to land, to each other, and to the past. The pathway leading to the circle, meanwhile, lists the names of Aboriginal veterans who were born in South Australia or the Northern Territory, or who served in a battalion or unit from South Australia.[56]

Yet, if much of the design of the memorial evokes elements of Indigenous cultures, the walls surrounding the memorial carry the insignia of the three defence services and the merchant navy. Moreover, the two bronze statues of a uniformed Indigenous serviceman and woman overlooking the ceremonial area are a 'borrowed' cultural form, in that there was no monumental statuary in pre-colonial Indigenous communities. Their positioning is meant to suggest that they are both the defenders of Australia and 'the keepers of a deeper knowledge about the land', but this reading is unlikely to occur to the random visitor.[57] Rather, the statues are reminiscent of the three infantrymen (one white, one black, one Latino) installed at the Vietnam Wall in Washington DC – statues installed because the abstract and reflective memorial of the wall was deemed by critics to be too unheroic.[58]

The ceremonies performed at this South Australian memorial are again a cross-cultural fusion. At the 2015 Reconciliation Week ceremony, a military brass and woodwind band played the traditional Christian hymns of remembrance: 'The Lord's My Shepherd', 'Now Thank We All Our God', 'Abide with Me', 'Oh God Our Help in Ages Past' and 'Eternal Father Strong to Save'. The music also included 'What a Friend We Have in Jesus', a chorus possibly popularised in mission communities. The ceremony also concluded with the traditional triad: Laurence Binyon's Ode of

Remembrance, the minute's silence and the Last Post. But while much of this was Western in its cultural derivation, the ceremony began with a welcome to country and a smoking ceremony, and included a short address by Uncle Roy Mundine about his role as Indigenous Elder to the Australian Army. The wreaths laid by the audience were rarely the traditional laurel or floral wreaths, but rather books to be used in Indigenous education. Most notably, the ceremony included a song by Indigenous singer, Vonda Last, 'For Love of Country'.

A variant on this fusion of remembrance practices can be found in the Coloured Diggers Anzac Day march. In recent years the march has developed its own traditions.[59] These include wreath-laying in Redfern Park at the original First World War memorial, which is a mix of neoclassical statuary and an Anzac digger; a smoking ceremony and dances by painted warriors; and a march through the streets of Redfern led by Indigenous dancers accompanied by clap sticks, didgeridoos and banners declaring 'Honour, Recognition and Respect – Lest We Forget'. In recent years the concluding rally has ended at the Community Centre, with Christian hymns, prayers addressed to a god whose voice is 'in the Dreaming', speeches by community leaders and politicians, and an interpretive dance of the poem, 'The Coloured Digger'.[60]

Perhaps the most 'Indigenised' Anzac rituals are to be found in the Honouring Warriors Spirits ceremony, held in the precincts of the Australian War Memorial in November 2015. Like earlier ceremonies, such as Connecting Spirits, held in 2005 at the Coorong, South Australia, this involved the scattering, at the base of the Lone Pine tree, of soil collected from places on the Gallipoli peninsula where Indigenous soldiers might have fallen.[61] The ceremony aims to reconcile past Western practices of burial of the dead with the Indigenous belief that ceremonies surrounding death facilitate the spirit returning to its home. Sponsored by the Australian Army and attended by senior military figures, the ceremony's catafalque party consisted of Indigenous warriors (who were also serving ADF personnel). Clap sticks, didgeridoos and Torres Strait Islander drums provided music to accompany a traditional dance and the scattering of soil around the base of the tree. The ceremony ended traditionally with Binyon's Ode, the Last Post and the minute's silence, but the ode was read in English and an Indigenous language.[62]

The Yininmadyemi artwork in Hyde Park, Sydney, in contrast, has eschewed any traditional cultural references. This massive sculpture takes the form of seven bullets, made of marble and steel: four are erect and three are fallen. One of the standing bullets represents Albert's grandfather, Eddie, a prisoner of war in Italy in the Second World War who narrowly escaped execution when he was captured after an escape attempt. The fallen bullets are other prisoners, shot before their captors realised they were 'British'. Collectively, the bullets are intended, Albert says, to represent 'the fallen soldier, the men who survived and on return to this country were left to fall again'.[63] Conceptualised as a deliberately strong installation, the memorial is very masculine, even phallic; and it is hard to imagine it being identified by the passersby as a specifically Aboriginal memorial. Indeed, although there are discrete plaques describing the memorial's meaning, volunteer staff at the nearby Anzac Memorial questioned by the author said they are often asked what Yininmadyemi is.

The range and scope of commemorative activities invented over the past two decades have therefore adapted to varying degrees the traditional rituals of Anzac, positioning Indigenous military service within the mainstream national memory of war. At the same time, in the face of official resistance to recognition of the 'frontier wars', Indigenous communities have appropriated Anzac rituals in an effort to link service in the defence forces with this earlier violence:

what Noah Riseman and Elizabeth Furniss call the 'Anzac-isation' of the frontier wars.[64]

Many of these new rituals have a relatively short history, so it is difficult to predict how enduring they will be. As Jay Winter has reminded us, it is not states and organisations who remember. Rather, it is individuals who do so and 'when such people lose interest, or time, or for any other reason cease to act; when they move away or die, then the collective dissolves and so do the acts of remembrance'.[65] Hence, the future of 'Indigenised' Anzac commemoration depends, in part, on whether the collectives that invented these new 'traditions' are succeeded by generations that share their belief that war memory is an appropriate way to promote Indigenous claims in twenty-first-century Australia.

It is a matter for debate whether such strategies should include, as some activists wish, the installation of a national memorial to Indigenous military service on Anzac Parade in Canberra. Certainly a memorial to Indigenous service in this politically charged space, which forms an axis between the federal parliament and the Australian War Memorial, would constitute recognition at the very heart of national remembrance. But would this inclusion come at the price of incorporation into the dominant Anglo-Celtic narrative and a subsequent loss of authenticity? A number of the memorials already on Anzac Parade were inspired by 'bottom-up' lobbying, but once installed, they failed to evolve into dynamic sites of memory.[66] Except on an occasional anniversary, they do not engage members of the Australian population in personal and spontaneous acts of remembrance. Certainly there is nothing on Anzac Parade to rival the Vietnam Wall in Washington DC, where countless gifts left by visitors have invested the site with an ongoing and deep personal significance.[67] Hence, a national memorial to Indigenous service on Anzac Parade might become a sterile monument, an admittedly important gesture from the state, but possessing none of the organic authenticity that the Aboriginal memorial on Mount Ainslie has acquired after years of remembrance activities on that bush site.

Moreover, the installation of a national memorial to Indigenous military service on Anzac Parade might well invest these episodes of the past with a status superior to that of frontier conflict. As critics such as Marilyn Lake and Henry Reynolds have observed, in recent years Anzac has silenced other narratives of the past, such as 'our national civil and political traditions of democratic equality and social justice'.[68] It is not embracing the logic of 'erasure' or 'elimination', therefore, to caution that the official recognition of Indigenous military service with the framework of Anzac – and even an 'Indigenised Anzac' – carry this same risk: that other narratives and histories of the Aboriginal experience of violence might fail to find their due place in Australia's national memory.

Appendix 1

Serving Our Country Yarn Ups and Interviews

Australian Capital Territory

Canberra, 15–16 December 2015, Australian Institute of Aboriginal and Torres Strait Islander Studies

New South Wales

Dubbo, 16 June 2014, Aboriginal Employment Strategy Office

Moree, 19 June 2014, Dhiiyaan Aboriginal Centre

Newcastle, 10–14 March 2014, Yamuloong Conference Centre

Sydney, 19–21 March 2014, Redfern Community Centre

Tweed Heads, 22–25 April 2015, Minjungbal Aboriginal Cultural Centre and the Tweed Heads & Coolangatta RSL Sub Branch

Northern Territory

Alice Springs, 16–18 September 2015, Institute for Aboriginal Development

Darwin, 10–11 September 2015, Office of Senator Nova Peris and interviewees' residences; 11–16 August 2016, Larrakeyah Barracks, interviewees' residence and the Cavenagh Hotel

Katherine, 14 September 2015, North Australian Aboriginal Justice Agency

Queensland

Beenleigh, 3–4 April 2014, Yugambeh Museum Language and Heritage Research Centre

Brisbane, 31 March – 2 April 2014, Murri Ministry

Cairns, 7–9 April 2014, Pacific Hotel

Cherbourg, 4 July 2014, Ration Shed Museum

Thursday Island, 10 April 2014, Jardine Motel

Townsville, 14–16 April 2014, Relationships Australia and the Townsville Aboriginal and Torres Strait Islander Corporation

South Australia

Adelaide, 14 April 2015, Register of Aboriginal Veterans of South Australia

Port Lincoln, 11 April 2015, Port Lincoln Hotel

Raukkan, 13 April 2015, Community Council Building

Tasmania

Hobart, 22 October 2014, Tasmanian Aboriginal Centre

Launceston, 23–24 October 2014, Aboriginal Elders Council of Tasmania

Victoria

Melbourne, 2–3 March 2015, Lowitja Institute

Lake Condah, 7 March 2015, Lake Condah Mission

Western Australia

Albany, 31 August – 1 September 2015, Western Australian Museum

Broome, 7–8 September 2015, Nyamba Buru Yawuru Ltd

Derby, 7–8 September 2015, 6DBY Radio Station and Derby Cemetery

Jarlmadangah, 6 September 2015, Mt Anderson Station

Perth, 31 August – 1 September 2015, Kuditj Café and interviewee residence

Port Hedland, 3–4 September 2015, Wangka Maya Pilbara Aboriginal Language Centre

Further to the organisations listed above, who hosted and otherwise facilitated the Yarn Ups, we also wish to thank the following organisations and individuals who also assisted with contacts, interviews, and research undertaken around the country: Don Bowie in Cairns; Noeline Briggs-Smith and Jessica Duncan in Moree; Vernice Gillies and Malcolm Traill at the Western Australian Museum in Albany; Damian Bell and the Gunditj Mirring Traditional Owners Aboriginal Corporation in Heywood, Victoria; Jackie McDonald and Magali McDuffie in Tweed Heads; John Papalitsas and Christopher Edwards at NORFORCE in Darwin; Jennifer Petterson at DVA in Darwin; the Register of Aboriginal Veterans of South Australia; the Tasmanian Museum and Art Gallery; the Torres Strait Islander Heritage Museum on Thursday Island; Kate Walker in Perth; Julie Walker in Port Hedland; and the Winnunga Nimmityjah Aboriginal Medical Service in Canberra.

Oral history interviews

Where consent allows, edited recordings of the interviews listed here are publicly available on the Serving Our Country project website <ourmobserved.anu.edu.au/>. The project interviewers were: Mick Dodson, John Maynard, Allison Cadzow, Noah Riseman, Mary Anne Jebb, Samuel Furphy, Craig Greene, Siobhan McDonnell and Magali McDuffie.

Akee, George. Interviewed by Riseman, 11 November 2011, Thursday Island.

Akee, Helen. Interviewed by Dodson, 2 April 2014, Brisbane.

Allie, Harry. Interviewed by Riseman, 4 November 2011, Sydney.

Anderson, Dennis. Interviewed by Cadzow, Jebb and Greene, 24 September 2015, Canberra.

Anderson, George. Interviewed by Dodson and Greene, 1 April 2014, Brisbane.

Anderson, Shane and Bradley Whip. Interviewed by Riseman and Greene, 12 August 2016, Darwin.

Anu, Ezra. Interviewed by Riseman, 7 December 2013, Canberra.

Appo, Robert. Interviewed by Cadzow, Greene and McDuffie, 22 April 2015, Tweed Heads.

Arnold, Edna. Interviewed by Dodson and Cadzow, 4 March 2015, Apollo Bay.

Atkinson, Graham. Interviewed by Dodson and Greene, 22 April 2016, Melbourne.

_____. Interviewed by Dodson, Cadzow and Greene, 11 May 2017, Melbourne.

Bailey, Edward. Interviewed by Riseman, 11 April 2012, Canberra.

_____. Interviewed by Cadzow and Greene, 30 August 2014, Canberra.

Baron, John. Interviewed by Riseman, 7 December 2013, Sydney.

Bell, Laura and June Gill. Interviewed by Cadzow and Greene, 7 March 2015, Lake Condah.

Bell, Terry. Interviewed by Cadzow and Greene, 23 April 2015, Tweed Heads.

Bell, Tyrone. Interviewed by Dodson and Greene, 16 December 2015, Canberra.

Bingarape, Mial. Interviewed by Riseman, 7 November 2011, Cairns.

_____. Interviewed by Cadzow and Greene, 8 April 2014, Cairns.

Blair, Bob. Interviewed by Riseman, 4 November 2011, Rockhampton.

Blitner, Irma and Annie Lange. Interviewed by Cadzow and Greene, 16 August 2016, Darwin.

Booka, Edward. Interviewed by McDuffie, 25 April 2015, Tweed Heads.

Bowden, Cecil. Interviewed by Dodson, 21 March 2014, Sydney.

Bowie, Phillip. Interviewed by Dodson and Greene, 8 April 2014, Cairns.

Boyd, Leslie. Interviewed by Dodson, 9 April 2014, Cairns.

Braun, Dennis. Interviewed by Dodson, Cadzow and Greene, 16 September 2015, Alice Springs.

Briggs-Smith, Noeline. Interviewed by Cadzow and Greene, 19 June 2014, Moree.

Brown, Tony. Interviewed by Cadzow, 21 December 2015, Hobart.

Browning, Mary, Christine Morgan and Marcia Browning. Interviewed by Cadzow, Greene and McDuffie, 22 April 2015, Tweed Heads.

Cahill, Colin. Interviewed by Dodson and Greene, 11 September 2015, Darwin.

Calitz, Richard. Interviewed by Dodson, Cadzow and Greene, 22 October 2014, Hobart.

Cashman, Merle. Interviewed by Cadzow and Greene, 8 July 2014, Brisbane.

Chadburn, Reuben. Interviewed by Cadzow and Greene, 23 April 2015, Tweed Heads.

Christophersen, Don. Interviewed by Cadzow and Greene, 15 August 2016, Darwin.

Christophersen, Jane. Interviewed by Cadzow and Greene, 16 August 2016, Darwin.

Clarke, Kevin and Saunders, Hilary. Interviewed by Cadzow and Greene, 6 March 2015, Portland.

Clarke, Yvonne. Interviewed by Dodson, Cadzow and Greene, 5 March 2015, Warrnambool.

Conlan, Dawn. Interviewed by Maynard, 23 October 2014, Newcastle.

Conlan, Ruth. Interviewed by Cadzow and Greene, 23 April 2015, Tweed Heads.

Connors, Hilda. Interviewed by Maynard, 18 September 2014, Newcastle.

Cook, Dave. Interviewed by Riseman, 27 September 2012, Newcastle.

Coolburra, Edna. Interviewed by Dodson and Greene, 14 April 2014, Townsville.

Corpus, Louise. Interviewed by Dodson and Greene, 19 March 2014, Sydney.

Coyne, Lester. Interviewed by Cadzow and Jebb, 31 August 2015, Albany.

Culbong, Margaret. Interviewed by Riseman and Greene, 1 September 2015, Perth.

D'Antoine, Fenton. Interviewed by Dodson and Greene, 11 September 2015, Darwin.

Derschow, George and Jan Cowan. Interviewed by Dodson and Greene, 4 September 2015, Port Hedland.

Doolan, Gaye. Interviewed by Cadzow and Greene, 6 August 2014, Canberra.

Edgar, James. Interviewed by Dodson and Greene, 8 September 2015, Broome.

Edwards, John. Interviewed by Jebb, 31 August 2015, Albany.

Everett, Murray. Interviewed by Dodson, Cadzow and Greene, 24 October 2014, Launceston.

Farrell, Keith and Beryl Farrell and Kaye McPherson. Interviewed by Cadzow, 21 December 2015, Hobart.

Follent, Doris. Interviewed by Cadzow, Greene and McDuffie, 22 April 2015, Tweed Heads.

Frater, Joyce and Erica Eurell. Interviewed by Cadzow, Greene and McDuffie, 22 April 2015, Tweed Heads.

Garwood, Alana. Interviewed by Jebb and Cadzow, 16 December 2015, Canberra.

Gaykamangu, Warrk'Mattjun. Interviewed by Cadzow, Greene and McDonnell, 11 August 2016, Darwin.

Gibson, Patricia. Interviewed by Cadzow and Greene, 12 August 2016, Darwin.

Giles, Tamara. Interviewed by Cadzow and Greene, 5 May 2017, Sydney.

Gillies, Vernice. Interviewed by Cadzow and Jebb, 1 September 2015, Albany.

Gordon, Sue. Interviewed by Cadzow and Jebb, 1 September 2015, Perth.

Griffin, Steve. Interviewed by Maynard, 17 October 2014, Newcastle.

Gurruwiwi, Benjamin. Interviewed by McDonnell, 11 August 2016, Darwin.

Hall, Glen. Interviewed by Cadzow, 11 September 2015, Darwin.

Harradine, Lionel. Interviewed by Dodson, Cadzow and Greene, 5 March 2015, Framlingham.

Hayes, Francis. Interviewed by Dodson, Cadzow and Greene, 14 September 2015, Katherine.

Hayward, William. Interviewed by Dodson, Riseman and Greene, 1 September 2015, Perth.

Hill, Vera. Interviewed by Dodson and Greene, 31 March 2014, Brisbane.

Hinton, Valerie and Gladys Constantine. Interviewed by Cadzow and Greene, 5 May 2017, Sydney.

Hodge, Madeline. Interviewed by Cadzow, 3 April 2014, Beenleigh.

Hoffman, Tracey. Interviewed by Cadzow, 1 April 2014, Brisbane.

Holt, Leanne. Interviewed by Dodson, 14 March 2014, Newcastle.

Holt, Lyle. Interviewed by Cadzow and Greene, 15 December 2015, Canberra.

Honner, Sheree. Interviewed by Maynard, Riseman and Greene, 11 April 2015, Port Lincoln.

Humes, Glenda. Interviewed by Cadzow and Greene, 16 July 2014, Canberra.

Illin, Alec. Interviewed by Cadzow, 15 April 2014, Townsville.

Illin, Glenda. Interviewed by Cadzow and Greene, 16 April 2014, Townsville.

Janetzki (Albert), Linda. Interviewed by Cadzow and Greene, 14 April 2014, Townsville.

Jarrett, Kathryn. Interviewed by Cadzow, 4 April 2014, Beenleigh.

Jones, Stephen. Interviewed by Riseman and Greene, 18 November 2016, Canberra.

Kelly, Ray. Interviewed by Maynard, 10 March 2014, Newcastle.

Ketchell, Marsat. Interviewed by Riseman, 11 November 2011, Thursday Island.

Kinsela, John. Interviewed by Cadzow and Greene, 4 May 2017, Sydney.

Kinsela (Stewart), Yvonne. Interviewed by Cadzow and Greene, 4 May 2017, Sydney.

Knox, Les. Interviewed by Cadzow and Greene, 18 June 2014, Narrabri.

Kopusar, Pat. Interviewed by Cadzow and Jebb, 4 September 2015, Port Hedland.

Kropinyeri (Thompson), Leslie. Interviewed by Maynard, Riseman and Greene, 11 April 2015, Port Lincoln.

Kropinyeri, Robyn. Interviewed by Maynard, Riseman and Greene, 11 April 2015, Port Lincoln.

Lampard, Frank. Interviewed by Riseman, 28 November and 20 December 2013, Adelaide.

Landers, Terry (now deceased). Interviewed by Cadzow and McDuffie, 24 April 2015, Burleigh Heads.

Law, Eric. Interviewed by Cadzow and Greene, 4 July 2014, Cherbourg.

Leddie, Elgan and Simon Leddie. Interviewed by Cadzow, 31 March 2014, Brisbane.

Lees, Pattie. Interviewed by Cadzow and McDuffie, 2 December 2014, Canberra.

Leftwich, Fred. Interviewed by Dodson and Greene, 16 December 2015, Canberra.

Lester, John. Interviewed by Maynard and Greene, 12 March 2014, Newcastle.

Lockyer, Allen. Interviewed by Cadzow and Jebb, 4 September 2015, Port Hedland.

Lovegrove, Francis. Interviewed by Dodson, Maynard and Greene, 13 April 2015, Raukkan.

Lovett, John. Interviewed by Cadzow and Greene, 6 March 2015, Heywood.

Lowe, Robert and Daphne Lowe. Interviewed by Dodson, Cadzow and Greene, 5 March 2015, Warrnambool.

Mallard, Frank and Len Ogilvie. Interviewed by Riseman and Greene, 31 August 2015, Perth.

Malone, Claude. Interviewed by Cadzow and Greene, 8 July 2014, Brisbane.

Markham, Mick. Interviewed by Dodson, Cadzow and Greene, 14 September 2015, Pine Creek.

Marshall, Gordon. Interviewed by Cadzow and Jebb, 7 September 2015, Derby.

Marshall, Gordon and Glynis Marshall. Interviewed by Cadzow and Jebb, 7 September 2015, Derby.
Mayo, Desmond. Interviewed by Cadzow, 4 December 2014, Canberra.
_____. Interviewed by Dodson and Greene, 10 September 2015, Darwin.
McBride-Yuke, Linda. Interviewed by Riseman, 20 June 2010, Brisbane.
McCormack, Jeffrey. Interviewed by Riseman, 9 July 2012, Adelaide.
McDermott, Claude. Interviewed by Cadzow and Greene, 23 April 2015, Tweed Heads.
McDermott, James. Interviewed by Cadzow and Greene, 23 April 2015, Tweed Heads.
McDonald, Jackie. Interviewed by Cadzow and Greene, 23 April 2015, Tweed Heads.
McDonald, Jackie and Trish Borg. Interviewed by Cadzow, Greene and McDuffie, 22 April 2015, Tweed Heads.
McMillan, Mark. Interviewed by Riseman, Cadzow and Greene, 12 May 2017, Melbourne.
Mills, Kathleen. Interviewed by Dodson, 10 September 2015, Darwin.
Mills, Patrick. Interviewed by Cadzow and Greene, 9 April 2014, Cairns.
Minniecon, Ray. Interviewed by Dodson, Maynard and Greene, 20 March 2014, Sydney.
Morris, Ricky. Interviewed by Dodson and Furphy, 3 March 2015, Melbourne.
Muir, Muki. Interviewed by Cadzow and Greene, 12 September 2015, Darwin.
Mundine, Roy. Interviewed by Cadzow, Maynard and Greene, 21 March 2014, Sydney.

Munyarryun, Tommy. Interviewed by Cadzow, Greene and McDonnell, 11 August 2016, Darwin.

Murphy, Dorothy. Interviewed by Cadzow, 16 April 2014, Townsville.

Neal, Patricia. Interviewed by Dodson and Cadzow, 16 June 2014, Dubbo.

Nean, David (now deceased). Interviewed by Maynard, 24 October 2014, Newcastle.

Nicholson, Samantha and Alice Noonan. Interviewed by Cadzow and McDonnell, 12 August 2016, Darwin.

Oobagooma, Ashley. Interviewed by Cadzow and Jebb, 8 September 2015, Derby.

Orcher, Melita and Hazel Fisher. Interviewed by Dodson and Greene, 2 April 2014, Brisbane.

Paulson, Iris and Colleen Hurley. Interviewed by Dodson and Greene, 31 March 2014, Brisbane.

Pearce, Angela. Interviewed by Dodson, Cadzow and Maynard, 12 March 2014, Newcastle.

Peters, Dorothy. Interviewed by Dodson, Cadzow and Greene, 11 May 2017, Healesville.

Pike, Betty. Interviewed by Riseman, 12 April 2011, Melbourne.

Pitt, Edward. Interviewed by Cadzow and Greene, 19 June 2014, Moree.

Pitt, George. Interviewed by Dodson and Greene, 4 September 2015, Port Hedland.

Pittman, Mick. Interviewed by Riseman, 21 January 2010, Newcastle.

_____. Interviewed by Cadzow and Greene, 14 March 2014, Newcastle.

Pittman, Tab. Interviewed by Cadzow, 11 March 2014, Newcastle.

Pocock, Belinda and Hilda Prince. Interviewed by Jebb, 10 July 2014, Ipswich.

Powell, Ron. Interviewed by Maynard, 16 October 2014, Newcastle.

Puruntatameri, Patrick and Richard Narwirr. Interviewed by Riseman and McDonnell, 12 August 2016, Darwin.

Quakawoot, Mabel. Interviewed by Riseman, 5 June 2011, Mackay.

Ralph, Ron. Interviewed by Cadzow and Jebb, 2 September 2015, Mandurah.

Remaj, Geoff. Interviewed by Cadzow and Jebb, 1 September 2015, Albany.

Rigney, Clyde, Dorothy Shaw, Verna Koolmatrie and John Pearson. Interviewed by Dodson, Maynard and Greene, 13 April 2015, Raukkan.

Rogan, Colin. Interviewed by Dodson and Greene, 11 September 2015, Darwin.

Rose, June. Interviewed by Dodson, Maynard and Greene, 11 March 2014, Newcastle.

Sandow, Estelle. Interviewed by Dodson, Cadzow and Greene, 1 April 2014, Brisbane.

Saunders, Hilary. Interviewed by Cadzow and Greene, 6 March 2015, Portland.

Scrutton, John. Interviewed by Dodson, Cadzow and Greene, 10 September 2015, Darwin.

Scully, Boyd (now deceased). Interviewed by Cadzow and Greene, 10 September 2015, Darwin.

Shaw, Geoff. Interviewed by Cadzow and Greene, 18 September 2015, Alice Springs.

Shaw, Jacqueline. Interviewed by Riseman, 27 September 2012, Cairns.

Sibosado, Ann. Interviewed by Dodson and Greene, 4 September 2015, Port Hedland.

Simon, Victor. Interviewed by Dodson, Cadzow and Greene, 21 March 2014, Sydney.

Slockee, Victor. Interviewed by Cadzow, 24 April 2015, Tweed Heads.

Smallwood, Denis. Interviewed by Cadzow and Greene, 23 April 2015, Tweed Heads.

Stanley-Taylor, Cecilia and Dorothy Murray. Interviewed by Cadzow, 16 April 2014, Townsville.

Stasiuk, Glen. Interviewed by Dodson, Riseman and Greene, 1 September 2015, Perth.

Summers, Joyce. Interviewed by Cadzow, Greene and McDuffie, 22 April 2015, Tweed Heads.

Summers, Noel. Interviewed by Cadzow and Greene, 2 April 2014, Brisbane.

Sumner, Major. Interviewed by Dodson, Maynard and Greene, 13 April 2015, Raukkan.

Syron, Gordon. Interviewed by Dodson, Maynard and Greene, 21 March 2014, Sydney.

Tang Wei, James and JK Stracke. Interviewed by Dodson and Greene, 7 September 2015, Broome.

Templar, Gloria. Interviewed by Cadzow and Greene, 24 October 2014, Launceston.

Terare, Malcolm. Interviewed by McDuffie, 25 April 2015, Tweed Heads.

Thingle, Jonah. Interviewed by Cadzow, Greene and McDonnell, 11 August 2016, Darwin.

Tipo, Clinton. Interviewed by Dodson and Greene, 7 April 2014, Cairns.

Togo, Geoffrey. Interviewed by Cadzow, Greene and McDuffie, 22 April 2015, Tweed Heads.

Townson, Chris. Interviewed by Riseman, 26 September 2012, Townsville.

_____. Interviewed by Cadzow, 15 April 2014, Townsville.
Tripp, Marjorie (now deceased). Interviewed by Dodson, Cadzow and Greene, 14 April 2015, Adelaide.
Trynes, Matt. Interviewed by Cadzow and Kate MacFarlane, 16 December 2015, Canberra.
Urquhart, Narelle. Interviewed by Dodson and Greene, 3 April 2014, Beenleigh.
Walker, Julie. Interviewed by Dodson and Jebb, 3 September 2015, Port Hedland.
Ware, Rose. Interviewed by Cadzow and Greene, 10 April 2014, Thursday Island.
Waters, Gladys. Interviewed by Cadzow and Greene, 8 July 2014, Brisbane.
Watson, John, Gordon Marshall and Anne Milgin. Interviewed by Cadzow and Jebb, 6 September 2015, Jarlmadangah.
Weston, Thelma. Interviewed by Cadzow and Greene, 16 December 2016, Canberra.
Whitton, Paulette. Interviewed by Maynard, 19 March 2014, Sydney.
Williams, Clarence. Interviewed by Cadzow and Greene, 23 April 2015, Tweed Heads.
Williams, David. Interviewed by Riseman, 9 July 2012, Sydney.
Williams, Laurel. Interviewed by Dodson, Maynard and Greene, 11 March 2014, Newcastle.
Williamson, Jean. Interviewed by Cadzow, 11 March 2015, Melbourne.
Woods, Eliza and Aden Eades. Interviewed by Cadzow and Jebb, 1 September 2015, Albany.

Appendix 2

Commemoration of Aboriginal and Torres Strait Islander military service

For the purpose of this listing, 'commemoration' has been taken to include major examples of commemorative activities in the public domain, including marches on Anzac Day, war memorial construction, museum exhibitions, cultural productions (film, television and theatre) and ceremonies/rituals focused on the commemoration of Indigenous military service. This list does not claim to be definitive, given the plethora of local and national commemorative activities in recent years.

Year	Location	Activity
1925	Raukkan/Point McLeay, SA	Commemorative stained-glass window, funded by the local Aboriginal community, installed in the mission church.
1931	Callan Park, Rozelle, NSW	Memorial replica of Sydney Harbour Bridge created by First World War Aboriginal returned soldier Douglas Grant.
1934	Walhallow, NSW	Memorial gateway erected to commemorate the Aboriginal residents of Walhallow station who fought in the First World War.
1936	Flinders Island, Tas.	Flinders Island Soldiers' Memorial (cenotaph) unveiled by Minister for Lands.
1937	Cape Barren Island, Tas.	Cape Barren Island Soldiers' memorial (pedestal with plaque) unveiled.
1951	Cherbourg mission, Queensland	Honour Board unveiled commemorating 48 men from settlement who served in two world wars.

Year	Location	Activity
1952	Wagga Wagga	Second World War returned soldier Reg Saunders speaks at Anzac Day march.
1953	Adelaide, SA	Aboriginal Private Stephen Dodd carries the Korean War banner in Adelaide's Anzac Day march.
1969	Anzac Memorial, Sydney	Memorial service held on National Aborigines Day to honour Aboriginal servicemen and women. The ceremony is led by Nyoongar man, and Korean War veteran, Ken Colbung. Wreaths also laid at the cenotaph in Martin Place.
1985	Melbourne	National Aboriginal and Islander Ex-Services Association organise Anzac Day march in Northcote after being denied permission by RSL to march separately in main Anzac Day march. Same Association stages Aboriginal Memorial Service at Shrine of Remembrance, Melbourne during NAIDOC Week.
1988	Canberra	Memorial (large rock and plaque) installed on Mount Ainslie by non-Aboriginal Canberra resident Honor Thwaites. Aboriginal curator and activist Djon Mundine, organises memorial of 200 hollow log coffins commemorating all the Indigenous people who, since 1788, lost their lives defending their land. Later installed in the National Gallery, Canberra.
1991	Burleigh Heads, Queensland	Yugambeh Aboriginal war memorial (rock and plaque) erected by Kombumerri Aboriginal Corporation in memory of Yugambeh men and women who served from the First World War to the Gulf War.
1993	Canberra	Protests at failure to fly Indigenous flags at ceremonial burial of Unknown Soldier, Australian War Memorial.
1993	Gold Coast, Queensland	About 50 Aboriginal people under leadership of Kombumerri group lead Anzac Day march.

Year	Location	Activity
1993	Canberra	Too Dark for the Lighthorse exhibition, Australian War Memorial. Researched by David Huggonson.
1993	Brisbane	Black Diggers march.
1995	Moree, NSW	Memorial plaque dedicated to 22 Kamilaroi servicemen erected in Moree Cemetery. Local Kamilaroi historian Noeline Briggs-Smith spent over two decades researching this history.
1995	Yirrkala, Arnhem Land, NT	Memorial (large rock with plaque) erected to commemorate Yolngu men who served in northern Australia as part of the Northern Territory Special Reconnaissance Unit during the Second World War.
1995	Inala, Queensland	Plaque unveiled commemorating Aboriginal Second World War RAAF pilot Leonard Waters.
1996	Taree, NSW	After considerable resistance from the Greater Taree City Council and local RSL, the Commonwealth Bank contributes funds for a memorial plaque to honour Koori soldiers. The plaque is hung in the Commonwealth Bank for four years. When the bank moves the plaque is relocated to the Manning Mall shopping centre. Later it is moved again to the Anglican Church and then, in 2007, to a Memorial Wall and Garden erected in the Manning Gardens Public School.
1996	Boggabilla, NSW	The Leonard Waters Memorial Park named in recognition of Leonard Waters; it includes a rock with two plaques.
1996		*The Coolbaroo Club* documentary (director Roger Scholes) tells the story of the Coolbaroo Club, formed in Perth in the wake of the Second World War when returned Aboriginal servicemen were excluded from drinking at the RSL.

Year	Location	Activity
1997–	Horn Island, Torres Strait	The Torres Strait Heritage Museum profiles Torres Strait Islander involvement in the defence of the nation.
1999	Launceston, Tas.	Memorial plaque for Aboriginal veterans, organised by Australians for Reconciliation Tasmania, the Launceston RSL and Department of Veterans' Affairs, is unveiled on Remembrance Day.
1999	Canberra	Memorial service during NAIDOC Week at Mt Ainslie memorial.
1999	Cairns and Brisbane	*The Sunshine Club*, an award-winning musical (Wesley Enoch and John Rodgers), set in Brisbane, features an Aboriginal serviceman who, on his return from the Second World War, starts the Sunshine Club, a place where black and white can meet and, most importantly, dance.
1999	Point Pearce, SA	Narungga War Memorial (pedestal with plaque) installed.
2000	Canberra	Department of Veterans' Affairs building renamed Lovett Tower after an Aboriginal family, 21 members of whom have served in war and peacekeeping operations since the First World War.
2000	Perth	A granite rock and memorial plaque erected in Kings Park and Botanic Garden, in memory of Aboriginal and Torres Strait Islander Australians who gave their lives while serving with Australian armed forces.
2000	Tasmania	Re-dedication of 1937 memorial commemorating Cape Barren Island First World War soldiers. The re-dedication included a new honour roll of 23 Second World War ex-servicemen.
2001	Perth	WA Aboriginal and Torres Strait Islander Veterans and Services Association lead Perth's Anzac Day march.

Year	Location	Activity
2001	Thursday Island, Torres Strait	Memorial dedicated, with Commonwealth government assistance, to the services of the Torres Strait Light Infantry Battalion.
2001	Fremantle, WA	Plaque unveiled at Monument Hill in honour of Aboriginal men and women who served in conflict.
2002	East Victoria Park, Perth	An RSL Aboriginal memorial (black granite rock) unveiled, dedicated to the memory of Aboriginal servicemen and women of the Victoria Park district.
2003		*The Forgotten* ABC documentary, by Glen Stasiuk, about Aboriginal military service.
2003	St George, Queensland	Pilots Memorial unveiled, honouring two Aboriginal Second World War pilots, John Jackson and Leonard Waters.
2004	Canberra	Aboriginal and Torres Strait Islander Veterans and Services Association (ATSIVSA) with the support of the Australian War Memorial, begins annual Anzac Day ceremonies at the memorial on the side of Mt Ainslie.
2005	WA	John Schnaars establishes Honouring Indigenous War Graves, placing many headstones throughout Western Australia for those indigenous veterans who otherwise would not have been recognised; and also creating a wall with individual plaques for Indigenous soldiers from the two world wars.
2006	Melbourne	Koorie elder Dot Peters encourages Victorian RSL to organise ceremony at Shrine during National Reconciliation Week. Department of Veterans' Affairs starts organising similar events in other cities, except Hobart and Darwin.

Year	Location	Activity
2006	Whim Creek, Pilbara, WA	Monument (semi-circle of stones) established by Doreen Lockyer and Lockyer family to commemorate her father and four uncles who fought in the Second World War. A memorial service is now held at the site every year, conducted by the Pilbara Regiment, with the support of local government and the community to recognise servicemen from the Pilbara region.
2006	Cape Barren Island, Tas.	Gloria Templar commemorates Aboriginal servicemen from Cape Barren Island, who served in the two world wars and Vietnam, with a quilt produced as part of the 'Through Our Eyes' project consisting of seven quilts made by members of the Aboriginal Elders Council.
2006	Redfern, Sydney	A church service is organised by Aboriginal Pastor Ray Minniecon on Anzac Day, attended by about 30 people. This is a precursor to the 2007 Coloured Diggers march.
2007	Redfern, Sydney	Coloured Diggers march, on the afternoon of Anzac Day, attended by about 300 people.
2007	National	Department of Veterans' Affairs, in conjunction with local Indigenous organisations, starts to host commemorative services in most capital cities during Reconciliation Week.
2008	Redfern, Sydney	Coloured Diggers Project formed to establish an Aboriginal and Torres Strait Islander veterans' honour board and develop a sculpture.
2009–	Shrine of Remembrance, Melbourne	Exhibition on 'Indigenous Australians at war from the Boer War to the present'. Exhibition tours regional Victoria from 2011–2014 and nationally thereafter.

Year	Location	Activity
2009	Toomelah, NSW	Memorial unveiled listing the names of 21 Toomelah and district Aboriginal veterans who served in the two world wars and Vietnam.
2009	Cherbourg, Queensland	Cherbourg War Memorial (copper board) lists all the members of the community who served in the two world wars. Boards honouring those who served in the Korean and Vietnam wars added in 2012.
2010	Warrnambool, Victoria	Plaque unveiled to commemorate Aboriginal soldiers from the south-west of Victoria. Memorial prompted by Warrnambool teacher and historian Peter Bakker and Koorie elder Rob Lowe senior.
2010	Coffs Harbour, NSW	March to recognise the contribution of Aboriginal and Torres Strait Islander servicemen and women; sponsored by the North Coast chapter of the Aboriginal and Torres Strait Islander Veterans and Services Association in Coffs Harbour, with the support of the Coffs Harbour RSL Branch.
2011	North Bondi, Sydney	North Bondi War Memorial (black granite wall) dedicated by RSL sub-branch to Aboriginal officer Reginald Saunders.
2011	Darwin	Exhibition at Darwin Military Museum on NORFORCE and 'Nackeroos' of Second World War.
2012	Concord West, Sydney	On the Kokoda Track Memorial Walkway memorial plaque installed commemorating Aboriginal servicemen who fought in the Battle of Kokoda.

Year	Location	Activity
2012	Karrakatta, Perth	Memorial wall unveiled at the Karrakatta Cemetery, commemorating Aboriginal servicemen killed in conflict and buried overseas during the two world wars. The memorial is located in the Aboriginal and Torres Strait Islander Keeping Place at Karrakatta Cemetery, a purpose-designed building holding the remains of Aboriginal people previously stored in museums in the state and around the country.
2012	Narooma, NSW	Memorial unveiled at the Narooma RSL dedicated to Aboriginal and non-Aboriginal servicemen and women. Tony Albert appointed the Australian War Memorial's first Indigenous official war artist, and the first to be deployed with NORFORCE.
2013	Adelaide	Aboriginal and Torres Strait Islander War Memorial unveiled at Torrens Parade Ground. A joint inititiative of local Indigenous communities, state government and the wider Adelaide community.
2014	National	*Black Diggers* play explores Indigenous military service in the First World War.
2014	National	NAIDOC week adopts theme of Serving Country: Centenary & Beyond.
2014	NSW	Wartime Legends, a Centenary of Anzac initiative, profiles Aboriginal and Torres Strait Islanders' military service during the First World War, and includes an online 'How to' guide for schools, local RSLs, businesses, government agencies and local councils to incorporate commemorations of Aboriginal and Torres Strait Islanders' military service in their activities from 2014 to 2018.

Year	Location	Activity
2015	Hobart	Exhibition at Tasmanian Museum and Art Gallery, 'The Islanders: For Freedom and Honour', details the history of Tasmanian Aboriginal servicemen in the First World War.
2015	Cherbourg, Queensland	Honour Board, incorporating the names of the 47 men from the Barambah Mission who served in the First World War, unveiled on Anzac Day. The adjacent park which was named ANZAC Park, is renamed 'The Boys from Barambah ANZAC Park'. 'The Boys from Barambah' exhibition opened at the Ration Shed.
2015	Meningie, SA	Meningie Memorial Park, featuring a 15-metre mural of local Aboriginal First World War soldiers, opens.
2015	Sydney	Major artwork (four standing bullets and three fallen shells), Yininmadyemi, by Aboriginal artist Tony Albert, installed in Hyde Park at initiative of Sydney City Council.
2015	Canberra	Australian War Memorial names gallery after Reg Saunders.
2016	Canberra	Australian War Memorial opens exhibition 'For Country, For Nation', exploring Aboriginal and Torres Strait Islander experiences during wartime and peace. Honouring Warrior Spirits ceremony, including the scattering of soil gathered at Gallipoli, sponsored by the Australian Army, in Australian War Memorial precinct.
2016	National	National Reconciliation Week promotion of Aboriginal and Torres Strait Islander Australians who served in Australia's armed forces in every military conflict since the Boer War (1899–1902) while being denied civil rights.

Year	Location	Activity
2016	Bathurst Island, NT	Bronze statue of Matthias Ulungurra, who captured the first Japanese prisoner on Australian soil, unveiled.
2016	Western Australia	Publication of *They Served with Honour: Untold Stories of Western Australian Aboriginal Servicemen at Gallipoli*, by WA Department of Aboriginal Affairs.
2017		Exhibition at National Archives of Australia, 'Facing Two Fronts: The fight for respect'.

Contributors

Mick Dodson AM, a member of the Yawuru peoples, is Director of the National Centre for Indigenous Studies at the Australian National University. Mick Dodson has been a prominent advocate on land rights and other issues affecting Aboriginal and Torres Strait Islander peoples, as well as a vigorous advocate of the rights and interests of Indigenous peoples around the world. Among his many prominent public offices, he has served as Commissioner on the Human Rights Commission (1993–98); was Counsel assisting the Royal Commission into Aboriginal Deaths in Custody (1988–90); a member of the Victorian Equal Opportunity Advisory Council; secretary of the North Australian Legal Aid Service; and chair of council of the Australian Institute of Aboriginal and Torres Strait Islander Studies (AIATSIS). Mick participated in crafting the text of the Declaration on the Rights of Indigenous Peoples in the United Nations Working Group on Indigenous Populations (WGIP), and the Inter-sessional Working Group of the Human Rights Commission which was adopted overwhelmingly in 2007 by the United Nations General Assembly. In 2009, Mick Dodson was named Australian of the Year by the National Australia Day Council.

Samuel Furphy is a Research Fellow in the National Centre of Biography, School of History, at the Australian National University. He has a particular interest in biography as a historical methodology, and his research has spanned Australian colonial history, Aboriginal history, British imperial history and the history of humanitarianism. He is a research editor for the *Australian Dictionary of Biography* and from 2014 to 2017 he was the recipient of an Australian Research Council early career fellowship on Aboriginal protectors in early colonial Australasia.

Geoffrey Gray is an adjunct professor of history at the University of Queensland. He is author of *A Cautious Silence: The Politics of Australian Anthropology* (2007); *Abrogating Responsibility: Vesteys Anthropology, and the Future of Aboriginal People* (2015); and co-editor (with Doug Munro and Christine Winter) of a special issue of the *Journal of Historical Biography* on the theme 'Telling Academic Lives' (vol. 16, 2014). He has written extensively on Aboriginal history and the history of anthropology. He is currently completing a book on senior academic appointments in Australia and New Zealand.

Siobhan McDonnell is a Research Fellow at the National Centre of Indigenous Studies and a Lecturer in Pacific Studies, at the Australian National University. She is a legal anthropologist who has spent 20 years working in Indigenous Australia and in the Pacific. Siobhan's scholarly interests include: constitutional law and rights for Indigenous Australians; how 'deficit discourse' frames engagement with Indigenous Australians; climate change and gender in the Pacific; land reform and Indigenous land rights; disaster management in the Pacific; and the manner in which concepts of 'paradise' frame foreign engagement in the Pacific. Siobhan's recent publications include (with Mick Dodson), 'Indigenous People as linked to Place, the Race power in the *Tasmanian Dam Case*', in Michael Coper, Heather Roberts and James Stellios (eds), *The Tasmanian Dam Case 30 Years On: An Enduring Legacy* (2017); and a co-edited book on land issues in Melanesia, *Kastom, Property and Ideology: Land Transformations in Melanesia* (2017).

John Maynard is a Worimi man from NSW. He is currently Director of the Purai Global Indigenous and Diaspora Research Centre and Chair of Aboriginal Studies at the University of Newcastle. His publications, which concentrate on the intersection of Aboriginal political and social relations, and the history of Australian race relations, include *Fight for Liberty and Freedom* (2007); *The Aboriginal Soccer Tribe* (2011); *Aborigines and the 'Sport of Kings'* (2013); *True Light and Shade: An Aboriginal Perspective of Joseph Lycett's Art* (2014); and (with Victoria Haskins) *Living with the Locals* (2016). He has held several major positions, including as Deputy Chairperson of AIATSIS.

Tristan Moss completed his PhD at the Strategic and Defence Studies Centre at the Australian National University in 2015, for which he won the CEW Bean Prize for Military History. His first book, *Guarding the Periphery: The Australian Army in Papua New Guinea, 1951–75*, was published by Cambridge University Press in 2017. In 2013–14 Dr Moss co-authored (with Joan Beaumont) the text for the Department of Veterans' Affairs commemorative website, 'The Thai-Burma Railway and Hellfire Pass'. He is currently a researcher on the Official Histories of Australian Operations in Iraq, Afghanistan and East Timor.

Shannyn Palmer graduated with a PhD in History from the Australian National University in 2017. Her research focuses upon place – both physical environments and the ways in which they are created and made meaningful by people – as fertile ground for thinking and writing histories of colonialism and cultural encounter. She lived in Alice Springs in the Northern Territory for four years and undertook fieldwork with Anangu, recording oral histories in Pitjantjatjara language, inspired by life on Angas Downs cattle station. Her thesis examines the ways in which this desert pastoral station was made – and unmade – by Anangu and others in their encounters with one another over half a century.

Noah Riseman is an Associate Professor of History at Australian Catholic University in Melbourne. He specialises in the history of marginalised social groups in the military, particularly Indigenous and LGBTI Australians. He has also done comparative work on Indigenous military service in the United States, Canada and New Zealand. He is the author of the similarly titled books *Defending Country: Aboriginal and Torres Strait Islander Military Service since 1945* (with Richard Trembath, 2016), *In Defence of Country: Life Stories of Aboriginal and Torres Strait Islander Servicemen & Women* (2016) and *Defending Whose Country? Indigenous Soldiers in the Pacific War* (2012).

Notes

Chapter 1: Serving Our Country

1 The current route was adopted in 2011.

2 Morris Janowitz, 'Military Institutions and Citizenship in Western Societies', *Armed Forces and Society*, vol. 2, no. 2, 1976, pp. 185–204.

3 Noah Riseman, 'Introduction: Diversifying the black diggers' histories', *Aboriginal History*, vol. 39, 2015, p. 137.

4 This term gained wide currency with the publication of John Keegan's *The Face of Battle*, Jonathan Cape, London, 1976.

5 Morag Loh and Judith Winternitz, *Dinky-Di: The contributions of Chinese immigrants and Australians of Chinese descent to Australia's defence forces and war effort, 1899–1988*, Australian Government Publishing Service, Canberra, 1989; Craig Wilcox, 'Irish Volunteer and Militia Corps in Australia' and John Connor 'Irish Soldiers in the First AIF', in *Irish-Australian Studies: Papers delivered at the seventh Irish–Australian Conference July 1993*, Rebecca Pelan (ed.), Crossing Press, Sydney, 1994, pp. 311–18, 319–24; Elena Govor, *Russian Anzacs in Australian History*, UNSW Press in association with the National Archives of Australia, Sydney, 2005; Mark Dapin, *Jewish Anzacs*, NewSouth Publishing, Sydney, 2017.

6 Anthony Bergin, *The ethnic composition of the Australian Defence Force, management, attitudes and strategies*, Working Paper no. 11, Australian Defence Force Academy, Canberra, 1993; Hugh Smith, 'Minorities and the Australian Army: Overlooked and Underrepresented?' in *A Century of Service: 100 Years of the Australian Army*, Peter Dennis, and Jeffery Grey (eds), Army History Unit, Department of Defence, Canberra, 2001, pp. 129–49.

7 Joan Beaumont, 'Remembering the heroes of Australia's wars; from heroic to post-heroic memory' in *Heroism and the Changing Character of War: Towards post-heroic warfare,* Sibylle Scheipers (ed.), Palgrave Macmillan, Basingstoke, Hants, pp. 340–2; Liz Reed, *Bigger Than Gallipoli: War, history and memory in Australia*, University of Western Australia Press, Perth, 2004, especially pp. 59–62, 71–82, 143–51.

8 For overviews of Aboriginal and Indigenous history, see: Ann McGrath, 'Contested Ground: What Is Aboriginal History?' in *Contested Ground: Australian Aborigines under the British Crown*, Ann McGrath (ed.), Allen & Unwin, Sydney, 1995, pp. 359–97; Bain Attwood, 'The founding of Aboriginal History and the forming of Aboriginal history', in *Aboriginal History*, vol. 36, 2012, pp. 119–71; Miranda Johnson, 'Writing Indigenous Histories Now', *Australian Historical Studies,* vol. 45, no. 3, 2014, pp. 317–30.

9 John Maynard, 'Circles in the Sand: An Indigenous Framework of Historical Practice', *Australian Journal of Indigenous Education*, vol. 36, Supplement, 2007,

p. 117. See also his *Fight for Freedom and Liberty: The Origins of Australian Aboriginal Activism*, Aboriginal Studies Press, Canberra, 2007.

10 These aspects feature also in histories which have been written collaboratively with non-Aboriginal historians and which draw closely on Aboriginal people's accounts. See for example: Heather Goodall, *Invasion to Embassy: Land in Aboriginal Politics in New South Wales 1770–1972*, Allen & Unwin, Sydney, 1996; Richard Broome, *Aboriginal Australians*, 4th edition, Allen & Unwin, Sydney, 2010; Ken Hampton and Christobel Mattingley, *Survival in Our Own Land: 'Aboriginal' Experiences in 'South Australia' since 1836*, Wakefield Press, Adelaide, 1988; Alick Jackomos and Derek Fowell (eds), *Living Aboriginal History of Victoria: Stories in the oral tradition*, Cambridge University Press, Melbourne, 1991; Jay and Peter Read (eds), *Long Time Olden Time, Aboriginal Accounts of Northern Territory History*, IAD Press, Alice Springs, 1991.

11 Maria Nugent, 'Aboriginal family history: Some reflections', *Australian Cultural History*, vol. 22, pp. 143–54; see also Fabri Blacklock, 'Telling it Our Way: Koori History in NSW', *Australian Cultural History*, vol. 23, 2003, pp. 112–14.

12 Bill Neidjie, *Story About Feeling*, Magabala Books, Broome, 1989; Ann McGrath and Mary Anne Jebb (eds), *Long History, Deep Time: Deepening histories of place*, ANU Press, Canberra, 2015.

13 To name only some of the important early works: Henry Reynolds, *The Other Side of the Frontier: Aboriginal resistance to the European invasion of Australia*, Penguin, Melbourne, 1982; Richard Broome, 'The Struggle for Australia: Aboriginal-European Warfare, 1770–1930' in Michael McKernan and M Browne (eds), *Australia: Two centuries of war and peace*, AWM in association with Allen & Unwin, Canberra, 1988, pp. 92–120; Bruce Elder, *Blood on the Wattle: Massacres and maltreatment of Aboriginal Australians since 1788*, Child & Associates, Sydney, 1988; *The Encyclopaedia of Aboriginal Australia*, Aboriginal Studies Press in association with AIATSIS, Canberra, 1994; McGrath 1995; Jeffrey Grey, *A Military History of Australia*, rev. edn, Cambridge University Press, Melbourne, 1999; and John Connor, *The Australian Frontier Wars, 1788–1838*, UNSW Press, Sydney, 2002.

14 For the Native Mounted Police, see Tim Rowse, 'The moral world of the Native Mounted Police', *Law and History*, forthcoming 2018.

15 Noah Riseman, 'The Rise of Indigenous Military History', *History Compass*, vol. 12, no. 12, 2014, pp. 902.

16 Alan Powell, *Australia's Northern War*, Melbourne University Press, Melbourne, 1988; Kay Saunders, 'Aboriginal and Torres Strait Islander labour in northern Australia during the Second World War', *Labour History*, vol. 69, 1995, pp. 131–48; Russell McGregor, *Indifferent Inclusion: Aboriginal people and the Australian nation*, Aboriginal Studies Press, Canberra, 2011.

17 David Huggonson's many publications include: 'The dark diggers of the AIF', *Australian Quarterly*, vol. 61, no. 3, 1989, pp. 352–7; 'Villers-Bretonneux: A strange name for an Aboriginal burial ground', *Journal of the Royal Historical Society of Queensland*, 1991, pp. 285–8; 'Aboriginal POW's of World War One', *Newsletter Historical Society of South Australia*, no. 105, 1993, pp. 9–10, no. 106, 1993, pp. 8–11; 'Aborigines and the aftermath of the Great War', *Australian Aboriginal*

Studies, vol. 1, 1993, pp. 2–9. For Chris Coulthard-Clark, see 'Aborigines in the first AIF', *Army History Journal*, vol. 286, 1973, pp. 21–6; 'Aboriginal medal winners', *Sabretache*, vol. 18, 1977 pp. 244–8; and 'On the track of the trackers', *Sabretache*, vol. 21, 1980.

18 Robert Hall, *The Black Diggers: Aborigines and Torres Strait Islanders in the Second World War*, Allen & Unwin, Sydney, 1989; *Fighters from the Fringe: Aborigines and Torres Strait Islanders recall the Second World War*, Aboriginal Studies Press, Canberra, 1995. The first work built on Hall's earlier *Aborigines and Torres Strait Islanders in the Second World War*, Strategic and Defence Studies Centre, Australian National University, Canberra, 1987.

19 Alick Jackomos and Derek Fowell, *Forgotten Heroes: Aborigines at war from the Somme to Vietnam*, Victoria Press, Melbourne, 1993.

20 Desmond Ball (ed.), *Aborigines in the Defence of Australia*, ANU Press, Canberra, 1991.

21 Rod Pratt, 'Queensland Aborigines in the First AIF', *Sabretache*, vol. 31, Jan./March 1990, pp. 18–22; April/June 1990, pp. 16–19; July/Sept. 1990, pp. 26–9; Oct./Dec. 1990, pp. 36–8; Heather Goodall, 'Not such a respected soldier: The impact of WWI on Aborigines in NSW', *Teaching History*, 1987, vol. 21, no. 4, pp. 3–6.

22 For example, Bill Cohen's *To My Delight: The autobiography of Bill Cohen, a grandson of the Gumbangarri*, Aboriginal Studies Press, Canberra, 1987; Tom Gray, *Icon of the North: The legend of Tom Gray*, Access Press, Perth, 1995; Tom Lowah, *Eded Mer: My life*, Rams Skull Press, Kuranda, 1991; Joe McGinness, *Son of Alyandabu: My fight for Aboriginal rights*, Queensland University Press, Brisbane, 1991.

23 Rory O'Connor, *Yugambeh: In defence of our country*, Kombumerri Aboriginal Corporation for Culture, Runaway Bay, 1991; George Bray, Kenny Laughton and Pat Foster, *Aboriginal Ex-servicemen of Central Australia*, IAD Press, Alice Springs, 1995; Doreen Kartinyeri, *Ngarrindjeri Anzacs*, South Australian Museum and Raukkan Council, Adelaide, 1996.

24 Ken Inglis, *Sacred Places: War memorials in the Australian landscape*, Melbourne, Miegunyah Press, 1998, 2nd edn, 2008, p. 421.

25 Ann Curthoys, 'National narratives, war commemoration and racial exclusion in a settler society: the Australian case' in *The Politics of War Memory and Commemoration*, TG Ashplant, G Dawson and M Roper (eds), London, Routledge, 2000, pp. 128–44.

26 Philippa Scarlett, *The Lock Family in World War One: How service records contribute to Darug history*, Indigenous Histories, Canberra, 2008; Scarlett, *Aboriginal and Torres Strait Islander Volunteers for the AIF: The Indigenous Response to World War One*, Indigenous Histories, Canberra, 2015; Scarlett (with Mark Newman and Sally Lawrence), *The Boys from Barambah: The Story of the Black Diggers of Barambah-Cherbourg of World War I*, Ration Shed Museum, Murgon, 2015; Jan James, *Forever Warriors*, J James, Perth, 2010; Government of Western Australia, 'They Served with Honour, <https://www.daa.wa.gov.au/community-development/they-served-with-honour/>; Victorian State Government, 'Aboriginal Victorians Involvement in World War I', <anzaccentenary.vic.gov.au/history/aboriginal-australians-involvement-world-war/>.

27 Noah Riseman, Kristyn Harman and Allison Cadzow (eds), special section on Aboriginal War Service in *Aboriginal History*, vol. 39, 2015.

28 Noah Riseman, 'Exploited Soldiers: Navaho and Yolngu Units in the Second World War', *Journal of Northern Territory History*, vol. 19, 2008, pp. 60–81; Riseman,'"Japan Fight, Aboriginal people fight; European people fight": Yolngu Stories from World War II', *Australian Journal of Indigenous Education*, vol. 37, 2008, pp. 65–72; Riseman, *In Defence of Country: Life stories of Aboriginal and Torres Strait Islander servicemen and women*, ANU Press, Canberra, 2016; Riseman and Richard Trembath, *Defending Country: Aboriginal and Torres Strait Islander military service since 1945*, University of Queensland Press, Brisbane, 2016.

29 Noah Riseman, *Defending Whose Country? Indigenous Soldiers in the Pacific War*, University of Nebraska Press, Lincoln, ME, 2012; Riseman,'The Vietnam War and Indigenous Service in Australia and the United States' in *New Perceptions of the Vietnam War: Essays on the war, the South Vietnamese experience, the diaspora and the continuing impact*, Nathalie Nguyen (ed.), McFarland & Company, Jefferson, NC, 2015, pp. 203–28; Timothy C Winegard, *Indigenous Peoples of the British Dominions and the First World War*, Cambridge University Press, New York, 2012. See also the special issue of *Wicazo Sa Review*, Noah Riseman (ed.), vol. 32, no. 1, 2017.

30 Riseman 2014, p. 901.

31 For research drawing on the Blackman brothers' service and letters see Tim Winegard, 'A Case Study of Indigenous Brothers in Arms during the First World War', *Australian Army Journal*, vol. 6, no. 1, 2009, pp. 191–206.

32 Jean Bou and Peter Dennis, *The Australian Imperial Force*, vol. 5 in *The Centenary History of Australia and the Great War*, Oxford University Press, Melbourne, 2016, p. 95.

33 Lynn Abrams, *Oral History Theory*, Milton Park, Routledge, 2010, p. 103.

34 Alessandro Portelli, *The Death of Luigi Trastulli and Other Stories: Form and meaning in oral history*, State University of New York Press, Albany, 1991, p. 51.

35 Alistair Thomson, *Anzac Memories: Living with the legend*, Oxford University Press, 1994, new edition, Monash University Publishing, Melbourne, 2013; also his 'Anzac Memories Revisited: Trauma, memory and oral history' in *The Oral History Review*, vol. 42, issue 1, 2015, pp. 1–29.

36 Serving Our Country website <ourmobserved.anu.edu.au>.

37 Lorina Barker, '"Hangin' out" and "Yarnin": Reflecting on the Experience of Collecting Oral Histories', *History Australia*, vol. 5, no. 1, 2008, pp. 9.1–9.9.

38 A companion volume of oral history and photographic images provisionally titled *Our Mob Served* is also planned.

39 For Marianne Hirsch on post-memory see <www.postmemory.net/>.

40 Many of the Serving our Country interviews can be found at <ourmobserved.anu.edu.au/>. The full database is, as of 2017, held on the Data Commons of the Australian National University with a view to transferring it to AIATSIS in the future.

41 The exclusion from (white) hotels and city streets in the evenings, as well as police harassment, are vividly recalled in *The Coolbaroo Club* (Steven Kinnane, Lauren Marsh, and Roger Scholes, 1996).

42 Glen Stasiuk, 'Warriors then, warriors still: Aboriginal soldiers in the 20th century', *Journal of Indigenous Issues*, vol. 7, no. 3, 2004, pp. 3–11.
43 Fiona Nicoll, 'War by Other Means: The Australian War Memorial and the Aboriginal Tent Embassy in national space and time' in *The Aboriginal Tent Embassy: Sovereignty, Black Power, Land Rights and the State*, Gary Foley, Andrew Schaap and Edwina Howell (eds), Routledge, London, 2014, pp. 279–80.

Chapter 2: Race, citizenship and military service

1 Tom Wright, *Black Diggers*, Playlab Production, South Brisbane, 2015, pp. 22–3.
2 For a succinct summary of the protectorate see Richard Broome, *Aboriginal Australians*, 4th edition, Allen & Unwin, Sydney, 2010, pp. 51–3. For the impact of anti-slavery movements in Australia and other colonies see Catherine Hall, *Civilising Subjects: Metropole and colony in the English imagination 1830–1867*, University of Chicago Press, Chicago, 2002.
3 Great Britain, Parliament, House of Commons, Report of the Parliamentary Select Committee on Aboriginal Tribes (British Settlements), William Ball, London, 1837, p. 10.
4 Penelope Edmonds, *Urbanizing Frontiers: Indigenous people and settlers in 19th-century Pacific Rim cities*, University of British Colombia Press, Vancouver, 2010.
5 Heather Goodall, *Invasion to Embassy: Land in Aboriginal politics in NSW, 1770–1972*, Allen & Unwin, Sydney, 1996.
6 This legislation was termed an Act to provide for the Protection and Management of the Aboriginal Natives of Victoria (1869).
7 Andrew Gunstone, 'Indigenous people and Stolen Wages in Victoria, 1869–1957', in *Indigenous Participation in Australian Economies II: Historical engagements and current enterprises*, Natasha Fijn, Ian Keen, Christopher Lloyd and Michael Pickering (eds), ANU E Press, Canberra, p. 184.
8 Anna Haebich, *Broken Circles: Fragmenting Indigenous families 1800–2000*, Fremantle Arts Centre Press, Perth, 2000, p. 166.
9 Report of the Parliamentary Select Committee 1837, p. 118.
10 See *Aboriginal Protection and Prevention of the Sale of Opium Act 1897* (Qld), regulations of September 1899.
11 John Chesterman and Brian Galligan, *Citizens without Rights: Aborigines and Australian citizenship*, Cambridge University Press, Melbourne, 1997, p. 40.
12 Noel Loos, 'A Chapter of Contact: Aboriginal-European Relations in North Queensland 1606–1992', in Henry Reynolds (ed.), *Race Relations in North Queensland*, James Cook University, Cairns, 1993, p. 50. See also Rosalind Kidd, *The Way We Civilise: Aboriginal affairs – the untold story*, University of Queensland Press, Brisbane, 1997.
13 Chesterman and Galligan 1997.
14 Russell McGregor, *Indifferent Inclusion: Aboriginal people and the Australian nation*, Aboriginal Studies Press, Canberra, 2011, p. xix.
15 McGregor 2011, p. xx.
16 McGregor 2011, p. xx.
17 Article 51(xxvi) of the Constitution stated that the parliament should have the power to make laws for the peace, order and good government of the

Commonwealth with respect to 'The people of any race, other than the aboriginal race in any State, for whom it is deemed necessary to make special laws' <www.foundingdocs.gov.au/amendment-amid-17.html>.

18 *Parliamentary Electorates and Elections Act 1912* (NSW); Chesterman and Galligan 1997, p. 135.

19 *Northern Territory Representation Act 1922* (Cth) section 7; Northern Territory Electoral Regulations, Commonwealth Statutory Rules 1922, No. 154 (22).

20 See discussion of the Victorian electoral records in Chesterman and Galligan 1997, p. 14; Bain Attwood and Andrew Markus, *The 1967 Referendum: Race, power and the Australian constitution*, Aboriginal Studies Press, Canberra, 2007, p. 4.

21 Chesterman and Galligan 1997, p. 92.

22 Brian Galligan, 'The Fabrication of Aboriginal Voting', *Inside Story*, 22 December 2016, <insidestory.org.au/the-fabrication-of-aboriginal-voting/>.

23 Galligan 2016.

24 Chesterman and Galligan, 1997, pp. 91–2.

25 McGregor 2011, p. xxiv.

26 McGregor 2011, p. xxiv.

27 Richard Broome, *Aboriginal Australians: A history since 1788*, 4th edition, Allen & Unwin, 2010, pp. 195–6.

28 Jessica Horton, '"Willing to fight to a man": The First World War and Aboriginal activism in the Western District of Victoria', *Aboriginal History*, vol. 39, 2015, pp. 203–22.

29 See discussion in *Bringing Them Home: National inquiry into the separation of Aboriginal and Torres Strait Islander children from their families*, Commonwealth of Australia, Sydney, 1997, pp. 131–5 <www.humanrights.gov.au/sites/default/files/content/pdf/social_justice/bringing_them_home_report.pdf>.

30 Aborigines Act 1890 Alteration of Regulations 1899 (Vic).

31 *Aborigines Act Amendment Act 1911* (WA).

32 *Aborigines Protection Act 1911* (NSW), section 11. See also Peter Read, *The Stolen Generations: The removal of Aboriginal children in New South Wales 1883 to 1969*, Government Printer, Sydney, 1981.

33 See Victoria Haskins, '& So We are "Slave Owners!": Employers and the NSW Aborigines Protection Board Trust Funds', *Labour History*, vol. 88, 2005, pp. 147–64, 149; Heather Goodall, '"Assimilation begins in the home": The State and Aboriginal women's work as mothers in New South Wales, 1900s to 1960s', *Labour History*, vol. 69, 1995, pp. 75–101; and Inara Walden, '"That Was Slavery Days": Aboriginal Domestic Servants in New South Wales in the Twentieth Century', *Labour History*, vol. 69, 1995, pp. 196–209.

34 See discussion of parliamentary debates in Haskins 2005, p. 152. See also *Bringing Them Home* report 1997, pp. 41–2.

35 Section 13(A) *Aborigines Protection (Amendment) Act, New South Wales 1915.*

36 Haskins 2005. See also Goodall 1995; Walden 1995.

37 Victoria Haskins, '"A better chance"? – sexual abuse and the apprenticeship of Aboriginal girls under the NSW Aborigines Protection Board', *Aboriginal History*, vol. 28, 2004, p. 43.

38 *Defence Act 1903–1909* (Cth), section 138(1)(b).

39 *Defence Act 1903–1910* (Cth), section 61(h).
40 Timothy Winegard, *Indigenous Peoples of the British Dominions and the Dominions and the First World War*, Cambridge University Press, New York, p. 87.
41 *Naval Defence Act 1910* (Cth), section 5.
42 *Air Force Act 1923* (Cth), section 3 (3).
43 Philippa Scarlett, *Aboriginal and Torres Strait Islander Volunteers for the AIF: The Indigenous response to World War One*, Indigenous Histories, Canberra, 2015, p. 15.
44 AIF Military Regulations Circular 113, 1917; Military Order 200 (2) May 1917.
45 Quoted in Scarlett 2015, p. 15.
46 Many attestations included the statement that 'I have associated with white people all my life.' See Scarlett, 'Aboriginal service in the First World War: Identity, recognition and the problem of mateship', *Aboriginal History*, vol. 39, 2015, p. 168.
47 See, for example, the differing perspectives of Tim Rowse, *White Flour, White Power: From rations to citizenship in central Australia*, Cambridge University Press, Melbourne, 1998; McGregor 2011; Anna Haebich, *Spinning the Dream: Assimilation in Australia 1950–1970*, Fremantle Press, Perth, 2008.
48 Commonwealth of Australia, Aboriginal Welfare: Initial conference of Commonwealth and State Aboriginal authorities, Canberra, 21–23 April 1937 <aiatsis.gov.au/sites/default/files/catalogue_resources_/20663.pdf>.
49 *Aboriginals Preservation and Protection Act 1939* (Qld).
50 Noah Riseman and Richard Trembath, *Defending Country: Aboriginal and Torres Strait Islander military service since 1945*, University of Queensland Press, Brisbane, 2016, p. 59.
51 Chesterman and Galligan 1997, p. 128.
52 John Lovett, interview, 6 March 2015.
53 Robert Hall, *The Black Diggers: Aborigines and Torres Strait Islanders in the Second World War*, Allen & Unwin, Sydney, 1989, p. 9.
54 David Huggonson, 'The dark diggers of the AIF', *The Australian Quarterly*, vol. 61, no. 3, pp. 352–7.
55 *Commonwealth Electoral (War-time) Act 1940*, section 6.
56 *Election Acts Amendments Act 1930* (Qld), section 8.
57 Chesterman and Galligan 2007, p. 172.
58 Rowse 1998, p. 114.
59 Broome 2010, pp. 208–9.
60 *Social Services Act (Cth) 1959*, section 24.
61 *Welfare Ordinance Act 1953* (NT), sections 4, 8, 14 and 15.
62 Chesterman and Galligan 1997, pp. 158, 160.
63 Attwood and Markus 2007, p. 121.
64 McGregor 2011, pp. 147–51. This issue was also mentioned frequently in Yarn Ups recorded for the Serving Our Country project.
65 Chesterman and Galligan 1997, p. 190.
66 Chesterman and Galligan 1997, p. 196.
67 *Aboriginal Land Rights Act 1976* (NT).
68 Rosalind Kidd, *Hard Labour, Stolen wages: National report on Stolen Wages*, Australians for Native Title and Reconciliation, Rozelle, NSW, 2007.

Chapter 3: The South African 'Boer War'

1 The *Brisbane Courier*, 11 February 1902, p. 5.
2 *Courier* 1902, p. 5.
3 Australian War Memorial, 'Australia and the Boer War, 1899–1902' <www.awm.gov.au/atwar/boer/>.
4 Dennis Judd and Keith Surridge, *The Boer War: A history*, IB Tauris, London, 2003, p. 79.
5 George Witton, *Scapegoats of the Empire: The true story of Breaker Morant's Bushveldt Carbineers*, Angus & Robertson, Sydney, 1982, p. 5.
6 See CN Connolly, 'Manufacturing spontaneity: The Australian offers of troops for the Boer War', *Historical Studies*, vol. 18, no. 70, 1978, pp. 106–17.
7 Thomas Pakenham, *The Boer War*, Abacus Books, London, 1991, p. 249. See also Kit Denton, *For Queen and Commonwealth*, Australians at War series, vol. 5, Time-Life Books, Sydney, 1987; Jeffrey Grey, *A Military History of Australia*, Cambridge University Press, Melbourne, 1990, pp. 57–60; Craig Wilcox, *Australia's Boer War: The war in South Africa, 1899–1902*, Oxford University Press, Melbourne, 2002.
8 Henry Reynolds, 'Colonial Cassandras: Why weren't the warnings heeded?' in Henry Reynolds and Marilyn Lake, *What's Wrong with ANZAC? The militarisation of Australian history*, NewSouth Books, Sydney, 2010, p. 56.
9 Douglas Newton, *Hell-Bent: Australia's leap into the Great War*, Scribe Publications, Melbourne, 2014, p. 23.
10 Henry Reynolds, *Unnecessary Wars*, NewSouth Books, Sydney, 2016, p. 155.
11 Heather Goodall, 'Winning overseas, losing at home', *Land Rights News*, vol. 4, no. 2, 1988, pp. 32–3; Heather Goodall, *Invasion to Embassy: Land in Aboriginal politics in New South Wales, 1770–1972*, Allen & Unwin, Sydney, 1996, p. 155.
12 Susan Johnston, 'The New South Wales Government Policy Towards Aborigines 1880–1904', MA thesis, University of Sydney, 1970, p. 76.
13 *The Australian Aborigines Advocate*, 31 October 1919, p. 2.
14 New South Wales Register of Aboriginal Reserves, 1875–1904, 2/29349, NSW State Archives; EJ Telfer, *Amongst Australian Aborigines – Forty Years of Missionary Work*, Fraser & Morphet Pty Ltd, Melbourne, 1939, p. 54.
15 *Coffs Harbour Advocate*, 26 May 1926, p. 2.
16 Goodall 1988, p. 32.
17 AIATSIS, 'Rare photo of Indigenous involvement in the Boer War' <aiatsis.gov.au/explore/articles/rare-photo-indigenous-involvement-boer-war>.
18 Australian War Memorial estimate conversation with Michael Bell; see also Peter Bakker, 'Australia's Dark Troopers in the Boer War', Conference Presentation, Brothers and Sisters in Arms Conference, Australian Catholic University, Melbourne, 25 June 2015.
19 Michael Bell, 'The Story of William Charles Westbury Aboriginal Soldier, The Boer War and First World War' Australian War Memorial website <www.awm.gov.au/articles/blog/william-charles-westbury>.
20 John Maynard, 'Fighting for Country' in *(In)Visible: The First Peoples and war*, Education Resource Kit, Lake Macquarie City Art Gallery, Lake Macquarie, 2015, p. 8.
21 *The Advertiser* (Adelaide), 28 August 1914, p. 9.

22 *The Leader*, 26 June 1915, p. 20.

23 John Ramsland, *Major-General Sir Neville Reginald Howse VC: Manning River pioneering doctor and war hero*, Manning Valley Historical Society, Taree, 2014, p. 6.

24 Ramsland 2014, pp. 6–7.

25 Alfred Polson, Boer War Dossiers, 1901–1902, B4418, item barcode 686089, NAA.

26 David Huggonson, 'Aborigines and the aftermath of the Great War', *Australian Aboriginal Studies*, no. 1, 1993, p. 8.

27 Patricia O'Brien, 'The gaze of the ghosts: European images of Aboriginal women in New South Wales and Port Phillip 1800–1860' in J Kociumbas (ed.), *Maps, Dreams, History: Race and representation in Australia*, Braxus Publishing, Sydney, 1998, p. 321.

28 Victoria Haskins, 'Could you see to the return of my daughter – Fathers and daughters under the New South Wales Aborigines Protection Board child removal policy', *Australian Historical Studies*, vol. 34, no. 121, 2003, p. 109.

29 Beverley Gulambali Elphick, and Don Elphick, *The Camp of Mercy: An historical and biographical record of the Warangesda Aboriginal Mission/Station, Darlington Point, New South Wales*, Gulambali Aboriginal Research, Canberra, 2004, p. 26. See also Philippa Scarlett, 'Boer War: Another Aboriginal soldier confirmed', *Indigenous Histories*, 7 February 2013 <indigenoushistories.com/2013/02/07/boer-war-another-aboriginal-soldier-confirmed/>.

30 Elphick and Elphick 2004, p. 26.

31 *The West Australian*, 28 November 1901, p. 5, quoted in Peter Bakker, 'Australia's dark troopers in the Boer War'.

32 The *Brisbane Courier*, 21 December 1899, pp. 5–6, cited in Dale Kerwin, 'The lost trackers: Aboriginal servicemen in the 2nd Boer War', *Sabretache*, vol. 54, no. 1, 2013, p. 6.

33 Henry Reynolds, *Why Weren't We Told? A personal search for the truth about our history*, Penguin Books (Viking), Melbourne, 1999, p. 144.

34 Jonathan Richards, *The Secret War: A true history of Queensland's Native Police*, University of Queensland Press, St Lucia, 2008, p. 39.

35 Richards 2008, p. 81.

36 Richards 2008, p. 8.

37 Clint Bracknell, 'Bobby Roberts: Intermediary and Outlaw of Western Australia's south coast' in *Brokers and Boundaries – Colonial Exploration in Indigenous Territory*, Maria Nugent, Tiffany Shellam, Shino Konishi and Allison Cadzow (eds), ANU Press, Canberra, 2016, pp. 126–7.

38 *Portland Guardian*, 8 January 1902, p. 3; *The Cumberland Argus and Fruitgrowers Advocate*, 11 January 1902, p. 5.

39 Craig Wilcox, *The Boer War: Australians and the war in South Africa, 1899–1902*, National Archives of Australia, Canberra, 2000, p. 40; telegram from Police Magistrate Burketown enquiring if half-castes are acceptable as recruits for Imperial Bushmen's Contingent, 1900, MP744/11, 1900/2878, NAA.

40 Kerwin 2013, pp. 4–12.

41 *The Register* (Adelaide), 8 January 1902, p. 4.

42 *Australian Town and Country Journal*, 1 February 1902, p. 30.

43 Lord Kitchener's cable in *The Age*, 18 July 1901, Correspondence files, A8, 1901/20/12, NAA.
44 Kerwin 2013, p. 8.
45 Dispatch of Bush Trackers by Mr Willis on SS *Euryalus*, NAA A8, 1902/25/71.
46 Arthur Conan Doyle, *The Great Boer War*, Smith, Elder, & Co., London, 1900, pp. 479– 83.
47 Judd and Surridge 2003, p. 80.
48 *Barrier Miner* (Broken Hill), 12 May 1900, p. 2.
49 *The New Zealand Herald*, 5 October 1899, p. 5.
50 Lynette Russell, '"The singular transcultural space": Networks of ships, mariners, voyagers and "native" men at sea, 1790–1870', in Jane Carey and Jane Lydon (eds), *Indigenous Networks – Mobility, Connections and Exchange*, Routledge, London, 2014, p. 97.
51 Philippa Scarlett, 'More on William Stubbings, Indigenous Boer War veteran', Indigenous Histories website, 15 April 2013 <indigenoushistories.com/2013/04/15/more-on-william-stubbings-indigenous-boer-war-veteran/>; Philippa Scarlett, 'William Stubbings: Aboriginal soldier of the Boer War', Indigenous Histories website <indigenoushistories.com/2013/03/28/william-stubbings-aboriginal-soldier-of-the-boer-war-2/>.
52 Philippa Scarlett, 'Jack Alick Bond: Boer War Aboriginal soldier', Indigenous Histories website, 23 April 2014 <indigenoushistories.com/2014/04/23/jack-alick-bond-boer-war-aboriginal-soldier/>.
53 Scarlett 2014.
54 Scarlett 2014.
55 'John Searle', National Boer War Memorial Association Inc. website <www.bwm.org.au/site/John_Searle.php>.
56 Edward Kennedy, *The Black Police of Queensland*, John Murray, London, 1902. Kennedy's account was subsequently taken up by AL Haydon in *The Trooper Police of Australia: A record of mounted police work in the Commonwealth from the earliest days of settlement to the present time*, A Melrose, London, 1911. See also Gary Presland, *For God's Sake Send the Trackers: A history of Queensland trackers and Victoria police*, Victoria Press, Melbourne, 1998; Dale Kerwin, 'Aboriginal heroes: episodes in the colonial landscape', Queensland Historical Atlas website <www.qhatlas.com.au/content/aboriginal-heroes-episodes-colonial-landscape>.
57 Kennedy 1902.
58 Kennedy 1902, pp. 171–3.
59 Kennedy 1902, pp. 171–3.
60 AIATSIS, 'Rare photo of Indigenous involvement in the Boer War'.
61 *The Sydney Morning Herald*, 17 January 1902, p. 7. See also Philippa Scarlett, 'Aboriginal trackers: Boer War', Indigenous Histories website, 2 May 2013 <indigenoushistories.com/2013/05/02/aboriginal-trackers-boer-war/>.
62 *The Age* (Melbourne), 3 August 1901, p. 13.
63 *Age* 1901, p. 13.
64 *The Mercury and Weekly Courier* (Victoria), 18 January 1901, p. 2; *The Standard* (Port Melbourne), 26 January 1901, p. 4.
65 *Mercury* 1901, p. 2; *Standard* 1901, p. 4.

66 This account was taken from *Mercury* 1901, p. 2; *Standard* 1901, p. 4.
67 Rob Droogleever, Desert Column, 'Boer War trackers remembered in Brisbane', 3 June 2012. The Desert Column – Australian Light Horse Studies Centre aims to present an accurate history as chroniclers of early Australian military developments from 1899 to 1920. The site currently holds over 12 000 entries. See <alh-research.tripod.com/Light_Horse/>.
68 Bill Woerlee, Desert Column Website – Boer War trackers remembered in Brisbane, posted 3 June 2012.
69 Richards 2008, pp. 220–268.
70 George Valder, Repatriation of Australians from South Africa, 1907, p. 23, A1, 1911/20405, NAA.
71 Valder 1907, p. 3.
72 Valder 1907, p. 18.
73 Valder 1907, p. 18.
74 Valder 1907, p. 18.
75 Kerwin 2013, p. 11.
76 Valder 1907, p. 19.
77 Valder 1907, p. 18.
78 Geoffrey Blainey, 'Foreword', in Max Chamberlain and Robin Droogleever, *The War with Johnny Boer – Australians in the Boer War*, Australian Military History Publications, Sydney, 2003, p. xvii.
79 Pealr Gibbs, quoted in Bain Attwood, *The Struggle for Aboriginal Rights*, Allen & Unwin, St Leonards, 1999, p. 97.

Chapter 4: The First World War

1 Details of 978 Indigenous servicemen can be found on the website of the Australian War Memorial, People Profiles/Indigenous service.
2 Australian War Memorial People Profiles/Indigenous Service (78 records); National Archives of Australia, Australian Indigenous Servicemen World War I Database, B2455 (920 Records); John Maynard Personal Database from AWM Records focused on personal stories of Indigenous servicemen (740 Records).
3 Noeline Briggs-Smith, interview, 19 June 2014.
4 Gordon Syron, interview, 21 March 2014.
5 *The Northern Star*, 2 September 1915, p. 5.
6 *The Chronicle* (SA), 6 March 2015, p. 38.
7 Timothy Winegard, *Indigenous Peoples of the British Dominions and the First World War*, Cambridge University Press, Cambridge, 2012, p. 135; Noah Riseman and Richard Trembath, *Defending Country: Aboriginal and Torres Strait Islander military service since 1945*, University of Queensland Press, Brisbane, 2016, pp. 6–7.
8 David Huggonson, 'The Dark Diggers of the AIF', *The Australian Quarterly*, vol. 61, no. 3, 1989, pp. 352–7; Philippa Scarlett, 'Against the Act', *Wartime – Official Magazine of the Australian War Memorial*, Issue 76, Spring 2016, p. 26; Rod Pratt, '"By cripes! I'll fight for white Australia!": Queensland Aborigines in the First A.I.F.', Master of Literary Studies thesis, Griffith University, 1990, p. 37.
9 Email correspondence, 26 November 2016.
10 B2455, item bar code 4375191, NAA; B2455, 3000716, NAA.

11 Scarlett 2016, pp. 26–30.
12 See Joan Beaumont, *Broken Nation: Australians in the Great War*, Allen & Unwin, Sydney, 2013, pp. 20–6.
13 'Aborigines in camp', *Hamilton Spectator*, 12 April 1916, cited in Lachlan Grant, 'The Fighting Gunditjmara: Indigenous people have fought for country and for nation, from frontier wars to world wars', *Wartime: Official magazine of the Australian War Memorial*, Issue 77, 2016, pp. 18–24.
14 *The Kalgoorlie Miner*, 24 October 1917, p. 4.
15 *The Cairns Post*, 6 July 1917, p. 4.
16 *The Cairns Post*, 30 June 1917, p. 4.
17 Phillip Bradley, *Australian Light Horse – The Campaign in the Middle East 1916–1918*, Allen & Unwin, Sydney, 2016, p. 8.
18 Indigenous World War I folders, private research by Margaret Beadman (hereafter Margaret Beadman records); B2455, 3047729, NAA.
19 B2455, 7127525, NAA; Margaret Beadman records.
20 B2455, 1789944, NAA; Margaret Beadman records.
21 Marilyn Lake and Henry Reynolds, *What's Wrong With ANZAC? The militarisation of Australian history*, NewSouth Publishing, Sydney, 2010; Carolyn Holbrook, *ANZAC: The unauthorised biography*, NewSouth Publishing, Sydney, 2014.
22 B2455, 1907589, NAA.
23 B2455, 3505023, NAA.
24 B2455, 5833509, NAA.
25 B2455, 3083615, NAA.
26 B2455, 1794132, NAA.
27 B2455, 11605041, NAA.
28 B2455, 3168962, NAA.
29 B2455, 4375046, NAA.
30 B2455, 8033821, NAA; B2455, 8087260, NAA; B2455, 8399911, NAA; B2455, 3457363, NAA.
31 Doreen Kartinyeri, *Ngarrindjeri Anzacs*, South Australian Museum, Adelaide, 1996, p. 41.
32 Kartinyeri 1996, p. 44.
33 Kartinyeri 1996, p. 44.
34 B2455, 8195463, NAA.
35 B2455, 8198576 and 11616229, NAA.
36 *Raymond Terrace Examiner*, 23 August 1918, p. 3.
37 Citation by J Gellibrand, AWM 28/1/17 Part 2, AWM.
38 Correspondence from Charles Tednee Blackman, 1915–1919, PRO1679, AWM.
39 The *Queensland Times*, 15 May 1918, p. 1.
40 *Our Aim*, August 1917.
41 B2455, 4730033, NAA.
42 B2455, 3168240, NAA; Margaret Beadman records.
43 2843 Charles Ethelbert Hite, Australian Red Cross Society records, 1DRL/0428, AWM.
44 B2455, 3122751, NAA.
45 6158, Private Brooks, Frederick, Australian Red Cross Society records, 1DRL/0428, AWM.

46 B2455, 3168240, NAA.
47 Charles Bean, *The Official History of Australia in the War of 1914–18, vol. III, The Australian Imperial Force in France: 1916*, Angus & Robertson, Sydney, 1939, p. 728.
48 B2455, 3168240, NAA.
49 B2455, 7360074, NAA; William Allan Irwin <oldsite.awm.gov.au/images/collection/pdf/RCDIG1068568--20-.pdf>.
50 Charles Bean, *Official History of Australia in the War of 1914–18*, vol. VI, *The A.I.F. in France 1918*, Angus & Robertson, Sydney, 1942, p. 819.
51 B2455, 8036851, NAA; Ewan Rose <oldsite.awm.gov.au/images/collection/pdf/RCDIG1068614--63-.pdf>.
52 B2455, 4817817, NAA; Harry Thorpe <oldsite.awm.gov.au/images/collection/pdf/RCDIG1068298--97-.pdf>.
53 B2455, 4817817, NAA.
54 B2455, 8198896, NAA; 4230 Thomas Amos Lewis, Australian Red Cross Society records, 1DRL/0428, AWM.
55 Geoffrey Blainey, *The Story of Australia's People – The Rise and Rise of a New Australia*, Penguin, Melbourne, 2016, p. 247; see also Stephen Garton, *The Cost of War: Australians return*, Oxford University Press, Melbourne, 1996, pp. 143–60.
56 B2455, 3097163, NAA.
57 Blainey, 2016, p. 247.
58 B2455, 4375413, NAA.
59 Leanne Holt, interview, 12 March 2014.
60 Kartinyeri 1996, p. 27.
61 LD Scott, 'White Australia – Aspects of Policy – "Keep Country British"', *The News* (Adelaide), 17 June 1925, p. 6.
62 Victoria Haskins and John Maynard, 'Sex, Race and Power – Aboriginal Men and White Women in Australian History', *Australian Historical Studies*, vol. 36, no. 126, October 2005, pp. 191–216; see also Katherine Ellinghaus, *Taking Assimilation to Heart – Marriages of White Women & Indigenous Men in the United States & Australia, 1887–1937*, University of Nebraska Press, Lincoln, 2006.
63 Graham Jenkin, *Conquest of the Ngarrindjeri – The Story of the Lower Murray Lakes Tribes*, Rigby, Adelaide, 1985, p. 230; see also Haskins and Maynard, 'Sex Race and Power', pp. 191–216.

Chapter 5: The home front in the First World War

1 Ernest Scott, *Australia during the War*, vol. 11, *Official History of Australia in the War of 1914–1918*, Angus & Robertson, Sydney, 1936.
2 WEH Stanner, *After the Dreaming*, Australian Broadcasting Commission, Sydney, 1969.
3 See for example, Michael McKernan, *The Australian People and the Great War*, Nelson, Melbourne, 1980; Melanie Oppenheimer, *All Work, No Pay: Australian civilian volunteers in war*, Ohio Productions, Walcha, NSW, 2002; Michael Tyquin, *Madness and the Military: Australia's experience of the Great War*, Australian Military History Publications, Loftus, NSW, 2006; Marina Larsson, *Shattered ANZACs: Living with the scars of war*, UNSW Press, Sydney, 2009.

4 John Connor, Peter Stanley and Peter Yule, *The War at Home, Centenary History of Australia and the Great War*, Oxford University Press, Melbourne, 2015, pp. 198–200.

5 See for example Richard Broome, *Aboriginal Victorians: A history since 1800*, Allen & Unwin, Sydney, 2005; Peter Biskup, *Not Slaves, Not Citizens: The Aboriginal problem in Western Australia, 1898–1954*, University of Queensland Press, Brisbane, 1973; Heather Goodall, *Invasion to Embassy: Land in Aboriginal Politics in New South Wales, 1770–1972*, Allen & Unwin, Sydney, 1996; Anna Haebich, *For Their Own Good: Aborigines and government in the southwest of Western Australia, 1900–1940*, 2nd edition, University of Western Australia Press, Perth, 1992.

6 Andrea Gerrard and Kristyn Harman, 'Lives Twisted out of Shape! Tasmanian Aboriginal soldiers and the aftermath of the First World War', *Aboriginal History*, vol. 39, 2015, pp. 183–201; Jessica Horton, '"Willing to Fight to a Man": The First World War and Aboriginal activism in the Western District of Victoria', *Aboriginal History*, vol. 39, 2015, pp. 203–22; Patricia Grimshaw and Hannah Loney, '"Doing Their Bit Helping Make Australia Free": Mothers of Aboriginal Diggers and the Assertion of Indigenous Rights', *Provenance: The Journal of Public Record Office Victoria*, no. 14, 2015.

7 Joan Beaumont, *Broken Nation: Australians in the Great War*, Allen & Unwin, Sydney, 2013, p. xvi.

8 Connor, Stanley and Yule 2015, pp. 12–17.

9 New South Wales, 'Report of the Board for the Protection of Aborigines for year 1914', p. 3, 'To Remove and Protect', AIATSIS online database <aiatsis.gov.au/collections/collections-online/digitised-collections/remove-and-protect> (hereafter AIATSIS).

10 New South Wales, 'Report of the Board for the Protection of Aborigines for year 1915', p. 2, AIATSIS.

11 Anna Haebich, *Broken Circles: Fragmenting Indigenous families 1800–2000*, Fremantle Arts Centre Press, Perth, 2000, pp. 182–3.

12 South Australia, 'Report of the Protector of Aborigines for the Year Ended June 30, 1915', p. 3, AIATSIS.

13 Peggy Brock, *Outback Ghettos: Aborigines, institutionalisation and survival*, Cambridge University Press, Cambridge, 1993, p. 89; see also, South Australia, 'Report of the Protector of Aborigines for the year ended June 30, 1917', p. 15, AIATSIS.

14 South Australia, 'Report of the Protector of Aborigines for the year ended June 30, 1916', p. 14, AIATSIS; South Australia, 'Report of the Protector of Aborigines for the year ended June 30, 1917', p. 17, AIATSIS.

15 Brock 1993, p. 89.

16 Queensland, 'Annual Report of the Chief Protector of Aboriginals for the Year 1914', p. 4, AIATSIS; Queensland, 'Annual Report of the Chief Protector of Aboriginals for the Year 1915', p. 5, AIATSIS.

17 Queensland, 'Annual Report of the Chief Protector of Aboriginals for the Year 1915', p. 7, pp. 14–15, AIATSIS.

18 Raymond Evans, *Loyalty and Disloyalty: Social Conflict on the Queensland Homefront, 1914–18*, Allen & Unwin, Sydney, 1987, p. 96; see also *Cairns Post*, 7 November 1916, p. 4.

19 Queensland, 'Annual Report of the Chief Protector of Aboriginals for the Year 1918', p. 4, AIATSIS.

20 Dawn May, *Aboriginal Labour and the Cattle Industry: Queensland from white settlement to the present*, Cambridge University Press, Melbourne, 1994.

21 Biskup 1973, p. 109.

22 Broome 2005, pp. 202–3.

23 *Hamilton Spectator*, 6 August 1917, p. 3.

24 New South Wales, 'Report of the Board for the Protection of Aborigines', 1920, p. 3, AIATSIS; New South Wales, 'Report of the Board for the Protection of Aborigines', 1921, p. 5, AIATSIS.

25 Haebich 2000, pp. 182–3.

26 Quoted in Richard Egan, *Neither Amity nor Kindness: Government policy towards Aboriginal people of NSW 1788 to 1969*, R. Egan, Sydney, 2012, p. 117.

27 Heather Goodall, 'Not Such a Respected Soldier: The impact of World War 1 on Aborigines in New South Wales', *Teaching History*, vol. 21, no. 4, 1987, p. 4.

28 South Australia, *Progress Report of the Royal Commission on the Aborigines: Together with minutes of proceedings, evidence, and appendices*, REE Rogers, Government Printer, Adelaide, 1913, p. 37.

29 Robert Foster, '"Endless Trouble and Agitation": Aboriginal Activism in the Protectionist Era', *Journal of the Historical Society of South Australia*, no. 28, 2000, pp. 22–4; see also Doreen Kartinyeri, *Ngarrindjeri Anzacs*, Aboriginal Family History Project, South Australian Museum and Raukkan Council, Adelaide, 1996, pp. 24–5.

30 Alan Powell, *Far Country: A short history of the Northern Territory*, Melbourne University Press, Melbourne, 1982, p. 161; Haebich 2000, p. 191.

31 Haebich 2000, p. 191.

32 Northern Territory of Australia, 'Report of the Administrator for the Year ending 30th June 1918', p. 11, AIATSIS.

33 Northern Territory of Australia, 'Report of the Administrator for the Year 1914–15', p. 28, AIATSIS.

34 *Barrier Miner* (Broken Hill, NSW), 7 March 1915, p. 4.

35 Biskup 1973, pp. 153–5.

36 Evans 1987, p. 40.

37 *Brisbane Courier*, 31 August 1915, p. 9.

38 *Telegraph* (Brisbane), 18 October 1915, p. 3.

39 *Bathurst Times*, 23 April 1915, p. 2.

40 *Echuca and Moama Advertiser and Farmers' Gazette*, 29 May 1915, p. 3.

41 New South Wales, 'Report of the Board for the Protection of Aborigines for Year 1915', p. 4, AIATSIS.

42 *Sydney Mail*, 7 April 1915, p. 42.

43 New South Wales, 'Report of the Board for the Protection of Aborigines for Year 1915', p. 3, AIATSIS.

44 Queensland, 'Annual Report of the Chief Protector of Aboriginals for the Year 1916', pp. 3, 12, AIATSIS.

45 Mark Newman, Sally Lawrence and Philippa Scarlett, *The Boys from Barambah: The story of the Black Diggers of Barambah-Cherbourg of World War I*, The Ration Shed Museum, Murgon, Queensland, 2015.
46 See for example, *The Farmer and Settler* (Sydney), 2 May 1916, p. 3.
47 *Echuca and Moama Advertiser and Farmers' Gazette*, 1915, p. 3.
48 Newman, Lawrence, and Scarlett 2015, p. 21.
49 *Advertiser* (Adelaide), 28 August 1914, p. 9.
50 See Kartinyeri 1996.
51 Jimmie Barker and Janet Mathews, *The Two Worlds of Jimmie Barker: The life of an Australian Aboriginal, 1900–1972*, Australian Institute of Aboriginal Studies, Canberra, 1977, p. 87.
52 *Register* (Adelaide), 26 May 1919, p. 7.
53 'Papers relating to No. 3027 Private R. W. Carter', South Australian Red Cross Information Bureau Collection, SRG 76/1/230, SLSA.
54 *Register* (Adelaide), 2 August 1919, p. 10.
55 'Aboriginal Welcome Home', *Queanbeyan Age and Queanbeyan Observer*, 12 September 1919, p. 6.
56 Samuel Furphy, 'Waters, Leonard Victor (1924–1993)', in *Australian Dictionary of Biography* website <adb.anu.edu.au/biography/waters-leonard-victor-len-24662>.
57 *Daily Observer* (Tamworth, NSW), 16 May 1919, p. 1.
58 Queensland, Reports of Aboriginals Department: 1919, pp. 5–6; 1920, p. 5, AIATSIS; David Huggonson, 'Aborigines and the Aftermath of the Great War', *Australian Aboriginal Studies*, no. 1, 1993, p. 4.
59 Haebich 1992, pp. 184–5.
60 David John Gilbert, 17 April 1919, quoted in Clem J Lloyd and Jacqueline Rees, *The Last Shilling: A history of repatriation in Australia*, Melbourne University Press, Melbourne, 1994, p. 107.
61 Gerrard and Harman 2015, p. 198.
62 Queensland, 'Annual Report of the Chief Protector of Aboriginals for the Year 1918', p. 4, AIATSIS.
63 Queensland, 'Annual Report of the Chief Protector of Aboriginals for the Year 1919', p. 4, AIATSIS.
64 Rod Pratt, 'Queensland's Aborigines in the First Australian Imperial Force' in *Aboriginal Peoples and Military Participation: Canadian and international perspectives*, P Whitney Lackenbauer, R Scott Sheffield and Craig Leslie Mantle (eds), Canadian Defence Academy Press, Kingston, Ontario, 2007, p. 232.
65 'Fisher Frank', B2455, item bar code 3900597, NAA.
66 Queensland, 'Annual Report of the Chief Protector of Aboriginals for the Year 1919', p. 4, AIATSIS.
67 Pratt, 'Queensland's Aborigines in the First Australian Imperial Force', p. 232.
68 David Huggonson, 'Aboriginal Trust Accounts in Queensland: How "Protection" Became "Oppression",' *The Australian Quarterly*, vol. 62, no. 4, 1990, pp. 367–8; Noah Riseman, 'Enduring Silences, Enduring Prejudices: Australian Aboriginal Participation in the First World War', in *Endurance and the First World War: Experience and legacies in New Zealand and Australia*, David Monger, Katie Pickles, and Sarah Murray (eds), Cambridge Scholars Publishing, Newcastle upon Tyne, 2014, pp. 188–9.

69 Patricia Grimshaw, Elizabeth Nelson and Sandra Smith, *Letters from Aboriginal Women in Victoria, 1867–1926*, History Department, University of Melbourne, Melbourne, 2002, pp. 251–3.
70 Bruce Ferguson to Board, 7 May 1919, Board for the Protection of Aborigines Correspondence Files, VPRS 1694, Unit 7, Bundle 1, 1919, ff. 547–48, Public Record Office of Victoria.
71 Marilyn Lake, *The Limits of Hope: Soldier settlement in Victoria, 1915–38*, Oxford University Press, Melbourne, 1987, p. 244.
72 Andrea Gerrard, 'Open to All Who Served or Was It? Soldier settlement for Tasmanian Aboriginal soldiers', *Tasmanian Historical Studies*, no. 20, 2015, pp. 29, 38.
73 Huggonson 1993, p. 7; Simon Flagg and Sebastian Gurciullo, *Footprints: The journey of Lucy and Percy Pepper*, Public Record Office Victoria; National Archives of Australia, Melbourne; Canberra, 2008, pp. 57–78, 100.
74 Bruce Scates and Melanie Oppenheimer, *The Last Battle: Soldier settlement in Australia, 1916–1939*, Cambridge University Press, Melbourne, 2016, p. 61.
75 Scates and Oppenheimer 2016, pp. 60–5.
76 Philippa Scarlett, *Aboriginal and Torres Strait Islander Volunteers for the AIF: The Indigenous response to World War One*, 2nd edition, Indigenous Histories, Macquarie, ACT, 2012, p. 44.
77 Haebich 1992, p. 224.
78 Huggonson 1993, p. 7.
79 'Lake Condah Reserve', *Argus* (Melbourne), 13 October 1921, p. 8.
80 'Aborigines' Rights', *Portland Guardian*, 20 July 1925, p. 3.
81 John Eustace Bews, quoted in John Maynard, *Fight for Liberty and Freedom: The origins of Australian Aboriginal activism*, Aboriginal Studies Press, Canberra, 2007, p. 127.

Chapter 6: The rise of the modern Aboriginal political movement, 1924–39

1 Jessica Horton, '"Willing to fight to a man": The First World War and Aboriginal Activism in the Western District of Victoria', *Aboriginal History*, vol. 39, 2015, p. 203.
2 Horton 2015, p. 210.
3 Horton 2015, p. 211.
4 Horton 2015, p. 211.
5 Horton 2015, p. 212.
6 'Lake Tyers Report', Minutes of Meetings of the Board, 1907–1921, B314, f. 343, NAA.
7 B314, NAA.
8 Horton 2015, p. 204.
9 Joseph G Tucker, Special Report, 14 October 1922, *Federal Surveillance of Afro-Americans (1917–1925): The First World War, the Red Scare and the Garvey Movement*, Microfilm, Lamont Library Index film A563, Harvard University.
10 *Morning Bulletin* (Rockhampton), 11 June 1921, p. 10.
11 *The Argus* (Melbourne), 25 December 1920, p. 4.
12 Christian W McMillen, *Making Indian Law*, Yale University Press, New Haven, 2007, p. 24.

13 McMillen 2007, p. 22.
14 *The Daylight*, 26 June 1922, p. 461.
15 *Daylight* 1922, p. 461.
16 Heather Goodall, 'Winning overseas, losing at home', *Land Rights News*, vol. 4, no. 2, 1988, pp. 32–3; Bruce Scates and Melanie Oppenheimer, *The Last Battle: Soldier settlement in Australia, 1916–1939*, Cambridge University Press, Melbourne, 2016.
17 Goodall 1988, pp. 32–3.
18 Heather Goodall, 'Not Such a Respected Soldier – The Impact of World War One on Aborigines in New South Wales', *Teaching History: Journal of the History Teachers' Association of New South Wales*, vol. 21, issue 4, 1987, pp. 3–6.
19 *A Guide to New South Wales State Archives Relating to Aboriginal People*, The Archives Authority of New South Wales, Sydney, 1998, p. 67.
20 Goodall 1987, pp. 3–6.
21 *Sunday Times* (Perth), 4 September 1921, p. 6.
22 *Sunday Times* (Perth), 30 October 1921, p. 12.
23 Richard Broome, *Aboriginal Australians* (2nd edition), Allen & Unwin, Sydney, 1994, p. 166. See also Bain Attwood, *The Struggle for Aboriginal Rights*, Allen & Unwin, Sydney, 1999.
24 Peggy Brock, 'Pastoral Stations and Reserves in South and Central Australia, 1850s to 1960s' in *Aboriginal Workers*, A McGrath, K Saunders and J Huggins (eds), *Australian Society for Labour History* (Special Issue), Sydney, 1995, p. 111.
25 *The Newcastle Sun*, 7 October 1925, p. 3.
26 John Maynard, 'Garvey in Oz: The International Black Influence on Australian Aboriginal Political Activism' in *Anywhere But Here: Black intellectuals in the Atlantic world and beyond*, K Radcliffe, J Scott and A Werner (eds), University Press of Mississippi, Jackson, 2015, pp. 99–116; John Maynard, 'Marching to a Different Beat: The influence of the International Black Diaspora on Aboriginal Australia' in *Indigenous Networks – Mobility, Connections and Exchange*, J Carey and J Lydon (eds), Routledge, London, 2014, pp. 262–72; John Maynard, '"In the Interests of Our People": The influence of Garveyism on the rise of Australian Aboriginal political activism', *Aboriginal History*, vol. 29, 2005, pp. 1–22; John Maynard, 'Vision, Voice and Influence: The rise of the Australian Aboriginal Progressive Association', *Australian Historical Studies*, vol. 34, no. 121, 2003, pp. 91–105.
27 A659/1, 1943/1/1451, 27/11888, 456, NAA; *The Daylight*, 31 March 1928.
28 Fred Maynard to NSW Premier Jack Lang, 1927, Correspondence Files, A27/915, New South Wales Premier's Department, NSW State Archives.
29 Maynard to Lang 1927.
30 John Maynard, *Fight for Liberty and Freedom*, Aboriginal Studies Press, Canberra, 2007, p. 7.
31 Peter Dennis, Jeffrey Grey, Ewan Morris, Robin Prior with Jean Bou, *The Oxford Companion to Australian Military History*, Oxford University Press, Melbourne, 2008, pp. 504–05.
32 Robert A Hall, *Black Diggers*, Aboriginal Studies Press, Canberra, 1997, p. 3; Heather Goodall 1988, p. 33; Elissa Blake, interview with Wesley Enoch, *The Sydney Morning Herald*, 11–12 January 2014, p. 6.

33 The *Raymond Terrace Examiner and Lower Hunter and Port Stephens Advertiser*, 6 April 1923, p. 3.
34 The *Raymond Terrace Examiner*, 1923, p. 3.
35 *Warrnambool Standard*, 25 July 1917, p. 4.
36 *Warrnambool Standard*, 1917, p. 4.
37 See Horton 2015.
38 *The Portland Guardian*, 30 May 1921, p. 2.
39 Heather Goodall, 'A History of Aboriginal Communities in New South Wales, 1909–1939', PhD thesis, University of Sydney, 1982, p. 187.
40 *The Voice of the North*, 12 June 1925, p. 3.
41 *The Argus* (Melbourne), 11 June 1925, p. 6.
42 *The Daylight*, 29 February 1928, p. 294.
43 *The Dayligh*, 1928, p. 294.
44 *The Daylight*, 31 May 1928, p. 331.
45 *The Daylight*, 30 April 1928, p. 317.
46 *The Daylight*, 30 June 1928, p. 342.
47 *The Cairns Post*, 28 January 1933, p. 11.
48 *The Cairns Post*, 19 February 1920, p. 6.
49 *The Register* (Adelaide), 16 July 1925, p. 12.
50 John Ramsland and Christopher Mooney, *Remembering Aboriginal Heroes*, Brolga Press, Melbourne, 2006, p. 4.
51 *The Australian Aborigines Advocate*, 31 August 1917, p. 4.
52 Christopher D Coulthard-Clark, 'Grant, Douglas (1885?–1951)' in Bede Nairn and Geoffrey Searle (eds), *Australian Dictionary of Biography*, Melbourne University Press, Melbourne, 1983, pp. 76–7.
53 Ramsland and Mooney 2006, p. 7.
54 The Australian War Memorial, 'Stolen Years: Australian prisoners of war', <www.awm.gov.au/exhibitions/stolenyears/ww1/Germany/>.
55 Ramsland and Mooney 2006, p. 11.
56 *The Sun* (Sydney), 10 March 1923, p. 2.
57 Coulthard-Clark 1983, pp. 76–7.
58 *The Lithgow Mercury*, 8 February 1929, p. 3.
59 *Lithgow Mercury*, 1929, p. 3.
60 *The Lithgow Mercury*, 24 June 1929, p. 6.
61 *The Riverine Herald*, 2 September 1930, p. 3.
62 *The Newcastle Sun*, 7 December 1927, p. 8.
63 *The Workers' Weekly*, 24 September 1931, p. 2.
64 Jack Horner, *Bill Ferguson: Fighter for Aboriginal Freedom*, Jack Horner, 1994, p. 27.
65 *The Sydney Morning Herald*, 4 April 1928, p. 24.
66 Heather Goodall and Allison Cadzow, *Rivers and Resilience – Aboriginal People on Sydney's Georges River*, UNSW Press, Sydney, 2009, p. 126.
67 Goodall and Cadzow 2009, p. 125.
68 Bain Attwood and Andrew Marcus, *The Struggle for Aboriginal Rights – A Documentary History*, Allen & Unwin, Sydney, 1999, p. 87.
69 *The Workers' Weekly*, 20 December 1938, p. 3.

70 Bain Attwood and Andrew Marcus, *Thinking Black – William Cooper and the Australian Aborigines League*, Aboriginal Studies Press, Canberra, 2004, p. 34.
71 Alick Jackomos, *Forgotten Heroes – Aborigines at War From the Somme to Vietnam*, Victoria Press, Melbourne, 1993, p. 9.
72 Attwood and Marcus 2004, p. 51.
73 Attwood and Marcus 2004, p. 92.
74 Attwood and Marcus 2004, p. 112–13.
75 Attwood and Marcus 2004, p. 112.
76 Heather Goodall, *Invasion to Embassy*, Allen & Unwin, Sydney, 1996, pp. 236–8.
77 Bain Attwood, *Rights for Aborigines*, Allen & Unwin, Sydney, 2003, p. 41.
78 *Sunday Times* (Perth), 21 October 1921, p. 18.
79 Blackman, cited in Philippa Scarlett, 'Aboriginal service in the First World War: Identity, recognition and the problem of mateship', *Aboriginal History*, vol. 39, 2015, p. 163.

Chapter 7: Australian military forces in the Second World War

1 Australian Government, Department of Veterans' Affairs website, 'Indigenous Australians at war' <www.dva.gov.au/i-am/aboriginal-andor-torres-strait-islander/indigenous-australians-war>. At the time of publication this estimate was under review by the Australian War Memorial and will possibly be increased.
2 See Joan Beaumont, *Australia's War 1939–45*, Allen & Unwin, Sydney, 1996, pp. 41–3.
3 Memorandum, Enlistment of Aborigines, 11 July 1940, MP508/1 275/750/1310, NAA.
4 Robert Hall, *Black Diggers: Aborigines and Torres Strait Islanders in the Second World War*, Allen & Unwin, Sydney, 1989, pp. 8–10; 'No admission of Aborigines', *Sydney Morning Herald*, 7 January 1939, p. 17. Hall's is the definitive account of Aboriginal and Torres Strait Islander service in the Second World War and the authors acknowledge their debt to him.
5 W Forgan Smith to Prime Minister Robert Menzies, 20 September 1939, A1608 D45/2/3, NAA.
6 Hall 1989, p. 10.
7 Chris Clark, 'Indigenous service in Australia's armed forces in peace and war', Australian War Memorial website <www.awm.gov.au/articles/indigenous-service/report-executive-summary/>.
8 FG Shedden, Secretary, Department of Defence, to Secretary, Department of Air, 'Enlistment of Foreigners in the Australian Services', 25 January 1940, A2671 45/1940, NAA.
9 RG Menzies, War Cabinet Agendum 45/1940, 'Enlistment of Aliens and British Subjects of Non-European Descent in the Australian Defence Forces', 24 February 1940, A2671 45/1940, NAA.
10 Paul Hasluck, *The Government and the People, 1939–41*, vol. I of *Australia in the War of 1939–1945*, Series 4 (Civil), Australian War Memorial, Canberra, pp. 613, 220.
11 This decision had been conveyed to various commands by the Secretary of the Military Board on 6 May 1940: MP508/1, 275/750/1310, NAA.
12 Author indecipherable to Northern, Eastern, Southern and Western Commands, 29 May 1940, MP508 275/750/1310, NAA.

13 GOC Western Command to Secretary, Military Board, Melbourne, section 60(h) Defence Act, 7 May 1940, MP508/1, 275/750/1310, NAA.

14 Anna Shnukal, 'Torres Strait Islanders', in *Multicultural Queensland 2001: 100 years, 100 communities: A century of contributions*, Maximilian Brandle (ed.), The State of Queensland (Department of Premier and Cabinet), Brisbane, 2001, p. 9.

15 Hall 1989, pp. 20–1; Angela Burger, *Neville Bonner, A Biography*, Macmillan, Melbourne, 1979, p. 20.

16 Secretary, Aborigines Welfare Board, to Deputy Assistant Adjutant General, Victoria Barracks, Sydney, 13 June 1940, SP459/1 527/2/4541, NAA.

17 Hall 1989, p. 17.

18 APA Burdeu to Prime Minister Menzies, 7 July 1940, MP 508/1 275/750/1310, NAA.

19 Alexander Mair, Premier, to Prime Minister, 23 July 1940, A1608 D45/2/3, NAA.

20 William Ferguson, Aborigines Progressive Association, to Prime Minister Menzies, 8 July 1940, A663 0130/1/186, NAA.

21 The Year Book of 1944–45 states there were 71 895 Aborigines at 30 June 1944, of whom 47 014 were 'full-blood', a category which the military authorities refused to consider eligible for military service (Australian Bureau of Statistics, Canberra, 1945).

22 *The Encyclopaedia of New Zealand*, 'The 28th (Māori) Battalion' <www.teara.govt.nz/en/nga-pakanga-ki-tawahi-maori-and-overseas-wars/page-5>.

23 Hall 1989, p. 12.

24 Superintendent, Cherbourg Aboriginal Settlement, to B Corser, Parliament House, 4 July 1940, MP508/1 275/750/699, NAA.

25 See Hall 1989, p. 18. Clarrie Combo, who was the subject of the Aborigines Welfare Board's complaint of 13 June, was allowed to enlist. See Brigadier i/c Eastern Command, to Secretary, Aborigines Welfare Board, 21 June 1940, SP459/1 527//4541, NAA.

26 FA McBride, Army, to Prime Minister Menzies, 17 August 1940, A1608 D45/2/3, NAA; Hall 1989, p. 17.

27 GCN Miles Adjutant-General, to Secretary, Military Board, 24 July 1940, B6681 214/1940, NAA.

28 Prime Minister Menzies to Premier NSW, MP508/1 275/750/1310; Miles to Secretary, Military Board, 24 July 1940; Secretary, Military Board, to various commands, received 13 August 1940, MP 508/1 275/750/1310, NAA.

29 Hall 1989, pp. 20–1, 114.

30 Hall 1989, p. 18.

31 For McGuire, see Brian Willis, Aborigines and the Defence Forces in Western Australia in World War II, MPhil thesis, University of Western Australia, 1995, pp. 14–15.

32 Tristan Moss, *Guarding the Periphery: The Australian Army in Papua New Guinea, 1951–1975*, Cambridge University Press, Cambridge, 2017, pp. 20–1.

33 DCGS, 'Employment of Torres Strait Islanders on Military Duty at Thursday Island', 4 January 1941, MP508/1 247/704/56, NAA.

34 Reg Ball, *Torres Strait Force 1942 to 1945: The defence of Cape York-Torres Strait and Merauke in Dutch New Guinea*, Australian Military History Publications, Sydney, 1996, p. 10; Hall 1989, p. 32.

35 Hall 1989, p. 35.
36 Memorandum, 'Conditions of Service, Native Units', 7 July 1942, MP742/1 247/1/1290, NAA; Hall 1989, p. 38.
37 GOC First Army, to LHQ, 15 January 1943, MP742/1 240/1/51, NAA.
38 HQ First Army, to LHQ, 15 January 1943, MP742/1 240/1/51, NAA.
39 GOC, 15 January 1943, MP742/1 240/1/51, NAA.
40 See 'Torres Strait Force Op Instn 28', 27 October 1943, AWM54 628/2/3, AWM.
41 Donald F Thomson, 'War-Time Exploration in Dutch New Guinea', *The Geographical Journal*, vol. 119, no. 1, 1953, p. 9.
42 Hall 1989, p. 52.
43 Hall 1989, discusses concerns over pay at length, pp. 42–54.
44 'Minutes of conference AAG First Aust Army and Mr McCracken, Public Service Commissioner, Q'Land State Government', no date, AWM54, 628/1/1A, AWM.
45 Statement by Prime Minister, 'Torres Strait Islander members of the Forces', 20 March 1944, A2671, 145/1944, NAA.
46 Willis 1995, pp. 22–35.
47 See Dudley McCarthy, *South-West Pacific Area First Year Kokoda to Wau*, vol. V of *Australia in the War of 1939–1945*, Series I (Army), Australian War Memorial, Canberra 1959, p. 84.
48 Donald Thomson, 'Report on the Organisation of the Northern Territory Coastal Patrol and the Special Reconnaissance Unit', April 1943, AA1966/5, 386, NAA.
49 Thomson 1943.
50 Peter Stanley, *Invading Australia: Japan and the battle for Australia, 1942*, Viking, Melbourne, 2008, p. 142.
51 Peter Dennis et. al., *The Oxford Companion to Australian Military History* (2nd edition), Oxford University Press, Melbourne, 2008, p. 4.
52 Hall 1989, p. 97.
53 Thomson, 'Report on the Organisation of the Northern Territory Coastal Patrol'.
54 Noah Riseman, *Defending Whose Country? Indigenous soldiers in the Pacific War*, University of Nebraska Press, Lincoln and London, 2012, p. 52.
55 Tommy Munyarryun, interview, 11 August 2016; Warrk'Mattjun Gaykamangu, interview, 11 August 2016.
56 Chris Clarke, 'A question of numbers – Second World War', Australian War Memorial website <www.awm.gov.au/indigenous-service/report-second-world-war/>.
57 John Barrett, *We Were There: Australian soldiers of World War II tell their stories*, Viking, Melbourne, 1987, pp. 24–5.
58 Quoted in Robert Hall, *Fighters from the Fringe: Aborigines and Torres Strait Islanders recall the Second World War*, Aboriginal Studies Press, Canberra, 1995, pp. 157, 159.
59 John Lester, interview, 12 March 2014. Paulette Whitton also suggested that her uncle enlisted more for employment than a desire to serve his country: interview, 19 March 2014.
60 Australian War Memorial, 'Captain Reginald Walter "Reg" Saunders', Australian War Memorial website <www.awm.gov.au/people/P302/>.
61 Quoted in Hall 1995, pp. 63–4.

62 John Lovett, interview, 6 March 2015.
63 Quoted in Hall 1995, p. 93.
64 Hall 1989, p. 25; Rosie Ware, interview, 10 April 2014.
65 Aden Eades, interview, 1 September 2015.
66 James McDermott, interview, 3 April 2014.
67 Alex Kruger and Gerard Waterford, *Alone on the Soaks: The life and times of Alec Kruger*, IAD Press, Alice Springs, 2007, pp. 121–2.
68 Michael Sawtell, Committee for Aboriginal Citizenship, to Prime Minister Menzies, 21 October 1939, A1608 D45/2/3, NAA.
69 Hall 1989, p. 11.
70 Hall 1989, pp. 22, 65.
71 Hall 1989, pp. 61, 68.
72 Ron Ralph, interview, 2 September 2015.
73 Tristan Moss and Georgina Fitzpatrick, 'Crimes against Captured Airmen' in Georgina Fitzpatrick, Tim McCormack and Narrelle Morris, *Australia's War Crimes Trials 1945–51*, Brill Nijhoff, Lieden and Boston, 2016, p. 235.
74 Australian War Memorial, 'Indigenous Australian Servicemen', Australian War Memorial website <www.awm.gov.au/encyclopedia/aborigines/indigenous/>; Hall 1989, p. 84.
75 Quoted in Hall 1995, p. 93.
76 Quoted in Hall 1995, pp. 76–7.
77 Court-Martial of Alexander Bell, 9 January 1943, A471 29781, NAA. Bell's complaints were also reported widely in the press. See for instance 'Aboriginal Gunner went AWL [sic]: "difficult to settle down"', *Argus*, 7 January 1943, p. 4.
78 Court-Martial of John Mortimer Ceissman, 8 July 1944, A471, 57893, NAA.
79 Court-Martial of Russell Raymond Amato, 22 June 1943, A471, 39593, NAA.
80 'Penong Aborigine Shows Efficiency in Drill', *West Coast Sentinel*, 5 September 1941, p. 3.
81 'Went on "Walkabout": Aborigine Admonished', *Daily Mercury*, 6 January 1942, p. 1.

Chapter 8: Labour and surveillance in northern Australia, 1939–45

1 Christine Choo, *Mission girls: Aboriginal women on Catholic missions in the Kimberley, Western Australia, 1900–1950*, University of Western Australia Press, Perth, 2001, p. 178.
2 Kirstie Close, 'Invisible Labourers: Cape Bedford (Hopevale) Mission and the "Paradox" of Aboriginal Labour in the Second World War', MA thesis, University of Melbourne, 2009, p. 7.
3 Jonathan Richards, '"What a howl there would be if some of our folk were so treated by an enemy": The evacuation of Aboriginal people from Cape Bedford Mission, 1942', *Aboriginal History*, vol. 36, 2012, p. 21.
4 Kay Saunders, 'Inequalities of Sacrifice: Aboriginal and Torres Strait Islander Labour in Northern Australia during the Second World War', *Labour History*, no. 69, 1995, p. 133.
5 KE Read, 'Effects of the Pacific War in the Markham Valley, New Guinea', *Oceania*, vol. XVIII, no. 2, 1947, pp. 95–116, at p. 100. See also Ian Hogbin, *Transformation Scene*, Routledge & Kegan Paul, London, 1951, pp. 11–12.

6 Former Superintendent Naylor to Commandant of Military Forces at Townsville, 28 January 1942, 6066/1/88, AWM.
7 John Curtin to Forde, 24 July 1942, MP729/6, 29/401/626, NAA.
8 Security (Brisbane) to Director-General of Security (Canberra), 16 July 1942, MP729/6, 29/401/626, NAA.
9 Robert Hall, *Black Diggers: Aborigines and Torres Strait Islanders in the Second World War*, Allen & Unwin, Sydney, 1989, p. 132.
10 Quoted in Dawn May, *Aboriginal Labour and the Cattle Industry*, Cambridge University Press, Melbourne, 1994, p. 149.
11 Penny Edwards and Shen Yuanfeng (eds), *Lost in the Whitewash: Aboriginal-Asian encounters in Australia 1901–2001*, Humanities Research Centre, ANU, Canberra, 2003.
12 Memo to Commissioner of Police, 5 November 1942, CC 993, 592/43, State Records of Western Australia (SROWA).
13 Memo to Minister for the North-West, 21 January 1943, ACC 993, 102/43, SROWA.
14 Carrodus to AL Driver, Administrator (NT), 15 July 1946, F1, 1946/767, NAA.
15 AP Elkin to Prime Minister Curtin, 2 April 1942, MP508/1, 240/701/217, NAA.
16 Geoffrey Gray, *Abrogating Responsibility: Vesteys, anthropology and the future of Aboriginal people*, Australian Scholarly Publishing, Melbourne, 2015, pp. 3–5. For scholarship examining the relationship between Aboriginal people and the Northern Territory pastoral industry see: Frank Stevens, *Aborigines in the Northern Territory Cattle Industry*, ANU Press, Canberra, 1974; Ann McGrath, *Born in the Cattle*, Allen & Unwin, Sydney, 1987; Deborah Bird Rose, *Hidden Histories: Black stories from Victoria River Downs, Humbert River and Wave Hill Stations*, Aboriginal Studies Press, Canberra, 1991; Tim Rowse, *White Flour, White Power: From rations to citizenship in central Australia*, Cambridge University Press, Melbourne, 1998; May 1994; Mary Anne Jebb, *Blood, Sweat and Welfare: A history of white bosses and Aboriginal pastoral workers*, University of Western Australia Press, Nedlands, 2002.
17 For example, see Bruce Shaw, *Banggaiyerri: The story of Jack Sullivan*, Aboriginal Studies Press, Canberra, 1983.
18 All Japanese people, from pearlers to bankers, were interned: Yuriko Nagata, *Unwanted Aliens: Japanese internment in Australia*, University of Queensland Press, Brisbane, 1996.
19 Deborah Bird Rose, *Hidden Histories*, Aboriginal Studies Press, Canberra, 1991, p. 159.
20 May 1994, p. 148.
21 Paddy Roe quoted in Liz Thompson (ed.), *Aboriginal Voices: Contemporary Aboriginal artists, writers and performers*, JB Books, Adelaide, 1990, p. 31.
22 May 1994, p. 148.
23 David Mowaljarlai and Jutta Malnic, *Yorro Yorro: Everything standing up alive: Spirit of the Kimberley*, Magabala Books, Broome, WA, 1993, p. 122.
24 Ronald M Berndt and Catherine H Berndt, 'Native labour and welfare in the Northern Territory', Adelaide (typescript/carbon copy), July 1946, pp. 259–60.
25 Berndt and Berndt 1946, p. 262.
26 Andrew Markus, *Governing Savages*, Allen & Unwin, Sydney, 1990, pp. 130–43.

27 Appendix B, Minutes of Conference on Native Affairs, HQ NT Force, 24 April 1945, EP 73/1/12/205.
28 See also Peter and Jay Read, *Long Time, Olden Time: Aboriginal accounts of Northern Territory history*, Institute for Aboriginal Development Publications, Alice Springs, 1991, p. 132; Jolly Read and Peter Coppin, *Kangkushot: The life of Nyamal Lawman Peter Coppin*, Aboriginal Studies Press, Canberra, 1999, pp. 54–5; Mowaljarlai and Malnic 1993, p. 120–4; Wandjuk Marika and Jennifer Isaacs, *Wandjuk Marika: Life story, as told to Jennifer Isaacs*, University of Queensland Press, Brisbane, 1995, pp. 66–70.
29 Berndt & Berndt 1946, pp. 263–5.
30 Quoted in Read & Read 1991, p. 132.
31 Berndt & Berndt 1946, pp. 261–2.
32 Berndt & Berndt 1946, p. 269. See also Geoffrey Gray, '"We Know the Aborigines are Dying Out": Aboriginal People and the Quest to Ensure their Survival, Wave Hill Station, 1944', *Health & History*, vol. 16, no. 1, 2014, pp. 10–18.
33 Berndt & Berndt 1946, p. 275.
34 FGG Rose, *Australia Revisited: the Aborigines' Story from Stone Age to Space Age*, Seven Seas Books, Berlin, 1968, p. 142. See also Hall 1989, pp. 174–5.
35 Noah Riseman, *Defending Whose Country? Indigenous soldiers in the Pacific War*, University of Nebraska Press, Lincoln, 2012, p. 73.
36 William De Maria, 'White Welfare: Black Entitlement: the Social Security Access Controversy, 1939–59', *Aboriginal History*, vol. 10, 1986, pp. 25–39; Gray 2015, pp. 258–9.
37 Superintendent Milingimbi Mission to Acting Director, 5 March 1943, AA1978/215, NAA.
38 Robert Hall 1989, p. 174.
39 Martin Thomas, 'Unpacking the testimony of Gerald Blitner: Cross-cultural Brokerage and the Arnhem Land Expedition', in Martin Thomas and Margot Neale (eds), ANU Press, Canberra, 2011, pp. 385–6; cf. Irma Blitner and Anne Lange, interview, 12 August 2016.
40 Judith Elton, 'Comrades or Competition? Union Relations with Aboriginal workers in the South Australian and Northern Territory Pastoral Industries, 1878–1957', PhD thesis, University of South Australia, 2007, p. 152.
41 Gray 2015, pp. 192–4.
42 Saunders 1995, pp. 131–48.
43 Gamanbarr in *Thomson of Arhem Land*, 2001, directed by John Moore, Icarus Films <http://icarusfilms.com/if-thom>.
44 Tex and Nelly Camfoo, *Love Against the Law: The autobiographies of Tex and Nelly Camfoo*, Aboriginal Studies Press, Canberra, 2000, p. 40.
45 Marika 1995, pp. 66–70.
46 See also Jeremy Long, *The Go-Betweens*, 1992, pp. 40–3; Hall 1989, p. 121; Riseman 2012, pp. 58–9; and Jack Ellis and Lorraine Gardner, 'Cox Peninsula during World War II' <wagait.nt.gov.au/wp-content/uploads/2015/11/Cox-Peninsula-during-World-War-II-Compiled-by-Jack-Ellis-and-Lorraine-Gardner-as-part-of-the-Anzac-Centenary-Programe.pdf>.

47 'NT prepares to honour Indigenous people's efforts in the second world war', *The Guardian*, 14 October 2015 <www.theguardian.com/australia-news/2015/oct/14/nt-prepares-to-honour-indigenous-peoples-efforts-in-darwin-bombing>.

48 Beatrice Kerinaiua with Magdalen Kerinaiua, *Ngirramini ngini karri, Ngiyarringani Kapani, yimamani parlingarri (purraputimali) = Memories of my father, Louie Munkara told by Beatrice Kerinauia*, Nguiu Nginingawila Literature Production Centre, Nguiu, NT, 1986, pp. 1–34.

49 Marika 1995, pp. 65–7. See also Noah Riseman, 'Defending Whose Country? Yolngu and the Northern Territory Special Reconnaissance Unit in the Second World War', *Limina*, vol. 13, 2007, pp. 79–91.

50 Jenny Rich, 'Lampu Ngmeiua, Charlie One (1920–1974)', *Australian Dictionary of Biography* website, Australian National University <adb.anu.edu.au/biography/lampungmeiua-charlie-one-10782/text19121>.

51 For the creation of the NTSRU see Donald Thomson, 'Report of the Northern Territory Coastal Patrol and the Special Reconnaissance Unit 1941–1943', edited by John Mulvaney <press-files.anu.edu.au/downloads/press/p72311/pdf/article0110.pdf>. For the history of the NAOU, Richard and Helen Walker, *Curtin's Cowboys, Australia's Secret Bush Commandos*, Allen & Unwin, Sydney, 1988.

52 Australian Government, Department of Veterans Affairs, 'Indigenous service' <www.anzacportal.dva.gov.au/history/conflicts/australia-and-second-world-war/resources/all-australian-homefront-19391945-0>.

53 Monument Australia, 'Nackeroo Memorial' <monumentaustralia.org.au/themes/conflict/ww2/display/80257-nackeroo-memorial>.

54 Thomson to GS McIlroy, 7 December 1942, Stanner to McIlroy, 22 December 1942, A705, 68/1/700, NAA.

55 'Notes on meeting held at the office of I[nspector] G[eneral] of A[dministration] on 8/1/43 to discuss the above question [employment of Aboriginal Labour]', F1, 42/435, NAA. See also report 'Participation in the War Effort by Australian Aboriginals', by Captain FR Morris, Controller of Native Personnel, NT Force, 8 September 1945, MP742/1, 164/1/209, NAA; Report, Administration of Native Affairs Section – Care and Guidance of Native Races by Army, HQ NT Force, 23 April, 1945, by acting WOW Charles Duffy, F1, 42/435, NAA. Elkin was also consulted, as was the Papuan government anthropologist FE Williams, and EWP Chinnery, ex-government anthropologist in New Guinea and Commonwealth Advisor on Native Affairs and director of the Northern Territory Native Affairs Branch.

56 Gillian Cowlishaw, 'Helping Anthropologists', *Canberra Anthropology*, vol. 13, no. 2, 1990, pp. 1–28.

57 Geoffrey Gray 2015, pp. 197–239.

58 Peggy Brock, 'Pastoral stations and reserves in South and Central Australia, 1850s/1950s', *Labour History*, no. 69, 1995, p. 111.

59 'No. 2 Boss', *West Australian*, 14 November 1944, p. 3.

60 Marika 1995, pp. 65–7.

61 See Berndt and Berndt 1946, passim; also RM Berndt and CH Berndt, *Nigger on the Woodheap.* Unpublished manuscript, copy in possession of author.

62 Ronald M Berndt and Catherine H Berndt, *The World of the First Australians*, Aboriginal Studies Press, Canberra, 1988, pp. 510–11.

63 Lyn A Riddett, 'Kine, Kin and Country: The Victoria River District of the Northern Territory 1911–1966', PhD thesis, James Cook University, 1989. See also Ewan Morris, '"Like Bends in an Old Tree"? Aboriginal workers and white pastoralists on Victoria River Downs station, 1930–1965', BA Hons thesis, Australian National University, Canberra, 1990.
64 Quilty to Prime Minister, 10 February 1943, CRS F1 43/24, NAA.
65 Quilty 1943. See also Lyn A Riddett, 'Aboriginal Employment in the Pastoral Industry (N.T. 1930–1966)' in *Employment and Unemployment: A collection of papers*, Deborah Wade-Marshall and Peter Loveday (eds), North Australia Research Unit Monograph, ANU, Canberra, 1985, p. 205. See also Gordon Sweeney, 'Patrol of Stations in Timber Creek and Wave Hill Districts. September-October 1947'. Copy in AIATSIS, PMS 1794.
66 Ronald M Berndt and Catherine H Berndt, *The World of the First Australians: Aboriginal traditional life, past and present* (first edition), Ure Smith, Melbourne, 1965, p. 325.
67 Ronald M Berndt, 'The Concept of Protest within an Aboriginal Context' in *A Question of Choice: Australian Aboriginal dilemmas*, RM Berndt (ed.), University of Western Australian Press, Perth, 1971, p. 30.
68 Ronald M Berndt and Catherine H Berndt, *End of an Era: Aboriginal labour in the Northern Territory*, Australian Institute of Aboriginal Studies, Canberra, 1987, p. xi.
69 Ronald M Berndt and CH Berndt, *A Northern Territory Problem*, Mimeo, University of Sydney, 1948, p. 66; Peter Biskup, *Not Slaves, Not Citizens*, University of Western Australia Press, Perth, 1973, pp. 162ff; Don McLeod, *How the West Was Lost*, self-published, Port Hedland, 1984; Read and Coppin 1999, passim. See also Brian Willis, 'Restriction and Control of Aborigines in Western Australia during World War Two', *Westerly*, vol. 40, no. 4, 1995, pp. 86–96.
70 Bill Harney interviewed by Mel Pratt, 'Natives new era', *The Sydney Morning Herald*, 15 January 1944, p. 7.
71 *Annual Report of the Commissioner for Native Affairs*, Year end 30 June 1944. Government Printer, Perth, p. 1.

Chapter 9: The Second World War home front

1 Regina Ganter, *Mixed Relations: Asian-Aboriginal contact in North Australia*, University of Western Australia Press, Perth, 2006, pp. 216–17.
2 William Jack Scully, Second Australian Imperial Force Dossiers, 1939–1947, B883, DX945, NAA. See also Peter Forrest, 'The life and death of William Scully,' Territory Stories website <hdl.handle.net/10070/244398>.
3 Margaret Somerville, Peter Forrest and Sheila Forrest, *They Crossed a Continent: The story of a wartime exodus from Croker Island to Sydney*, 3rd edition, Shady Tree, Darwin, 2011, p. xiii.
4 Claire Henty-Gebert, *Paint Me Black: Memories of Croker Island and other journeys*, Aboriginal Studies Press, Canberra, 2005, p. 16.
5 Somerville, Forrest and Forrest 2011, p. xx.
6 Henty-Gebert 2005, pp. 17–21.
7 Somerville, Forrest and Forrest 2011, p. xxi.

8 Christine Choo, *Mission Girls: Aboriginal women on Catholic missions in the Kimberley, Western Australia, 1900–1950*, University of Western Australia Press, Perth, 2001, p. 252.
9 Boyd Scully, interview, 10 September 2015.
10 Gordon Briscoe, *Racial Folly: A twentieth-century Aboriginal family*, ANU Press, Canberra, 2010, pp. 19–21.
11 Jane Christophersen, interview, 16 August 2016.
12 Connie Nungulla McDonald and Jill Finnane, *When You Grow up*, Magabala Books, Broome, WA, 1996, p. 41.
13 Nungulla McDonald and Finnane 1996, pp. 36–37.
14 Elsie Roughsey, *An Aboriginal Mother Tells of the Old and the New*, Paul Memmott and Robyn Horsman (eds), McPhee Gribble, Melbourne, 1984, pp. 42, 49.
15 Choo 2001, p. 251.
16 George Derschow and Jan Cowan, interview, 4 September 2015.
17 Ganter 2006, p. 224.
18 Eugene Perez, *Kalumburu: The Benedictine Mission and the Aborigines, 1908–1975*, Kalumburu Benedictine Mission, Wyndham, WA, 1977, pp. 103–9; Choo 2001, pp. 265–73.
19 Eugene Perez, *Kalumburu War Diary*, Rosemary Pratt and John Millington (eds), Artlook Books, Perth, 1981, pp. 129–30.
20 Perez 1981, p. 131.
21 Western Australia, 'Annual Report of the Commissioner of Native Affairs for the Year Ended 30th June, 1944', pp. 5–6, 'To Remove and Protect', AIATSIS online database <aiatsis.gov.au/collections/collections-online/digitised-collections/remove-and-protect>.
22 Noah Riseman, *Defending Whose Country?: Indigenous soldiers in the Pacific War*, University of Nebraska Press, Lincoln, NE, 2012, pp. 71, 88.
23 Alyssa Bates, 'Remembering the bombing of Milingimbi', ABC News Online <www.abc.net.au/news/2016-05-31/milingimbi-wwii-history-indigenous-nt-community-bombed-japanese/7465020>.
24 Irma Blitner and Annie Lange, interview, 16 August 2016.
25 Elizabeth Osborne, *Torres Strait Islander Women and the Pacific War*, Aboriginal Studies Press, Canberra, 1997, pp. 35–7.
26 Elizabeth Osborne, 'Torres Strait Islander Women: An Interpretation of Some Recollections on Their Experiences during the Pacific War, 1942–1945', *Northern Perspective*, 18, no. 2, 1995, p. 32.
27 Thursday Island State High School, *Torres Strait at War: A recollection of wartime experiences*, Thursday Island State High School, Thursday Island, 1988, pp. 36–7.
28 Elizabeth Osborne 1997.
29 Rosie Ware, interview, 10 April 2014.
30 Doris Pilkington, *Under the Wintamarra Tree*, University of Queensland Press, Brisbane, 2002, p. 42.
31 Furley Gardner, quoted in Stuart Rintoul, *The Wailing: A national black oral history*, William Heinemann Australia, Melbourne, 1993, p. 215.
32 Anna Haebich, *Broken Circles: Fragmenting Indigenous families 1800–2000*, Fremantle Arts Centre Press, Perth, 2000, p. 20.

33 HE Thonemann, *Tell the White Man: The life story of an Aboriginal lubra*, Collins, London and Sydney, 1949, p. 144.
34 Frederick Rose, *The Wind of Change in Central Australia: The Aborigines at Angas Downs, 1962*, Akademie-Verlag, Berlin, 1965, pp. 24–5.
35 *Courier-Mail* (Brisbane), 8 October 1942, p. 4.
36 Sally Hodson, 'Making a Rural Labour Force: The Intervention of the State in the Working Lives of Nyungars in the Great Southern, 1936–1948', *Studies in Western Australian History*, vol. 14, 1993, pp. 33–4.
37 Richard Broome, *Aboriginal Victorians: A history since 1800*, Allen & Unwin, Sydney, 2005, p. 232.
38 Fiona Davis, *Australian Settler Colonialism and the Cummeragunja Aboriginal Station: Redrawing boundaries*, First Nations and the Colonial Encounter, Sussex Academic Press, Eastbourne, UK, 2014, p. 135.
39 Peggy Brock, *Outback Ghettos: Aborigines, institutionalisation and survival*, Cambridge University Press, Cambrige, UK, 1993, pp. 104–5.
40 South Australia, 'Report of the Aborigines Protection Board, 1943', p.1, AIATSIS.
41 South Australia, 'Report of the Aborigines Protection Board, 1944', p.1, AIATSIS.
42 *Courier-Mail* (Brisbane), 8 June 1944, p. 3.
43 Alick Jackomos and Derek Fowell, *Forgotten Heroes: Aborigines at war, from the Somme to Vietnam*, Victoria Press, Melbourne, 1993, p. 43.
44 Jackamos and Fowell 1993, p. 37.
45 EM Fisher, 'Elphick, Gladys (1904–1988)', *Australian Dictionary of Biography* website <adb.anu.edu.au/biography/elphick-gladys-12460>.
46 Dot Collard and Beryl Hackner, *Busted out Laughing: Dot Collard's story / as told to Beryl Hackner*, Magabala Books, Broome, WA, 2003, p. 43.
47 *Telegraph* (Brisbane), 22 June 1940, p. 20.
48 Jan (Kabarli) James, *Forever Warriors*, J. James, Northam, WA, 2010, pp. 154, 284, 287.
49 David Huggonson, 'Our Women and the War Effort', *Koori Mail*, 12 July 1995, p. 21.
50 Sue Hardisty (ed.), *Thanks Girls and Goodbye!: The story of the Australian Women's Land Army 1942–45*, Viking O'Neil, Melbourne, 1990, p. 151.
51 Hardisty 1990, pp. 12, 34–5.
52 Mabel Edmund, *No Regrets*, UQP Black Australian Writers, University of Queensland Press, Brisbane, 1992, p. 9.
53 Gladys Waters, unpublished memoir, privately held; see also Samuel Furphy, 'Waters, Leonard Victor (1924–1993)', *Australian Dictionary of Biography*, forthcoming.
54 See Eli Daniel Potts and Annette Potts, *Yanks Down Under, 1941–45: The American impact on Australia*, Oxford University Press, Melbourne, 1985.
55 Alice Nannup, *When the Pelican Laughed*, Lauren Marsh and Stephen Kinnane (eds), Fremantle Arts Centre Press, Perth, 1992, p. 177.
56 Kate Darian-Smith, *On the Home Front: Melbourne in wartime: 1939–1945*, 2nd edition, Melbourne University Press, Melbourne, 2009, p. 216.
57 Darian-Smith 2009, p. 190.
58 Stephen Kinnane, *Shadow Lines*, Fremantle Arts Centre Press, Perth, 2003, pp. 310–11.

59 Len Watson, quoted in Potts and Potts 1985, p. 404.
60 Western Australia, 'Annual Report of the Commissioner of Native Affairs 1943–44', p. 6, AIATSIS.
61 Western Australia, 'Annual Report of the Commissioner of Native Affairs, 1944–45', p. 15, AIATSIS; see also 'Woman Imprisoned', *The West Australian*, 24 August 1944, p. 3.
62 FI Bray, Commissioner of Native Affairs, to Lieut. Col. Gibson, 16 June 1942, ACC 993 919/42, SROWA.
63 Kay Saunders, *War on the Homefront: State intervention in Queensland 1938–1948*, University of Queensland Press, Brisbane, 1993, pp. 77–9.
64 Potts and Potts 1985, p. 368.
65 Victoria Grieves, 'Children born of war: a neglected legacy of troops among civilians', *The Conversation*, 12 August 2014 <theconversation.com/children-born-of-war-a-neglected-legacy-of-troops-among-civilians-29845>; see also Karen Hughes, 'Mobilising Across Colour Lines: Intimate encounters between Aboriginal women and African American and other allied servicemen on the World War II home front', *Aboriginal History*, vol. 40, 2017, pp. 41–73.
66 Queensland, 'Report of the Director of Native Affairs 1943', p. 2, AIATSIS.
67 *Northern Star* (Lismore, NSW), 20 August 1942, p. 4.
68 Davis 2014, p. 135; see also 'Aboriginal Concert', *Riverine Herald* (Echuca, Vic.), 19 September 1945, p. 1.
69 Davis 2014, p. 117.
70 Davis 2014, p. 125.
71 Jack Horner, 'Patten, John Thomas (Jack) (1905–1957)', *Australian Dictionary of Biography* website <adb.anu.edu.au/biography/patten-john-thomas-jack-7980>.
72 Jackomos and Fowell 1993, p. 47.
73 Jackomos and Fowell 1993, p. 35.
74 Kathryn Jarrett, interview, 4 April 2014.
75 June Rose, interview, 11 March 2014.
76 Margaret Tucker, *If Everyone Cared*, quoted in Jackomos and Fowell 1993, p. 37.
77 Haebich 2000, p. 288; citing Darryl Kickett personal communication (1999).
78 Cecil Bowden, interview, 21 March 2014; see also Anna Haebich and Doreen Mellor (eds), *Many Voices: Reflections on experiences of Indigenous child separation*, National Library of Australia, Canberra, 2002, pp. 52–3; *Koori Mail*, 9 May 2007, p. 36.
79 Robert Hall, 'Hughes, Timothy (1919–1976)', *Australian Dictionary of Biography* website <adb.anu.edu.au/biography/hughes-timothy-10567>; see also 'The land looks good to Tim', *Mail* (Adelaide), 30 October 1954, p. 5.
80 Rintoul 1993, p. 325.
81 Lester Coyne, interview, 31 August 2015; see also Vernice Gillies, interview, 1 September 2015.
82 Eliza Woods and Aden Eades, interview, 1 September 2015; see also 'Frederick Eades,' B883, WX34262, NAA.
83 *Portland Guardian*, 17 July 1944, p. 2.
84 *Portland Guardian*, 20 October 1949, p. 3.
85 Lachlan Grant, 'The Fighting Gunditjmara', *Wartime: Official magazine of the Australian War Memorial*, October 2016, p. 24.

86 John Lovett, interview, 6 March 2015; see also Margaret Burin, 'Equal on frontline, rejected on return: battle for an Aboriginal veteran's justice', ABC News Online, 29 May 2012, <www.abc.net.au/local/stories/2012/05/29/3513177.htm>.

Chapter 10: Opening the military door, 1945–65

1 Human Rights and Equal Opportunity Commission Australia, National Inquiry into the Separation of Aboriginal and Torres Strait Islander Children from Their Families, *Bringing Them Home: Report of the national inquiry into the separation of Aboriginal and Torres Strait Islander children from their families*, Human Rights and Equal Opportunity Commission, Sydney, 1997, p. 34.

2 See Robin Gerster, *Travels in Atomic Sunshine: Australia and the Occupation of Japan*, Scribe Publications, Melbourne, 2008.

3 Quoted in Cameron Forbes, *The Korean War: Australia in the giants' playground*, Macmillan, Sydney, 2010, pp. 285–6.

4 Gladys Waters, interview, 8 July 2014; Robert Hall, *Fighters from the Fringe: Aborigines and Torres Strait Islanders recall the Second World War*, Aboriginal Studies Press, Canberra, 1995, p. 170; Donald Edward Waters, B883, QX51818, NAA.

5 See AWM 146170; AWM F07526, 'BCOF on Parade in Japan'.

6 'Kenneth Colbung', *Message Stick*, produced and directed by Kelrick Martin, produced by the Australian Broadcasting Corporation (ABC), 2004. See also Private Kenneth Colbung, Royal Australian Infantry Corps, interviewed by Bill Bunbury for ABC Radio National *Hindsight* for program 'Korea, 1950–1953, The Forgotten War', AWM S01906.

7 Charles Mene, in Hall 1995, p. 101.

8 'Protest', *Examiner* (Launceston), 28 March 1946, p. 1.

9 'Aboriginal officer hits at Army ban', *The Daily News* (Perth), 26 March 1946, p. 6.

10 See 'Action by RSL', *National Advocate* (Bathurst, NSW), 13 March 1945, p. 3.

11 'R.S.L. Suggests Aboriginal Unit', *The Age* (Melbourne), 10 November 1951, p. 2; 'Aboriginal Battalion Suggested', *Queensland Times* (Ipswich), 5 November 1951, p. 1; 'Aboriginal battalion suggested', *The Advertiser* (Adelaide), 5 November 1951, p. 2.

12 Australian Military Forces Minute Paper, 'Enlistment of Aborigine in ARA', signed Director of Personnel Administration, 20 May 1949, MP742/1, 275/1/696, NAA.

13 MP742/1, 275/1/696, NAA.

14 See A816, 72/301/23, NAA.

15 A4949, C2391, NAA.

16 A816, 72/301/23, NAA. For more on National Service in the 1950s, see Pam Maclean, 'An Almost Universal Scheme of National Service in Australia in the 1950s', *Australian Journal of Politics & History*, vol. 52, no. 3, 2006, pp. 378–97.

17 Noel Loos and Koiki Mabo, *Eddie Koiki Mabo: His life and struggle for land rights*, University of Queensland Press, Brisbane, 1996, p. 83.

18 Noel Tovey, *Little Black Bastard: A story of survival*, Hachette Australia, Sydney, 2004, p. 144.

19 Tovey 2004, p. 147.

20 Jeffrey Grey, *A Military History of Australia*, Cambridge University Press, Cambridge, UK, 1990, pp. 193–5.

21 See Peter Dennis and Jeffrey Grey, *Emergency and Confrontation: Australian military operations, Malaya and Borneo, 1950–1966*, Allen & Unwin in association with the Australian War Memorial, Sydney, 1996.

22 Grace Vogler, 'Cecil Charles Anderson', The Premier's Anzac Prize 2015 <education.qld.gov.au/students/grants/.../anzac/.../28-april-cecil-charles-anderson.docx>.

23 Charles Mene, in Hall 1995, pp. 106–7.

24 For the Korean War generally see Robert O'Neill, *Australia in the Korean War 1950–1953, Volume 1, Strategy and Diplomacy*, Australian War Memorial and the Australian Government Publishing Service, Canberra, 1981; *Volume 2, Combat Operations*, Australian War Memorial and the Australian Government Publishing Service, Canberra, 1985; Richard Trembath, *A Different Sort of War: Australians in Korea 1950–53*, Australian Scholarly Publishing, Melbourne, 2005.

25 Private Cedric 'Ned' Egglestone and Don McLeod, Royal Australian Infantry Corps, interviewed by Bill Bunbury, 3 September 1998, RSL Reservoir, interviewed for ABC Radio National *Hindsight* for program 'Korea, 1950–1953, The Forgotten War', AWM S01907.

26 Pat Owen, in Alick Jackomos and Derek Fowell, *Forgotten Heroes: Aborigines at war from the Somme to Vietnam*, Victoria Press, Melbourne, 1991, p. 73.

27 Len Ogilvie, interview, 31 August 2015. See also Leonard Ogilvie, interviewed by John Bannister, 10 February 2004, 26869, IWM, London; Leonard Ogilvie, interviewed by John Bannister, 25 May 2001, *Bringing Them Home Oral History Project*, TRC 5000/274, NLA.

28 Private Cedric 'Ned' Egglestone and Don McLeod, AWM S01907.

29 Pat Owen, in Jackomos and Fowell 1991, p. 73.

30 Ken Colbung, 'The Spirit Has More Strength', in *Speaking from the Heart*, Sally Morgan (ed.), Fremantle Press, Perth, 2007, p. 74.

31 Private Kenneth Colbung, Royal Australian Infantry Corps, interviewed by Bill Bunbury for ABC Radio National *Hindsight* for program 'Korea, 1950–1953, The Forgotten War', S01906, AWM. See also Ken Colbung, interview with Kerrie Jean Ross, *Awaye!*, ABC Radio National, 27 August 2007 <www.nma.gov.au/exhibitions/first_australians/resistance/yagan/awaye_audio_program_transcript>.

32 Glenda Humes, interview, 16 July 2014.

33 Private Cedric 'Ned' Egglestone and Don McLeod, AWM S01907.

34 Glenda Humes 2014.

35 Quoted in Noah Riseman and Richard Trembath, *Defending Country: Aboriginal and Torres Strait Islander military service since 1945*, University of Queensland Press, Brisbane, 2016, p. 46.

36 Noah Riseman, 'Aboriginal military service and assimilation', *Aboriginal History*, vol. 38, 2014, pp. 163–8; Riseman and Trembath 2016, pp. 28–30.

37 Colbung 2007, p. 75.

38 Riseman and Trembath 2016, pp. 93–120; Noah Riseman, 'Escaping Assimilation's Grasp: Aboriginal women in the Australian women's military services', *Women's History Review*, vol. 24, no. 5, 2015, pp. 757–75.

39 Mabel Quakawoot, interview, 5 June 2011.

40 Doris Follent, aka Sue Bellear, interview, 22 April 2015.

41 Thelma Weston, Workshop: Women and Services – Defending Country Conference, 2 December 2014, ANU, Canberra.
42 'Your Career – Women's Services', *Dawn*, 16, no. 8, August 1967, p. 12.
43 Len Ogilvie, interview, 31 August 2015. See also Leonard Ogilvie, TRC 5000/274, NLA.
44 Sue Gordon, interview, September 2015. See also Sue Gordon, interview with Noah Riseman, 25 November 2010, TRC 6260/5, NLA.
45 David Cook, interview, 20 January 2010. See also Noah Riseman, *In Defence of Country: Life stories of Aboriginal and Torres Strait Islander servicemen and women*, ANU Press, Canberra, 2016, p. 37.
46 David Cook welfare file, courtesy of David Cook.
47 David Cook service record, service number 214933, Central Army Records Office, courtesy of NAA.
48 See Noah Riseman, 'The stolen veteran: institutionalisation, military service, and the Stolen Generations', *Aboriginal History*, vol. 35, 2011, pp. 57–77.
49 Geoff Shaw, interview, 17 September 2015.
50 Reuben Chadburn, interview, 23 April 2015.
51 David Cook, interview, 20 January 2010.
52 Mial Bingarape, interview, 8 April 2014; Mial Bingarape, interview, 7 November 2011.
53 Mial Bingarape, interview, 8 April 2014.

Chapter 11: The Vietnam War

1 For histories of Australia's Vietnam War see Peter Edward, *Australia and the Vietnam War*, NewSouth Publishing, Sydney, 2014; John Murphy, *Harvest of Fear: A history of Australia's Vietnam War*, Allen & Unwin, Sydney, 1993; Paul Ham, *Vietnam: The Australian war*, HarperCollins, Sydney, 2007.
2 See Alistair Thomson, *Anzac Memories: Living with the legend*, 2nd ed., Monash University Publishing, Melbourne, 2013; 'Anzac Stories: Using Personal Testimony in War History', *War & Society*, vol. 25, no. 2, 2006, pp. 1–21.
3 Noah Riseman, 'The Stolen Veteran: Institutionalisation, Military Service and the Stolen Generations', *Aboriginal History*, vol. 35, 2011, pp. 57–77.
4 See Rosalind Kidd, *Trustees on Trial: Recovering the stolen wages*, Aboriginal Studies Press, Canberra, 2006; Andrew Gunstone, *The Government Owes a Lot of Money to Our People: A history of Indigenous stolen wages in Victoria*, Australian Scholarly Publishing, Melbourne, 2009.
5 Frank Mallard, interview, 31 August 2015. See also Frank Mallard, interview with Noah Riseman, 24 November 2010, Perth, ORAL TRC 6260/2, NLA.
6 Claude Malone, interview, 8 July 2014.
7 Fenton D'Antoine, interview, 11 September 2015.
8 Phillip Prosser, interview with John Bannister, 22 January 2000, Perth, 'Bringing Them Home Oral History Project', TRC 5000/183, NLA. See also Phil Prosser, 'Show Respect', in *Speaking from the Heart*, Sally Morgan (ed.), Fremantle Press, Perth, 2007, p. 139.
9 Edna Coolburra, interview, 14 April 2014.
10 *National Service Act 1964*, section 18(e).

11 *National Service Act Regulations*, 1964, section 18.
12 Des Mayo, interview, 10 September 2015.
13 David Nean, interview, 24 October 2014.
14 Les Kropinyeri, interview, 11 April 2015.
15 Alec Illin, interview, 15 April 2014.
16 George Anderson, interview, 1 April 2014.
17 Geoff Shaw, interview, 18 September 2015.
18 See Noah Riseman, '"Describing misbehaviour in Vung Tau as 'mischief' is ridiculously coy": Ethnographic Refusal, Reticence and the Oral Historian's Dilemma', *Oral History Review*, vol. 45, 2018 (forthcoming).
19 Vic Simon, interview with Fabri Blacklock, City of Sydney Oral History Program, 25 November 2013.
20 Thomas 'Buddy' Lea interview, *SpeakingOut*, ABC Online.
21 Des Mayo, 10 September 2015.
22 Roy Mundine, interview, 21 March 2014.
23 Tom Holm, *Strong Hearts, Wounded Souls: Native American Veterans of the Vietnam War*, University of Texas Press, Austin, 1996.
24 David Nean, interview, 24 October 2014.
25 Edna Coolburra 2014.
26 Clarence Williams, interview, 23 April 2015.
27 Rob Bryant, interview with Fabri Blacklock, City of Sydney Oral History Program, 27 December 2013.
28 Glenn James, interview with Ina Bertrand, Melbourne, Victorians at War – Oral History Project, 23 January 2001.
29 Geoff Shaw 2015.
30 George Anderson 2014.
31 Edna Coolburra 2014. See also Sandy MacGregor, as told to Jimmy Thomson, *No Need for Heroes*, CALM Pty Limited, Sydney, 1993, pp. 89–90.
32 George Bostock, interview with Noah Riseman, 18 June 2010, Brisbane.
33 Claude Malone 2014.
34 See James E Westheider, *The African American Experience in Vietnam: Brothers in arms*, Rowman and Littlefield, Lanham, MD, 2008; James E Westheider, *Fighting on Two Fronts: African Americans and the Vietnam War*, New York University Press, New York, 1997.
35 Frank Mallard, ORAL TRC 6260/2 NLA.
36 Edna Coolburra 2014. See also MacGregor 1993, pp. 89–90.
37 See Ham 2007, pp. 278–88; Mark Dapin, *The Nashos' War: Australian National Servicemen and Vietnam*, Viking, Melbourne, 2014, pp. 199–205.
38 Frank Mallard 2015.
39 Des Mayo, 10 September 2015.
40 David Nean 2014. See also John Kinsela, interview, 4 May 2017.
41 See Brendan O'Keefe, *Medicine at War: Medical aspects of Australia's involvement in Southeast Asia 1950–1972*, Allen & Unwin in association with the Australian War Memorial, Sydney, 1994; David Bradford, *The Gunners' Doctor: Vietnam Letters*, Random House Australia, Sydney, 2007.

42 Bobby Baker, in Kevin Cook and Heather Goodall, *Making Change Happen: Black and white activists talk to Kevin Cook about Aboriginal, union and liberation politics*, ANU E Press, Canberra, 2013, p. 33.

43 Patricia O'Shane, in Stuart Rintoul, *The Wailing: A national Black oral history*, William Heinemann, Melbourne, 1993, p. 46.

44 Margaret Culbong, interview, 1 September 2015.

45 See Gary Foley, 'Black Power in Redfern 1968–1972', The Koori History Website, <www.kooriweb.org/foley/essays/essay_1.html>; Ann Turner (ed.), *Black Power in Australia: Bobby Sykes versus Neville Bonner*, Heinemann Educational Australia, Melbourne, 1975; Kathy Lothian, 'Seizing the Time: Australian Aborigines and the Influence of the Black Panther Party, 1969–1972', *Journal of Black Studies*, vol. 35, no. 4, March 2005, pp. 179–200; Kathy Lothian, 'Moving Blackwards: Black Power and the Aboriginal Embassy' in *Transgressions: Critical Australian Indigenous histories*, Ingereth Macfarlane and Mark Hannah (eds), ANU E Press, Canberra, 2007, pp. 19–34; Kathleen Lothian, '"A blackward step is a forward step": Australian Aborigines and Black Power, 1969–1972', Master's thesis, Monash University, 2002.

46 'At the Court of Petty Sessions Held at Albany Before H.J. Ryan, Esq., S.M. This 22nd Day of November, 1971; Date of Decision: 13th December, 1971, Between: Nigel Frederick Spitz, Commonwealth Police, Complainant, and Mervyn Eades, Defendant', A2354, 1968/1, NAA.

47 For more on the Eades case, see Noah Riseman, 'The Curious Case of Mervyn Eades: National Service, Discrimination and Aboriginal People', *Australian Journal of Politics & History*, vol. 59, no. 1, 2013, pp. 64–80.

48 James Tang Wei, interview, 7 September 2015.

49 David Nean 2014.

50 George Anderson 2014.

51 Ray Minniecon, interview, 20 March 2014. Joseph Minniecon did two tours in Vietnam: 6/1965–6/1966 and 12/1967–12/1968, but according to the nominal roll it was within four units.

52 Chris Dixon, 'Redeeming the Warrior: Myth-Making and Australia's Vietnam Veterans', *Australian Journal of Politics and History*, vol. 60, no. 2, 2014, pp. 214–28; Ann Curthoys, 'Vietnam: Public Memory of an anti war movement' in *Memory and History in 20th-century Australia*, Kate Darian-Smith and Paula Hamilton (eds), Oxford University Press, Oxford, 1994, pp. 113–34.

53 Ray Orchard, in Rintoul 1993, p. 306. See also Alec Illin, 2014.

54 Dapin 2014, pp. 338–40.

55 Alistair Thomson, 'Anzac Stories: Using Personal Testimony in War History', *War & Society*, vol. 25, no. 2, 2006, pp. 1–21; Alistair Thomson, 'Anzac Memories Revisited: Trauma, Memory and Oral History', *Oral History Review*, vol. 42, no. 1, 2015, pp. 1–29.

56 Geoff Shaw 2015.

57 Eric Law, interview, 4 July 2014.

58 Edna Coolburra 2014.

59 Dave Cook, interview, 20 January 2010; see also Noah Riseman, *In Defence of Country: Life stories of Aboriginal and Torres Strait Islander servicemen and women*, ANU Press, Canberra, 2016, p. 53.

60 Des Mayo, interview, 4 December 2014.
61 James Tang Wei 2015.
62 Prosser, 146.
63 James Tang Wei 2015.
64 Des Mayo, 10 September 2015.
65 Dave Cook 2010; Riseman 2016, p. 43.
66 Robyn Kropinyeri, interview, 11 April 2015.
67 FB Smith, 'Agent Orange: The Australian Aftermath' in *Medicine at War*, pp. 281–363.
68 Commonwealth Department of Veterans' Affairs, 'Morbidity of Vietnam Veterans: A study of the health of Australia's Vietnam veteran community', Commonwealth Department of Veterans' Affairs, Canberra, 1998.
69 Victor Slockee, interview, 24 April 2015.
70 Des Mayo, 10 September 2015.
71 Michael Markham, interview, 14 September 2015.
72 Robyn Kropinyeri 2015.
73 Geoff Shaw 2015.
74 Laurel Williams, interview, 11 March 2014.
75 Claude Malone 2014. See also Eric Law, interview, 4 July 2014.
76 James Tang Wei 2015.
77 Les Kropinyeri, interview, 11 April 2015.
78 Patrick Mills, interview, 9 April 2014.
79 'Army's first Indigenous Elder', Australian Army website <www.army.gov.au/Our-people/Army-Indigenous-community/Armys-first-Indigenous-Elder>. See also Roy Mundine, interview, 21 March 2014; Thomas 'Buddy' Lea, *SpeakingOut* interview, ABC Online; Frank Mallard 2015; Frank Mallard, ORAL TRC 6260/2, NLA.
80 George Bostock, interview with Noah Riseman, 18 June 2010, Brisbane; Bob Blair, interview, 22 June 2010; Graham Atkinson, in Jackomos and Fowell, *Forgotten Heroes: Aborigines at war from the Somme to Vietnam*, Victoria Press, Melbourne, 1991, p. 72; Graham Atkinson, BOSTOCK_G01-016549, AIATSIS; Michael Markham 2015; John Kinsela, interview with Fabri Blacklock, City of Sydney Oral History Program, 14 November 2013; Glenn James, in Jackomos & Fowell 1991, p. 69; Glenn James, interview with Ina Bertrand, Melbourne, Victorians at War – Oral History Project, 23 January 2001; Geoff Shaw, interview, 18 September 2015; Geoff Shaw in *I Hope the War Will Be Over Soon*, directed by John Ruane, produced by Juniper Films, 1988.
81 Ray Minniecon, interview, 20 March 2014.
82 Edna Coolburra 2014. See also Charles Wooley, 'Blood brothers: kidney donation', *60 Minutes*, Channel Nine, produced by Stephen Taylor, 19 August 2001.
83 Roy Mundine 2014.
84 Des Mayo 2014.

Chapter 12: Servicewomen

1 Noah Riseman, 'Escaping Assimilation's Grasp: Aboriginal women in the Australian women's military services', *Women's History Review*, vol. 24, issue 5, 2014, pp. 757–75.

2 Noah Riseman and Richard Trembath, *Defending Country: Aboriginal and Torres Strait Islander military service since 1945*, UQP, Brisbane, 2016, chapter 4, pp. 93–120. See Sarah Tomkins, 'An assessment of the effect of government and military policies on the ability of Indigenous Australians to enlist in Armed Forces since Federation', Australian War Memorial Internships, unpublished report, 2014.

3 Karen Hughes, 'Mobilising Across Colour Lines: Intimate encounters between Aboriginal women and African-American and other allied servicemen on the World War II home front', *Aboriginal History*, vol. 41, Dec 2017, pp. 57–8.

4 Kimberlé Crenshaw, 'Mapping the Margins: Intersectionality, identity politics, and violence against women of color', *Stanford Law Review*, vol. 43, no. 6, 1991, p. 1243; Crenshaw, *On Intersectionality: Essential writings of Kimberlé Crenshaw*, The New Press, New York, 2012; Patricia Hill Collins, *Black Feminist Thought: Knowledge, consciousness and the politics of empowerment*, Unwin Hyman, Boston, 1990.

5 Riseman, 2014; Grace Poulin, *Invisible Women: WWII Aboriginal servicewomen in Canada*, DG Poulin, Thunder Bay, 2007.

6 Larissa Behrendt, 'Women's Work: The inclusion of the voice of Aboriginal women', *Legal Education Review*, no. 169, 1995 <www.austlii.edu.au/au/journals/LegEdRev/1995/9.html>.

7 Jan Bassett, '"Ready to serve": Australian Women and the Great War', *Journal of the Australian War Memorial*, vol. 2, 1983, pp. 8–16.

8 Philippa Scarlett, 'An Indigenous Nurse in WW1: Marion Leane Smith', Indigenous Histories website <indigenoushistories.com/2013/10/30/an-indigenous-nurse-in-world-war-one-marion-leane-smith-smith/>.

9 See Janette Bomford, *Soldiers of the Queen: Women in the Australian Army*, Oxford University Press, Melbourne, 2001, pp. 1–2. Other key works on women in the defence forces include Lorna Ollif, *Women in Khaki*, Ollif Publishing Company, Sydney, 1981; Patsy Adam-Smith, *Australian Women at War*, 2nd edition, Penguin, Melbourne, 1996; Jan Bassett, *Guns and Brooches: Australian Army nursing from the Boer War to the Gulf War*, Oxford University Press, Melbourne, 1992; Joyce Thomson, *The WAAAF in Wartime Australia*, Melbourne University Press, Melbourne, 1991; Clare Stevenson and Honor Darling (eds), *The WAAAF Book*, Hale & Iremonger, Sydney, 1984; Ann Howard, *You'll Be Sorry!*, Tarka, Sydney, 1990; Shirley Fenton-Huie, *Ships Belles: The story of the Women's Royal Australian Naval Service in War and Peace, 1941–1985*, Watermark Press, Sydney, 2000; Margaret Curtis-Otter, *WRANS*, Naval History Society of Australia, Sydney, 1976.

10 Jan James, *Forever Warriors*, J. James, Perth, 2010, p. 249; Margaret Phyllis Mills, Service Cards for Petty Officers and Men, 1911–1970, A6770, MILLS MP, NAA.

11 Rosina Parfitt, B884, WF97218, NAA; Linda Lester, RAAF Personnel Files of NCO and other ranks, 1921–1948, A9301, 174865, NAA; Alick Jackomos and Derek Fowell, *Forgotten Heroes: Aborigines at war from the Somme to Vietnam*, Victoria Press, Melbourne, 1993, p. 34.

12 Alana Garwood, interview, 16 December 2015.

13 Florence Madge Stewart, Citizen Military Forces Personnel Dossiers, 1939–1947, B884, VF397904, NAA.

14 Helen Annie McDonald, B884 VF513768, NAA.
15 Bomford, 2001; Ruth Ford, 'Lesbians and loose women: female sexuality and the women's services during WW2' in Joy Damousi and Marilyn Lake (eds), *Gender and War: Australians at war in the twentieth century*, Cambridge University Press, Melbourne, 1995, pp. 81–104.
16 Betty Ellen Ray, A9301, 111812, NAA; Dorothy Pearl Nicholls, B884, NF463648, NAA.
17 Winifred Emma Iselin, B884, QF143254, NAA; Robert Hall, *Fighters from the Fringe: Aborigines and Torres Strait Islanders recall the Second World War*, Aboriginal Studies Press, Canberra, 1995, p. 121.
18 Ivy Edith Myrtle Bell, A9301, 94524, NAA.
19 Pat Kopusar, interview, 4 September 2015; Ella May Thompson B884, WF41865, NAA.
20 Betty Pike, interview, 12 April 2011.
21 Pike 2011.
22 Hall 1995, p. 121.
23 Jim Fletcher, *Clean Clad and Courteous*, J Fletcher, Sydney, 1989.
24 Hall 1995, p. 130.
25 Kathleen Jean Mary Walker, B884, QF267190, NAA.
26 Kathie Cochrane, *Oodgeroo*, University Queensland Press, Brisbane, 1994, pp. 10–13; *Tribune*, 19 July 1945, p. 4.
27 Roberta Sykes (ed.), *Murawina: Aboriginal women of high achievement*, Double Day, Sydney, 1993, p. 151.
28 Alice Lovett, A9301, 95994, NAA.
29 Jackomos and Fowell 1993, p. 39.
30 Her other friends working in munitions were: Mary King, Eileen Watson and Connie Alberts.
31 Jackomos and Fowell 1993, p. 41.
32 Jackomos and Fowell 1993, p. 40.
33 Jean Elizabeth Stewart, A9301, 174955, NAA.
34 Jean Williamson, interview, 11 March 2015.
35 Elizabeth Pike, *Power of Story: Spirit of the Dreaming*, John Garratt, Melbourne, 2011, pp. 4–6.
36 Hughes 2017.
37 *The Dawn*, vol. 13, no. 6, 1964, p. 13; vol. 15, no. 10, 1966, p. 6. See also, *The Dawn*, vol. 13, no. 4, 1964, p. 1.
38 Pattie Lees, Presentation, Defending Country Conference, ANU, Canberra, 2 December 2014.
39 Tracey Hoffman, interview, 1 April 2014.
40 Gwendolyn Etter-Lewis, 'Black Women's Life Stories: Reclaiming self in narrative texts' in Sherna Berger Gluck and Daphne Patai (eds), *Women's Words: The feminist practice of oral history*, Routledge, New York, 1991, p. 48; Sherry Thomas 'Digging beneath the surface: oral history techniques', *Women's Oral History: A frontier reader*, Susan Armitage with Patricia Hart and Karen Weathermon (eds), Frontiers & University of Nebraska Press, Lincoln, 2002, pp. 53–5, 59.

41 Kathleen Ryan, '"I Didn't Do Anything Important": A pragmatist analysis of the oral history interview', *The Oral History Review*, vol. 36, no. 1, 2009, pp. 25–44. See also Juliette Pattinson, '"The thing that made me hesitate": re-examining gendered intersubjectivities in interviews with British secret war veterans', *Women's History Review*, vol. 20, no. 2, 2011, pp. 251–2.
42 Marjorie Tripp, interview, 14 April 2015.
43 Tripp in *For Love of Country*, directed by Malcolm McKinnon, produced by Reconciliation South Australia, 2011.
44 Gaye Doolan, interview, 6 August 2014; ANU Inspiring Women, ANU Gender Institute, Canberra, 2013 <genderinstitute.anu.edu.au/quiet-defiance>.
45 Anna Haebich, *Broken Circles: Fragmenting Indigenous families 1800–2000*, Fremantle Arts Centre Press, Perth, 2000.
46 Pattie Lees, interview, 2 December 2014; Pattie Lees, interviewed by Colleen Hattersley, 13 June 2001, Brisbane, 2663460, NLA; 'Responses to the apology' [sound recording], State Library of Queensland, 2009 <www.youtube.com/watch?v=Anl5mX3BTVk>.
47 Sue Gordon, interview, 2 September 2015; Sue Giller, Army Personnel Files, B2458, F58056, NAA.
48 Sue Gordon, Workshop on Gender in the Services, Defending Country Conference, ANU, Canberra, 2 Dec 2014. See also Noah Riseman, *In Defence of Country: Life stories of Aboriginal and Torres Strait Islander servicemen and women*, ANU Press, Canberra, 2016; Gordon interviewed by Noah Riseman, 25 November 2010, Perth, 5018270, NLA; Riseman and Trembath, 2016, pp. 104–8.
49 Gordon 2015; Lees 2001.
50 Thelma Weston, interview, 16 December 2016.
51 Weston 2016.
52 Eileen McHughes interviewed by Bill Marsh, One River, Goolwa, 2013 <pandora.nla.gov.au/pan/136770/20140212-0000/oneriver.com.au/same-as-the-river/index.html>. See also Dianne Bell, *Listen to Ngarrindjeri Women Speaking: Kungun Ngarrindjeri Miminar Yunnan*, Spinifex Press, Melbourne, 2008, p. 62.
53 Linda Albert, interview, 15 April 2014. Linda Janetzki requested use of her maiden name, Albert, to recognise the connection with the Albert family service history.
54 Albert 2014.
55 Tripp 2015.
56 Bronwyn Fredericks, comments, Serving Our Country panel, NAISA, University of Honolulu, 21 May 2016.
57 Riseman and Trembath 2016, p. 94.
58 Lees 2014.
59 Doolan 2014.
60 Albert 2014.
61 Bronwyn Lowe, 'Reflections on gender and memory: Personal experiences of women of the WAAAF during the Second World War', *Melbourne Historical Journal*, vol. 39, no. 1, 2011, p. 162.
62 Thelma Weston, Workshop on Gender in the Services, 2014.
63 Sue Gordon in Riseman 2016, pp. 66–7.
64 Ruth Ford, 'Disciplined, punished and resisting bodies: Lesbian women and the Australian armed services, 1950s–60s', *Lilith*, vol. 9, 1996, pp. 70–1.

65 Gordon and Doolan, Workshop on Gender in the Services, 2014.
66 Ford 1995, p. 96.
67 Workshop on Gender in the Services, 2014.
68 Workshop on Gender in the Services, 2014.
69 Workshop on Gender in the Services, 2014.
70 See Lorina Barker, '"Hangin out" and "Yarnin": Reflecting on the experience of collecting oral histories', *History Australia*, vol. 5, no. 1, 2008, pp. 09.1–09.9.
71 Doris Follent, interview, 22 April 2015.
72 Tripp 2015.
73 Ann McGrath, *Born in the Cattle: Aborigines in cattle country*, Allen & Unwin, Sydney, 1987, chapter 4, 'Black Velvet', pp. 68–94; Liz Conor, *Skin Deep: Settler impressions of Aboriginal women*, UWA Press, Perth, 2016, pp. 289–93; bell hooks, '"Selling Hot Pussy": Representations of Black female sexuality in the cultural marketplace', *Black Looks: Race and representation*, South End Press, Boston, 1992, pp. 61–78. See also Patricia Hill Collins 1990.
74 Doolan, Presentation, Defending Country, ANU, Canberra, 2 December 2014.
75 Riseman 2016, p. 72.
76 Gordon, Workshop on Gender in the Services, 2014.
77 Gordon 2015.
78 Albert 2014.
79 Maria Nugent, 'Sites of segregation/sites of memory: Remembrance and "race" in Australia', *Memory Studies*, vol. 6, no. 3, 2013, p. 307.
80 Cecilia Stanley-Taylor, interview, 16 April 2014.
81 Stanley-Taylor 2014.
82 Albert 2014; Stanley-Taylor 2014; Pattie Lees, Workshop on Gender in the Services, 2014.
83 Christine Reghenzani 2015, *Women in the ADF: Six decades of policy change (1950 to 2011), Summer Scholars Paper*, 27 November, Australian Parliamentary Library Papers.
84 Tracey Hoffman, 2014.

Chapter 13: Ex-service activism after 1945

1 Phillip Prosser, ORAL TRC 5000/183, NLA. See also Phil Prosser, 'Show Respect', in *Speaking from the Heart*, Sally Morgan (ed.), Fremantle Press, Perth, 2007, p. 140.
2 Phil Prosser, in *The Forgotten*, directed by Glen Stasiuk, originally aired as an episode of *Message Stick* on the ABC, 27 April 2003. See also Prosser 2007, pp. 140–1.
3 See Jennifer Clark, *Aborigines & Activism: Race, Aborigines & the coming of the Sixties to Australia*, University of Western Australia Press, Perth, 2008; John Chesterman, *Civil Rights: How Indigenous Australians won formal equality*, University of Queensland Press, Brisbane, 2005; Frances Peters-Little, Denise Haslem and Robert Lewis, *Vote Yes for Aborigines: The 1967 Referendum and the fight for Aboriginal citizenship rights*, Ronin Films, Canberra, 2007.
4 General Secretary, RSL to JB Chifley, Prime Minister, 20 November 1946 in RSL papers, series 1, MSS 6609, box 158, file 2248c, NLA. See also *Argus* (Melbourne), 2 November 1946.

5 Joe McGinness, *Son of Alyandabu: My fight for Aboriginal Rights*, University of Queensland Press, Brisbane, 1991, pp. 30–50; Sue Taffe, 'The Cairns Aborigines and Torres Strait Islander Advancement League and the Community of the Left', *Labour History*, no. 97, 2009, pp. 149–67; 'Elia Ware', *Collaborating for Indigenous Rights*, National Museum of Australia <indigenousrights.net.au/people/pagination/elia_ware>.

6 No name or date of speech – simply 'Kath Walker', in papers of Oodgeroo Noonuccal, Box 30, University of Queensland Library. See also 'Kath Walker', *This Is Your Life*, 1980, 25 min.; Oodgeroo Noonuccal, in Hall, *Fighters from the Fringe: Aborigines and Torres Strait Islanders recall the Second World War*, Aboriginal Studies Press, Canberra, 1995, p. 118.

7 Oodgeroo Noonuccal, in Hall 1995, pp. 130–1.

8 See Noah Riseman, 'Escaping Assimilation's Grasp: Aboriginal Women in the Australian Women's Military Services', *Women's History Review*, vol. 24, no. 5, 2015, pp. 762–3. See also *Shadow Sister: A film biography of Australian Aboriginal poet Kath Walker, M.B.E*, directed and produced by Frank Heimans, Cinetel Productions, 1977, 53 min.

9 Linda McBride-Yuke, interview, 20 June 2010. See also Linda McBride-Yuke, 'Journey of a Lifetime: From the Sticks to the State Library – an Aboriginal Editor's Story', *Journal of the Association for the Study of Australian Literature*, vol. 14, no. 3, 2014, p. 2.

10 For more on OPAL and QCAATSI, see Rita Huggins and Jackie Huggins, *Auntie Rita*, Aboriginal Studies Press, Canberra, 1994, pp. 83–102.

11 Linda McBride-Yuke 2010.

12 Mavis Thorpe Clark, *The Boy from Cumeroogunga: The story of Sir Douglas Ralph Nicholls, Aboriginal leader*, Hodder and Stoughton, Sydney, 1979, pp. 116–23.

13 Clark 1979, pp. 116–23. See also Richard Broome, 'Nicholls, Sir Douglas Ralph (Doug) (1906–1988)', *Australian Dictionary of Biography* website <adb.anu.edu.au/biography/nicholls-sir-douglas-ralph-doug-14920>.

14 Herbert Stanley Groves, B883, NX200798, NAA.

15 Jack Horner, *Seeking Racial Justice: An insider's memoir of the movement for Aboriginal advancement, 1938–1978*, Aboriginal Studies Press, Canberra, 2004, pp. 14–21.

16 Faith Bandler and Len Fox, *The Time Was Ripe: A history of the Aboriginal-Australian Fellowship, 1956–69*, Alternative Publishing Co-operative, Sydney, 1983. See also 'Subject files', ASIO, A6122, item 156/REFERENCE COPY, NAA.

17 See Russell McGregor, *Indifferent Inclusion: Aboriginal people and the Australian nation*, Aboriginal Studies Press, Canberra, 2011, pp. 101–12.

18 See McGinness 1991, pp. 71–83; Faith Bandler, *Turning the Tide: A personal history of the Federal Council for the Advancement of Aborigines and Torres Strait Islanders*, Aboriginal Studies Press, Canberra, 1989; Sue Taffe, *Black and White Together, FCAATSI: The Federal Council for the Advancement of Aborigines and Torres Strait Islanders, 1958–1973*, University of Queensland Press, Brisbane, 2005.

19 Bandler 1989, p. 98.

20 Linda McBride-Yuke 2010.

21 Ken Colbung, 'The Spirit Has More Strength', in Morgan 2007, p. 75.

22 On Black Power and the Aboriginal Tent Embassy, see Gary Foley, 'Black Power in Redfern 1968–1972', The Koori History Website <www.kooriweb.org/foley/essays/essay_1.html>; Kathy Lothian, 'Seizing the Time: Australian Aborigines and the Influence of the Black Panther Party, 1969–1972', *Journal of Black Studies*, vol. 35, no. 4, 2005, pp. 179–200; Kathy Lothian, 'Moving Blackwards: Black Power and the Aboriginal Embassy' in *Transgressions: Critical Australian Indigenous histories*, Ingereth Macfarlane and Mark Hannah (eds), ANU Press, Canberra, 2007, pp. 19–34; *Embassy Days*, aired as an episode of *Message Stick*, ABC, 2008; Gary Foley, Andrew Schaap and Edwina Howell (eds), *The Aboriginal Tent Embassy: Sovereignty, Black Power, Land Rights and the State*, Routledge, Abingdon, UK, 2014.

23 Kathie Cochrane, *Oodgeroo*, University of Queensland Press, Brisbane, 1994, pp. 80–5. On the split in FCAATSI, see Taffe 2005, pp. 219–313.

24 Kath Walker, in *Embassy Days* 2008.

25 Oodgeroo Noonuccal, *My People*, 3rd ed., The Jacaranda Press, Brisbane, 1990; Cochrane 1994, pp. 119–20.

26 Richard Broome, *Fighting Hard: The Victorian Aborigines Advancement League*, Aboriginal Studies Press, Canberra, 2015, chapter 7.

27 Broome 2015, chapter 8.

28 Colbung 2007, pp. 76–7. Ken Colbung, interview with Kerrie Jean Ross, *Awaye!*, ABC Radio National, 27 August 2007 <www.nma.gov.au/exhibitions/first_australians/resistance/yagan/awaye_audio_program_transcript>.

29 Colbung 2007, pp. 76–7.

30 ABC television news and current affairs programs, K1129, item 1821482, NAA.

31 'Kenneth Colbung', *Message Stick*, produced and directed by Kelrick Martin, produced by the ABC, 2004. See also Ken Colbung, interview with Kerrie Jean Ross, 27 August 2007; Colbung 2007, p. 77.

32 Ken Colbung, interview with Kerrie Jean Ross, 27 August 2007.

33 K1129, 1821484, NAA.

34 K1129, 1821486, NAA.

35 K1129, 1093624, NAA.

36 Margaret Culbong 2015.

37 'Kenneth Colbung', *Message Stick,* 2004.

38 Gerry Bostock, 'Gerry Bostock's Story', LivingNow website <www.livingnow.com.au/articles/living-with-spirit/gerry-bostock%25e2%2580%2599s-story>; 'Best Foot Forward', *Message Stick*, produced by the ABC, 2005.

39 Lyn Brignell, 'Brindle, Kenneth (Ken) (1931–1987)', *Australian Dictionary of Biography* website <adb.anu.edu.au/biography/brindle-kenneth-ken-12255>.

40 Bandler and Fox 1983, pp. 81–92.

41 Bandler 1989, p. 135.

42 Brignell 2007.

43 Linda McBride-Yuke 2010.

44 Gary Murray, 'Murray, John Stewart (1922–1989)', *Australian Dictionary of Biography* website <adb.anu.edu.au/biography/murray-john-stewart-15824/text27023>; Broome 2015.

45 'Faith, Len Culbong Story', Desperate Measures series, episode 14, produced NITV, 2013.
46 Margaret Culbong 2015.
47 'Faith, Len Culbong Story' 2013.
48 Margaret Culbong 2015.
49 'Faith, Len Culbong Story' 2013; Margaret Culbong 2015. On John Pat, see Peter N Grabosky, *Wayward Governance: Illegality and its control in the public sector*, Australian Institute of Criminology, Canberra, 1989, chapter 5 <www.aic.gov.au/publications/previous%20series/lcj/1-20/wayward/ch5t.html>.
50 'Faith, Len Culbong Story' 2013.
51 Quentin Beresford, *Rob Riley: An Aboriginal leader's quest for justice*, Aboriginal Studies Press, Canberra, 2012, p. 75.
52 Beresford 2012. See also Fiona Skyring, *Justice: A History of the Aboriginal Legal Service of Western Australia*, UWA Publishing, Perth, 2011.
53 Beresford 2012, p. 75.
54 Graham Atkinson, in Jackomos and Fowell 1991, p. 72. See also Graham Atkinson, AIATSIS, BOSTOCK_G01-016549.
55 Phillip James Prosser interviewed by John Bannister in the *Bringing Them Home* oral history project, TRC 5000/183, NLA.
56 Sue Gordon, ORAL TRC 6260/5, NLA; Sue Gordon, interview, 1 September 2015; Riseman 2016, pp. 57–88; Riseman and Trembath 2016, pp. 104–8.
57 Bob Blair, interview, 22 June 2010.
58 Frank Lampard, interview, 28 November 2013 and 20 December 2013; Geoff Shaw, interview, 18 September 2015; Patricia Lees, TRC 5000/300, NLA; Harry Allie, interview, 4 November 2011; Chris Townson, interview, 26 September 2012; George Bostock, interview with Noah Riseman, 18 June 2010, Brisbane; Mabel Quakawoot, interview, 5 June 2011; Jacqueline Shaw, interview, 27 September 2012; Riseman and Trembath 2016, pp. 103–4; Neil Macdonald, interview with Noah Riseman, 3 and 5 December 2009, Canberra; Riseman 2016, pp. 27; 142–3; 169–71.

Chapter 14: North-West Mobile Force

1 Paul A Rosenzweig, *Ever Vigilant: The regimental history of the North West Mobile Force 1981–2001*, North West Mobile Force, Australian Army, 2001; Trevor Tough, *Kimberley Squadron Norforce: The first twenty years*, Hesperian Press, Perth, 2015; Noah Riseman and Richard Trembath, *Defending Country: Aboriginal and Torres Strait Islander military service since 1945*, University of Queensland Press, Brisbane, 2016, pp. 143–57.
2 Desmond Ball (ed.), *Aborigines in the Defence of Australia*, ANU Press, Sydney, 1991; Riseman and Trembath 2016, p. 144.
3 Riseman and Trembath 2016, pp. 145–6.
4 Department of Defence, *Norforce: Modern warrior, traditional values*, Department of Defence, Canberra, 2013.
5 'Soldiers Key Role', *Koori Mail*, 8 April 2009, p. 60.
6 Department of Defence 2013, pp. 70–86.
7 'Diverse tasks in hostile terrain', *Canberra Times*, 30 November 1994, p. 36; Scott

Fuller, Pilbara Regiment, Port Hedland stated there were no Aboriginal people in the Squadron in 2014, email correspondence, 31 August 2015.

8 Riseman and Trembath 2016, pp. 147–8.

9 '51st Battalion, Far North Queensland Regiment', Australian Army website <www.army.gov.au/our-people/units/forces-command/2nd-division/51st-battalion-far-north-queensland-regiment>.

10 'Garma Festival', *NORFORCE News*, no. 14, December 2001, p. 35.

11 Tough 2012, pp. 147–76.

12 Riseman and Trembath 2016, p. 155; *Sydney Morning Herald*, 31 October 2008 <www.smh.com.au/national/military-to-end-role-in-nt-intervention-20081031-5f8i.html>.

13 Frances and Howard Morphy 'Thwarted Aspirations: The political economy of a Yolngu outstation 1972 to the present' in Nicolas Peterson and Fred Myers (eds), *Experiments in Self-Determination: Histories of the outstation movement in Australia*, ANU Press, Canberra, 2016, p. 303.

14 Paul Toohey, 'Once More Warriors', *The Australian Magazine*, 23–24 September 2000, pp. 16–20, 22. See also Rosenzweig 2001, p. 262.

15 Munyarryun 2016. See also *NT News*, 27 August, 2016, p. 33.

16 Munyarryun 2016.

17 Puruntatameri's artworks are held in the Museum of Victoria, National Gallery of Victoria, National Maritime Museum and National Gallery of Australia collections.

18 Robert Hall, *Black Diggers*, Aboriginal Studies Press, 1997, p. 100; Noah Riseman, '"Japan Fight, Aboriginal people Fight, European people Fight": Yolngu Stories from World War II', *Australian Journal of Indigenous Education*, vol. 37, issue 51, 2008, pp. 65–6.

19 Patrick Freddy Puruntatameri and Richard Narwirr, interview, 12 August 2016.

20 Warrk'Mattjun Gaykamangu, interview, 11 August 2016.

21 Donald Thomson, compiled by Nicolas Peterson, *Donald Thomson in Arnhem Land*, Miegunyah Press, Melbourne, 2003, especially 'The Special Reconaissance Unit', pp. 194–229.

22 Benjamin Gurruwiwi, interview, 11 August 2016.

23 *NT News*, 1 October 1981, cited in Adrian Harrison, 'Aboriginal Involvement in the Army Reserve', in *Service Delivery to Remote Communities*, Peter Loveday (ed.), North Australia Research Unit (NARU), ANU, Darwin, 1982, p. 138.

24 Reg Davies, Diary of the First Aboriginal Recruit Course, October 1981, appendix 4 in Rosenzweig 2001.

25 Mary Anne Jebb (ed.), *Mowanjum: 50 years a community*, Mowanjum Aboriginal Community and Mowanjum Artists Spirit of the Wandjina Aboriginal Corporation, Derby, 2008, pp. iv–v.

26 Jebb 2008, p. 152.

27 Ashley Oobagooma, interview, 8 September 2015.

28 Oobagooma 2015.

29 Daisy Utemorrah, *Dunbi the Owl*, compiled by Pamela Lofts, Scholastic, Sydney, 1983. See also Elkin Umbagai 'Tumbi the Owl', in *Visions of Mowanjum: Aboriginal writings from the Kimberley*, Rigby, Sydney, 1980, p. 74.

30 Many thanks to Mary Anne Jebb for her advice and suggestions regarding this section.
31 Oobagooma 2015.
32 Davies, in Rosenzweig 2001, p. 355.
33 Oobagooma 2015.
34 Rhys Jones and Betty Meehan 'The Arnhem Salient' in Ball (ed.), 1991, pp. 148–50.
35 Mary Anne Jebb, *Blood, Sweat and Welfare: A history of white bosses and Aboriginal pastoral workers*, University of Western Australia Press, Perth, 2002, p. 306.
36 Oobagooma 2015.
37 Gaykamangu 2016.
38 Munyarryun 2016; Rosenzweig 2001, p. 295.
39 Munyarryun 2016.
40 Samantha Muller, citing: Bakamana Yunupingu and Helen Watson, 1986, pp. 6–7, in '"Two Ways": Bringing Indigenous and Non-Indigenous Knowledges Together' in *Country, Native Title and Ecology*, Jessica Weir (ed.), ANU Press, Canberra, 2012.
41 Riseman and Trembath, 2016, pp. 149, 156–7.
42 Debbie Hohaia, 'The Potential Benefits to the Australian Defence Force Educational Curricula of the Inclusion of Indigenous Knowledge Systems', PhD thesis, Charles Darwin University, 2016, p. 66.
43 Munyarryun 2016.
44 Munyarryun 2016.
45 Thingle 2016.
46 Munyarryun 2016.
47 Munyarryun 2016.
48 Munyarryun 2016. See also 'Ramingining Elders responses', *Green Left Weekly*, 28 November 2011 <www.greenleft.org.au/content/aboriginal-elders-reject-%C3%A2%C2%80%C2%98another-decade-discrimination%C3%A2%C2%80%C2%99>.
49 Gaykamangu 2016.
50 Puruntatameri and Narwirr 2016.
51 Davies in Rosenzweig 2001, p. 358. Emphasis in original.
52 Harrison 1982, p. 142
53 Hohaia 2016, p. 269.
54 Puruntatameri and Narwirr 2016.
55 Gurruwiwi 2016. Also Thingle 2016.
56 I Barnes and John S Lotu, 'The Aboriginal Soldier: Ideal for the RFSU', *NORFORCE News*, no. 2, pp. 11–15, cited in Rosenzweig 2001, p. 131.
57 Tough 2015, p. 153; Rosenzweig 2001, pp. 292, 300.
58 Puruntatameri and Narwirr 2016.
59 Thingle 2016.
60 Oobagooma 2015.
61 Elgan Leedie, personal communication, Cherbourg, 11 July 2015.
62 Leedie, 2014.
63 Toohey 2000, pp. 20–2.
64 Gary Oakley, personal communication with the author, 2015.

65 *The Age*, 5 March 2005 <www.theage.com.au/news/National/A-very-special-kind-of-force-minds-the-north/2005/03/04/1109700672482.html#>.
66 Gurruwiwi 2016.
67 Leedie 2014.
68 David Hancock, 'Putting on the Green Skin: Australia's Indigenous Army', *Australian Geographic*, no. 93, 2010, p. 74.
69 Hancock 2010, p. 77.
70 Many thanks to Shannyn Palmer for generously sharing her perspectives on country and kin, and the expansion of family connections, with the author.
71 Puruntatameri 2016.
72 Gaykamangu 2016.
73 Jones and Meehan, 1991, p. 146; Kathy Marks, 'Brothers in Arms', *Sydney Morning Herald* (Good Weekend), 10 December 2011, p. 22.
74 Patricia Gibson, interview, 12 August 2016.
75 Gaykamangu 2016.
76 Thingle 2016.
77 Ben Bohane, 'The Black Watch', *The Bulletin*, 3 March 1998, p. 32.
78 Gaykamangu 2016.

Chapter 15: The Australian Defence Force, 1990s to 2017

1 Robert Hall, 'Aborigines and Torres Strait Islanders in the Armed Forces' in Peter Dennis et al., *The Oxford Companion to Australian Military History*, Oxford University Press, Melbourne, 2008, p. 5; David Horner, *Making the Australian Defence Force*, The Australian Centenary History of Defence, vol. 4, Oxford University Press, Melbourne, 2001, pp. 327–8.
2 Horner 2001, p. 228.
3 Horner 2001, p. 225.
4 Owen Hartley and Rachel Utley (eds.), *Major Powers and Peacekeeping: Perspectives, priorities and the challenges of military intervention*, Ashgate, Aldershot, UK, 2006, p. 1.
5 Horner 2001, p. 241.
6 Chris Townson, interview, 15 April 2014. See also Chris Townson, interview, 26 September 2012.
7 Townson 2012. See also Riseman and Trembath 2016, pp. 160–2.
8 Townson 2014.
9 Townson 2014.
10 Horner 2001, p. 245.
11 Robert Syron, interviewed by Fabri Blacklock, 3 October 2013, City of Sydney Oral History Program <www.sydneyoralhistories.com.au/robert-syron/>.
12 Syron 2013.
13 Syron 2013.
14 Horner 2001, p. 7.
15 'Australia's Military Involvement in Afghanistan since 2001: A chronology', Parliamentary Library, Commonwealth of Australia, available at <www.aph.gov.au/About_Parliament/Parliamentary_Departments/Parliamentary_Library/pubs/BN/1011/MilitaryInvolvementAfghanistan>.

16 Ricky Morris, interview, 3 March 2015.
17 Riseman and Trembath 2016, pp. 163–4.
18 Dennis Smallwood, interview, 23 April 2015. While issues of mental health resulting from 'peacekeeping' operations is a common thread across the memories of those who served, it is important to note that some people interviewed for the Serving Our Country project who served in the same conflicts did not discuss mental health or psychological trauma. Rather, they emphasised the positive experiences they had while serving and the opportunities that arose for them as a result. See Lyle Holt, interview, 15 December 2015; Colin Rogan, interview, 11 September 2015.
19 Townson 2014.
20 Syron 2013.
21 Syron 2013.
22 Robert Hall, *Fighters from the Fringe: Aborigines and Torres Strait Islanders in the Second World War*, Aboriginal Studies Press, Canberra, 1995; Riseman and Trembath 2016; Noah Riseman, *In Defence of Country: Life stories of Aboriginal and Torres Strait Islander servicemen and women*, ANU Press, Canberra, 2016.
23 Philippa Scarlett, 'Aboriginal service in the First World War: Identity recognition and the problem of mateship', *Aboriginal History*, vol. 39, 2015, pp. 163–81.
24 I am very grateful to Professor Tim Rowse for his thoughtful comments on an earlier draft, which were helpful in finessing the arguments made here.
25 Morris 2015.
26 Smallwood 2015.
27 Morris 2015.
28 Riseman and Trembath 2016, p. 122.
29 Riseman and Trembath 2016, p. 140.
30 Riseman and Trembath 2016, p. 140.
31 Horner 2001, pp. 318–19.
32 Horner 2001, p. 321.
33 Miranda Johnson, 'Reconciliation, indigeneity, and postcolonial nationhood in settler states', *Postcolonial Studies*, vol. 14, no. 2, 2011, p. 188.
34 Damien Short, *Reconciliation and Colonial Power: Indigenous rights in Australia*, Ashgate, Aldershot, UK, p. 2.
35 Riseman and Trembath 2016, p. 165.
36 Anthony Bergin, Robert Hall, Roger Jones and Ian McAllister, 'The Ethnic Composition of the Australian Defence Force: Management, attitudes & strategies', prepared for Director General Recruiting, Headquarters Australian Defence Force, 2 vols, Unisearch, February 1993.
37 Riseman and Trembath 2016, p. 167.
38 Email communication, Directorate of Indigenous Affairs (DIA), Department of Defence, 14 February 2017.
39 Department of Defence website, 'Army Aboriginal Community Assistance Program (AACAP) information brief' <www.defence.gov.au/publications/080502_AACAP.pdf>.
40 Morris 2015.
41 Reconciliation Australia website, Defence Reconciliation Action Plan 2007 <www.reconciliation.org.au/raphub/wp-content/uploads/raps/federal/department%20of%20defence%20rap.pdf>.

42 Australian Bureau of Statistics, 'Population Distribution Aboriginal and Torres Strait Islander Australians', 15 August 2007 <www.ausstats.abs.gov.au/Ausstats/subscriber.nsf/0/377284127F903297CA25733700241AC0/$File/47050_2006.pdf>.

43 Email communication, DIA 2017.

44 Lisa Phelps quoted in Sergei De Silva-Ranasinghe, 'Defence and Indigenous Affairs: An untold story', *Policy*, vol. 30, no. 1, 2014, p. 45. The current head of DIA is Michael Howell.

45 Keith Thomas and Steve Bell, 'Competing for the Best and Brightest: Recruitment and Retention in the Australian Defence Force', *Security Challenges*, vol. 3, no. 1, 2007, pp. 97–118; Damien Short, 'When sorry isn't good enough: Official remembrance and reconciliation in Australia', *Memory Studies*, vol. 5, no. 3, 2012, pp. 293–304.

46 Damien Short, 'Australian Aboriginal Reconciliation: The Latest Phase in the Colonial Project', *Citizenship Studies*, vol. 7, no. 3, 2003, pp. 302–4. See also Damien Short 'Reconciliation, Assimilation and Indigenous Peoples', *International Political Science Review*, vol. 24, no. 4, 2003, pp. 502–3.

47 Email communication, DIA 2017. See also 'ADF Indigenous Entry Pathways', pamphlet produced by Defence Indigenous Affairs <www.defence.gov.au/CoDE/indigenous>.

48 Email communication, DIA 2017.

49 Defence Reconciliation Action Plan 2015–2018, Department of Defence, p. 5 <www.defence.gov.au/diversity/_Master/docs/drap/DRAP.pdf>.

50 Email communication, DIA 2017.

51 See Australian Army website, 'Army's first Indigenous Elder' <www.army.gov.au/our-people/army-indigenous-community/armys-first-indigenous-elder>.

52 Department of Defence, 'Cultural Awareness' <www.defence.gov.au/Diversity/Indigenous/support/cultural-awareness.asp>.

53 Lisa Phelps quoted in De Silva-Ranasinghe 2014, p. 46.

54 'Norforce: a spirit of brotherhood', *The Sydney Morning Herald*, 15 March 2012 <www.smh.com.au/entertainment/norforce-a-spirit-of-brotherhood-20120314-1v1xs.html>.

55 'Norforce', *Sydney Morning Herald*, 2012.

56 Stephen (aka Steve) Jones, interview, 18 November 2016.

57 Phelps quoted in De Silva-Ranasinghe 2014, p. 46.

58 Morris 2015.

59 Department of Defence website, 'A Proud History: Over a century of service to Australia' <www.defencejobs.gov.au/indigenous/proud-history>.

Chapter 16: Commemoration

1 Ken S Inglis, *Sacred Places: War memorials in the Australian landscape*, Miegunyah Press, Melbourne, 1998, p. 48.

2 Inglis 1998, p. 188.

3 'Memorial to the Natives', *News* (Adelaide), 18 August 1925, p. 9.

4 Noah Riseman, 'Aboriginal military service and assimilation', *Aboriginal History*, vol. 38, 2014, p. 160.

5 'War Memorial Unveiled by the Governor', *Sydney Morning Herald*, 5 August 1931, p. 12.

6 Australian Government, Department of Veterans' Affairs et. al., 'The Islanders' <the-islanders.net/>.

7 Noah Riseman, 'Evolving Commemorations of Aboriginal and Torres Strait Islander Military Service', *Wicazo Sa Review*, vol. 32, no. 1, 2017, pp. 80–101.

8 Riseman 2017.

9 Inglis 1998, pp. 352–8, 375.

10 The Cherbourg memory website <cherbourgmemory.org/>.

11 *Wagga Wagga Daily Advertiser*, 26 April 1952, p. 1; Riseman 2017.

12 See documentaries *No Bugles No Drums*, 1990 <www.youtube.com/watch?v=A3BQdK-drkM>; and *Aeroplane Dance*, 1994 <www.screenaustralia.gov.au/the-screen-guide/t/aeroplane-dance-1994/4801/>; Catherine Freyne, 'Recognising Military Service' <www.sydneybarani.com.au/sites/recognising-military-service/>; Riseman 2017.

13 See Maria Nugent, 'Aboriginal Family History', *Australian Cultural History*, no. 23, 2003, pp. 143–54; Fabri Blacklock, 'Telling It Our Way: Koori History in NSW', *Australian Cultural History*, no. 23, 2003, pp. 155–60.

14 'Ruxton plans to stop Aboriginal group march', *Canberra Times*, 5 March 1985, p. 3.

15 Riseman 2017.

16 *Canberra Times*, 20 March 1985, p. 9.

17 Noah Riseman and Richard Trembath, *Defending Country: Aboriginal and Torres Strait Islander military service since 1945*, University of Queensland Press, Brisbane, 2016, pp. 171–2.

18 Riseman and Trembath 2016, p. 172.

19 Riseman 2017.

20 Anne Brennan, 'Lest We Forget: Military Myths, Memory and Canberra's Aboriginal and Torres Strait Islander Memorial', *Memory Connection*, vol. 1, no. 1, 2011, p. 36.

21 For the argument that the increased governmental interest in Anzac Day was a response to the 1988 controversies see Mark McKenna, 'Anzac Day: How did it become Australia's National Day?', in *What's Wrong with Anzac: The militarisation of Australian history*, Marilyn Lake and Henry Reynolds (eds), University of New South Wales Press, Sydney, 2010, pp. 110–34.

22 Paul Keating, Redfern speech, 10 December 1992, transcript available at <antar.org.au/sites/default/files/paul_keating_speech_transcript.pdf>. The Keating government completed the process begun in the 1980s of paying compensation for Indigenous ex-service personnel who had been underpaid during the war and in 1994 presented service medals to Aboriginal Australians who had patrolled the remote north Australian coast.

23 'Aborigines call for recognition of their people's sacrifice', *Canberra Times*, 12 November 1993, p. 7.

24 Liz Reed, *Bigger than Gallipoli: War, history and memory in Australia*, University of Western Australia Press, Perth, 2004, pp. 9, 144.

25 Reed 2004, pp. 144, 151.

26 'Honouring Indigenous War Graves Incorporated' website <www.hiwg2005.websyte.com.au/>.
27 Riseman and Trembath 2016, p. 172; Dot Peters, interview, 11 May 2017.
28 Shrine of Remembrance website, 'Indigenous Australians at War from the Boer War to the present' <www.shrine.org.au/Exhibitions/Travelling-Exhibitions/Indigenous-Australians-at-war>.
29 'The Sunshine Club' Wikipedia entry <en.wikipedia.org/wiki/The_Sunshine_Club>.
30 'Seems Like Yesterday' AusStage website entry <ausstage.edu.au/pages/event/4246>.
31 'The Forgotten Aboriginal War Veterans No Longer Forgotten', *Message Stick*, ABC Online.
32 Frank Lampard, quoted in Reconciliation South Australia website, 'Aboriginal and Torres Strait Islander War Memorial Unveiled' <www.reconciliationsa.org.au/news/reconciliation/aboriginal-and-torres-strait-islander-war-memorial-unveiled>.
33 Marj Tripp, interview, 14 April 2015. For the Register of Aboriginal Veterans of South Australia see Reconciliation South Australia website <www.reconciliationsa.org.au/learn/ravsa>.
34 Letter to author from Kyam Mayer, SA Minister for Aboriginal Affairs and Reconciliation, 28 July 2015.
35 Frank Lampard, speaking at 'Defending Country' conference, Australian National University, Canberra, December 2014.
36 Ray Minniecon, interview, 14 March 2014.
37 Riseman 2017.
38 City of Sydney website, 'Coloured Digger March' <www.cityofsydney.nsw.gov.au/learn/sydneys-history/anzac-centenary/coloured-diggers-march>.
39 For details see Ray Minniecon, interview, 8 November 2013, City of Sydney Oral History Program website <cdn.sydneyoralhistories.com.au/wp-content/uploads/Minniecon-Ray.pdf>.
40 City of Sydney website, Eora Journey – The People's Journey, Sydney <www.cityartsydney.com.au/projects/eora-journey/>.
41 The subtitle echoes the limerick: 'There was a young lady of Riga/Who rode with a smile on a tiger/They returned from the ride/With the lady inside/And the smile on the face of the tiger.'
42 Information provided by Professor Peter Stanley and Dr Peter Londey, November 2016.
43 Australian War Memorial website, 'Too Dark for the Light Horse' <www.awm.gov.au/visit/exhibitions/toodark>. The Resource Book can be found at <www.awm.gov.au/sites/default/files/education/box/03_res_book.pdf>.
44 Australian War Memorial website, 'Indigenous commemoration for the Centenary' <www.awm.gov.au/about/our-work/projects/indigenous-commemoration>.
45 Emma Kelly, 'Australian War Memorial gallery named in honour of Indigenous soldier Reg Saunders', *Canberra Times*, 11 November 2015 <www.canberratimes.com.au/act-news/australian-war-memorial-gallery-named-in-honour-of-indigenous-soldier-reg-saunders-20151111-gkw2zb.html>. The Memorial meanwhile headed off criticism that the original gargoyles of an Indigenous man and women in its courtyard should be removed on the grounds that they were

racist: Primrose Riordan, 'Indigenous gargoyles to stay at the Australian War Memorial', *Canberra Times*, 4 June 2015 <www.canberratimes.com.au/act-news/indigenous-gargoyles-to-stay-at-australian-war-memorial-20150604-ghgitz.html>.

46 For the 'history wars', see Riseman 2017.

47 Paul Daley, 'Australian War Memorial': The remarkable rise and rise of the nation's secular shrine', *The Guardian*, 19 May 2015 <www.theguardian.com/australia-news/postcolonial-blog/2015/may/19/australian-war-memorial-the-remarkable-rise-and-rise-of-the-nations-secular-shrine>.

48 'Australian War Memorial unveils new Rover Thomas painting Ruby Plains Massacre 1', *Canberra Times*, 3 March 2017 <www.canberratimes.com.au/act-news/canberra-life/australian-war-memorial-unveils-new-rover-thomas-painting-ruby-plains-massacre-1-20170302-gupa63.html>.

49 Bruce Kapferer, *Legends of People, Myths of State: Violence, intolerance and political culture in Sri Lanka and Australia*, Smithsonian Institution Press, Washington, 1988.

50 I acknowledge the insights that follow to Tim Rowse's perceptive discussion of this issue in 'Indigenous Heterogeneity', *Australian Historical Studies*, vol. 45, no. 3, 2014, pp. 297–310.

51 Rowse 2014, p. 299.

52 Cavanagh and Wolfe quoted in Rowse 2014, pp. 298–9.

53 Rowse 2014, p. 302.

54 Rowse 2014, p. 310.

55 Miranda Johnson, 'Writing Indigenous Histories Now', *Australian Historical Studies*, vol. 45, no. 3, 2014, p. 324.

56 Government of South Australia, 'I am the Forgotten Soldier', The Aboriginal and Torres Strait Islander War Memorial Appeal booklet, copy provided to author by SA Minister for Aboriginal Affairs and Reconciliation, 28 July 2015.

57 Government of South Australia 2015.

58 Kristin Ann Hass, *Carried to the Wall: American Memory and the Vietnam Veterans Memorial*, University of California Press, Berkeley, 1998, pp. 15, 18.

59 Themes have included Aboriginal women, prisoners of war, Vietnam veterans and the Unknown Soldier, Minniecon 2014.

60 Creative Spirits website, 'Anzac Day Coloured Digger March' <www.creativespirits.info/aboriginalculture/history/anzac-day-coloured-digger-march>.

61 In the 'Connecting Spirits' ceremony soil from the grave of Private Rufus Gordon Rigney in Belgium was returned to his country in the Coorong to commemorate the 90th anniversary of Anzac Day. The soil had been collected by students of the Mount Barker School.

62 A short video of part of the ceremony can be found at the Department of Defence website <video.defence.gov.au/play/3752#>.

63 Tony Albert, interview, 18 November 2013, City of Sydney Oral History Program <www.sydneyoralhistories.com.au/tony-albert/>.

64 Elizabeth Furniss, 'Timeline History and the Anzac Myth: Settler Narratives of Local History in a North Australian Town', *Oceania*, vol. 71, no. 4, 2001 p. 289; Riseman 2017.

65 Jay Winter, *Remembering War: The Great War between memory and history in the twentieth century*, Yale University Press, New Haven, 2006, p. 4.
66 See Joan Beaumont, 'Remembering the Heroes of Australia's Wars: From Heroic to Post-Heroic Memory', in Sibylle Scheipers (ed.), *Heroism and the Changing Character of War*, Palgrave Macmillan, Basingstoke; New York, 2014, pp. 339–42.
67 Hass 1998, p. 63.
68 Lake and Reynolds 2010, p. viii.

Index

Index